CAMBRIDGE GREEK AND LATIN CLASSICS

AF167683

HOMER
ODYSSEY
BOOKS XIII AND XIV

EDITED BY
A. M. BOWIE
The Queen's College, Oxford

CAMBRIDGE
UNIVERSITY PRESS

CAMBRIDGE
UNIVERSITY PRESS

University Printing House, Cambridge CB2 8BS, United Kingdom

One Liberty Plaza, 20th Floor, New York, NY 10006, USA

477 Williamstown Road, Port Melbourne, VIC 3207, Australia

314-321, 3rd Floor, Plot 3, Splendor Forum, Jasola District Centre, New Delhi - 110025, India

79 Anson Road, #06-04/06, Singapore 079906

Cambridge University Press is part of the University of Cambridge.

It furthers the University's mission by disseminating knowledge in the pursuit of education, learning and research at the highest international levels of excellence.

www.cambridge.org
Information on this title: www.cambridge.org/9780521159388

© Cambridge University Press 2013

First published 2013

A catalogue record for this publication is available from the British Library

Library of Congress Cataloging in Publication data
Homer.
[Odyssey. Books 13–14]
Odyssey. Books XIII and XIV / edited by A. M. Bowie, The Queen's College, Oxford.
pages   cm. – (Cambridge Greek and Latin Classics)
Includes bibliographical references and index.
ISBN 978-0-521-76354-7 (hardback)
1. Odysseus (Greek mythology) – Poetry.   1. Bowie, Angus M.   II. Title.
PA4025.A6B69   2013
883′.01 – dc23   2013016365

ISBN 978-0-521-76354-7 Hardback
ISBN 978-0-521-15938-8 Paperback

For
Pat Easterling

CONTENTS

PREFACE

When considering which books of the *Odyssey* I might offer a commentary on, I discovered that all the most popular books were already spoken for, so it seemed a good idea to investigate the merits of the less popular second half of the epic. Books 13–14 were chosen, in part because they contain the hinge between the account of Odysseus' wanderings and the return to the 'real' world, but more because they are the ones which in the past have received the least complimentary criticism, as being too leisurely and devoid of incident. Episodes like that in Eumaeus' farmstead had considerable influence on later literature, but the magical world of the wanderings has long been of greater fascination. There is a slow revaluation of the second part taking place, and this commentary attempts to add to that. I set myself the task of rescuing the reputation of these books, by seeking where their merits lie and gaining a sense of what it is that the poet is here doing with the epic genre. My particular interest has been in the way this part of the *Odyssey* seems to take a radically new direction for epic, by giving major roles to 'lower status' figures and the facts of everyday life, with some aristocratic figures acting as the arch-villains of the piece. This goes along with a critical view of what was achieved by the Trojan War.

It will soon be seen that this is a resolutely 'unitarian' edition. This is not just a personal predilection. The fact that the 'Analysts' have never succeeded in creating an account of the text that most can agree on does not necessarily invalidate the method, but the second part of the *Odyssey* in particular reveals itself as very tightly constructed, and though there are indeed problems in the narrative they are not such as lead me to think that there is a basic inconsistency in the episodes. Many traditions of oral literature – and whether our *Odyssey* was composed orally or with the help of writing, it is still heavily marked by oral tradition – are characterised by inconsistencies which could be condemned in a written text, but which are and were tolerated by the societies which produced the works. I have therefore given little space to discussion of the various deletions which have been proposed for these books.

Beside the literary analyses, the Introduction and notes provide a good deal of help with the Homeric language, especially from a historical perspective. This is not the result of a desire to deluge the reader with philological erudition, but of a conviction that, if one has an idea of how linguistic forms and constructions came about, they are more comprehensible and so easier to learn and retain.

As with my edition *Herodotus VIII*, I have again to thank pupils at the JACT Summer School for being guinea pigs for the commentary on book XIII. Philomen Probert very kindly read the account of the Homeric dialect

ix

and improved it in no small measure; the final decisions and the errors are mine and mine alone. By her acuity as copy-editor, Dr Iveta Adams improved the work greatly in terms of presentation, consistency and accuracy. I am grateful too to Queen's College and the Faculty of Classics for the granting of sabbatical leave. Finally, as all contributors to this series have found, the Editors are remarkably unstinting in their willingness to read, encourage, advise and, perhaps most important of all, where a submission fails to meet the well-conceived conventions and aims of the series, criticise. One cannot but be deeply grateful. Furthermore, Pat Easterling has provided me with guidance of all kinds from my undergraduate days onwards, and it is to her that this volume is humbly dedicated.

ABBREVIATIONS

I ANCIENT AUTHORS AND WORKS

Abbreviations of ancient authors and inscriptional collections are largely those of LSJ, of journals those of *L'année philologique*. Eustathius is quoted from G. Stallbaum, *Eustathii archiepiscopi Thessalonicensis commentarii ad Homeri Odysseam*, 2 vols. in 1, Leipzig 1825–6 (repr. Hildesheim, 1970), conveniently available on the *Thesaurus Linguae Graecae*.

II MODERN WORKS

A–H–C   Ameis, F. A., Hentze, K. and Cauer, P. (eds.), *Homers Odyssee: für den Schulgebrauch erklärt*, Leipzig 1868–1922.

Beekes   Beekes, R., *Etymological dictionary of Greek*, 2 vols., Leiden 2009.

CHO   *A commentary on Homer's Odyssey* (1–8 ed. A. Heubeck, S. R. West and J. B. Hainsworth; 9–16 ed. A. Heubeck and A. Hoekstra; 17–24 ed. J. Russo, M. Fernández-Galiano and A. Heubeck), Oxford 1985–93.

DCPP   Lipiński, E. (ed.), *Dictionnaire de la civilisation phénicienne et punique*, Turnhout 1992.

EA   Moran, W. L. (ed.), *The Amarna Letters*, Baltimore and London 1992.

Ebeling   Ebeling, H. (ed.), *Lexicon Homericum*, 2 vols., Leipzig 1885.

EM   Gaisford, T. (ed.), *Etymologicum magnum*, Oxford 1848.

GEF   M. L. West (ed.), *Greek epic fragments from the seventh to the fifth centuries* B C, Cambridge, MA 2003.

GH   Chantraine, P., *Grammaire homérique*, 2 vols., Paris 1948–53.

GP   Denniston, J. D., *The Greek particles*, 2nd edn, Oxford 1954.

K–G   Kühner, R. and Gerth, B., *Ausführliche Grammatik der griechischen Sprache*, 2 vols., 3rd edn, Hannover 1890–1904.

LfgrE   *Lexikon des frühgriechischen Epos*, Göttingen 1955–2010.

OCD   Hornblower, S., Spawforth, A. and Eidinow, E. (eds.), *Oxford classical dictionary*, 4th edn, Oxford 2012.

Smyth   Smyth, H. W., *Greek grammar* (rev. by G. M. Messing), Harvard 1956.

Stanford   Stanford, W. B., *The Odyssey of Homer*, 2 vols., London 1947–8.

Epic fragments are quoted from *GEF*. See now also M. L. West 2013.

INTRODUCTION

The main fault of the *Odyssey* is that at many points the narrative content is drawn out to excessive length. At these points one feels that
the monumental singer is consciously and almost painfully elaborat-
ing his material so as to make a great poem which will match the
scale of the *Iliad* ... It is in conversations between some of the main
characters – between the suitors and Telemachus, or the disguised
Odysseus and Eumaeus or later Penelope herself – that a certain lack
of tension, an excessive leisureliness, become intrusive.[1]

Thus wrote Geoffrey Kirk sixty years ago, expressing a view which is still
alive in the way that the second half of the poem tends to be less prized and
studied than the first.[2] Recent criticism has however moved to an assessment of the *Odyssey* which is closer to Aristotle's summary, where the sen-
sational aspects of books 6–12 are ignored:

A man is away from home for many years, jealously watched by Poseidon, and has lost his followers; moreover, at home his affairs are such
that his property is being wasted by suitors and plots are being laid
against his son; he comes home in dire distress, and after disclos-
ing himself makes an attack and destroys his enemies without being
killed himself. That is what is proper to the action; the rest of the
poem is episodes.[3]

To borrow Lowe's trenchant words, 'appreciation of the *Odyssey* has
been dogged by our perverse modern tendency to see the poem's secondary narrative as primary, and vice versa – as if IX–XII are the "essential"
Odyssey, and the remaining twenty books mere narrative appendages'.[4]
    It will be the task of this commentary to contribute to this rehabilitation
of the second half.

---

[1] Kirk 1962: 357–8.
[2] In 1960, Lord had been more appreciative, commenting on 'the masterly inter-
weaving of plots by following the lead of the elementary forces in the story itself'
(repeated in 2000: 181). A further dissenting voice was Rutherford 1992: 9–16.
The *Iliad* does of course contain lengthy discussions, such as that in book 9 about
the return of Achilles, but these concern issues central to the story, not false tales
or minor exploits.
[3] *Poet.* 1455b17–23.
[4] Lowe 2000: 134. Cf. Redfield 2009: 278: 'the plot of the *Odyssey* is in its second
half; the first part of the poem is all prelude'.

1 BOOKS 13–14 AND THE SECOND HALF
OF THE *ODYSSEY*

1.1 'Closure' and transition

'Books 13–14' cover the transition between the end of the wanderings and the beginning of the long series of episodes on Ithaca. The division into books is almost certainly post-Homeric, and may even be the result of commercial considerations:[5] it has therefore no especial authority. The most natural place for a pause in this part of the epic would be 13.93, where the sun rises on Ithaca: if the *Odyssey* was, as is possible, performed over two days, this would have made a good opening for the second morning.[6] However, a notable technique employed in making the transition from the 'fairy-tale' world of the wanderings to the 'real' world of Ithaca is the use of a number of 'closural' techniques,[7] which suggest at a number of points that we are coming to the close of the episode, but the actual end is constantly deferred in a variety of ways.

The end of book 12 closes Odysseus' story, but not quite the context in which it stands, the evening meal in Alcinous' palace: that closure comes very soon, as the Phaeacians all head for bed (13.17). A new day then sees the beginning of the final preparations for Odysseus' night-time departure. That day then rapidly passes in the text, but not for Odysseus who is impatient to depart.[8] Night falls once again (13.35), at which point warm farewells are exchanged and the ship is packed with gifts. Odysseus is put to sleep in the boat (13.75–6), and his sleep is especially deep, being described as 'unwaking, very like death' (13.80). The conjunction of night, sleep, death and departure looks classically closural, and this sense is reinforced by the way in which 13.89–92 recall the very first lines of the epic, again suggesting that 'part one' is coming to its close. We are not

---

[5] Cf. Commentary p. 91.

[6] We are at about the mid-point of the *Odyssey*, numerically and in terms of the plot, and if the *Iliad* was performed over three days (cf. Taplin 1992), the *Odyssey* could have been fitted into two: cf. Taplin 1992: esp. 19, 27, 31; Olson 1995: 233–4.

[7] 'Closure' is a technical term of narratology which applies to the bringing of a *narrative* to a conclusion. It is different therefore from the way in which a *text* ends with its final full stop, in that it is an artificial conclusion because there will always have been events subsequent to the last one narrated. Closure therefore is an artistic means of giving the sense that things have come to a close, even though they must 'in fact' have continued, because time does not stop. There are a wide range of such techniques, the most obvious being nightfall, a marriage ('and they lived happily ever after'), the end of a journey, death and so on.

[8] This day, on which rather little happens, may seem a little awkward, but it is necessary because Odysseus could not decently be sent on his way after a night of story-telling. Odysseus' own impatience with the length of the day acknowledges, with gentle humour on the poet's part, any impatience the reader might feel.

however allowed to indulge too much in this sense of an imminent ending, because these closural features are counterpointed by the emphasis
on the great vigour and energy of the ship's progress through the sea as it
moves the story on to its next stage (13.76–8, 81–8): the combination of
peaceful calm and frenetic activity prevent any notion of a closure.

The boat arrives on Ithaca and the day breaks, suggesting a new start
(13.93–5), but the expected final departure of the Phaeacians is deferred
for a full description of the cave of Phorcys.[9] Still, the combination of daybreak, the depositing of the gifts and the departure of the Phaeacians looks
like the end of the Phaeacian episode and the start of the Ithacan phase.
However, Homer has a further surprise up his sleeve: right in the middle
of the line where the Phaeacians leave (13.125), the story switches suddenly to Olympus for Poseidon's angry outburst to Zeus about the threat
to his reputation from Odysseus' escape to Ithaca. It becomes clear that
things in the narrative are far from finished where the Phaeacians are concerned, as Poseidon and Zeus plan punishment for their persistent saving
of mariners from the dangers of the sea. We then duly return to Scherie
for what really does look like the end of the role of the Phaeacians in the
epic. But even here, things are not quite as they seem, because closure of
this episode is perennially deferred by the fact that it is not clear what is
to happen next. Poseidon has threatened to put a mountain on the city
of the Phaeacians, but the text leaves it quite unclear whether he does
or not:[10] having decided this is the best plan, he turns the ship to stone
but then leaves (13.164), and no more is said of him. We are left with the
Phaeacians standing anxiously round their altars wondering, like us, what
will happen next: for the Phaeacians, there will have been a closure of
some sort, a repenting by Poseidon or their destruction, but the audience
is denied knowledge of what this closure was. Again, the sense of incom-
pleteness is reinforced by the way that this episode ends, as it began, in the
middle of a line, where we return to Odysseus on the shore (13.187).

This too seems like a new start: Odysseus is back on Ithaca and can begin
his campaign to regain his home and kingship. Homer however immediately makes it clear that things are not that simple, by having Athena make
the island unrecognisable to him (13.188–90). For the audience, the journey is over, but for Odysseus there is no closure yet: he is convinced that
he has been fooled by the Phaeacians and has more adventures ahead of
him (13.200–2). Athena then arrives and we might expect a speedy free-
ing of Odysseus from his delusion, but Athena is herself in disguise, as a
shepherd, and confuses him further by saying that the island *is* Ithaca but

---

[9] A poet keen to finish with the Phaeacians and get on to the next episode could
have left the description of the cave until they had gone.
[10] Cf. 13.165–87n.

describing it in an unfamiliar way. It is then another 150 lines before she finally dispels the mist and Odysseus is convinced that he is indeed home (13.352–3). The audience's perceptions and Odysseus' are now aligned, and the Ithacan part of the epic is clearly under way, though quite where it began is, one now realises, far from clear.

The whole narrative of these 350 or so lines has thus been constructed so that we are given a constant sense that the Phaeacian episode is coming to a conclusion, by the motifs of nightfall, farewells, sleep, death, daybreak, destruction and arrival; but at the same time, the closure never quite comes and uncertainty about the fate of the Phaeacians lingers for ever.[11]

Once the Ithacan episode is under way and Odysseus is transformed from honoured hero to destitute beggar, books 13–14 will begin his transition from beggar to king that culminates in book 23. Odysseus begins on the shore, and at the start of book 14 he moves inland to Eumaeus' farmstead; thence, in book 17, he will move to his home and eventual triumph. There is thus a tripartite structure to the second half, which sees Odysseus move from the seashore to an intermediate place and then to a central position. The sea, the uncultivated wild area, is the opposite of the palace, the centre of human society and civilisation. Eumaeus' farm is then a mid-point between the two: it is separated from the sea, but is still out in the wilds; it is a work of human hands, but not one as sophisticated as a palace; and it contains a society too, but this is essentially one of pigs not of human beings.

This pattern of three-fold transition is in fact one which structures much of the plot of the epic in various ways.[12] In the narrative of the poem as a whole, this 'sea–land' transition can be analysed in two ways. First, there is the pattern 'sea–Scherie–Ithaca'. His wanderings show Odysseus in the grip of the wildness of the sea, in a world which is characterised by the bestial and the fantastic, and where many of the things which normally typify human society, such as cities,[13] sacrifice, agriculture and sailing, are missing. The Cyclopes 'have no meeting-places where decisions are taken

[11] One might compare the way that the closure of the whole epic, with Odysseus' victory and the resolution of the quarrel with the Suitors' relatives, is to be set against the fact that Odysseus will have to leave again to wander to the saltless and sealess land spoken of by Teiresias (11.119–37).

[12] For what follows, cf. especially Segal 1962; Vidal-Naquet 1981. Lowe 2000: 135 notes of many of the episodes in the epic that 'generally they follow the recurrent pattern of a simple linear route from beach or harbour to homestead, city, or palace'. This pattern thus lies at the heart of the macro- and micro-narratives of the poem.

[13] Aeolus has a polis (10.13), but it is a floating island inhabited only by one family, where brothers and sisters are given in marriage to each other and feast constantly.

nor laws; they dwell on the tops of high mountains in hollow caves, and each one rules over his wife and children' (9.112–15). The Cyclops eats his meat raw, without sacrifice, and Odysseus' men are forced to make abnormal sacrifices (cf. 9.231–2, 12.353–73). Though they belong to the world of the sea, these people do not sail: 'the Cyclopes have no ships with painted prows, nor craftsmen to build them ships' (9.125–6). In the land of the Laestrygonians, 'there appeared the works of neither oxen nor men' (10.98).[14]

That Scherie is a transitional phase is shown by the fact that these human features now appear, but in a way that blends the world of men and the fantasy world of the sea. They have a demos and a polis (6.3), but all is not entirely like the human world: they sacrifice normally, as if the gods needed to be contacted by the smoke of sacrifice, but the gods dine with them (7.200–3); they sail, but their ships have magical properties (8.564–71); they are agriculturalists, but 'the fruits of the trees never rot nor fail in winter or summer; they exist all year-round. As the west wind continually blows, some are growing and others ripening . . .' (7.117–19).

It is only when we reach Ithaca that all these activities take place in the normal human way.

Secondly, this pattern can also be seen in a broader spread of the story. In this second form, Calypso's island, where Odysseus is at the start (1.48–51), is 'the *omphalos* of the sea' (1.50), that is, the most 'sea-y' place.[15] Ithaca, which was the final term in the last scheme, is now the middle term: as an island, it is insufficiently earthy. The final term is then the land to which Teiresias says Odysseus must travel when he has killed the Suitors: 'travel then, with a well-poised oar, until you come to men who do not know the sea, do not eat their food mixed with salt, and do not know ships with their painted prows, nor well-poised oars' (11.121–5). There he must sacrifice to Poseidon. This land, with no traces of the sea, is thus the very opposite of Calypso's island.

A similar pattern of transition from a wild to a cultural status can also be seen in the development of Odysseus himself.[16] Again, there are two phases. At the end of book 5, he escapes from the sea and sleeps under leaves 'as when a man hides a torch in black ash at the edge of a field, where there are no neighbours nearby, preserving the seed of the fire' (5.488–90): he is barely of the human world. He then meets the members of the royal family hierarchically, first the princess, then the queen, then the king. His diplomacy enhances his status, and finally his stories lead the Phaeacians to treat him like the great warrior and adventurer that he

---

[14] Cf. also 9.106–11, 123.
[15] Cf. the way the *omphalos* at Delphi represented the very centre of the earth.
[16] On Odysseus' changing identity, cf. Kahane 2005: 138–50.

is.[17] He then repeats this pattern on Ithaca, beginning as a very destitute beggar and steadily building up his importance: he meets a servant and then his son in Eumaeus' farmstead, and then another servant, Eurycleia, and finally his wife in the palace. His real identity is revealed (22.35–41),[18] and he sleeps with his wife in the centre of the palace in the bed built round Athena's olive-tree, a position which is the absolute opposite of that at the end of book 13.

In 13.341–3, Athena explains her absence during Odysseus' wanderings as the result of not wanting to annoy her uncle Poseidon, and underpinning these moves from sea to land is the opposition between those two gods, who, in some traditions, broadly represent the cultural world of man and the world of nature.[19] In a number of stories, they come into conflict, and the victor is Athena: at Athens, according to later tradition, she and her cultivated olive-tree were preferred for the patronage of the city to Poseidon and his more elemental salt-spring and war-horse. Similarly in the *Odyssey*, Odysseus escapes from the ravages of the sea through the kind of high intelligence that is also associated with Athena: as she says in 13.296–9, 'we are both clever: you are the best amongst men at scheming (*boulē*) and speaking, and I am famous amongst all the gods for cunning (*mētis*) and cleverness'. A great theme of the *Odyssey* is this triumph of intelligence over more brutal, threatening powers: Odysseus overcomes powerful figures like the Cyclops and, with Athena's help, a horde of Suitors, because he is cleverer than they are.

Books 13 and 14 therefore not only move Odysseus from fantasy world to reality, but also inaugurate his transition from voyager to king in his palace.

1.2 Disguise, recognition, narrative

Athena's disguising of Ithaca at the start of the Ithacan episode inaugurates another crucial motif which will run like a thread through the narrative of the second half.[20] The scene between Odysseus and Athena

---

[17] There is also a countervalent motion to this increase in status, in that in his stories he goes from being the Iliadic hero at the start to shipwrecked and alone on Scherie.

[18] In the battle, he dons heavy armour (22.122–4), thus returning to his old Iliadic status.

[19] Cf. esp. Detienne and Vernant 1978: 187–213. This is in fact a little schematic. Though they can be opposed, they sometimes act in concert, as in Eur. *Tr.* 48–97 (cf. perhaps *Od.* 4.499–511); nor does the simple nature/culture divide work for say Soph. *OC* 712–15, where Poseidon is perhaps attributed with the invention of the oar, elsewhere said to be Athena's gift.

[20] Cf. Aristotle's description of the poem as having ἀναγνώρισις... διόλου 'recognition throughout' (*Poet.* 1459b15). For recognition on Scherie, cf. Murnaghan

sets the pattern for the subsequent use of the motif in two different ways.[21] First, the detailed aspects of the disguises and recognitions foreshadow the four main meetings and recognitions of the second half of the poem, that is, those between Odysseus and (in order of recognition) Telemachus, Eurycleia, Eumaeus (and Philoetius) and Penelope. Athena appears in two disguises, one male, as a princely young shepherd, and one female, as a mature woman, and each disguise looks forward to two later recognitions. Her appearance as a shepherd-prince looks forward first, in her guise of a young prince, to the meeting with Telemachus, and second, in her guise of a shepherd, to the meeting with the swineherd Eumaeus.[22] Her second disguise, as 'a fair, tall woman, skilled in fine works' (13.288–9), then looks forward both to the admirable housekeeper Eurycleia, and also to Penelope: the phrase quoted is one used to denote excellence in Homeric women.[23] Book 13 thus acts as a *mise en abyme*[24] for the whole of the second half. Not only does this give a pleasing structure to the narrative, but it may also have acted as an aide-memoire for the poet, encapsulating the double sequence of low- and high-status meetings which are to inform the second part. It also functions as an indication to the audience of how the plot is to unfold. We thus get an insight of how the poet went about composing his long epic, taking the important structural features of the story and generating from them smaller and larger episodes.

The meeting of Odysseus and Athena allows us to isolate a very simple narrative matrix consisting of a three-fold scheme with the elements 'disguise', 'recognition' and 'narrative', which Homer will reuse and modify in a variety of different ways throughout the rest of the poem. When a

1987: 91–103. On recognition in literature generally, cf. Cave 1997; on this much discussed aspect of the *Odyssey*, cf. Stewart 1976; Murnaghan 1987; Goldhill 1991: 1–68; Steiner 2010: 20–2. On the ancient scholars' treatment of the theme, cf. N. J. Richardson 1983. Eustathius 2.214.9–10 writes that 'Odysseus was recognised in unexpected and greatly varied ways (παραδόξως καὶ πολυτρόπως) by all those who recognised him, and no recognition is completely like any other'.

[21] For the structural study of the *Odyssey*, cf. especially Arend 1933 (review in A. M. Parry 1971: 404–7); Thornton 1970: 38–57; Fenik 1974; Nagler 1974; M. W. Edwards 1975; B. B. Powell 1977; Foley 1990: 240–77, 1991: 1–60; Reece 1993; Lord 2000: 68–98, and 158–85 on the *Odyssey*.

[22] This link is strengthened by the repetition of the description of her as a mature woman in the Telemachus scene (16.157–8 = 13.288–9). Both the shepherd and Telemachus carry spears (13.225 and 16.40). Cf. 13.217–50n. *sub fin.*

[23] Cf. 13.289n.

[24] *Mise en abyme*, a phrase from French heraldry, is used to refer to a passage of a text which contains within itself a smaller version of the whole. For instance, the opening quarrel of the *Iliad*, in which Agamemnon and Chryses quarrel over the girl Chryseis, mirrors the main tale of the quarrel over Helen, and indeed the coming quarrel over Briseis. The equivalent expression in English for *mise en abyme* is 'infinite regress', and the word refers to those heraldic shields which have a smaller shield on them, which itself contains a yet smaller shield and so on to infinity.

person's identity is sought or discussed, narrative is regularly used to put
off the recognition of the disguised figure, so that the story continues to
unfold without reaching the recognition which must bring the scene to a
close. Disguise is thus essential to the continuation of the narrative, but
recognition threatens it, and the various deceptive narratives which pop-
ulate the books of the second half are what permits a substantial epic to
come about. The basic plot of stories like the *Odyssey* is the eventual recognition between husband and wife,[25] but this can only be given interest
and substance if the theme of disguise is exploited and the recognition
deferred. Narration thus becomes an unavoidable aspect of the story. Narration is of course by definition an unavoidable aspect of almost any story,
but in the *Odyssey* it is narration by the 'secondary narrators' in the story
which carries a good deal of the burden of informing and extending the
plot.

In book 13 one can see how this matrix works to allow the poet to
create a lengthy episode out of very simple elements when, in order to
delay the revelation of the island's and her own identity, Athena disguises
the appearance of Ithaca and herself takes on the appearance of a noble
young shepherd. Athena eventually reveals to Odysseus that the island is
in fact Ithaca, but maintains its disguise and gives a fictional description
of it (13.37–49): its identity is thus established but not its appearance.
Odysseus is pleased to hear it is Ithaca, but now obscures his real identity,[26] replying with a tale which constructs a false one. At this point, Athena
reveals herself and that she knows who Odysseus is. This repeats the treatment of the island: her identity is revealed, but her real appearance is still
hidden behind another disguise. Odysseus eventually returns to the question of the identity of the island, and this time Athena, having described it
in terms familiar to us from Homer's own description (13.96–112), dispels
the mist and reveals its true nature. Where Odysseus had earlier 'rejoiced
and was delighted that Athena had told him it was his land' (13.251–2), he
now 'rejoiced and was delighted with the land of his fathers' (13.353–4):
he is no longer relying on hearsay. Thus, the identity of all the major elements of the scene, goddess, mortal and island, is finally established, after
the delays through false narratives; the story moves on, with Odysseus now
being actually disguised for his encounters in Eumaeus' farm and in the
palace.

In book 14, this matrix of disguise, identity and narrative recurs, though
the identity revealed is a false one and the true recognition is put off until a

---

[25] For detailed comparison of the *Odyssey* and Sanskrit epic treatments of this
theme, cf. N. Allen 2009.
[26] Odysseus' caution before an unknown and possibly divine figure contrasts
with the Suitors' continual carelessness about Odysseus' identity, despite warnings
that he might be a god (cf. 17.483–7, 18.353–5) and other indications that he may
be other than he seems; cf. Murnaghan 1987: 67–90.

later stage. Its operation can most efficiently be appreciated in a schematic summary of the conversation between Eumaeus and the beggar:

A1 Odysseus: *identity* of your master? (115–20).

A2 Eumaeus: *narrative* of Penelope's mistrust of beggars (121–30); *narrative* of Odysseus' presumed fate, including *revelation* of his name (131–47; NB 144).

B1 Odysseus: *oath* that Odysseus will return (148–64).

B2 Eumaeus: *rejection* of Odysseus' return; *narrative* of Telemachus (165–84).

A1 Eumaeus: your *identity*? (185–90).

A2 Odysseus: *narrative* of beggar's life (191–359), including r*evelation* of fictional name (14.204) and *narrative* about Odysseus (321–35).

B2 Eumaeus: *rejection* of Odysseus' return and *narrative* of his fate (360–77), his own present life and trick played by the Aetolian (378–89).

B1 Odysseus' *promise*: 'kill me if Odysseus does not return'; Eumaeus' horrified *rejection* (390–408).

There is a simple ABAB pattern, with variations. The first A concerns Odysseus' identity, the second that of the beggar, but they are of course the same person and so this disparity between the audience's knowledge and Eumaeus' generates much of the gentle humour of the scene. In each case, narrative is used to develop the sections by deferring or deflecting awkward questions, while conveying information between the two men, true or false.

The beggar's second false tale, of how he got a cloak on a cold night at Troy (468–502), does not explicitly raise the question of Odysseus' identity, but still does so implicitly, as Odysseus tells a story about himself serving with Odysseus, who provides the clever idea for getting the cloak. We have again play with the question of the identity of the beggar/Odysseus, and again the centrepiece is a narrative.

The recognition-scene involving Telemachus makes less use of narrative, but again uses a matrix, this time of 'parent and child', which figures in the two similes which frame the episode, and is used four times. When Telemachus arrives, Eumaeus

went up to his master (ἄνακτος) ...Just as a loving father welcomes his son who has come from a far-off land in the tenth year of his absence, an only son and dear for whom he has suffered a great deal, so the god-like swineherd embraced and kissed passionately Telemachus who looked like a god. (16.14–21)

In the simile a father welcomes a child, but in the story the welcomer is not Telemachus' father, and the 'master' is not Odysseus.[27] Telemachus addresses Eumaeus as ἄττα (16.31; cf. 57, 130), a word, derived from IE *atta* 'father', which is used generally by younger men to older,[28] and again excludes Odysseus from his parental role. We begin then with a disjunction.

In the second phase, father and son encounter each other for the first time, but there is no recognition: Telemachus addresses his father simply as 'stranger' (16.44), and turns to seek information about him from Eumaeus, who gives a brief narrative (16.57–67). When father and son do talk, the lack of recognition is again marked by the language: Odysseus talks of himself as if of another person, wishing that 'Odysseus himself might come' (16.101), and Telemachus needlessly tells Odysseus about his father (16.119–20).

Athena arrives and seems to herald the revelation of Odysseus' identity by telling Odysseus to 'speak to your son' (16.168), and restoring him to his proper appearance.[29] However, expectations of a recognition are defeated, because Telemachus, frightened by the change, turns away and again refers to Odysseus as 'stranger' (16.181). Odysseus reveals his identity (16.188–95), but Homer surprises us again by having Telemachus reject the identification, and Odysseus sits dejectedly down. The possibility arises that Telemachus, like Eumaeus, is not yet to recognise his father, but this is immediately dispelled as Telemachus embraces his father and a parent-and-child simile brings the identification to a close: 'they cried shrilly, more sadly than birds, sea-eagles or vultures with curved talons, whose children countrymen have taken away before they are fledged' (16.215–18).

Recognition has been achieved, and Odysseus finally replaces Eumaeus as 'dear father' (16.222).[30]

So far we have had one scene involving identity where Odysseus is known to another person but does not initially recognise her; one where he knows the other, who does not recognise him (a pattern replicated with the other swineherds); and one where one person of a pair recognises

---

[27] The juxtaposition in 20 of the synonymous epithets θεοειδέα of Telemachus and δῖος of Eumaeus strengthens the link between master and servant.

[28] Cf. also *Il.* 9.607, 17.561 (Achilles and Menelaus to Phoenix); *Od.* 17.6, 599, 21.369 (Telemachus to Eumaeus).

[29] This reverses the pattern of the revelation of Ithaca, where its identity is first revealed and then its true appearance.

[30] There is a poignant relationship between the sadness felt by father and son on their reunion, achieved through the mediation of a countryman, and that felt by the birds at the loss of their children through countrymen. This clash conveys something of the bitter-sweet nature of this reunion and the mixture of delight mingled with a sense of loss that accompanies it.

him when the second is absent. The aged dog, Argos, provides another variant (17.290–327), whereby Argos and Odysseus recognise each other, but Eumaeus is, though present, excluded (17.304–5). Again, narrative is used to give substance to the scene, as Homer tells of Argos' recent history (17.290–9), and Eumaeus describes his glorious past (17.312–23). That a dog is the only mortal creature who immediately recognises Odysseus throws into relief the lack of perception of the humans, in an almost humorous way.[31]

The recognition by Penelope, to which all is tending, is given especial prominence.[32] The recognition by Eumaeus is given two stages, that by Penelope is spread over three phases, in books 19, 20 and 23. There is also a crescendo in the phases, from lack of recognition in 19, to 'virtual' recognition in 20, to actual recognition in 23.[33] These stages also frame the other recognitions: within the first is the recognition by Eurycleia, and between the second and third that by Eumaeus and Philoetius. The staggered progress of the recognition increases the pathos and allows Homer twice to treat the scene of a face-to-face meeting between husband and wife.

The first phase repeats the pattern of the scene with Telemachus and Eumaeus: two people are unaware of Odysseus' identity, and one eventually realises who he is.[34] The pattern is four sets of ABC, the last syncopated, with narrative again prominent, and 'gifts' as a linking motif:

A1 103–5 Penelope *asks* 'Who are you?'

B1 106–22 Odysseus *responds* diverting question to *description* of good ruler.

C1 123–61 Penelope's *sad story* of her life and the trick with the web.

A2 162–3 Penelope *asks* 'Who are you?'

B2 164–203 Odysseus *responds*, a *story* about *gifts* to Odysseus in Crete.

C2 204–13 Penelope *weeps*.

[31] The strongest reactions to the recognition of Odysseus are given by Argos on his squalid dung-heap and Queen Penelope in the centre of the house: Argos dies, and 'Penelope's knees and heart went limp, as she recognised the signs which Odysseus made clear to her' (23.205–6), a line that is used of the death of warriors in the *Iliad* (e.g. 21.115). Cf. Lord 2000: 177 for the theme in Yugoslav epic in which 'the return of the hero is associated with the death of one of the characters in his immediate circle upon recognition'.

[32] See most recently Levaniouk 2010.

[33] This crescendo is lost if one thinks that Penelope does, consciously or unconsciously, recognise Odysseus, as has been suggested e.g. by Harsh 1950; Amory 1963; Austin 1975: 205–36; Winkler 1990: 129–61; Ahl and Roisman 1996: 223–38. For a critique of this idea, cf. Emlyn-Jones 1984; Rutherford 1992: 33–8.

[34] On this type of recognition, where one family member conceals his or her identity from the others, Louden 2011: 72 says: 'to my knowledge, the only other ancient romances that feature this same subtype are Euripides' *Alcestis* and Kalidasa's *Shakuntala*, both of which use variants of the type'.

A3 213–19 Penelope *asks* Odysseus about Odysseus' clothing.
B3 220–57 Odysseus *responds, story* about Odysseus; his *gifts* to Odysseus.
C3 249–51 Penelope *weeps* and *denies* Odysseus' return.

B4 252–307 Odysseus' *story* about Odysseus collecting *gifts.*
C4 308–16 Penelope *denies* Odysseus' return.

Narrative plays a big role, each tale deferring the recognition, while always maintaining that possibility. The variety of the tales recalls the variety in those told to Eumaeus. Penelope's tale of the web mixes pathos with wry amusement; Odysseus' first smacks of tales told so often by beggars seeking a meal; his second is a poignantly humorous account of how the women admired Odysseus' clothes; the last blends falsehood with true aspects of the last stages of Odysseus' voyage.

Eurycleia's recognition falls into two parts, with what one might call a 'virtual' recognition[35] followed by an actual one:

A1 363–78 Eurycleia's sad *account* of Odysseus' likely existence.
B1 378–92 Eurycleia's 'virtual' *recognition* ('you are very like Odysseus'); *recognition of* scar.

A2 393–466 *Account* of Odysseus' scar.
B2 467–503 Eurycleia *recognises* Odysseus; Odysseus' suppression of her reaction.

The lengthy narration of the scar is a famous problem in Odyssean scholarship, but what has been said so far about narration suggests that it is an extreme example of the use of narrative to defer recognition.[36]

Eurycleia's 'virtual' recognition is then repeated for Penelope, in a different form. In this second stage of her recognition, revelation and reunion take place but only through dreams, imagery and imagination. Penelope tells how she dreamt that an eagle killed her geese and, as she lamented them, 'in a human voice' the eagle (19.545) identified itself as Odysseus: 'this is no dream (ὄναρ), it is propitious reality (ὕπαρ) ... Before I was an eagle, now I have come as your husband' (19.548–9). Odysseus then confirms the identification: 'Odysseus himself has said how things

[35] Another variant on the 'virtual' recognition is Irus' glimpse of Odysseus' powerful thighs when he tucks his garment up for the fight (18.66–75): he does not know it is Odysseus, but he knows he is in trouble.
[36] In terms of focalisation, it could be a piece of author-narration by Homer himself, making a change from the general use of character-narration in the other scenes; ποτε (19.393) would be the tale-teller's 'once upon a time'. Alternatively, it could be Eurycleia's memory: the narration follows a verb of perceiving, ἔγνω (19.392), whose subject is Eurycleia, and its length is explicable as what narratologists call a 'slow-down', where a brief event in the story, like a flash of memory, is expanded by the narrative over a much longer time. In favour of the latter is de Jong 1985, against Doherty 1995: 155–6; cf. also Köhnken 1976.

will end' (19.557). There is a meeting therefore, but only an imaginary one. This motif is then reused in a more intimate but still distanced manner.[37] Penelope wakes and reveals that 'this very night once more there lay by me a man like him, just as he was when he went with the army, and my heart rejoiced, for I did not think it was a dream (ὄναρ), but reality (ὕπαρ) at last' (20.88–90): Odysseus is now himself, not an eagle, but still a dream. Odysseus immediately has a comparable experience: 'but as she wept, godlike Odysseus heard her voice, and he pondered this, and it seemed to him in his heart that she recognised him and was standing by his head' (20.92–4).[38] Again, husband and wife are brought together but only in imagination: three more books are to pass before the true meeting.[39]

The recognition by Penelope then finally arrives in book 23, and a link to the previous scenes is provided by reference to her sleeping (23.18–19). The pattern is as follows:

A1 1–24 Eurycleia: *Odysseus has come*; Penelope *disbelieves, gods* made Eurycleia stupid.
A2 25–33 Eurycleia: *he is the beggar*; Penelope *overjoyed*.
A3 34–68 Eurycleia *saw evidence*; Penelope *sceptical*: *god* killed Suitors.
A4 69–84 Eurycleia *talks of scar*; Penelope *non-committal*; descends.

B1 85–152 Penelope *uncertain*. Telemachus *chides*, Odysseus mollifies.
B2 152–296 Odysseus *chides*; Penelope is *cautious* and orders bed. Odysseus falls for trick. Recognition!

---

[37] A link to the first stage is provided by a reference to a daughter or daughters of Pandareus (20.66–78, cf. 19.518–23; Schadewaldt 1959).

[38] At moments like these one can appreciate why some have proposed that Penelope has, more or less consciously, recognised Odysseus. This is to go too far however. Homer has found a way to express the complex psychological reactions of Penelope to the charismatic beggar: she can see similarities between him and Odysseus and may even hope he may turn out to be Odysseus, but she cannot allow herself to fall for her own desire that this might be the case.

[39] In the meantime, Eumaeus and Philoetius recognise Odysseus, again through the scar (20.185–239 and 21.188–229). Like Eurycleia and Penelope, Philoetius has a two-stage recognition: at 20.204–6, he says 'I broke into a sweat when I saw you...and I remembered Odysseus: I imagine he is wearing the same rags', before finally recognising him in book 21. A new sense of 'recognition' also appears, in Odysseus' acknowledgement of the worth of the two men. In the first episode, he says to Philoetius 'I myself recognise (γιγνώσκω) that there is wisdom in your heart' (20.228); and in the second Odysseus 'recognised (ἀνέγνω) the staunch heart in them' (21.205), before going on to say 'I recognise (γιγνώσκω) that to you alone of my servants is my coming welcome' (21.209–10). The Suitors' recognition will be brutally done: Odysseus throws off his rags and kills Antinous, revealing who he is (though without using his name; 22.1–41): on the difference between this recognition and the others, see Murnaghan 1987: 56–90.

Here, with another virtuoso display of narrative *uariatio,* Homer manages under 'A' to get four different variations on the theme of Penelope's reaction to Eurycleia's news. Husband and wife then meet again in the hall, and Homer gives us two bites at the cherry of recognition, the climax coming as a result of detailed narration of Odysseus' construction of his bed.[40] The tricking of Odysseus by a woman 'skilled in fine works' thus brings us right back to book 13, and the similar scene with Athena.[41]

It should be clear now that these repeated scenes concerning identity and repetition are not just the product of a laborious attempt to bulk out the epic, but are central to the story. The story itself, at bottom, is very simple: a man comes home in disguise and reclaims his wife. For that story to be of interest to an audience in a hall, by a camp-fire or at a festival, it has to be expanded, and the poet of the *Odyssey* seems to have set himself to show how it is possible to introduce into it a whole range of variations on the theme that is at the heart of the work: 'Who is the beggar?'[42] The false tales and other narratives are designed to provoke a variety of different reactions, which are fitted to their contexts: humour in Odysseus' to Athena and Eumaeus, pathos in those to Penelope and in her stories, a sense of loss in Eumaeus' stories about himself and Argos, and so on. As Lowe puts it, 'the *Odyssey* is the most encyclopaedic *compendium* of technical plot devices in the whole of ancient storytelling, and one of the most dazzling displays of narrative fireworks anywhere in literature'.[43]

The desire for a more prompt ending, felt by those who find the stories over-long and unnecessary, is not however a totally inappropriate response, just an incomplete one. As a result of the desire for completeness in a story, the audience naturally wants an episode or the whole story brought to its satisfactory conclusion with the recognition of Odysseus; but there is the complementary response which does not want the recognition to come, because this will inevitably bring the story to an end, and thus end the pleasure which the act of narrating it affords. We want

[40] The phrase σήματ' ἀναγνούσηι (23.206) is repeated from early in the first phase (19.250).

[41] The recognition by Laertes (24.205–355) contains many thematic similarities with the earlier scenes, especially with those involving Penelope (cf. Louden 2011: 90–2), and narrative is again involved in Odysseus' false tale about entertaining Odysseus (303–14), and in his brief account of the scar given in response to Laertes' request for a 'sign' (331–44; 345–6 ≈ 23.205–6 of Penelope). However, when compared with the earlier examples, there seems to be no particular originality about it.

[42] This question inaugurates the whole Penelope episode: 19.105 τίς πόθεν εἰς ἀνδρῶν; 'Who among men are you and where are you from?' Cf. also 1.170, 7.238, 10.325, 14.187, 15.264, 24.298.

[43] 2000: 129.

Penelope reunited with her husband, but we realise that her pleasure will be the end of ours. Thus, underlying the whole treatment of Odysseus' identity is a tension between narrative and recognition. Narration threatens recognition, because it prolongs the story and defers the recognition; but recognition in turn threatens narrative because, once Odysseus is recognised, the *Odyssey* is essentially at an end.

Finally, there is another, metaliterary, way of looking at the question of disguise and narrative in the *Odyssey*, which further justifies the amount of story-telling in the epic. We said above that these two motifs 'ran like a thread' through the narrative, and the metaphor was not casually chosen. Weaving is one of the commonest Indo-European metaphors for poetic composition,[44] and clothing plays a big part in our story, both in terms of disguise and in connection with the narratives that people tell. Athena says to Odysseus 'I have come here to weave with you a clever plan (μῆτιν ὑφήνω)' (13.303):[45] the plan they will weave is the narrative Homer will tell. Subsequently, Odysseus is disguised in filthy clothes by Athena, and it is this which allows the story to be extended as it is, the disguise preventing people from seeing the truth. In his discussions with Eumaeus, the question of his getting a cloak as a reward for his narratives about Odysseus is a frequent motif, as when Eumaeus warns him not to imitate other beggars: 'you would soon, old man, craft your story (παρατεκτήναιο) in a different way if one were to give you a cloak and tunic for clothes' (14.131): the verb contains the element *tekt-* found in words for 'craft, craftsman' (*archi-tektōn*, etc.). At 14.396, Odysseus suggests an arrangement, whereby if Odysseus returns he will get a cloak and tunic. His final story to Eumaeus and the swineherds is precisely aimed at getting a cloak and tells a story of how he did this once before. Later, Penelope promises to give the beggar a cloak and tunic if she finds he is telling the truth (17.549–50, 556–8). She herself tells the story of how she fooled the Suitors for three years by the stratagem of weaving and unpicking the fabric, with a story that she was creating a shroud for Laertes (19.137–52): 'I contrive tricks' (ἐγὼ δὲ δόλους τολυπεύω, 19.137), she says, and the verb means literally 'to card wool for spinning'. Narrative and garments thus frequently go together, and in each case the narrative is either a false tale or potentially false. The weaving of clothes and the weaving of false tales are thus parallel: disguise in the physical form of clothes and in the verbal form of lies is thus central both to the survival of the characters and to the 'fabric' of the story of the *Odyssey*. These ideas are set forth in books 13–14 and are developed through the second half.

[44] M. L. West 2007: 36–8.   [45] For the phrase, cf. 4.678, 739, 9.422, 13.386.

2 IDEOLOGY AND SOCIOLOGY:
A NEW TYPE OF EPIC?

The disguising of Odysseus as a beggar by Athena heralds a concentration in the second half on 'lower-status'[46] figures. As with the prevalence of leisurely conversations, this concentration looks unepic and suggests that the *Odyssey* is deliberately seeking to bring into the epic genre subjects which might be thought to be alien and even opposed to it: epic poetry, it seems to be saying, can be made out of such subject matter just as well as from more traditional tales of derring-do.

It is not possible to prove conclusively that the *Odyssey* was doing something new in thus concentrating on the world of the less privileged, because, apart from the *Iliad*, we have nothing previous to compare it with: the other Greek epics of which we have evidence all post-date the *Odyssey*. A full survey would be needed to establish the point, but the work of scholars who have surveyed various epic traditions suggests that humbler characters are usually found in epic only in subordinate roles. Bowra noted that a 'characteristic of heroic narrative is that on the whole it concentrates on the happy few and neglects the others'; of the few low-status characters whom he came across he wrote, 'though these humble characters may have roles of some importance, they are introduced mainly because they help the great and indeed display towards them that self-denying devotion which a hero expects from his servants'.[47] Of Ugaritic epic, Wyatt states trenchantly, 'epic is definitely *not* proletarian in its concerns!'[48] A character like Sargon, king of Babylon, may be brought up by herdsmen, but his main exploits are as a king; Gilgamesh may meet an Ale-wife, but she is a divinity more like Calypso than Eurycleia.

The admittedly very scanty fragments of the other early Greek epics suggest that the *Odyssey*'s interest in ordinary people is unusual for this genre. The only reference to a humble figure in the fragments is the shepherd who found the egg laid by Nemesis and brought it to Leda, but there is no evidence that he played a major role in the story.[49] There are grand figures who are compelled for various reasons to dress in rags: Adrastus fled from the defeat of the Seven εἵματα λυγρὰ φέρων ('wearing squalid clothes');[50] king Telephus came to the Greeks at Aulis as a beggar to get healing for

---

[46] I use this term *faute de mieux*. It refers as neutrally as possible to their social status in the majority of the poem. On the sociology of the *Odyssey*, see e.g. Donlan 1973; P. W. Rose 1975; Finley 1978; Farron 1979–80; A. T. Edwards 1993; Raaflaub 1997. On modern responses to the interest in lower status figures, cf. Hall 2008: 131–43.
[47] Bowra 1966: 53–4.   [48] N. Wyatt 2005: 247.
[49] *Cypria*, fr. 11 (= Apollod. *Bibl.* 3.10.7; *GEF* p. 90).
[50] *Thebaid*, fr. 11 (*GEF* p. 52).

his wound;[51] Odysseus entered Troy as a beggar;[52] and there are traditions about gods being forced to do menial work.[53] In *Epigoni*,[54] there
appeared Rhachius, 'the Ragged Man', who married Teiresias' daughter
Manto in accordance with an oracle: he might be an example of a man of
poor origins playing a major role, but we know too little of him. There
is no evidence however that these other epics concentrated on figures
like Eumaeus to anything like the extent that the *Odyssey* does.[55] To put
book 14 in context, the ways in which the *Odyssey* foregrounds lower-status
characters will be sketched here.

Having disguised his main character as a beggar, Homer opens book
14 with a detailed account of the way in which Eumaeus constructed his
farmstead to keep himself and his pigs safe from marauders and wild animals (14.6–20), and then describes how Odysseus came upon him making
himself a pair of sandals (14.23–4). Eumaeus' attention to his duties is thus
made plain from the very start, and this valuing of what Grover Cleveland
called 'the dignity of labour' will be a feature of the second part of the
poem.[56] Here the *Odyssey* contrasts with the Greek aristocratic ideology
that manual labour was beneath any dignity.[57]

The work of servants does not go unmentioned in the *Iliad*, but it is
usually referred to in a rather perfunctory way,[58] as at 9.658–62: 'Patroclus
ordered his comrades and handmaidens immediately to spread a thick
couch for Phoenix. They obeyed and spread the couch as he ordered, with

[51] *Cypria*, *Arg.* 7 (*GEF* pp. 72–4).
[52] *Ilias Parua*, *Arg.* 4 (*GEF* p. 122; cf. also p. 118 for the tragedy *Ptōkeia*).
[53] Cf. e.g. Panyassis, fr. 3 (*GEF* p. 194) on Apollo serving Admetus.
[54] Fr. 4 (*GEF* p. 58).
[55] Eumaeus is of course of royal birth originally (15.413–14), but for the *Odyssey*
he is simply a swineherd.
[56] The life and work of herdsmen is valued in the poem, but it is not romanti-
cised. A. T. Edwards says that 'though qualified by slavery and poverty, Eumaeus'
simple life presents a bucolic vision of great power' (1993: 63; cf. generally
60–70), but if slavery and poverty are not enough, the dangers from marauders
(e.g 14.262–5, 15.386–8 and 427–8) and wild animals bring such a claim into
question.
[57] Cf. e.g. Hdt. 2.167; Xen. *Oec.* 4.2–3; Pl. *Rep.* 495d-e; Arist. *Pol.* 1258b35–9,
1337b8–14. There are however a few instances in epic where aristocrats are
described as involved in such activities: Paris builds his palace (*Il.* 6.314–17),
Lycaon cuts wood for a chariot (21.37–8), Priam's sons tend his horses
(24.247–80), the Ithacan assembly is sent ἐπὶ ἔργα ἕκαστος (*Od.* 2.252), Odysseus
builds his bed-chamber (23.183–204) and Laertes tends his farm (24.205–12). Cf.
also 13.222; Strasburger 1997: 58–61.
[58] The longer *Iliad* uses *dmōai/-es* twelve times to the *Odyssey*'s eighty, and
amphipoloi thirteen times to the *Odyssey*'s sixty (both epics generally avoid the
blunter *doulos*; cf. 14.340n.). Very roughly, there is a reference to a slave or servant every 600 lines in the *Iliad*, and every 150 lines in the *Odyssey*. For an overview
of slavery in Homer, see Schmidt 2006.

fleeces and a rug and soft fabric of linen. There the old man lay down and waited for holy Dawn'. There is nothing quite like the scene where Eurycleia gives orders for the cleaning of the hall after the Suitors' dinner (20.147–63):[59]

> But Eurycleia, a goddess among women, daughter of Ops son of Peisenor, called to the maids and said, 'Wake up. Some of you sweep the house, and sprinkle it with water; put the purple rugs on the well-made seats; others wipe down all the tables with sponges, clean the mixing-bowls and the well-wrought double cups. Others, go for water to the fountain at once and bring it here quickly. The Suitors will not be absent for long; they will be here early, as it is a feast-day for everyone.' So she spoke, and they listened closely to her, as you can imagine, and obeyed: twenty of them went to the fountain with its black water, and the others worked skilfully about the house. The lordly men-servants also came in and chopped the firewood efficiently and skilfully. The women returned from the fountain, and after them came the swineherd with the three best pigs he had.

It is striking that so banausic an activity as cleaning up after a riotous dinner should be given such an extended and detailed treatment.[60] Furthermore, the sense of efficient organisation by the servant Eurycleia is clear,[61] and her importance is emphasised by the honorific way she is introduced: she is a 'goddess among women', a phrase normally reserved for the aristocracy, and is given a grand patronymic 'daughter of Ops son of Peisenor'. This imposing introduction is found only twice elsewhere amongst the twenty-nine occasions on which she is introduced, and both instances occur where her importance is again stressed: in 1.429 she makes her first appearance in the poem and her status in the household is emphasised, and in 2.347 her stewardship of Odysseus' great store-room is recounted. Its use here marks the importance of what she is doing.[62]

In the same way, the men are described by the paradoxical phrase *drēstēres agēnores* 'lordly manservants'. *Drēstēr*, literally 'a doer', is a rare word

---

[59] Nearest is the preparation of Priam's chariot in 24.265–80, but this passage, with its very unusual technical vocabulary, is important not so much for the acknowledgement of the work of servants as for marking, by a passage of an unusual nature, the crucial nature of this journey to get back his son's body.

[60] In the later *H.Dem.* 138–44, Demeter lists household tasks she might undertake, but there is no extended description of them.

[61] Stanford (ad loc.) is wrong to call her imperatives 'fussy' and herself 'excited'. There is nothing in the passage to suggest this.

[62] It tells us too of course that she was once of aristocratic birth, like Eumaeus, but her birth should not be interpreted as the reason for her excellence: the *Odyssey* makes it very clear that aristocratic birth alone is no guarantee of nobility of character.

in the *Odyssey*,[63] and means an ordinary slave: Pindar describes someone as a *therapōn* 'an attendant', not a *drēstēr*.[64] The epithet *agēnōr* 'manly' is used fourteen times of the Suitors (*mnēstēres*). The rhyming and metrically equivalent phrases *drēstēres/mnēstēres agēnores* thus implicitly pose the question of which group the epithet is better applied to, the aristocratic but evil Suitors or the humble woodmen who work studiously at their task.[65] The menial work of such people, we are reminded, when well carried out,[66] is essential to the smooth running of an aristocratic household. Stanford thus gets things the wrong way round when he says 'the epithet is not absurd: the servants of a noble palace may acquire some of the dignity of their surroundings' (Stanford ad loc.); it is rather they who give the palace such dignity as it has under the Suitors. This use of honorific epithets for Eurycleia and the workmen is of a piece with the way in which Eumaeus is described at the beginning of book 14 as 'the godlike swineherd' (14.3) and 'leader of men' (14.22):[67] again, the apparently paradoxical use of such epithets of a herdsman acts as a challenge to the aristocratic monopoly on such terms elsewhere.[68]

The description of Eumaeus' farmstead also allows him to take his place alongside the higher-status people whose residences are given especial treatment. The *Odyssey* devotes space to the spectacular palaces of Menelaus, which Telemachus compares to that of Zeus (4.71–5; cf. 43–6), of Alcinous with its immensely rich decoration and magical metal dogs (7.81–132), of Aeolus with its continual feasting and music (10.3–12), and of Odysseus (17.264–71),[69] and gives detailed pictures of the homes of Circe (10.210–19), Calypso (5.57–74) and the Cyclops (9.219–23).[70] Eumaeus' farm cannot compete in grandeur with these other settings, but

---

[63] Elsewhere, only at 16.248 and 18.76.   [64] *Py.* 4.287.

[65] Olson 1991–2 notes that servants' suggestions are not usually acted on, but passages like this show that their importance is indicated in other ways.

[66] The words 'efficiently' and 'knowledgeably' are used also of Odysseus in the making of his raft and bedroom: 5.245, 250, 259; 23.185, 193, 197. Cf. 15.319–24, where Odysseus as a beggar proudly lists his skills in making fires, chopping wood, carving, cooking and wine-pouring.

[67] Cf. 14.3n.

[68] The language of this passage is also unusual. κορέω (149) is very rare in Greek (Dem. 18.258 and Eupolis, fr. 167): in the *Iliad*, there is no sweeping. ῥαίνω (150) is used of wiping things spattered with blood or dust, but not of laying dust. A sponge (151) makes a single appearance, to wipe Hephaestus' fine physique after work (18.414). ἀμφιμάομαι (152) is not thought fit for literature again until the fourth century AD. Nonetheless, these ordinary words sit happily alongside august formulae such as δέπα ἀμφικύπελλα (cf. 13.57n.). In the language, as amongst the characters, the mundane rubs shoulders with the grand.

[69] 'Palace' may be too grand a word for Odysseus' house, whose precise dimensions are not clear from the text.

[70] On the relative importance of *oikoi* and *poleis* in Homer, cf. Scully 1990: 100–13.

it has merits of its own which make it no less significant. With its *prodromos* 'vestibule', *aulē* 'courtyard' and fine outlook, it recalls these grander houses, but what is more notable about it is its fitness for purpose: it is solid and well defended, with large stones and a defensive wall topped with thorny bushes, and though it has no magical dogs, those it does have are well up to their task, as Odysseus immediately discovers.

The way in which Eumaeus' home has served its purpose well is reinforced by an intertextual relationship between it and the only description of a building in the *Iliad*, that of the palace of Priam (6.242–50).[71] The intertexts create an implied comparison between the palace of the wealthiest man in the *Iliad* and the farmstead of a poor swineherd, and may also prompt the reflection that Eumaeus' sturdy farm has done more to protect his pigs than Priam's grand palace did to protect the Trojans. A humble dwelling thus takes its rightful place in epic verse.

Quotation of Iliadic passages is similarly used to suggest that the doings of the poor are of equal value to the more grandiose acts of the rich. When Eumaeus goes out to spend the night in the cold with his pigs, the language used mirrors that of warriors arming to go into battle: 'first, he slung his sword over his brawny shoulders and put on a thick cloak to keep out the wind. He also took the skin of a well-fed goat, and a sharp javelin to protect him against dogs and men' (14.528–31). This may be compared with *Il.* 3.334–8, of Paris: 'he slung his silver-studded bronze sword over his shoulders, and then his great, sturdy shield; ... he took his mighty spear, that fitted his grasp'. The contrast between the epithets for the arms is instructive: Paris puts on a sword which has silver nails, and grasps a huge spear; Eumaeus contents himself with a sword and a javelin that are 'sharp', the essential requirement in a battle, silver nails counting for nothing. The final phrase, 'to ward off dogs and men', reminds us that Eumaeus has to contend with wild beasts as well as enemies of his own kind.

Another activity normally reserved for higher-status characters is entertaining. Eumaeus is twice described as making a meal in book 14. In Greek, as in ancient Near Eastern and Indo-European epic, 'banquet' scenes are not casually employed, but are used to highlight key moments in the story,[72] so the fact that the swineherd Eumaeus should be involved in such scenes is of significance: 'Eumaios is unique in the poem in that he is a servant host.'[73] Indeed, his sacrifice, at thirty-nine lines, is the longest

---

[71] Munro, who noted the parallels, said the lines are 'almost a parody of the description of Priam's palace' (1901: ad 14.13–16). The shared phrases are 6.244 πεντήκοντ'... θάλαμοι ~ 14.15 πεντήκοντα σύες; 6.245, 249 ~ 14.14 πλησίον ἀλλήλων; 6.247 ἔνδοθεν αὐλῆς ~ 14.13 ἔντοσθεν δ' αὐλῆς; 6.248 δώδεκ'...θάλαμοι ~ 14.13 συφεοὺς δυοκαίδεκα.

[72] Cf. e.g. Grottanelli 1989; Vanstiphout 1992; Reece 1993; A. M. Bowie 2003; Sasson 2005: 227–8.

[73] Louden 1997: 100.

in the epic.[74] Furthermore, Eumaeus' meals are presented with the same attention to detail and employ the same kind of language as the grander feasts: there are only a very few signs that this is a rustic meal taking place in a farmstead and not a general's tent or a palace.[75] Eumaeus' generous meal given to a mere beggar demands as much attention and laudatory language as the entertainment by the wealthy of a noble visitor; the subsequent casual treatment of the beggar by the aristocratic Suitors and their generally excessive dining emphasise the point. This point is made again in a humorous way, when Eumaeus serves Odysseus and his fellow-herdsmen a 'fat five-year old pig' (ὗν ... πίονα πενταέτηρον, 14.419). This epithet recurs three times in epic with βοῦν 'ox', in sacrifices by Agamemnon (*Il.* 2.403, 7.315) and Autolochus (*Od.* 19.420), and the phrases πίονα or ἄρσενα πενταέτηρον seem to be formulaic at verse-beginning or -end. Five years is a good age at which to eat beef-cattle, but improbably old for a pig, so the use of the epithet seems to imply that Eumaeus' pig is just as good as Agamemnon's ox, the mild inappropriateness drawing attention to the point.

Finally, there is story-telling, criticised, as we have seen, by some for its prevalence in the second part. Here too however the *Odyssey* does something unusual. Story-telling is not uncommon in epic: in the *Iliad*, internal stories are told by figures like Glaucus (6.145–211), Diomedes (6.215–31), Phoenix (9.527–605), Nestor (11.668–762) and Agamemnon (19.86–136); and in the *Odyssey* by the likes of Nestor again (3.103–200), Menelaus (4.333–592) and Agamemnon (11.404–34). What is different is that in the second half 'lesser' figures also narrate. Odysseus as a beggar and Eumaeus tell each other lengthy tales, Eumaeus' being of a length comparable to Nestor's longest Iliadic tale (15.389–484).[76] The voice of epic narration in the *Odyssey* is thus no longer the preserve of the elite, as in the *Iliad*, but passes also to the other end of the social scale.[77]

Furthermore, the stories which Odysseus and Eumaeus tell each other are not traditional tales about elite members of society, nor about their own or their families' glorious past, such as Glaucus and Diomedes swap in the *Iliad*. Odysseus' tales are amusingly self-deprecating. In the first

---

[74] Next longest is the thirty-four lines of Nestor's sacrifice (3.430–63).

[75] Cf. 14.77, 78, 425nn.

[76] The point made in this paragraph relates strictly to the difference between the two epics, and does not imply that in 'reality' no beggar ever told stories. Lord 2000: 18 notes that in Yugoslavia the difference between beggars and other singers was that 'only beggars lived completely by singing'. That the same was true in early Greece exists at least as a possibility.

[77] Note too how the swineherd Eumaeus is given the role of appraising Odysseus' story-telling in 14.363, 509: Eumaeus 'has obviously attended enough epic performances to make him something of a connoisseur' (Doherty 1995: 72); cf. Louden 1997: 110.

(14.192–359), he tells how he became a good commander and went to Troy, but says nothing of any exploits there; he stresses his military skill, but his main tale of battle involves insubordination by his troops, an ignominious defeat and a life preserved only by abasing himself before the enemy king. He rebuilds his life in Egypt, but then throws everything away by foolishly following a Phoenician trader on a business venture. This epic narration culminates in destitution not *kleos*, a striking reversal of the norm. His second tale (14.462–506), of how he procured a cloak when on an ambush at Troy, is similarly self-mocking: pride in being on a mission with the likes of Odysseus and Menelaus is mixed with the stupidity of going out on a freezing night without a cloak.[78]

If Odysseus' tales are self-deprecatory, Eumaeus' story is remarkably low-genre, and even rather squalid (15.390–484). His nurse is seduced on the beach by a visiting Phoenician, and bribed to steal the king's son so that they can sell him at a good price; on her way out with the child, she pauses only to stuff three valuable goblets into her bosom. When she dies on the voyage, falling ignominiously into the bilge, she is unceremoniously heaved overboard for the seals and fish to eat.

There seems to be a deliberately bathetic, indeed unepic, quality to these tales, but they still entertain. The stories of ordinary people, Gray's 'short and simple annals of the poor', are thus shown to be as valid and instructive as, and of equal interest to, those of more aristocratic figures: in a world of great social change and the ever-present danger of raiding-parties and piracy, these stories would have been equally or indeed more 'relevant' to Homer's own audience than tales of heroic valour. The tale of the Nurse may have a squalid side, but there is also pathos in it: the Nurse's actions deprive Eumaeus of his home and royal status, but she was responding to a very natural desire to return to her own home, a desire which probably struck a chord with some of those listening to Homer.

The ideology of the *Odyssey*, and especially of its second half, thus represents a parity of status of the rich and the poor, and the sense that neither group has a monopoly on excellence. The Suitors represent the worst of the aristocracy and Melanthius, Melantho and the lascivious amongst the serving-maids the worst of the poor. The royal families of Ithaca, Pylos, Sparta and Scherie mark a peak of aristocratic excellence, and Eurycleia, Eumaeus and Philoetius of lower-status excellence. This parity is symbolised in three notable passages in the events leading up to the battle in

---

[78] That these speeches contain such unedifying stories surely makes very problematic the idea, put forward by Woodhouse, that these represent 'the real experiences of the real Odysseus on his way home from Troy' (1930: 132), which were superseded by the more fantastic tales that now make up the *Odyssey*.

the hall. First, Odysseus prays to Zeus for two signs of future success, one from Zeus and another from those in the palace (20.97–121). Zeus duly thunders, and a grinding-woman prays that she may be preparing the Suitors' last dinner. She is not just a lowly servant, but the weakest of them (20.110), still working because she has not been able to finish her quota. Thus Zeus, the highest god, and the lowliest servant-woman are brought together to affirm the gods' intention that Odysseus should succeed. Later, when he reveals himself to Eumaeus and Philoetius, Odysseus promises them that 'if the god subdues the Suitors at my hands, I shall give you both wives, and possessions and houses built beside mine; you will be brothers and companions (ἑτάρω) of Telemachus' (21.213–16).[79] Finally, when in the battle Telemachus fetches four shields, four pairs of spears and four helmets, the weapons of the aristocratic warrior, 'the two servants put on the fine armour, and stood with clever, cunning Odysseus' (22.114–15); when Odysseus has finished his arrows, he follows suit. The social gap between them is closed by the wearing of the same armour in the fight. The herdsmen thus move from their marginal rural context, in which we first meet Eumaeus, and become an integral part of the restored centre, with Eurycleia there to keep the place in good order.

In response to the complaints about the second half of the epic and books 13–14 especially, one can reply that the author of this poem has in fact produced a very radical and innovative kind of epic, which takes on the task of introducing into this 'high' genre 'low' characters, and seeks generally to avoid tales of aristocratic exploits in battle and elsewhere, in favour of stories of everyday life. Equally striking is the way in which the narrative in books 13 to 21 involves very little in the way of major or exciting events. There are long conversations, verbal sparring-matches, the throwing of food and other bad behaviour by the Suitors, and a competition to string the bow characterised by bickering and ill grace, but it is only when Odysseus reveals himself in the hall that exciting, 'epic', action begins. It has been a tour de force to construct nine books out of material so apparently unpromising for an epic.

3 THE *ODYSSEY* AND TROY

If the *Odyssey* is a very different kind of poem from the *Iliad* in its ideology, there is also a strong strand running through it which devalues any notion that the Trojan War was a great Greek triumph.[80] When Eumaeus talks of

---

[79] On *hetairos* in Homer, see Spahn 2006.
[80] This is not of course to say that the *Iliad* does no more than glorify the war, simply that the *Odyssey* opposes the common idea that Troy was a great pan-Hellenic triumph.

what Odysseus would have done for him as a good servant if he had not
died, he bursts out with 'I wish the tribe of Helen had perished utterly,
since she undid the knees of many men' (14.68–9). Later, he makes clear
the negative effects of the War on the household:[81]

> I have had no pleasant word or kindness from my mistress, since that
> plague, the arrogant Suitors, descended on our house. Servants take
> great pleasure in talking before their mistress, in asking the news,
> eating and drinking, and then taking something away to the coun-
> tryside, the kind of things that warm the servants' hearts. (15.374–9)

This is very much the attitude of the poem to the victory: it was not worth
it.[82] T. E. Lawrence described the poet of the *Odyssey* as 'a great but uncritical reader of the *Iliad*',[83] but there is a growing consensus that the *Odyssey*
was in fact far from uncritical of the *Iliad*. It presents, as we have seen, a
very different ideology, but it also seems to wish to 'cut down to size' the
war at Troy.

It does this in part by largely ignoring it. With the Phaeacians, Odysseus
begins his story from the moment that he left Troy: 'Come, I will tell of my
painful return, which Zeus gave me as I left Troy. A wind blew me from
Troy to the Cicones . . .' (9.37–9): he wastes no time on his war exploits.
To Eumaeus, he summarises the whole Trojan War and its aftermath in
three lines: 'there we sons of the Achaeans fought for nine years, and in
the tenth sacked the city of Priam and went home in our ships; the god scattered the Achaeans' (14.240–2). When Homer summarises his account to
Penelope, he completely ignores Troy: 'he began with how he first con-
quered the Cicones' (23.310).[84]

When it does tell stories from Troy, the *Odyssey* tends to ignore episodes
treated by the earlier epic ('Munro's Law'), and those it does tell have
a decidedly 'Odyssean' rather than 'Iliadic' flavour, involving trickery
rather than great deeds on the battlefield.[85] Helen's story of how Odysseus
entered Troy disguised as a poor menial in order to collect intelligence
and to slaughter a good number of Trojans (4.238–64) has resonances

---

[81] For Homer's picture of Ithaca during Odysseus' absence, see Jones 1992:
81–90.
[82] Cf. Penelope's Κακοΐλιον οὐκ ὀνομαστήν ('that evil city Ilium whose name is an
abomination' (19.260, 597; tr. Shewring)), and her lament that Odysseus' departure has destroyed her beauty (18.251–3, 19.124–6). Similarly, Demodocus' two
songs, of the quarrel between Odysseus and Achilles (8.72–82) and of the Trojan
Horse (8.487–534), cause Odysseus to cry like a woman who has lost her husband
in war.
[83] 1940: Introduction.
[84] There are other brief references in 8.219–20, 9.263–9, 504, 10.15–16,
11.168–9 and 19.182.
[85] On these stories, see Olson 1989.

with his disguised entry into his own palace; and Menelaus' curious tale of how he restrained the Greeks in the Horse from responding to Helen's imitation of their wives' voices (4.266–89) looks forward to his refusal to succumb to the temptation to tell Penelope of his arrival. The only Trojan episode Odysseus mentions to Eumaeus is the decidedly unheroic ambush on which he forgot his cloak (14.468–502): it is not even true.

The accounts of those who were at Troy also paint an almost unrelievedly gloomy picture. Nestor is particularly eloquent (3.103–200):[86] suffering at Troy was great, but even when Troy fell, the troubles did not cease, as the sons of Atreus fell out over whether to return immediately or make sacrifice to the gods; the drunken Greeks split in two, some returning, some waiting; and those who left again split in two. Many got back, but Agamemnon died after his return.

Telemachus compares Menelaus' palace to that of Zeus (4.71–5), but he demurs. While he was collecting all this wealth, his brother was killed:

> so it is not with any pleasure that I rule over these possessions...I suffered a great deal and I saw the decline of my prosperous house, which once contained many fine things. I would be happy to live in my palace with a third of my possessions, if the men who died at broad Troy far from horse-rearing Argos could be alive. (4.93–9)

Even in Sparta, with its elegant and wealthy life-style, there is gloom and sadness, as the success of Menelaus' expedition is seen as a disaster.

In the Underworld in book 11, we see the war's deleterious effects on the dead, many of whom come to Odysseus grieving.[87] Agamemnon gives a grim description of his murder and that of his men by Clytemnestra (11.404–34). When Odysseus imagines that Achilles must be as important amongst the shades as he was in life, he makes his famous and bitter reply: 'I would rather work the fields as a labourer for a landless man, who has almost no livelihood, than be king over all the souls of the dead' (11.489–91). Ajax, angered by Odysseus' victory in the contest for Achilles' arms, will not even speak to him, causing Odysseus to say 'how I wish I had not won in that competition, since because of it the earth closed over such a great man, who in physical beauty and exploits was second only to Achilles amongst the Danaans' (11.548–52). Just as Menelaus' wealth turned to dust in the aftermath of Troy, so Odysseus' famous victory in the contest turns out to have tragic consequences.

For the *Odyssey* therefore, the legacy of Troy is misery and implacable hatred, amongst the living and the dead. The war was not a glorious victory,

---

[86] On the following episodes in Pylos and Sparta, see especially Rutherford 1991–3.
[87] Cf. 11.388, 472, 542.

but led to the deaths of great men, the loss of some of the best years of their
lives for husbands and wives, the decline of great houses, the separation of
sons and fathers, the death of sons before fathers, disputes among former
allies and hatreds that survive the grave. It is perhaps no coincidence that
the destructive Sirens sing the story of Troy, which Odysseus must listen to
but not be detained by: listening to the story of Troy is, as it were, bad for
your health.[88]
    Against this grim canvas, the restoration of Odysseus' house, and his
reunion with his wife, son and servants, take on a greater significance. They
seem to represent an ideal against which to set the apparent grandeur of
foreign wars and travel, the cost of which is made all too clear. The *Odyssey*
replaces this grandeur of war and conquest as the subject of epic with the
importance of domestic life and personal ties. As Odysseus tells Calypso
when she offers him immortality, though Penelope is physically inferior to
her, his desire is to return to Ithaca (5.215–24). The meetings of Odysseus
with a shepherd and a swineherd in books 13 and 14 signal this importance
of everyday existence.

4 HOMERIC METRE

4.1 The metrical scheme

Greek metre[89] is 'quantitative', that is, it works by the varied alternation
of 'long' and 'short' syllables.[90] The ancients analysed Homer's metre as a
'dactylic hexameter', that is six 'feet', each based on a dactyl ($-\cup\cup$), which
they analysed into two parts, the 'princeps' ($-$) and the 'biceps' ($\cup\cup$). The
biceps can be substituted by a long syllable in all of the first five feet, thus
creating a 'spondee' ($--$).[91] The basic scheme is therefore:

$$-\underset{\smile}{\smile} \ -\underset{\smile}{\smile} \ -\underset{\smile}{\smile} \ -\underset{\smile}{\smile} \ -\underset{\smile}{\smile} \ -\underset{\smile}{}$$

This is a 'stichic' metre, i.e. one in which the same metrical pattern is
repeated in each line (*stikhos*); the lines are not grouped into stanzas.

---

[88] Cf. Pucci 1998: 1–6 and Dougherty 2001: 71–3.

[89] See generally M. L. West 1982, with 35–42 on the Homeric hexameter; also
1987, with 18–23 on Homer; 1997.

[90] The division of the line into syllables does not take account of word-division
or etymology. A syllable begins with a consonant if there is one and with the vowel if
not; the second of two consecutive consonants usually starts the following syllable.
Thus 13.18 ῥοδοδάκτυλος ἠώς is segmented ρο-δο-δακ-τυ-λο-ση-ως. Syllables ending
in a consonant are 'closed', in a vowel 'open'.

[91] This is less common in the fifth foot than elsewhere (La Roche 1898). Strictly
speaking, the metre should be called the 'dactylic hexameter catalectic', because
of the 'missing' final syllable.

The analysis of this metre as a 'hexameter' is however unlikely in histor-ical terms. More than 98 per cent of lines have a word-break ('caesura') in the third foot, either after the princeps or after the first short of the biceps. It seems therefore more likely that the line was originally a conjunction of two elements ('cola'), either –⏑⏑–⏑⏑– ('hemiepes') with ⏓⏓–⏑⏑–⏑⏑–– ('paroemiac'), or –⏑⏑–⏑⏑–⏑ with ⏑–⏑⏑–⏑⏑––.[92] This idea is supported also by the facts that these two cola are found independently in 'lyric' metres, and that many formulae have the shape of these cola: thus for the first pairing, cf. 13.139 τὸν δ' ἀπαμειβόμενος ¦ προσέφη νεφεληγερέτα Ζεύς; for the second 13.159 αὐτὰρ ἐπεὶ τό γ' ἄκουσε ¦ Ποσειδάων ἐνοσίχθων.

With the third-foot caesurae, the full scheme is thus either[93]

–⏓ –⏓ – ¦ ⏓ –⏓ –⏓ –⏓

or

–⏓ –⏓ –⏑ ¦ ⏑ –⏓ –⏓ –⏓

4.2 Rules of quantity ('prosody')

Syllables are described as 'short' when they contain a short vowel which is either open or followed by a single consonant.[94] They are 'long' when they contain a long vowel, a diphthong or a short vowel followed by two consonants.

There is an exception to the last rule in that when the two consonants are a combination of a plosive, i.e. π and its voiced and aspirated equiva-lents β and φ, and similarly τ, δ, θ, and κ, γ, χ, with a liquid (i.e. λ and ρ) then the syllable can remain short. This occurs at the start of a word (ποτῐ βρεφος), and when the two consonants are in the same word (Πᾰτρŏκλος); but not when the consonants are in different parts of a compound (always e.g. ἔκλεγω) or in two different words (ἐκ λογων).[95]

92 Cf. M. L. West 1973: 187–92; Hackstein 2010: 413–14.
93 A break after the first short of the third foot ('feminine' caesura) is more com-mon than one after the princeps ('masculine') by a proportion of 4:3. A few verses have no third-foot caesura but one after the princeps of the fourth. A caesura is usu-ally avoided between two short syllables in the fourth foot ('Hermann's Bridge'). For the purposes of scansion, no caesura can occur between an enclitic or a pro-clitic and the preceding or following word respectively.
94 'Light' and 'heavy' are sometimes preferred as the descriptions, since 'short' and 'long' belong more properly to vowels, and a vowel is not actually lengthened by being followed by two consonants. Strictly too, the syllable is not so lengthened: in τὸ σκότος, the syllable that is 'long' is τοσ not το (M. L. West 1982: 8–9). 'Short' and 'long' are used here as more familiar.
95 The combination is sometimes described as 'mute + liquid'. Not all of these combinations function so in Homer: this alternation is not found with βλ and γλ.

When two open vowels, which are not in a diphthong, come into contact, a number of things can happen:

(i) 'Elision': a short final vowel is lost, as in 13.1 οἱ δ' ἄρα πάντες.⁹⁶
(ii) 'Correption': a long vowel or diphthong is not lost but is shortened, as επεῖ and ικευ in 13.4 ὦ ὀδῦσευ ἔπεῖ ἴκευ ἐμὸν πότῖ. What happened was that the second vowel was consonantalised into a kind of glide, so that ἔπεῖ ἴκευ ἐμόν was pronounced /epeyikewemon/.⁹⁷
(iii) 'Synizesis': two vowels are run together into a single syllable; this happens regularly when ε is involved, as in 13.7 ὑμεῶν, 14.263 Αἰγυπτῖῶν.
(iv) 'Hiatus': a long vowel or diphthong can stand unchanged. This is often because the second word originally began with a digamma (ϝ = w), so that the hiatus came about only after the digamma was lost, which process began in Ionic perhaps before the eighth century.⁹⁸ Thus, in 1.248 τρυχοῦσῖ δὲ οἶκὸν was originally τρυχοῦσῖ δὲ ϝοῖκὸν. Once the digamma began to be lost however, because the poets were not historical linguists, they extended this possibility to places where there had been no digamma, as in 13.14 αὐτὲ ἄγειρομενοι, where ἀγειρόμενοι never began with ϝ.

There are a number of other apparent anomalies. Not all sequences of syllables will fit into the hexameter. For instance, words with sequences of ᴗᴗᴗ or ᴗ––ᴗ will not fit, and in order to accommodate such words 'metrical lengthening' was employed, whereby one vowel was artificially lengthened: thus 14.101 συβόσια (ᴗᴗᴗᴗ) became συβοσῖα; compare also ἀθανατος, ἀνερες and so on.⁹⁹

Sometimes vowels are lengthened before words that appear with initial single μ-, λ-, ν-, ρ-, ϝ-, because in some cases these originally began with an s- or w-, as e.g. μοῖρα < *smer-, ῥήγνυμι < *wrē-: so Il. 16.143 Πηλϊαδα (σ)μελίην, 5.327 κατα (σ)ρόον, 5.343 απō (σϝ)εō, and so on.¹⁰⁰ When the s- or w- was lost, poets found it useful to treat the resulting μ- etc. either as two consonants or as one depending on convenience, and this metrical facility was extended by analogy to words which did not have an original initial s- or w-, as in 13.51 ανα μέγαρον. It appears that these consonants could be slightly prolonged to produce lengthening.

Homer can lengthen a syllable in the princeps, sometimes when a final continuant (ν, ρ, ς) is treated as double, as in the last syllable of μέγαρον in 13.51 μέγαρον ὀφρ' εὐξάμενοι.

---

⁹⁶ This sometimes happens also with -αι and -οι.
⁹⁷ This sometimes happens internally, as in δήϊεν, υἱός.
⁹⁸ Cf. below 5.2 §2.2. The digamma is observed some 3,000 times and neglected some 600.
⁹⁹ Cf. W. F. Wyatt 1969.   ¹⁰⁰ Cf. GH 1.175–8.

Finally, there are a number of spellings which may hide much earlier forms.[101] ἀνδρότητα (–◡–◡), which will not fit the hexameter, is usually explained as hiding earlier *anṛtata (◡◡–◡), with r as a vocalic consonant.[102] Similarly, in 10.60 βῆν εἰς Αἰόλου κλυτὰ δώματα, Αἰόλου (–◡–) represents earlier *Αἰόλοο (< Αἰόλοιο).

4.3 Date

A number of formulae suggest that the hexameter may have been created around the fourteenth century BC.[103] The development of the vocalic sound ṛ > or, ar etc. has happened by the time of the Linear B tablets, so the formula νὺξ ἀμβρότη, which will not scan and must go back to *nux amṛta (–◡◡–), preserves the pre-Mycenean vocalic ṛ. Διΐφιλος preserves an original dative ending in -ei found in Mycenean and later replaced by the locative -i. In Mycenean, initial and intervocalic s has become h, but forms like ἀγχί-(h)αλος, ἐπι-(h)άλμενος preserve its original consonantal value, which has prevented the elision of the last syllable of the preposition.[104] Similarly, initial y became h and still appears in some forms in Mycenean: in Homer, ὥς (< *yōs) often makes position as if it had a consonant at the start, as in 14.251 θέος ὥς. If the formula ἀσπίδος ἀμφιβρότης was a later form of *aspidos amphimṛtas, it would refer to a form of shield popular before 1400. All of these are features of formulae, not simple anomalies, which suggests that they and so the hexameter go back at least to the Mycenean period.[105]

5 HOMERIC LANGUAGE

What follows is not a complete account of the Homeric dialect.[106] Its aim is to give the reader a sense of the salient aspects of the dialect and an

---

[101] See now however Barnes 2011 for the most recent discussion of this feature, supporting the idea that a metrical rather than a linguistic archaism is involved.
[102] For this, cf. below 5.2 §1.
[103] For the following, cf. M. L. West 1997: 233–7.
[104] That ἀγχί-(h)αλος 'near the sea' had an original initial s is shown by e.g. Lat. sal 'salt'.
[105] Cf. Meillet 1923; M. L. West 1973: 162–70; Nagy 1974. On the difficult question of how epic was performed, see M. L. West 1981: esp. 113–15 and 121–5: 'Homeric "singing" was truly singing, in that it was based on definite notes and intervals, but it was at the same time a stylized form of speech, the rise and fall of the voice being governed by the melodic accent of the words' (115). Also M. L. West 1992: 208–9, 328–9.
[106] The fullest account of the language of Homer is Chantraine, GH. Useful shorter accounts are: Palmer 1962; Hainsworth 1988; Janko 1992: 8–19; Horrocks 1997; Wachter 2000; Hackstein 2010. See the Glossary (pp. 234–7) for the explanation of technical terms.

indication of where historically its range and variety came from. It does not
therefore cover every aspect of the language, nor for the most part does
it consider features which are familiar from Attic, nor rarer exceptions or
unusual forms. Where these occur in books 13–14, they are dealt with in
the commentary. Many of the points here are controversial, but detailed
discussion has been avoided for the sake of comprehensibility.

5.1 The dialect mixture

As we have it, the language of epic is principally the Ionic dialect spoken
(with local variations) in Euboea, the islands of the eastern Aegean and
Asia Minor,[107] with an admixture of forms from the Aeolic dialect spoken
(with local variations) in Thessaly, Boeotia and northern islands like Les-
bos. The forms that are generally taken to be Aeolic are the following:[108]

(1) forms with π < IE *k^w: πίσυρες ('four'), πέλομαι ('be in motion, be'),
   as opposed to Ionic τέσσαρες and τέλομαι;
(2) the doubling of m, n, l, r after *s, where Ionic lengthens the preceding
   vowel, as in ἄμμες, ὔμμες for Ionic ἡμεῖς, ὑμεῖς; cf. Sanskrit yuṣman 'you';
(3) dative plurals in -εσσι;
(4) κεκλήγοντες, a perfect active participle with thematic -οντ- instead of
   -οτ-; cf. 14.30n;
(5) infinitives in -μεναι, -μεν;
(6) patronymics like Τελαμώνιος Αἴας;
(7) apocope of prepositions (see §7.5.3 below);
(8) 3rd person plurals in -εν, like ἤγερθεν for ἠγέρθησαν;
(9) athematic conjugation of contract verbs, as in φορήμεναι for φορεῖν, e.g.
   14.343 ὅρηαι.

The way in which Ionic and Aeolic have mixed can be seen even in individual words, such as 14.230 νέ-εσσι-ν, which has two Ionic features, the
shortening of νη- > νε- and the ephelcystic -ν, alongside the Aeolic suffix
-εσσι.

There are also some features which could come from Mycenean,[109] the
East Greek dialect found on the Linear B tablets, such as masculine genitive singulars in -αο and -οιο, genitive plurals in -άων and the ending -φι; a
number of words are shared with epic and the tablets, such as ἀμφιφορεύς,
ἄναξ, δέπας, φάσγανον. The resulting wide variety of forms available to the

---

[107] It is disputed how far West rather than East Ionic features are involved: cf.
Hackstein 2010: 401–2.
[108] Cf. Wathelet 1970; Haug 2002: 39–106, 145–64.
[109] The alternative is that they are simply archaisms.

poets is a clear sign that Homer's was an artificial dialect, not one spoken in everyday life. On the other hand, there are disputes as to the relationship between the two main dialect strands in the poems, Ionic and Aeolic. Ionic is clearly the dominant one in our texts, and many think there were parallel Ionic and Aeolic traditions, and that a dominant Ionic tradition borrowed a small number of features from the parallel Aeolic tradition for their metrical usefulness. There is however a school of thought that says that East Greek epic died out after the fall of the Mycenean palaces, and that the Greek poetic tradition was preserved in the Aeolic area in a so-called 'Aeolic phase', whence Ionic bards subsequently revived their own tradition. The balance of power seems currently to lie with the first school.

5.2 Some preliminary basics

The account of the Homeric dialect, and the linguistic parts of the commentary, will be more comprehensible if the following features of the history of the Greek language are kept in mind.

1 Roots. Greek words are built on 'roots', i.e. a basic building block, to which various prefixes and suffixes are added: these prefixes and suffixes indicate the function of the word in its sentence. So ἔ-λυ-ο-ν is augment (showing a past tense) + root + thematic vowel + personal ending, δί-δω-μι is reduplication + root + personal ending, λόγ-ο-ς is root + thematic vowel + nominative suffix, and so on. Roots contain consonants and vowels in a wide variety of shapes: CV, CVC, CCV, CVCC etc.

Roots appear in different 'grades' (the terms 'Ablaut' and 'vowel gradation' are sometimes used for this feature), that is, there are different vowels in the root. This phenomenon can be seen in the English groups *drive, drove, driven; drink, drank, drunk; fight, fought* and so on. Greek roots have three 'grades', *e-, o-* and zero- (i.e. no vowel, though see next paragraph). Using the simple CVC shape, exemplified by the root **pet-* 'fly', we have the three grades πετ-, ποτ-, πτ-, as e.g. in πέτ-ομαι, ποτ-έομαι, ἐ-πτ-όμην.

In roots involving *m* and *n*, the zero grade appears as an α, and in those involving *l* and *r*, as λα, αλ, ρα, αρ, because these were 'vocalic consonants', i.e. consonants with a vocalic element. This phenomenon can be heard in English *seven* (/sevᵉn/), where the second syllable is different from and weaker than the first, or in the Czech town of Brno (/bᵉrno/). These 'vocalic consonants' are transcribed m̥, n̥, l̥, r̥. Thus we have *e*-grade μέν-ος, *o*-grade μέ-μον-α, and zero-grade με-μα-ώς (from -mn̥-); τείν-ω, τόν-ος, τα-τός (from *tn̥-tos); βέλ-ος, βόλ-ος, βάλ-λω; δέρκ-ομαι, δέ-δορκ-α, ἔ-δρακ-ον.

In some instances, there are also short and long forms of the root: τί-θε-μεν, τί-θη-μι.

Other examples are: πέτ-ομαι, ποτ-ή, πτ-έρον; μέν-ω, μον-ή, μί-μν-ω; λείπ-ω, λέ-λοι-πα, ἔ-λιπ-ον; πείθ-ω, πέ-ποιθ-α, ἔ-πιθ-ον; στείχ-ω, στοῖ-χος, ἔ-στιχ-ον; δέρ-ω ('flay'), δορ-ά ('skin'), δέ-δαρ-μαι; σπεύδ-ω, σπουδ-ή; κλέ(Ϝ)-ος, κλύ-ω; δείκ-νυμι, δίκ-η.

2 Some important sound changes

2.1 ᾱ > η. Where Common Greek had an original long *a*, Homer's Ionic generalised a change to long *e*, so that original τιμά, which is preserved in say Doric dialects, became τιμή. (In Attic this change did not take place after ρ, ε, ι: so where Ionic has χώρη, οἰκίη, Attic has χώρᾱ, οἰκίᾱ etc.)

2.2 Digamma (Ϝ). All the Greek dialects inherited a *w*-sound, written in some dialect inscriptions with the letter digamma (Ϝ). In Ionic however this sound was lost before the eighth century. It was maintained in some dialects, such as Laconian, and its presence can also be reconstructed from other languages, such as Latin: that ἰδών had an initial digamma is suggested by Latin *uid-eo*, and that οἶκος did by Latin *uicus*.

2.3 *s*. This sound too was lost in certain circumstances, both at the start of the word and between vowels. In initial position, it became *h*, as in ἕξ (cf. Lat. *sex*), ἑπτά (Lat. *septem*). Between vowels its loss led to hiatus, and sometimes subsequent coalescing of the two vowels, so *ἵκεσο 'you came' > ἵκεο > ἵκου.

3 Laryngeals. This is a complex and contested subject, of which only the briefest account can be given here, in order to make the etymological remarks in the Commentary more comprehensible.[110] 'Laryngeals' are so called after a type of consonant found for example in Semitic languages (and most familiar in English in the 'glottal stop', heard for instance in the pronunciation of 'pattern' as /pa'rn/). They were posited to explain aspects of the IE vowel system and vowel gradation (§1 above), and then actually discovered in Hittite. Since cuneiform Hittite uses Akkadian symbols for a sound transcribed as *h*, laryngeals are represented with the same letter, and in the most commonly accepted theory there are three, written h_1 ('neutral' laryngeal), h_2 ('a-colouring'), and h_3 ('o-colouring'). Something of the way they created the vowel system can be seen in the following table:[111]

---

[110] Cf. Beekes 1969; Sihler 1995: 165–8.

[111] Matters are made more complex by the fact that PIE also had at least four long and short vowels, so it is not always clear whether a laryngeal is involved. I have tried to use examples where it is fairly clear one is.

initial position e- < h_1e-, as in *ed- 'eat' (ἔδομαι) < *h_1ed-
                            a- < h_2e-, as in *ag- 'lead' (ἄγω) < *h_2eg-
                            o- < h_3e-, as in *od- 'smell' (ὀδμή) < h_3ed-

long vowels $\bar{e}$ < eh_1, as in *$dh\bar{e}$- 'put' (τί-θη-μι) < *$dheh_1$-[112]
                        $\bar{a}$ < eh_2-, as in *$st\bar{a}$- 'stand' (Dor. ῐ-στᾱ-μι) < *$steh_2$-
                        $\bar{o}$ < eh_3-, as in *$d\bar{o}$- 'give' (δί-δω-μι) < *deh_3-

5.3 The Homeric dialect

1 Nouns

1.1 a-stems ('first declension')

1.1.1 In the genitive plural, we find both the Aeolic and early Greek άων and Ionic -εων (< -$\bar{a}s\bar{o}m$, which gave Latin -$arum$); -εων is from -ηων with the shortening of the η.

1.1.2 The original form of the dative plural was -ᾱσι, which became -ησι after the Ionic shift of ᾱ > η, and then -ηισι through the influence of the masculine form in -οισι; the latter gave rise by analogy also to -αισι. Forms in -αις are often to be explained as the result of the later Atticisation of the text.

1.1.3 In Greek, the masculine first-declension nouns have a special nominative singular in -ης, as in ποιητής, contrast Lat. $poeta$. There are also nominatives in -ᾰ, like νεφεληγερέτα.[113]

1.1.4 The genitive singular of these masculine nouns began as -ᾱο, but became first -ηο, and then by 'quantitative metathesis' (i.e. the exchange of quantity by the two vowels) -εω.

1.2 o-stems ('second declension')

1.2.1 In the genitive singular, we find -οιο, which goes back to IE *-$osyo$, and gave rise to -ου via -οο, when the y was lost (-οο was replaced by -ου in later texts, producing in some places unmetrical forms like 10.60 Αἰόλου).[114]

1.2.2 Dative plurals in -οις are in some cases probably old instrumentals, though they could also be more recent Attic forms (for the facts, cf. GH 1.194–6); those in -οισι are old locatives.

1.3 Third declension

1.3.1 s-stems. In words like γέν-ος etc., the stem suffix is -es/os-, the latter visible in the vocative Διό-γενες. The -s- was lost between vowels, and Homer keeps uncontracted forms where Attic contracts. Thus in the genitive there was a sequence

---

[112] One can see here how the presumption of a laryngeal in these cases of long vowels produces the common CVC form of Greek roots.
[113] Cf. Leukart 1994; Hajnal 1995; 13.139n.
[114] On this controversial point, cf. Willi 2008.

*γέν-εσ-ος > *γέν-εℎ-ος > γένεος (> Attic γένους); hence too
γένεῖ, γένεα, γενέων, γένεσσι, γενέεσσι.

1.3.2 *i*-stems

  1.3.2.1 πόλις has a range of forms. Beside a full set of forms in
  i (πόλις, πόλι, πόλιν, πόλιος, πόλῖ (< 1 + 1), πόλιες, πόλῖς
  (< -νς), πολίων, πολίεσσι), the old locative πόληϊ provided a stem for the creation of πόληος and πόλεος,
  πόληι, πόληες and πόληας.

  1.3.2.2 The word for 'son' is even more complex. The stem
  υἱ- gave υἷα, υἷος etc.; a stem υἱε- υἱέος. υἱός, an *o*-stem,
  is itself a new creation, based on the genitive plural υἱῶν (λόγος : λόγων :: *x* : υἱῶν, *x* = υἱός); it gave
  rise to υἱέ, υἱόν and υἱοῦ. The dative υἱάσι (14.206)
  was created on analogy with other kinship terms like
  πατράσι.

1.3.3 *u*-stems

  1.3.3.1 πολύς also mixes forms from a *u*-stem (πολύ-ν,
  πολέ(ϝ)-ος, πολέ(ϝ)-ες etc.) with those from an *o*-stem
  (πολλός, πολλόν etc.).

1.3.4 Diphthong stems

  1.3.4.1 βασιλεύς and other nouns with diphthong stems
  decline βασιλῆ(ϝ)-α, βασιλῆ(ϝ)-ος etc. (dative plural
  βασιλεῦσι); there are also genitive singulars in -εος like
  Τυδέος.

1.3.5 The name Zeus followed the IE pattern *dyēus, dyēm, diwos,
  diwi*: Ζεῦς, Ζῆν, Δι(ϝ)ός, Δι(ϝ)ί. Ζῆν was then regularised
  to Ζῆνα to make it look more like an accusative, and an
  accusative was created for the Δι- stem, Δί(ϝ)α.

1.3.6 The word for 'ship' has both long-vowel forms νῆυς, νῆα, νῆος
  etc., and the short-vowel forms νέα, νέος, νέες, νέας and, with
  the Aeolic ending, νέεσσι; the dative plural also appears as
  νηυσί.

2 Adjectives

2.1 Comparatives in -ιων can look unfamiliar because of the sound
  changes caused by the interaction of the -ι- with the last consonant
  of the stem: so ταχύς θάσσων < *θαχ-ίων;[115] μακρός μάσσων (< *μακ-
  ίων); βραχύς βράσσων; παχύς πάσσων.

3 Numerals

3.1 Note Aeolic ἴα 'one' (cf. 14.435n.), πίσυρες 'four' (cf. above §1.1).

---

[115] ταχ- comes about by 'Grassmann's Law': in certain circumstances, where
there were two consecutive aspirates, the first lost its aspiration, as also in θρίξ,
τριχός.

4 Pronouns

4.1 These are very complex, combining as they do Ionic, Aeolic and metrically lengthened forms, so a table may be the best way to illustrate them.

1st pers.	2nd pers.	Reflexive
Singular		
N. ἐγώ(ν)	σύ, τύνη	
A. ἐμέ, με	σε	ἑ(ϝ)ε, (ϝ)ε
G. ἐμέο (ἐμεῖο), μεῦ (Ionic), μευ, ἐμέθεν	σέο (σεῖο), σεῦ, σευ, σέθεν, τεοῖο (gen. of possessive τεός)	ἕο (εῖο), εὗ, ἕθεν
D. ἐμοί, μοι	σοί, τοι, τεΐν	ἑοῖ, οἷ
Dual		
N. νῶϊ (<acc. stem νώ + *ϝ1 'we')	σφῶϊ, σφώ	
A. νώ, νῶϊ	σφῶϊ, σφώ	σφωέ
G. νῶϊν	σφῶϊν, σφῶϊν	σφωΐν
D. νῶϊν	σφῶϊν, σφῶϊν	
Plural		
N. ἄμμες, ἡμεῖς	ὔμμες, ὑμεῖς	
A. ἄμμε, ἡμέας, ἥμεας	ὔμμε, ὑμέας	σφέ, σφας, σφέας
G. ἀμμέων, ἡμέων	ὑμμέων, ὑμέων	σφέων, σφείων, σφῶν
D. ἄμμιν, ἡμῖν, ἥμιν, ἧμιν	ὔμμι, ὑμῖν, ὔμιν, ὗμιν	σφίσι(ν), σφί(ν)

NB μιν, an accusative singular for all genders used also as a reflexive.

5 Possessive adjectives

5.1 'Your' is both τεός and σός (the latter from the reduced form of the root *τϝ-ός; cf. Lat. *tuus* < *tovos* < *tewos*). 'His, hers, its' is ἑός (< *σεϝός, cf. Lat. *suus*) and ὅς (< σϝ-ός); there is also σφός, which is used for both singular and plural.

6 Verbs

6.1 Reduplication

6.1.1 Reduplication is used in many languages to intensify a remark, and in IE verbs also to mark the repetition of an action (cf. βορβορύζω 'have tummy rumblings'). In IE languages, reduplication also has purely grammatical uses. We are used to it in the perfect (λέλυκα) and some presents (μίμνω), but in Homer it is also found in the aorist stems.

6.1.2 In the aorist, as in the perfect, the reduplicating vowel is ε
(and the zero grade is used): κέλ-ομαι ἐ-κέ-κλ-ετο (14.413);
τέρπ-ομαι τε-ταρπ-όμενος (14.244); πείθ-ω (παρ-)πε-πιθ-ών
(14.290).

6.1.3 Reduplication can take the form also of repetition of the root
in any of the three stems: present δαρ-δάπτ-ουσιν (14.92) <
*δαρ-δάρπτ-ω (related to δρέπω); μαρ-μαίρω (< *μαρ-μάρ-ίω);
παμ-φαίνω; aorist ἀγ-αγ-εῖν; perfect ὄρ-ωρ-ε.

6.1.4 The first consonant can be reduplicated with ι, as in δί-δω-μι,
λι-λαί-εται (13.31), βι-βάς; note also the slightly different ἀ-τι-
τάλλω (14.41) related to ἀταλός.

6.1.5 Where roots begin with ϝ- or σ-, the reduplication can be
obscured by subsequent sound changes: εἰλυμένα (< εἰλύω)
'wrapped' (14.136) is from ϝε-ϝλῦ-μένα which became
*εἰλῦμένα with the loss of the digammas; (κατα-)είμένον (< ἕνν-
υμι < ϝέσ-νυμι, cf. Latin ues-tis) 'clothed' (13.351) is similarly
from ϝε-ϝεσ-μένον.

6.2 Augment

6.2.1 The augment was originally an optional adverbial form,
which was later to be used compulsorily to emphasise that
a verb form was 'past'. In Homer, its optionality is very clear:
see 13.1 ἔφατο, but 13.3 φώνησεν.[116] The gnomic aorist (see
§9.2.1 below) usually has the augment.

6.2.2 Before roots beginning with digamma, the augment appears
as η-, as in ἀπ-ηύρα (< ἀπ-ήϝρα; cf. 13.132n.).

6.3 Personal endings

6.3.1 Active

6.3.1.1 1st p.s., 3rd p.s. Note the use of the athematic endings -μι, -σι (< -τι) in the subjunctive as well as the
optative: ἐθέλ-ωμι, φέρ-ησι.

6.3.1.2 2nd p.s. -θα appears frequently. It was taken from perfects like οἶσθα, and used first to distinguish between
the 2nd and 3rd p.s. of the imperfect of εἰμί, both
of which had become ἦς (< ἦσ-ς and ἦσ-τ); then
it was generalised to indicatives, subjunctives and
optatives.

6.3.1.3 3rd p.pl. In secondary tenses in Greek the ending
-nt (Lat. ama-nt etc.) loses its t, so *ἔβα-ντ etc. became
ἔβαν (13.17) etc. These forms co-exist in Homer with
later forms in -σαν.

<hr/>

[116] Though its use is not entirely arbitrary, cf. Mumm 2004.

6.3.2 Middle

6.3.2.1 2nd p.s. The primary singular endings were -μαι, -σαι, -ται, but -σαι lost its *s* between vowels (see above 5.2 §2.3), which led to the change -εσαι > -εαι in the second person, thus obscuring this regularity; cf. πειρήσεαι (13.336). There are also contracted forms in -ηι such as γνώσηι, usually found in elision before vowels and so possibly for earlier γνώσε(αι) etc.

6.3.2.2 The same loss occurred in athematic verbs, but the *s* was restored on the analogy of stems in a consonant: so, in the verb κεῖμαι, 2nd p.s. κεῖσαι was recreated from *κεῖαι on the analogy of e.g. ἦσ-σαι ἦσ-ται. We find also δύνασαι, παρίστασαι and so on. The same thing happened in the perfect: δίδοσαι etc.

6.3.2.3 There was a similar loss in the -σο of the secondary tenses: *ἐλύσα-σο > ἐλύσαο > ἐλύσω. This *s* is not restored except in a very few cases.

6.3.2.4 1st p.pl. Note -μεσθα alongside -μεθα, perhaps on analogy with the 2nd p.pl. ending -σθε.

6.3.2.5 3rd p.pl. In primary tenses, after a consonant we find -αται, as in τετεύχαται (14.138), which looks like a 3rd p.s., but in fact comes from 3 p.pl. -*ṇtai*.

6.3.2.6 In secondary tenses, the same thing happened: -*ṇto* became -ατο, so κορεσαίατο (14.28), κεχολώατο (14.282).

6.4 Iteratives in -σκω. The suffix -*sk*-, found for instance in English 'wash', denoted a repetition or continuation of an action, cf. φάσκω 'say'. It was productive in Ionic especially for past tenses, as imperfect ἔρδεσκες (13.350) and aorist εἴπεσκε (13.160).

6.5 Aorist

6.5.1 Athematic sigmatic aorist. These are the familiar ἔ-λυ-σ-α etc., with the aorist sign -*s*- added to the stem, followed by the personal endings.

6.5.2 Thematic aorist. These are built on the zero-grade root using the thematic vowel, and may be either unreduplicated, as in ἔ-λιπ-ο-ν, ἔσχον, ἔδρακον, or reduplicated, as in τε-ταρπ-ό-μενος (14.244), (παρ-)πε-πιθ-ών (14.290), ἔ-ειπ-ε (14.492n.).

6.5.3 Athematic asigmatic aorists. These can have either short vowels with zero grade, but no *s* (14.34 ἔ-φθῖ-το, ἔ-χῦ-το); or long vowels, sometimes alternating with short, as in ἔθηκα ἔθεμεν, sometimes not, as in ἔστην ἔστημεν.

6.5.4 Athematic root aorists. Unlike the thematic aorists, these have the endings simply added to the root, without the thematic vowel: γέν-το 'grasped', δέκ-το 'received', λέκ-το 'told' etc.[117]

6.5.5 For the so-called 'mixed' aorists like ἄξετε, cf. 14.414n.

6.6 Future

6.6.1 This is formed by the 'desiderative' suffix -s-, which expressed a desire for something to happen (compare in a different way English futures with 'I will').

6.6.2 There are also futures formed on the perfect stem, such as δεδέξομαι, κεχολώσεται; and on the aorist, such as πεφιδήσεται (< φείδομαι 'spare'), πεπιθήσω (< πείθω).

6.6.3 In disyllabic roots like καλε- 'call', the loss of the intervocalic sigma led to futures that were the same as the presents (e.g. καλέω). This pattern was then extended to other roots ending in l, n, r (e.g. στελ-έω, μεν-έω), and is also found in verbs in -ίζω (κομιῶ). There are also Aeolic futures in -ίσσω (ξενίσσουσι), and forms in -ξω (πολεμίξω).

6.7 Perfect and pluperfect

6.7.1 The pluperfect has three forms. Ones with secondary endings (13.170 ἐτέτυκ-το); thematic ones (14.471 ἄνωγ-ο-ν, γέγων-ε); and Attic–Ionic ones in -εα, -εας etc.

6.8 Moods

6.8.1 Subjunctive

6.8.1.1 A characteristic feature of the Homeric dialect is the subjunctive with a short vowel where Attic has a long vowel, as in 13.182 ἱερεύσομεν for ἱερεύσωμεν. This was originally a feature of athematic verbs, and especially their asigmatic aorists, which made a subjunctive simply by adding the thematic vowel: thus the present ἴ-μεν 'we go' had a subjunctive ἴ-ο-μεν, cf. ἴδ-μεν 'we know' with the subjunctive εἴδ-ο-μεν.

6.8.1.2 Short-vowel subjunctives are also found in s-aorists: τείσομεν, ἀμείψεται. Eventually, the long-vowel forms began to replace these, so that we have θήῃς and θήῃ alongside 13.164 θείομεν. In these long forms, there was then a shortening of the first vowel (θέωμεν) or contraction (θῆισι).

6.8.2 Optative

6.8.2.1 Athematic optative. These add an optative marker -ιη- or -ῑ- to the stem: for εἰμί (root *e(s)-), we have *ἐ-ίη-ν > εἴην, *ἐ-ί-μεν > εἴμεν.

---

[117] For the suggestion that they are old imperfects, cf. *GH* 1.296–7.

6.8.2.2 Thematic optative. Here -ι- is added after the thematic vowel, as 13.22 βλάπτοι, σπερχο-ί-ατ'; in contract verbs, καλέοι etc.

6.9 Verbal nouns

6.9.1 Infinitive. The -μεν and -μεναι endings, which are characteristic of the athematic infinitives, are also sometimes found with thematic stems, as ἀγέμεν, φερέμεν, εἰπέμεν, ἀγορευέμεναι. ἔμμεναι and ἔμμεν (< ἔσ-μεν(αι)) sometimes appear as ἔμεναι, ἔμεν.

6.9.2 Participles. For Aeolic perfect participles in -ων, cf. 14.30n.

7 Syntax

7.1 Number

7.1.1 Neuter plurals often have a plural verb, especially if the plural is made up of a number of individual items (as in 13.103–4 αἰπόλια ... βόσκοντ(αι), describing Odysseus' different flocks), or refers to complex structures like doors or chariots.

7.1.2 The dual is preserved in Homer, but it is often found combined with plural forms, as notably in Il. 21.115 χεῖρε πετάσσας ἀμφοτέρας 'having stretched out both hands', and 14.193–5 εἴη μὲν νῦν νῶϊν (dual) ... ἐδωδή ... κλισίης ἔντοσθεν ἐοῦσι | (plural) δαίνυσθαι ἀκέοντ(ε) (dual) 'would that we two had food ... to dine on quietly in the hut' (see the note on this passage).

7.2 Cases

7.2.1 Greek, like Latin, simplified the original IE case system, which consisted of nominative, vocative, accusative, genitive, dative, ablative, locative and instrumental. In Greek, the dative took over the functions of the locative[118] and instrumental,[119] and the genitive those of the ablative.[120]

7.2.2 Nominative. This is sometimes used as a vocative where two people are addressed, as Il. 3.276–7 Ζεῦ πάτερ ... | Ἠέλιός τε and Od. 19.406 γαμβρὸς ἐμὸς θυγάτηρ τε; or in expressions such as Il. 4.189 φίλος ὦ Μενέλαε.

7.2.3 Vocative. For old vocatives in -α used as nominatives, such as νεφεληγερέτα, cf. above §1.1.3.

---

[118] οἴκοι 'at home' preserves an old locative; cf. also 13.18n.
[119] Hence the use of the dative for the thing with which something is done: μαχαίραι 'with a knife'.
[120] Hence ὑπό + gen. of human agents, but a + ablative in Latin.

7.2.4 Accusative. This case can express the end, aim or result towards which an action is directed or proceeds.

7.2.4.1 We can distinguish 'external' and 'internal' accusatives. Contrast 'strike a man', where the man is the object of the action of striking, and 'strike a blow', where the blow is the result aimed at. For an internal accusative, cf. 13.384 φθίσεσθαι...οἶτον lit. 'to perish the fate'.

7.2.4.2 A special kind of internal accusative is the cognate accusative, where the object is etymologically related to the verb, as in 13.26 δαίνυντ(ο) ...δαῖτα 'they ate a meal', 13.50 κρητῆρα κερασσάμενος 'having mixed a mixing-bowl'.

7.2.4.3 Very common is the 'adverbial accusative', where neuter singulars and plurals of pronouns and adjectives are used as adverbs, as in 13.29 πολλά... κεφαλὴν τρέπε 'he often turned his head', 13.74 ἵνα νήγρετον εὕδοι 'so that he should sleep unwakingly'.

7.2.4.4 The accusative of respect as found in 14.177 δέμας καὶ εἶδος ἀγητός 'delightful as to (in) body and form' is already found in Homer but its origin is uncertain.

7.2.5 Genitive

7.2.5.1 The Greek genitive absorbed the functions of the ablative.

7.2.5.2 The genitive had as its main functions, when governed by a noun, to express some kind of relationship between things, and when governed by a verb, to delimit the sphere where an action takes place.

7.2.5.2.1 The use with nouns is seen in phrases like 13.104 ἱρὸν Νυμφάων, where the genitive indicates that the shrine belongs to the Nymphs, and in 'subjective' genitives like 'fear felt by lions', and 'objective' ones like 'fear of lions'.

7.2.5.2.2 Genitives of price, content, value also depend on the idea of relationship between things: ἕρκος ὀδόντων 'a fence (consisting) of teeth'; ὀκτὼ σταδίων τεῖχος 'a wall of eight stades'; ἱερὰ τριῶν ταλάντων 'offerings worth three talents'.

7.2.5.3 The adverbial uses of the genitive are clear in its use with verbs of touching (14.319 χειρὸς ἀναστήσας 'raising me by (taking) my hand'), desiring, reaching (14.229 Τροίης ἐπιβήμεναι 'come to Troy'), beginning, filling (14.28 κρειῶν κορεσαίατο 'satisfy themselves with meat'), perceiving (people), remembering, forgetting, concerning oneself with (14.3 βιό-τοιο... κήδετο 'was concerned for his livelihood') etc.; and most strikingly in phrases such as διέπρησσον πεδίοιο 'they made their way over the plain'. Hence we find the genitive used of time (14.161 τοῦδ' αὐτοῦ λυκάβαντος 'in this same month'): the 'genitive absolute' gives the time, conditions, cause etc. of an event.

7.2.5.4 The IE ablative indicated the point from which an action took place. So the Greek genitive is used with or without a preposition with verbs of separation, ceasing, removing, giving up, failing, being distant from (14.352 ἔα ἀμφὶς ἐκείνων 'I was far from them'). It is also used to mark the point of departure for a comparison, as in γυναικῶν περίειμι 'I surpass all women' ('I am superior from the point of view of all women').

7.2.6 Dative

7.2.6.1 The dative absorbed the functions both of the original locative case, which described where something happened, and also of the instrumental, which described what an action was done with and also expressed the ideas of association and conjunction.

7.2.6.2 Like the accusative, the 'pure' dative indicates the person concerned in an event. Compare 14.215–16 ἴδωμαι, | μή τί μοι οἴχονται... ἄγοντες 'let me see if they have gone away taking anything from me' i.e. to my disadvantage: the direct object of the taking is τι, the indirect 'me'. Thus the pure dative is used with verbs of helping, benefiting, hurting, (dis)pleasing, meeting, advising, commanding, obeying, comparing.

7.2.6.3 It is also found regularly as a dative of the agent with passive verbs, especially in the perfect and pluperfect, as in 13.28 λαοῖσι τετιμένος 'honoured by the people'.

7.2.6.4 As well as indicating the object etc. that something was done with, as in 14.452 πρίατο κτεάτεσσιν ἑοῖσιν 'he purchased with his own resources', the instrumental dative is used to indicate the cause of

or motive for something, as in 14.205–6 θεὸς ὣς
τίετο...ὄλβωι τε πλούτωι τε 'he was honoured like
a god because of his prosperity and wealth', and
also the manner in which it was done, as πολλῶι 'by
much'.

7.2.6.5 It also expresses association, as in 14.480 ἑτάροισιν
ἔλειπον 'I left it with my companions', and in the
so-called 'sociative' datives with αὐτός, as 14.76–7
παρέθηκ'... | θέρμ' αὐτοῖσ' ὀβελοῖσιν 'he put them
before him hot with their spits'.

7.2.6.6 The locatival dative (cf. Ἀθήνῃσι 'at Athens') is also
seen in expressions of time, as 14.314 δεκάτῃ...νυκτί
'on the tenth night'.

7.3 Demonstratives, articles, relatives

7.3.1 One major difference between Attic and Homer is that the
Attic article ὁ, ἡ, τό is in Homer still a demonstrative, 'that
man', 'he', 'she' etc.[121] E.g. 13.2 τὸν δ' αὖτ' Ἀλκίνοος ἀμείβετο
'to him Alcinous replied'. So in 13.1 οἱ δ' ἄρα πάντες means
strictly 'they, all of them' (that is, οἱ is not the article with
πάντες). Note also the appositional usage 13.187 ὁ δ' ἔγρετο
δῖος Ὀδυσσεύς 'he woke up, (did) divine Odysseus' (again, ὁ
is not the article).

7.3.2 This demonstrative often marks a contrast: 13.16 ὣς ἔφατ'
Ἀλκίνοος, τοῖσιν δ' ἐπιήνδανε μῦθος 'thus spoke Alcinous, and
they found his words pleasing'. The contrast can sometimes be in the actions of the same person, as in 13.162–4
ἐνοσίχθων | ...λᾶαν ἔθηκε·...ὁ δὲ νόσφι βεβήκει 'Poseidon
turned it to stone and he went away'.

7.3.3 There are however cases where the demonstratives are used
in ways which are getting very close to a proper article. Such
are cases with numbers, as 14.24–6 οἱ δὲ δὴ ἄλλοι | ᾤχοντ'
ἄλλυδις... | οἱ τρεῖς· τὸν δὲ τέταρτον ἀποπροέηκε πόλινδε 'the
other three went to different places, but the fourth he had
sent to the city'. Very close too is 14.235–6 τὴν γε στυγερὴν
ὁδόν...ἣ πολλῶν ἀνδρῶν ὑπὸ γούνατ' ἔλυσε, though there
remains an element of the demonstrative here in 'that well-
known expedition'. We really seem to have reached the article with a phrase like 14.12 τὸ μέλαν δρυὸς ἀμφικεάσσας 'having
cut off the bark of the wood all round'.

---

[121] Its later use as the article shows the same weakening in meaning that produced the article in Romance languages: the Latin demonstrative *ille* 'that' gave Fr.
le, la; Sp. *el, la*; It. *il, la*.

7.3.4 By another shift, these demonstratives become relatives, as in
13.54–5 θεοῖσιν | ἔσπεισαν μακάρεσσι, τοὶ οὐρανὸν εὐρὺν ἔχουσιν,
or with the relative placed first 14.80 ἔσθιε νῦν, ὦ ξεῖνε, τά τε
δμώεσσι πάρεστι, χοίρε' 'eat now, guest, those things/what servants have, pig-meat'. In 14.227 αὐτὰρ ἐμοὶ τὰ φίλ' ἔσκε, τά που
θεὸς ἐν φρεσὶ θῆκεν 'those things were dear to me, which I suppose the gods put into my mind', one can see both demonstrative and relative use.

7.3.5 The relatives ὅς and ὅστις are also used.

7.4 Pronouns

7.4.1 There is another demonstrative pronoun ὅς: in *Il.* 21.198,
Achilles lists Ocean as one of those bodies of water that could
not fight Zeus, ἀλλὰ καὶ ὃς δείδοικε Διὸς μεγάλοιο κεραυνόν 'but
even he feared mighty Zeus's thunderbolt'. This is sometimes
hard to distinguish from the relative ὅς, as can be seen from
14.288–90:

δὴ τότε Φοῖνιξ ἦλθεν ἀνὴρ ἀπατήλια εἰδώς,
τρώκτης, ὃς δὴ πολλὰ κάκ' ἀνθρώπους ἐεόργει·
ὅς μ' ἄγε παρπεπιθὼν ἧισι φρεσίν.

Then indeed a cunning Phoenician man came, a
greedy man, who did men great harm, who/he led me
on and persuaded me with his ideas.

The first ὅς is clearly a relative pronoun, but the second could
be either another relative (Homer can use a sequence of relatives thus) or a demonstrative.

7.5 Prepositions

7.5.1 Ancient and later scholars for long explained a phrase like
ἀνὰ δ' ἵστατο (13.56) as the splitting into its two constituent
parts by the particle of an original ἀνίστατο; thus it was called
tmesis 'cutting'. Historically, however, the opposite is the case:
compound verbs such as ἀνίστημι are later formations. What
we call 'prepositions' originally had an independent, quasi-
adverbial existence in the sentence, simply adding to it the
idea they expressed, such as 'up', 'down', 'around' etc. The
word 'preverb' is now preferred for this stage of the development of the use of these words. In fact, in some cases,
Homer's use of these preverbs represents a stage of Greek
earlier than that of the Mycenean tablets.[122]

[122] Cf. Horrocks 1984; against this idea, Hajnal 2004.

This earlier stage can be seen clearly in 13.438 ἐν δὲ στρόφος ἦεν ἀορτήρ 'and on it [the wallet] there was a belt', where
ἐν is clearly adverbial not prepositional; and 14.50 ἐστόρεσεν
δ' ἐπὶ δέρμα ἰονθάδος ἀγρίου αἰγός 'he spread over a skin of a
shaggy wild goat', where δέρμα is the object of the verb and
is not governed by ἐπί. In time, it was felt more and more
that the preverb belonged with the verb and ultimately it was
united with it. We can see an intermediate case in 14.65 θεὸς δ'
ἐπὶ ἔργον ἀέξηι 'the god increases his work', where ἐπί could be
adverbial, 'in addition', or part of a nascent compound verb
with ἀέξηι (compare 15.19 δόμων ἐκ κτῆμα φέρηται). Finally, in
13.138 λαχὼν ἀπὸ ληΐδος αἶσαν 'taking his portion from the
booty', we reach the stage where ἀπό is essentially a preposition. That the augment in Classical Greek comes in the vast
majority of verbs between the preverb and the verb is a vestige
of the original situation where the two parts were separate.

7.5.2 A similar thing happened with nouns. In earlier Greek, the
case of a word was determined simply by the function of the
noun in the sentence; the preverbs again added a measure of
precision. As time went on however, the preverbs were gradually thought to determine the case of the noun and were
largely put in front of it to show this. In 13.21 αὐτὸς ἰὼν διὰ
νηός 'going himself through the ship' one can see an intermediate case, where διά could be explained as either reinforcing
the local genitive ('himself in the ship going through it') or
governing it ('himself going through the ship').

7.5.3 An Aeolic feature of Homer's use of prepositions is 'apocope', whereby a shortened form is used: ἄν, ἀπ-, κάτ, πάρ,
ὑπ-. In certain cases, the last consonant of the preposition is
assimilated to the consonant that follows, so we find κάββαλε
(κάτ-βαλε), κὰδ δ' ἄρ' (13.73), κὰρ ῥόον, καμμονίη, κὰγ γόνυ,
κάλλιπε, καππεδίον.

8 Syntax: verbs

8.1 Voice

8.1.1 In IE there existed the active and the middle voices, 'the latter indicating the especial interest of the subject in the event
referred to by the verb, or that the action takes place in the
person of the subject'.[123] The IE passive developed out of the
intransitive middle, but in Greek the process was not mor-
phologically complete, since there are no separate passive

[123] Palmer 1962: 145.

forms for the present tense, λύομαι doing duty for both middle and passive, and in Homer there are no future passives in -(θ)ήσομαι. In Homer, as in a number of IE languages, the middle is still used for the passive, the idea of 'the action taking place in the person of the subject' being close to the idea of the passive, which indicates that the person undergoes the action: cf. 13.2 κηληθμῶι ἔσχοντο 'they were held in enchantment'.

8.1.2 Homer is unusual in having middle forms for verbs of perception such as ὁρῶμαι (cf. 14.343 ὅρηαι 'you see'), and ἀκούομαι; again the subject is particularly interested in the action. Compare the way that futures, which were created by the addition of a suffix expressing desire or will (see above §6.6.1), also tend to appear in the middle voice, because the subject is especially concerned in the action through his desire for it to happen.

9 Tenses

9.1 The verbal stems in IE were 'aspects', indicating the kind of action involved, rather than 'tenses', which convey the timing of the action. The basic distinctions were that the present denoted an action in progress (ἀποθνήισκει 'she is dying', ἀπέθνηισκε 'she was dying'), the aorist an action as a single event without reference to time (ἀπέθανε 'she died'), and the perfect a state reached in the past and still in force (τέθνηκε 'she is dead'). These distinctions are far from absolute however, and it is often hard to distinguish between the imperfect and the aorist.

9.2 Aorist

9.2.1 The use of the aorist as a 'timeless' form may explain the 'gnomic' aorist, which states a general truth, as in 14.463–4 οἶνος γὰρ ἀνώγει | ἠλεός, ὅς τ' ἐφέηκε πολύφρονά περ μάλ' ἀεῖσαι 'the maddening wine commands me, which makes (aorist) even the sensible man sing'. In 14.62–3 κτῆσιν ὄπασσεν, | οἷά τε ᾧ οἰκῆϊ ἄναξ εὔθυμος ἔδωκεν 'he gave me property of the sort a kindly master gives his servant', the first aorist marks what happened in the past, the second is gnomic.

9.2.2 This is common too in similes, as in that of the ploughman in book 13, which is in the present tense apart from 13.33 ἀσπασίως δ' ἄρα τῷ κατέδυ φάος ἠελίοιο 'the light of the sun sets to his great pleasure'.

9.2.3 This timeless aspect also accounts for cases in which Homer has an aorist where we might expect a present or a future. Compare 13.172–4 θέσφαθ' ἱκάνει | πατρὸς ἐμοῦ, ὃς ἔφασκε

Ποσειδάων' ἀγάσασθαι | ἡμῖν 'there were oracles from my
father, who used to say that Poseidon is/would be angry
with us'.

9.3 Perfect. Homeric perfects and pluperfects can express the idea that
an action was performed in an intensive or repeated fashion, which
is conveyed by the reduplication (see §6.1.1 above). This has essentially a present sense: τέτριγα 'I squeak', γέγηθα 'I rejoice'.

10 Moods

10.1 The subjunctive and optative have two basic functions, the voluntative and the prospective, though in neither mood is this an
impermeable distinction.[124]

10.2 Subjunctive

10.2.1 The voluntative subjunctive expresses the will of the
speaker, as in 13.215 ἀλλ' ἄγε δὴ τὰ χρήματ' ἀριθμήσω καὶ
ἴδωμαι... 'come on, I want to count my goods and see...'
The negative is μή.

10.2.2 The prospective, sometimes distinguished by the addition
of κε/ἄν, expresses an expectation, as in Il. 1.205 τάχ' ἄν
ποτε θυμὸν ὀλέσσηι '(I expect) he will soon lose his life';
6.459 καί ποτε τις εἴπηισι 'someone will say, I expect'. The
negative is οὐ.

10.3 Optative

10.3.1 The voluntative optative expresses a wish which, unlike
in Attic, can be unfulfilled: 14.468 εἴθ' ὣς ἡβώοιμι 'if only
I were as young'. This optative can also denote a polite
wish, as in 14.496-7 ἀλλά τις εἴη εἰπεῖν Ἀτρεΐδηι Ἀγαμέμνονι
'perhaps there might be someone who would go and tell
Agamemnon'. The negative is μή.

10.3.2 The prospective optative, with or without κε/ἄν, expresses
potentiality: 14.122-3 οὔ τις κεῖνον ἀνὴρ ἀλαλήμενος
ἐλθών | ἀγγέλλων πείσειε γυναῖκα 'no wanderer announ-
cing Odysseus is likely to persuade his wife'. The wish can
be for the present or past, as with the voluntative optative.
The negative is οὐ.

10.4 Future tense

10.4.1 Because of its desiderative origin and the closeness of its
use to that of the subjunctive, the future can be considered here; for the closeness, cf. Il. 6.459 καί ποτε τις εἴπηισι
'someone might say, I expect', which is followed by 462
ὥς ποτε τις ἐρέει 'thus perhaps someone will say'. Like the

---

[124] This is the traditional view, which is here kept for reasons of simplicity; but see
now, for a more complex analysis of indicative, subjunctive and optative, Willmott
2007.

prospective subjunctive, the future is also used with κε/ἄν: *Il.* 4.176 καί κέ τις ὧδ' ἐρέει 'someone will say'.

10.4.2 The voluntative sense is seen in 14.512 ἀτὰρ ἠῶθέν γε τὰ σὰ ῥάκεα δνοπαλίξεις 'but at dawn I want you to wrap your own rags around you'.

10.5 Infinitive

10.5.1 IE infinitives were originally verbal nouns in various cases (accusatives, genitives, ablatives, locatives), not related to the rest of the conjugation and without tense or voice; they expressed the root meaning of the verb. Traces of the use of infinitives as cases can sometimes be discerned in Homer.

10.5.2 A cognate accusative may be preserved in expressions like 13.160 βῆ ῥ' ἴμεν 'he went his way': for βαίνω with the accusative, cf. Pi. fr. 191 ἔβαινε Δωρίαν κέλευθον ὕμνων 'he took a Dorian path of songs'. One could see an accusative of respect in *Il.* 1.428 περὶ μὲν βουλὴν Δαναῶν, περὶ δ' ἐστὲ μάχεσθαι 'you are superior amongst the Greeks as to planning and as to fighting', where the infinitive has the same function as the noun βουλήν.

10.5.3 The use of infinitives in final and consecutive constructions points to the locative-dative used to indicate the end of an action, as in 13.33-4 κατέδυ φάος ἠελίοιο | δόρπον ἐποίχεσθαι 'the sun sets so that he goes to dinner', 15.457 νῆυς ἤχθετο... νέεσθαι 'the ship was loaded for departure'.

10.5.4 Used on their own, infinitives had the force of a command, ordering the realisation of the verb's sense: 13.307 σὺ δὲ τετλάμεναι καὶ ἀνάγκηι 'and you, bear up because you must'.

11 The complex sentence

11.1 Parataxis

11.1.1 One of the most striking features of Homer's Greek when compared with the later language is the way in which the connection between parts of a sentence is made much less specific. The elements are in 'parataxis', 'a setting beside each other', rather than linked 'syntactically' by conjunctions etc.[125] There is a simple example in 13.182 ταύρους... ἱερεύσομεν, αἴ κ' ἐλεήσηι 'let us sacrifice bulls (to

---

[125] Cf. generally *GH* ii.351-64 'La structure de la phrase complexe et la parataxe'. The preservation of parataxis would have been helped by the use of formulaic expressions in the composition of Homeric verse. The differences between Homer and later Greek may be due in part to the different syntactic choices made by oral and literate societies: there is no reason to imagine that the further back one went in time the more paratactic Greek was.

see) if he might pity us'. The audience is left to make the connections between the clauses, as again in 14.487–8 οὐ τοι ἔτι ζωοῖσι μετέσσομαι, ἀλλά με χεῖμα | δάμναται 'I shall not continue amongst the living; but the cold is killing me', where cause is implied. Sometimes the parataxis can produce passages that are difficult to explain and editors have come to suspect the transmitted texts, but there are a sufficient number of such cases to suggest that change is not necessary. There is a notable example in 14.85–9, on which see the Commentary.

11.1.2 What we now call 'constructions' developed out of the uses of the different kinds of moods, tenses etc. which we have been looking at, and there are numerous cases in Homer where one can see the 'construction' (syntax) beginning to emerge from the parataxis. Thus in 13.207–8 οὐδὲ μὲν αὐτοῦ | καλλείψω, μή πώς μοι ἔλωρ ἄλλοισι γένηται, the 'paratactic' translation is 'nor will I leave them here; may they not become prey to others', with a voluntative subjunctive; but we are very close to a purpose clause, 'I will not leave them here, so that…' In 13.363–4 ἀλλὰ χρήματα μὲν μυχῶι ἄντρου θεσπεσίοιο | θείομεν αὐτίκα νῦν, ἵνα περ τάδε τοι σόα μίμνηι, the ἵνα-clause means literally 'where (I hope) they might be safe', but this could easily slip into 'in order that they should be safe'.

11.2 Indirect statements

11.2.1 The accusative and infinitive construction is not found in Homer.

11.2.2 The conjunctions which introduce indirect speech in Greek (ὅ, ὅ τε, ὅτι, ὡς, οὕνεκα) were originally causal conjunctions. The ease with which this shift in meaning could happen can be seen in a sentence like *Il.* 2.255 ὀνειδίζων ὅτι οἱ μάλα πολλὰ διδοῦσιν, which is either 'reproaching him because they gave him a great deal' or 'reproaching him for the fact that…' (cf. *GH* II.288–92).

11.3 Indirect questions. These are introduced by εἰ (ἄν) and ἦ, and the mood is the same as in the direct question. The prospective and deliberative subjunctives and the oblique optative are also found, as in 13.415 ὤιχετο πευσόμενος μετὰ σὸν κλέος, εἴ που ἔτ' εἴης 'he went in search of news about you, whether you are still alive anywhere'.

11.4 Causal clauses. These are introduced by ὅ, ὅτι, ὅ τε, οὕνεκα.

11.5 Consecutive (result) clauses. These are expressed by the simple infinitive (see §10.5.3 above). There are only two examples in

Homer of the infinitive introduced by ὡς τε, and none of the Attic ὡστε + indicative.

11.6 Final (purpose) clauses

11.6.1 These are introduced by ἵνα, ὡς (usually with κε/ἄν) and ὄφρα (with κε but seldom) and, since they involve willing or expectation, use the voluntative or prospective subjunctive or optative. For examples, see under §11.1.2 above.

11.6.2 As in Attic, the optative is used after secondary tenses, and is much more common than the subjunctive.

11.6.3 Where optatives are found after primary tenses, this may be the result of the paratactic mode of composition, in which the two clauses were originally independent.[126]

11.7 Conditional clauses

11.7.1 Future conditions

11.7.1.1 In discussing the subjunctive, optative and future we saw how the distinctions between them were highly permeable. Nowhere is this better seen than in conditional clauses referring to the future, where all three moods can be used in both parts, in any combination between the parts, and with or without κε or ἄν, again in both parts. There are more than twenty possible combinations (not counting examples involving other tenses), most of which are found.

11.7.1.2 Something of this variety can be seen in the following examples:

11.7.1.2.1 *future* + *εἰ with subjunctive* (κε): 14.138–41 οὐ γὰρ ἔτ' ἄλλον | ἤπιον ὧδε ἄνακτα κιχήσομαι...οὐδ' εἴ κεν πατρὸς καὶ μητέρος αὖτις ἵκωμαι | οἶκον.

11.7.1.2.2 *optative (κε)* + *εἰ with optative* (κε): 14.131–2 αἶψά κε καὶ σύ, γεραιέ, ἔπος παρατεκτήναιο, | εἴ τίς τοι χλαῖνάν τε χιτῶνά τε εἵματα δοίη (cf. also 13.291–2, 14.402–5).

11.7.1.2.3 *εἰ with optative* + *future: Il.* 10.222–3 ἀλλ' εἴ τίς μοι ἀνὴρ ἅμ' ἕποιτο καὶ ἄλλος, | μᾶλλον θαλπωρὴ...ἔσται 'but if someone else would follow me, there will be greater comfort'.

---

[126] See Willmott 2007: 164–5 for a different explanation.

11.7.1.3 Note also the mixed conditional 14.56–7 οὔ μοι
θέμις ἔστ᾽, οὐδ᾽ εἰ κακίων σέθεν ἔλθοι, | ξεῖνον ἀτιμῆ-
σαι 'it is not right for me to show no concern for
a stranger, even if a more destitute man than you
were to come'.

11.7.2 Unreal conditions

11.7.2.1 The aorist is used in past unreal conditions as
in Attic: 13.137–8 ὅσ᾽ ἂν οὐδέ ποτε Τροίης ἐξήρατ᾽
Ὀδυσσεύς, | εἴ περ ἀπήμων ἦλθε '(a quantity of pos-
sessions) such as Odysseus would never have taken
from Troy, if he had returned without trouble';
14.67 τῶ κέ με πόλλ᾽ ὤνησεν ἄναξ, εἰ αὐτόθι γήρα 'thus
my master would have done me great benefits, if he
had grown old here'.

11.7.2.2 Unlike Attic, Homer also uses the potential
optative of 'unreal' present and past events: Il.
23.274–5 εἰ μὲν νῦν ἐπὶ ἄλλωι ἀεθλεύοιμεν Ἀχαιοί, | ἤ
τ᾽ ἂν ἐγὼ τὰ πρῶτα λαβὼν κλισίηνδε φεροίμην 'if we
Achaeans were competing in honour of another
man, I would certainly win and take the first prize
to my hut'; and Od. 2.185, with an implied protasis 'if you had died', οὐδέ κε Τηλέμαχον κεχολ-
ωμένον ὧδ᾽ ἀνιείης 'you would not now be provoking
Telemachus in his anger'.

11.7.3 General conditions

11.7.3.1 As in Attic, the protasis of a present general condition has the subjunctive, sometimes + κε/ἄν;
cf. 14.372–4 οὐδὲ πόλινδε | ἔρχομαι, εἰ μή πού τι
περίφρων Πηνελόπεια | ἐλθέμεν ὀτρύνηισιν 'and I don't
go to the city, unless wise Penelope happens to
encourage me to do so'.

11.7.3.2 Past general conditions have the optative.

11.8 Relative clauses

11.8.1 Indefinite or generalising relative clauses. The usual pattern is that in primary sequence there is the subjunctive,
usually with κε/ἄν or τε; and in secondary the optative,
without κε/ἄν.

11.8.1.1 With the subjunctive, cf. 13.31–2 ᾧ τε πανῆμαρ νειὸν ἀν᾽ ἕλκητον βόε οἴνοπε πηκτὸν ἄροτρον
'(the ploughman) for whom all day up and
down the fallow field his two dark oxen drag
his jointed plough' (this is common in comparisons); 14.214 ὅς τις ἁμάρτηι 'whoever sins'.

11.8.1.2 With the optative, cf. 21.414–15 οὔ τινα γὰρ τίεσκον...ὅτις σφέας εἰσαφίκοιτο 'they honoured no-one who came to them'.

11.8.2 Final relative clauses. This and the conditional sense (§11.8.3) are specialised versions of this generalising use, cf. 18.334–6 μή τί τοι τάχα Ἴρου ἀμείνων ἄλλος ἀναστῆι, | ὅς τίς σ'... | δώματος ἐκπέμψηισι '(take care that) a better man than Irus doesn't appear who might send you (i.e. in order to send you) out of the house'; 15.458 καὶ τότ' ἄρ' ἄγγελον ἧκαν, ὃς ἀγγείλειε γυναικί 'then they sent a messenger who could inform (i.e. to inform) his wife'. The future indicative is more common than the optative.

11.8.3 Conditional relative clauses. See §11.8.2 and cf. 13.213–14 Ζεύς...ὅς τε...ἀνθρώπους τίνυται..., ὅς τις ἁμάρτηι 'Zeus who punishes men, if anyone does wrong'; 13.291 κερδαλέος κ' εἴη καὶ ἐπίκλοπος, ὅς σε παρέλθοι 'he would be a clever and cunning man, who/if he could deceive you'.

11.9 Temporal clauses

11.9.1 With the subjunctive, cf. 13.155–7 ὁππότε κεν δὴ πάντες ἐλαυνομένην προΐδωνται | λαοὶ ἀπὸ πτόλιος, θεῖναι λίθον ἐγγύθι γαίης | νηΐ θοῆι ἴκελον 'when everyone is watching from the city walls the ship as it comes, make it a rock that looks like a ship'.

11.9.2 With the optative, cf. 14.169–70 θυμὸς ἐνὶ στήθεσσιν ἐμοῖσιν | ἄχνυται, ὁππότε τις μνήσηι κεδνοῖο ἄνακτος 'my heart is pained in my breast, when anyone mentions my excellent master'.

11.10 'Until'

11.10.1 In a purely temporal sense, these clauses have the subjunctive with or without κε/ἄν when referring to the future: Il. 3.290–1 μαχήσομαι... εἵως... κιχείω 'I shall fight until I find'.

11.10.2 The aorist indicative is used when referring to the past: 13.321 ἠλώμην, εἵως με θεοὶ κακότητος ἔλυσαν 'I wandered until the gods freed me from my trouble'.

11.10.3 The optative + κε/ἄν is found if there is an optative in the main clause (with one exception).

11.11 πρίν

11.11.1 In reference to the past, πρίν usually has the infinitive: 14.229 πρὶν μὲν γὰρ Τροίης ἐπιβήμεναι υἷας Ἀχαιῶν 'before the sons of the Achaeans went to Troy'.

11.11.2 The only time that an indicative is involved is when πρίν γε governs a clause introduced by ὅτε: 13.318–23

οὐδ' ἐνόησα … νηὸς ἐμῆς ἐπιβᾶσαν, πρίν γ' ὅτε … θάρσυνάς τ'
ἐπέεσσι 'and I didn't see you boarding my boat, until you
encouraged me with words…'

11.11.3 For future reference, the subjunctive is used, but without κε/ἄν: 10.174–5 οὐ γάρ πω καταδυσόμεθα … εἰς Ἄϊδαο
δόμους, πρὶν μόρσιμον ἦμαρ ἐπέλθῃι 'we shall not go down
to the house of Hades, until the allotted day comes'.

12 Particles

12.1 ἀτάρ, αὐτάρ can be adversative ('but', 'and yet') or progressive
('and then').

12.2 ἄρα/ἄρ/ῥα. One of Homer's favourite particles. It marks an interest in what is described, either amongst the characters, where it
can point to a sudden realisation ('so!', 13.209), or amongst the
audience, where it can mean 'as you can imagine' (13.1n.). ἄρα
is sometimes strengthened by other particles of a similar force: ἦ
ἄρα, ἦ ῥά νύ τοι, etc.

12.3 δέ. Note 'apodotic' δέ, that is δέ used apparently superfluously to
join a main clause to a subordinate one: 13.143–4 ἀνδρῶν δ' εἴ
πέρ τίς σε … | οὔ τι τίει, σοὶ δ' ἐστὶ καὶ ἐξοπίσω τίσις αἰεί 'if any man
dishonours you at all, you have a means of revenge in future'.
This may have been a feature of the spoken, informal language,
with slippage between subordinate and main clauses: cf. 'then'
in 'if you are allowed to do that, then everyone will want to'.[127]
It is called 'apodotic' because of its frequency in the apodosis of
conditional clauses. 'Only in Homer and Herodotus is apodotic
δέ really at home' (GP 177; cf. GH II.356–7).

12.4 ἦ is found only in speeches, meaning 'in truth, really' and the like,
sometimes combined with other particles: ἦ μήν, ἦ γάρ, etc.

12.5 μέν is not always followed by δέ. In γε μέν it is adversative, or concessive: 8.134 φυήν γε μὲν οὐ κακός ἐστι 'in build at least he is not
bad'.

12.6 οὖν. Almost only as ἐπεὶ οὖν (14.67) and ὡς οὖν.

12.7 περ. See 13.130n.

12.8 τε

12.8.1 τε 'and' is, like Latin -que, < kʷe-.[128]

12.8.2 Beside its connective sense, τε is also very frequently used
to indicate permanent or typical characteristics: 13.300–1
ἦ τέ τοι αἰεὶ | … παρίσταμαι 'I who always stand beside you'.

12.9 τοι is a datival form of τυ, and is usually found in speeches with
a sense like 'mark you', often reminding a character or audience

---

[127] Cf. Slings 1998.   [128] See the magisterial Ruijgh 1971.

of something that may have slipped their minds: 13.341 ἀλλά τοι οὐκ ἐθέλησα Ποσειδάωνι μάχεσθαι 'I didn't want to fight Poseidon, mind'.

5.4 Bones of the Homeric dialect

This section lists the more common features of the Homeric dialect which differ from Attic usage.

1st declension: feminines
    -αων, -εων genitive plurals
    -ησι, -ῃσι, -αισι dative plurals
1st declension: masculines
    -α nominative singulars (νεφεληγερέτα)
    -αο, -εω genitive singulars
2nd declension
    -οιο genitive singulars
    -οισι dative plurals
3rd declension
    πόλις, πόλι, πόλιν, πόλιος (and πόληος, πόλεος), πόλι (and πόληϊ); πόλιες (and πόληες), πόλῑς (and πόληας), πολίων, πολίεσσι
    πολύς has u-stem forms (πολύ-ν, πολέος, πολέες etc.), and ο-stems (πολλός, πολλόν etc.)
    Ζεῦς, Ζῆν (and Ζῆνα, Δία), Διός, Διί
Numerals
    ἴα 'one', πίσυρες 'four'
Pronouns
    1st person
        ἐμέο, μεῦ, ἐμέθεν genitive singular
        ἄμμες, ἄμμιν 'we', beside ἡμεῖς, ἡμῖν
    2nd person
        τύνη nominative
        σέο, σεῦ, σέθεν, τεοῖο genitive singular
        τοι, τεῖν dative singular
        ὔμμες, ὔμμι 'you', beside ὑμεῖς, ὑμῖν
    3rd person and reflexive
        ἑ, ἑε, μιν accusative singular
        ἕο, εὗ, ἕθεν genitive singular
        ἑοῖ, οἷ dative singular
        σφέ, σφας, σφέας accusative plural
        σφέων, σφείων, σφῶν genitive plural
Possessive adjectives
    τεός and σός 'yours'

ἑός, ὅς 'his, hers, its'
Demonstratives
    The Attic article ὁ, ἡ, τό is in Homer still a demonstrative, 'that
    man', 'he', 'she' etc.: τὸν δ᾿ αὖτ᾿ Ἀλκίνοος ἀμείβετο 'to him Alcinous
    replied'.
Verbs
    Augment: frequently omitted (φώνησεν).
    2nd person singular active
        -θα (οἶσθα etc.)
    2nd person singular middle-passive
        -εαι and -ηι (from -εσαι) as πειρήσεαι and γνώσηι
        -αο and -ω (from -ασο) as ἐλύσαο and ἐλύσω
    3rd person plural middle-passive
        -αται, -ατο (τετεύχαται 'they have been made', κεχολώατο 'they
        were angry'). Distinguish these forms from 3rd-person *singu-*
        lars in -αται, -ατο.
Aorists
    Reduplicated aorists: τεταρπόμενος 'rejoicing', (παρ-)πε-πιθ-ών
    'obeying'.
Subjunctives
    Homeric subjunctives regularly have a short vowel where Attic
    has a long vowel, as ἀμείβεται for ἀμείβηται, ἴομεν for ἴωμεν.
Infinitives
    -μεν, -μεναι, as ἀγέμεν, ἔμμεν, εἰπέμεν; ἀγορευέμεναι, ἔμμεναι.
Particles
    δέ: note the frequent use of δέ apparently superfluously to join main
    clauses to subordinate clauses, as in 13.143–4 ἀνδρῶν δ᾿ εἴ πέρ τίς
    σε...| οὔ τι τίει, σοὶ δ᾿ ἐστὶ καὶ ἐξοπίσω τίσις αἰεί 'but if any man dis-
    honours you at all, you have a means of revenge in future', where
    the second δέ would not be used in Attic prose. This is called
    'apodotic' δέ because of its frequency in the apodosis of condi-
    tional clauses (see §12.3 above).

6 HISTORY OF THE TEXT

Uncertainty surrounds the 'text' (in the broadest sense) of the *Odyssey*
(and indeed the *Iliad*) throughout a good deal of its history, particularly
in the early period.[129] We do not know when the figure of Odysseus and

---

[129] This is a major and contested subject, which can only be touched on here.
See e.g. Cauer 1923: 9–135; T. W. Allen 1924: 202–327; Pasquali 1952: 201–47;
Davidson 1962; Fraser 1972: 447–79; S. R. West, *CHO* I.33–48; Janko 1992: 20–38;
Haslam 1997.

the tales of his adventures were joined: some of them could have come from the Argonautic tradition, some from the Near East. We do not know for certain where or when the poems reached something like their current form. The dialect mixture points to Ionian-speaking parts, and Asia Minor has generally been thought to be the broad area, but the case for Euboea is now made more strongly.[130] The traditional date for their composition is the late eighth century, but a date later in the seventh now has growing support. We do not know whether one poet or more than one was responsible, nor whether the composition involved original creation or some form of compilation of earlier versions, nor whether the same poet or poets produced both epics.[131] Uncertain too is whether he/they composed the poems orally, in writing or in a mixture of the two: comparative evidence from outside Greece suggests that poets can adapt their speed to make dictation possible, and writing can contribute to the generation of poems on a grander scale than normal. The fact that the linguistic development of the Homeric language stopped at a very early stage, difficult to date but most likely in the eighth or early seventh century, is best explained by the development being stopped by the recording of the texts in writing.[132] The reason why oral epics were transmuted into written texts is lost to us: was it perhaps on the initiative of a wealthy patron with knowledge of the written epics of the Near East?

We do know that in mid sixth-century Athens there were competitions instituted by the Peisistratids at the Panathenaea, when rhapsodes such as the 'Homeridae' from Chios recited the poems,[133] but the tradition of a 'Peisistratean recension'[134] made for those competitions is hard to evaluate: it could mean simply that Peisistratus collected a set of texts which were used to judge the performance of the reciters. How far rhapsodes altered the text at other performances is also unknowable. And yet, despite all the possible ways in which variation could have been introduced into the texts of the poems, and despite a host of minor textual variants, it is striking that the 'city' texts of the two poems collected in the third and second centuries from places as far apart as Marseilles, Crete, Cyprus and Sinope on the Black Sea coast offer essentially similar versions.[135]

Part of the difficulty here is that, during the period down to the fifth century, the transmission will have been predominantly oral. Textual transmission thereafter becomes more important, though we have to wait until

---

[130] See M. L. West 1988: 165–72; Powell 1997.
[131] On the 'Homeric Question', see Turner 1997.   [132] Cf. Janko 1982.
[133] Cf. Plato's *Ion* for a fourth-century picture of these men.
[134] For the evidence on this, see Jensen 1980: 207–26; also Janko 1992: 29–32; for the ancient evidence, see [Pl.] *Hipparch.* 228B, Lycurg. *in Leocr.* 102.
[135] Such copies of the *Odyssey* are known from Argos and Marseilles, alongside one known as 'Aeolic'; cf. T. W. Allen 1924: 283–96.

the third century for our first surviving papyrus manuscripts, which are
very fragmentary indeed. Greater light begins to dawn, however. The first
person to have produced an 'edition' (*ekdosis*) of Homer was the late fifth-
century poet Antimachus of Colophon,[136] but this seems not to have been
an edition in the sense of a scholarly treatment of textual matters.[137] The
trail-blazer in this area was Zenodotus of Ephesus, described as the first
diorthōtes ('reviser') of Homer, who flourished in the first half of the third
century. He was the first head of the Library at Alexandria, and began
the study of differing copies of the text in order to establish an authoritative version.[138] The evidence we have of early Ptolemaic texts which he
would have studied shows that they differed from later papyri in having
lines not found in the later tradition ('plus verses'), different readings
and omissions; however, they did not apparently have episodes in a different order.[139] Zenodotus did not however leave a commentary explaining
his textual choices or his method of working, but he did invent the *obelus*
('spit') written as '—' in the margin) to mark lines he thought should not
be in the text.

By tradition, the next great Homeric scholar, Aristophanes of Byzan-
tium, was a pupil of Zenodotus; he also was Librarian at Alexandria.[140]
He lived in the second half of the third century and into the second. His
method was not always to expunge lines from the text he thought spurious, but to use signs in the margins to indicate his judgements: lines he
'athetised', i.e. suspected but did not delete, were marked with the *kerau-
nion* (T); an *asteriskos* (※) marked repeated lines he thought more appropriate in one place rather than another, and so on. He may well have been
the first to accentuate the text in order to distinguish between homonyms,
and famously put the 'limit' (*peras*) of the *Odyssey* at 23.296.[141]

The most significant follower of Aristophanes was another head of the
Library, Aristarchus of Samothrace, who died around the middle of the
second century.[142] His great addition to scholarship on Homer and other
texts was the significant use of commentaries (*hypomnēmata*), something
which seems to have been rare before him. He is thus effectively the father
of scientific scholarship, though his comments can today seem to depend

---

[136] Pfeiffer 1968: 94.
[137] Critical discussion of Homer begins of course before this. For instance, in the
late sixth century, Theagenes of Rhegium and others produced allegorical readings
of Homer, and in Aristophanes' *Daitaleis* (fr. 233K–A), there is a discussion of the
meaning of obscure Homeric expressions.
[138] See Pfeiffer 1968: 105–19; Nickau 1977; S. R. West, *CHO* 1.41–4.
[139] On the Homeric papyri, see S. R. West 1967; Sutton 1991; Haslam 1997.
[140] Cf. Pfeiffer 1968: 171–81.
[141] An example of Aristophanes' criticism can be found in 13.158n.
[142] See Lehrs 1882; Ludwich 1884–5; Pfeiffer 1968: 210–19.

too much on subjective criteria such as decorum.[143] Like Zenodotus and Aristophanes he used marginal signs, adding a number of his own;[144] these were linked to his notes in the commentary. Given that not many of Aristarchus' and others' suggested readings made it into the later texts, it would appear that these editions kept a transmitted text and used the commentary in a separate roll to record emendations etc. A good deal of his and others' scholarly work is preserved in the marginal notes and interlinear comments (*scholia*) of the tenth-century Venetus A codex of the *Iliad*,[145] thanks to the work of the later scholars such as Didymus, Aristonicus, Herodian and Nicanor. Also important for the preservation of their work are the Byzantine lexica such as the *Suda*, and the voluminous and still extant commentary of Eustathius, the twelfth-century bishop of Thessalonica.[146]

It would seem that a relatively standard, 'vulgate'[147] text was created in this period. The papyri continue to show variants and lines which are not in this vulgate, but the differences are fewer than before. It is this tradition which is behind the medieval tradition of our manuscripts. The papyrus roll was gradually replaced by the 'codex', or book with pages, and papyrus itself by parchment, prepared animal skins; the earliest Homeric texts on the latter date from the third century AD. By sometime in the late eighth century AD a new more economical script ('minuscule') was developed replacing the capital ('majuscule') script used until then for book-texts, and this is the origin of the scripts used for Greek today. Many manuscripts were recopied in minuscule in this period. Most of our manuscripts of Homer were copied in Italy in the fourteenth and fifteenth centuries.[148] In 1488, the first printed copy of the *Iliad* and *Odyssey* was produced in Florence by Demetrius Damilas, aided by Demetrius Chalcondylas.

The text printed here text is my own, but does not depend on fresh scrutiny of the manuscript evidence. It is punctuated for readability, and a small *apparatus criticus* points to the more important cases where manuscripts and/or scholars disagree on what should be printed.

---

[143] Cf. for instance 13.320–3, 333–8, 14.495nn.
[144] He used the *asteriskos* differently: the scholia on 14.398–401 say 'these lines are marked as spurious with "asterisks" since they were transferred from later lines' (i.e. 430–3).
[145] Unfortunately, there is no comparable manuscript for the *Odyssey*, so the scholia on this poem are less copious than those on the *Iliad*. On the manuscripts of the *Odyssey*, see the brief account in Haslam 1997: 94–5. The earliest dates to the tenth century. On the Homeric scholia, see Nagy 1997.
[146] Cf. van der Valk 1971–87; Kazhdan and Franklin 1984: 115–95.
[147] On the problems with this term, see Haslam 1997: 63–4.
[148] On these, cf. Haslam 1997: 87–99.

SIGLA

a   a variant reading found in one or more MSS
b   another variant found in yet other MSS
c   a third such variant
p   a reading found in a papyrus

ΟΜΗΡΟΥ ΟΔΥΣΣΕΙΑΣ Ν–Ξ

Reaction to Odysseus' tales and preparations for departure

Ὣς ἔφαθ᾽, οἱ δ᾽ ἄρα πάντες ἀκὴν ἐγένοντο σιωπῆι,
κηληθμῶι δ᾽ ἔσχοντο κατὰ μέγαρα σκιόεντα.
τὸν δ᾽ αὖτ᾽ Ἀλκίνοος ἀπαμείβετο φώνησέν τε·
"ὦ Ὀδυσεῦ, ἐπεὶ ἵκευ ἐμὸν ποτὶ χαλκοβατὲς δῶ
ὑψερεφές, τώ σ᾽ οὔ τι πάλιν πλαγχθέντα γ᾽ ὀίω   5
ἂψ ἀπονοστήσειν, εἰ καὶ μάλα πολλὰ πέπονθας.
ὑμέων δ᾽ ἀνδρὶ ἑκάστωι ἐφιέμενος τάδε εἴρω,
ὅσσοι ἐνὶ μεγάροισι γερούσιον αἴθοπα οἶνον
αἰεὶ πίνετ᾽ ἐμοῖσιν, ἀκουάζεσθε δ᾽ ἀοιδοῦ·
εἵματα μὲν δὴ ξείνωι ἐϋξέστηι ἐνὶ χηλῶι   10
κεῖται καὶ χρυσὸς πολυδαίδαλος ἄλλα τε πάντα
δῶρ᾽, ὅσα Φαιήκων βουληφόροι ἐνθάδ᾽ ἔνεικαν·
ἀλλ᾽ ἄγε οἱ δῶμεν τρίποδα μέγαν ἠδὲ λέβητα
ἀνδρακάς, ἡμεῖς δ᾽ αὖτε ἀγειρόμενοι κατὰ δῆμον
τεισόμεθ᾽· ἀργαλέον γὰρ ἕνα προικὸς χαρίσασθαι."   15
ὣς ἔφατ᾽ Ἀλκίνοος, τοῖσιν δ᾽ ἐπιήνδανε μῦθος.
οἱ μὲν κακκείοντες ἔβαν οἶκόνδε ἕκαστος·
ἦμος δ᾽ ἠριγένεια φάνη ῥοδοδάκτυλος Ἠώς,
νῆάδ᾽ ἐπεσσεύοντο, φέρον δ᾽ εὐήνορα χαλκόν.
καὶ τὰ μὲν εὖ κατέθηχ᾽ ἱερὸν μένος Ἀλκινόοιο,   20
αὐτὸς ἰὼν διὰ νηὸς ὑπὸ ζυγά, μή τιν᾽ ἑταίρων
βλάπτοι ἐλαυνόντων, ὁπότε σπερχοίατ᾽ ἐρετμοῖς·
οἱ δ᾽ εἰς Ἀλκινόοιο κίον καὶ δαῖτ᾽ ἀλέγυνον.
τοῖσι δὲ βοῦν ἱέρευσ᾽ ἱερὸν μένος Ἀλκινόοιο
Ζηνὶ κελαινεφέϊ Κρονίδηι, ὃς πᾶσιν ἀνάσσει.   25
μῆρα δὲ κήαντες δαίνυντ᾽ ἐρικυδέα δαῖτα
τερπόμενοι· μετὰ δέ σφιν ἐμέλπετο θεῖος ἀοιδός,
Δημόδοκος, λαοῖσι τετιμένος. αὐτὰρ Ὀδυσσεὺς
πολλὰ πρὸς ἠέλιον κεφαλὴν τρέπε παμφανόωντα,
δῦναι ἐπειγόμενος· δὴ γὰρ μενέαινε νέεσθαι.   30
ὡς δ᾽ ὅτ᾽ ἀνὴρ δόρποιο λιλαίεται, ὧι τε πανῆμαρ
νειὸν ἀν᾽ ἕλκητον βόε οἴνοπε πηκτὸν ἄροτρον·

---

4 ἧκες a: ἦλθες b   14 ἄνδρα κατ᾽ a   16 μῦθος: θυμῶι a: θυμός b   27 θεῖος: δῖος
a   32 ἀνέλκοντες a

ἀσπασίως δ' ἄρα τῶι κατέδυ φάος ἠελίοιο
δόρπον ἐποίχεσθαι, βλάβεται δέ τε γούνατ' ἰόντι·
ὡς Ὀδυσῆ' ἀσπαστὸν ἔδυ φάος ἠελίοιο.   35
αἶψα δὲ Φαιήκεσσι φιληρέτμοισι μετηύδα,
Ἀλκινόῳ δὲ μάλιστα πιφαυσκόμενος φάτο μῦθον·
"Ἀλκίνοε κρεῖον, πάντων ἀριδείκετε λαῶν,
πέμπετέ με σπείσαντες ἀπήμονα, χαίρετε δ' αὐτοί.
ἤδη γὰρ τετέλεσται ἅ μοι φίλος ἤθελε θυμός,   40
πομπὴ καὶ φίλα δῶρα, τά μοι θεοὶ Οὐρανίωνες
ὄλβια ποιήσειαν· ἀμύμονα δ' οἴκοι ἄκοιτιν
νοστήσας εὕροιμι σὺν ἀρτεμέεσσι φίλοισιν.
ὑμεῖς δ' αὖθι μένοντες ἐϋφραίνοιτε γυναῖκας
κουριδίας καὶ τέκνα· θεοὶ δ' ἀρετὴν ὀπάσειαν   45
παντοίην, καὶ μή τι κακὸν μεταδήμιον εἴη."
    ὡς ἔφαθ', οἱ δ' ἄρα πάντες ἐπήινεον ἠδ' ἐκέλευον
πεμπέμεναι τὸν ξεῖνον, ἐπεὶ κατὰ μοῖραν ἔειπε.
καὶ τότε κήρυκα προσέφη μένος Ἀλκινόοιο·
"Ποντόνοε, κρητῆρα κερασσάμενος μέθυ νεῖμον   50
πᾶσιν ἀνὰ μέγαρον, ὄφρ' εὐξάμενοι Διὶ πατρὶ
τὸν ξεῖνον πέμπωμεν ἑὴν ἐς πατρίδα γαῖαν."
    ὡς φάτο, Ποντόνοος δὲ μελίφρονα οἶνον ἐκίρνα,
νώμησεν δ' ἄρα πᾶσιν ἐπισταδόν· οἱ δὲ θεοῖσιν
ἔσπεισαν μακάρεσσι, τοὶ οὐρανὸν εὐρὺν ἔχουσιν,   55
αὐτόθεν ἐξ ἑδρέων. ἀνὰ δ' ἵστατο δῖος Ὀδυσσεύς,
Ἀρήτηι δ' ἐν χερσὶ τίθει δέπας ἀμφικύπελλον
καί μιν φωνήσας ἔπεα πτερόεντα προσηύδα·
"χαῖρέ μοι, ὦ βασίλεια, διαμπερές, εἰς ὅ κε γῆρας
ἔλθηι καὶ θάνατος, τά τ' ἐπ' ἀνθρώποισι πέλονται.   60
αὐτὰρ ἐγὼ νέομαι· σὺ δὲ τέρπεο τῶιδ' ἐνὶ οἴκωι
παισί τε καὶ λαοῖσι καὶ Ἀλκινόωι βασιλῆϊ."

Departure and journey to Ithaca

ὡς εἰπὼν ὑπὲρ οὐδὸν ἐβήσετο δῖος Ὀδυσσεύς·
τῶι δ' ἅμα κήρυκα προΐει μένος Ἀλκινόοιο
ἡγεῖσθαι ἐπὶ νῆα θοὴν καὶ θῖνα θαλάσσης.   65
Ἀρήτη δ' ἄρα οἱ δμωιὰς ἅμ' ἔπεμπε γυναῖκας,
τὴν μὲν φᾶρος ἔχουσαν ἐϋπλυνὲς ἠδὲ χιτῶνα,

57 χειρὶ a   63 ἐβήσατο a

τὴν δ' ἑτέρην χηλὸν πυκινὴν ἄμ' ὄπασσε κομίζειν·
ἡ δ' ἄλλη σῖτόν τ' ἔφερεν καὶ οἶνον ἐρυθρόν.
    αὐτὰρ ἐπεί ῥ' ἐπὶ νῆα κατήλυθον ἠδὲ θάλασσαν,   70
αἶψα τά γ' ἐν νηΐ γλαφυρῆι πομπῆες ἀγαυοὶ
δεξάμενοι κατέθεντο, πόσιν καὶ βρῶσιν ἅπασαν.
κὰδ δ' ἄρ' Ὀδυσσῆϊ στόρεσαν ῥῆγός τε λίνον τε
νηὸς ἐπ' ἰκριόφιν γλαφυρῆς, ἵνα νήγρετον εὕδοι
πρυμνῆς. ἂν δὲ καὶ αὐτὸς ἐβήσετο καὶ κατέλεκτο   75
σιγῆι· τοὶ δὲ καθῖζον ἐπὶ κληῖσιν ἕκαστοι
κόσμωι, πεῖσμα δ' ἔλυσαν ἀπὸ τρητοῖο λίθοιο.
εὖθ' οἱ ἀνακλινθέντες ἀνερρίπτουν ἅλα πηδῶι,
καὶ τῶι νήδυμος ὕπνος ἐπὶ βλεφάροισιν ἔπιπτε,
νήγρετος ἥδιστος, θανάτωι ἄγχιστα ἐοικώς.   80
    ἡ δ', ὥς τ' ἐν πεδίωι τετράοροι ἄρσενες ἵπποι,
πάντες ἄμ' ὁρμηθέντες ὑπὸ πληγῆισιν ἱμάσθλης,
ὑψόσ' ἀειρόμενοι ῥίμφα πρήσσουσι κέλευθον,
ὣς ἄρα τῆς πρώιρη μὲν ἀείρετο, κῦμα δ' ὄπισθε
πορφύρεον μέγα θῦε πολυφλοίσβοιο θαλάσσης.   85
ἡ δὲ μάλ' ἀσφαλέως θέεν ἔμπεδον· οὐδέ κεν ἴρηξ
κίρκος ὁμαρτήσειεν, ἐλαφρότατος πετεηνῶν·
ὣς ἡ ῥίμφα θέουσα θαλάσσης κύματ' ἔταμνεν,
ἄνδρα φέρουσα θεοῖσ' ἐναλίγκια μήδε' ἔχοντα,
ὃς πρὶν μὲν μάλα πολλὰ πάθ' ἄλγεα ὃν κατὰ θυμόν,   90
ἀνδρῶν τε πτολέμους ἀλεγεινά τε κύματα πείρων·
δὴ τότε γ' ἀτρέμας εὗδε, λελασμένος ὅσσ' ἐπεπόνθει.
    εὖτ' ἀστὴρ ὑπερέσχε φαάντατος, ὅς τε μάλιστα
ἔρχεται ἀγγέλλων φάος Ἠοῦς ἠριγενείης,
τῆμος δὴ νήσωι προσεπίλνατο ποντοπόρος νηῦς.   95
    Φόρκυνος δέ τίς ἐστι λιμήν, ἁλίοιο γέροντος,
ἐν δήμωι Ἰθάκης· δύο δὲ προβλῆτες ἐν αὐτῶι
ἀκταὶ ἀπορρῶγες, λιμένος ποτιπεπτηυῖαι,
αἵ τ' ἀνέμων σκεπόωσι δυσαήων μέγα κῦμα
ἔκτοθεν· ἔντοσθεν δέ τ' ἄνευ δεσμοῖο μένουσι   100
νῆες ἐΰσσελμοι, ὅτ' ἂν ὅρμου μέτρον ἵκωνται.
αὐτὰρ ἐπὶ κρατὸς λιμένος τανύφυλλος ἐλαίη,
ἀγχόθι δ' αὐτῆς ἄντρον ἐπήρατον ἠεροειδές,
ἱρὸν Νυμφάων, αἳ Νηϊάδες καλέονται.

68 ὄπασσε: ἔπεμπε a   75 πρυμνῆς Bekker: πρύμνη MSS   76 ἕκαστος a   84
πρώιρη Rochefort: πρύμνη MSS   88 ἔτετμεν a

ἐν δὲ κρητῆρές τε καὶ ἀμφιφορῆες ἔασι   105
λάϊνοι· ἔνθα δ' ἔπειτα τιθαιβώσσουσι μέλισσαι.
ἐν δ' ἱστοὶ λίθεοι περιμήκεες, ἔνθα τε Νύμφαι
φάρε' ὑφαίνουσιν ἁλιπόρφυρα, θαῦμα ἰδέσθαι·
ἐν δ' ὕδατ' ἀενάοντα. δύω δέ τέ οἱ θύραι εἰσίν,
αἱ μὲν πρὸς βορέαο καταιβαταὶ ἀνθρώποισιν,   110
αἱ δ' αὖ πρὸς νότου εἰσὶ θεώτεραι· οὐδέ τι κείνηι
ἄνδρες ἐσέρχονται, ἀλλ' ἀθανάτων ὁδός ἐστιν.
   ἔνθ' οἵ γ' εἰσέλασαν, πρὶν εἰδότες. ἡ μὲν ἔπειτα
ἠπείρωι ἐπέκελσεν ὅσον τ' ἐπὶ ἥμισυ πάσης,
σπερχομένη· τοῖον γὰρ ἐπείγετο χέρσ' ἐρετάων.   115
οἱ δ' ἐκ νηὸς βάντες ἐϋζύγου ἤπειρόνδε,
πρῶτον Ὀδυσσῆα γλαφυρῆς ἐκ νηὸς ἄειραν
αὐτῶι σύν τε λίνωι καὶ ῥήγεϊ σιγαλόεντι,
κὰδ δ' ἄρ' ἐπὶ ψαμάθωι ἔθεσαν δεδμημένον ὕπνωι,
ἐκ δὲ κτήματ' ἄειραν, ἅ οἱ Φαίηκες ἀγαυοὶ   120
ὤπασαν οἴκαδ' ἰόντι διὰ μεγάθυμον Ἀθήνην.
καὶ τὰ μὲν οὖν παρὰ πυθμέν' ἐλαίης ἀθρόα θῆκαν
ἐκτὸς ὁδοῦ, μή πώ τις ὁδιτάων ἀνθρώπων,
πρὶν Ὀδυσῆ' ἐγρέσθαι, ἐπελθὼν δηλήσαιτο.

Poseidon's desire to punish the Phaeacians

αὐτοὶ δ' αὖ οἴκόνδε πάλιν κίον. οὐδ' ἐνοσίχθων   125
λήθετ' ἀπειλάων, τὰς ἀντιθέωι Ὀδυσῆϊ
πρῶτον ἐπηπείλησε, Διὸς δ' ἐξείρετο βουλήν·
"Ζεῦ πάτερ, οὐκέτ' ἐγώ γε μετ' ἀθανάτοισι θεοῖσι
τιμήεις ἔσομαι, ὅ τε με βροτοὶ οὔ τι τίουσι,
Φαίηκες, τοί πέρ τοι ἐμῆς ἔξ εἰσι γενέθλης.   130
καὶ γὰρ νῦν Ὀδυσῆ' ἐφάμην κακὰ πολλὰ παθόντα
οἴκαδ' ἐλεύσεσθαι, νόστον δέ οἱ οὔ ποτ' ἀπηύρων
πάγχυ, ἐπεὶ σὺ πρῶτον ὑπέσχεο καὶ κατένευσας.
οἱ δ' εὕδοντ' ἐν νηΐ θοῆι ἐπὶ πόντον ἄγοντες
κάτθεσαν εἰν Ἰθάκηι, ἔδοσαν δέ οἱ ἄσπετα δῶρα,   135
χαλκόν τε χρυσόν τε ἅλις ἐσθῆτά θ' ὑφαντήν,
πόλλ', ὅσ' ἂν οὐδέ ποτε Τροίης ἐξήρατ' Ὀδυσσεύς,
εἴ περ ἀπήμων ἦλθε, λαχὼν ἀπὸ ληΐδος αἶσαν."

112 ἀνέρες ἔρχονται a   115 τοίων pa   135 ἄσπετα: ἀγλαὰ a

τὸν δ' ἀπαμειβόμενος προσέφη νεφεληγερέτα Ζεύς·
"ὢ πόποι, ἐννοσίγαι' εὐρυσθενές, οἷον ἔειπες.   140
οὔ τί σ' ἀτιμάζουσι θεοί· χαλεπὸν δέ κεν εἴη
πρεσβύτατον καὶ ἄριστον ἀτιμίῃσιν ἰάλλειν.
ἀνδρῶν δ' εἴ πέρ τίς σε βίῃ καὶ κάρτεϊ εἴκων
οὔ τι τίει, σοὶ δ' ἐστὶ καὶ ἐξοπίσω τίσις αἰεί.
ἔρξον ὅπως ἐθέλεις καί τοι φίλον ἔπλετο θυμῶι."   145
τὸν δ' ἠμείβετ' ἔπειτα Ποσειδάων ἐνοσίχθων·
"αἶψά κ' ἐγὼν ἔρξαιμι, κελαινεφές, ὡς ἀγορεύεις·
ἀλλὰ σὸν αἰεὶ θυμὸν ὀπίζομαι ἠδ' ἀλεείνω.
νῦν αὖ Φαιήκων ἐθέλω περικαλλέα νῆα
ἐκ πομπῆς ἀνιοῦσαν ἐν ἠεροειδέϊ πόντωι   150
ῥαῖσαι, ἵν' ἤδη σχῶνται, ἀπολλήξωσι δὲ πομπῆς
ἀνθρώπων, μέγα δέ σφιν ὄρος πόλει ἀμφικαλύψαι."
τὸν δ' ἀπαμειβόμενος προσέφη νεφεληγερέτα Ζεύς·
"ὢ πέπον, ὡς μὲν ἐμῶι θυμῶι δοκεῖ εἶναι ἄριστα·
ὁππότε κεν δὴ πάντες ἐλαυνομένην προΐδωνται   155
λαοὶ ἀπὸ πτόλιος, θεῖναι λίθον ἐγγύθι γαίης
νηΐ θοῆι ἴκελον, ἵνα θαυμάζωσιν ἅπαντες
ἄνθρωποι, μέγα δέ σφιν ὄρος πόλει ἀμφικαλύψαι."
αὐτὰρ ἐπεὶ τό γ' ἄκουσε Ποσειδάων ἐνοσίχθων,
βῆ ῥ' ἴμεν ἐς Σχερίην, ὅθι Φαίηκες γεγάασιν.   160
ἔνθ' ἔμεν'· ἡ δὲ μάλα σχεδὸν ἤλυθε ποντοπόρος νηῦς,
ῥίμφα διωκομένη. τῆς δὲ σχεδὸν ἦλθ' ἐνοσίχθων,
ὅς μιν λᾶαν ἔθηκε καὶ ἐρρίζωσεν ἔνερθε,
χειρὶ καταπρηνεῖ ἐλάσας· ὁ δὲ νόσφι βεβήκει.
οἱ δὲ πρὸς ἀλλήλους ἔπεα πτερόεντ' ἀγόρευον   165
Φαίηκες δολιχήρετμοι, ναυσικλυτοὶ ἄνδρες.
ὧδε δέ τις εἴπεσκεν, ἰδὼν ἐς πλησίον ἄλλον·
"ὢ μοι, τίς δὴ νῆα θοὴν ἐπέδησ' ἐνὶ πόντωι
οἴκαδ' ἐλαυνομένην; καὶ δὴ προὐφαίνετο πᾶσα."
ὡς ἄρα τις εἴπεσκε· τὰ δ' οὐκ ἴσαν ὡς ἐτέτυκτο.   170
τοῖσιν δ' Ἀλκίνοος ἀγορήσατο καὶ μετέειπεν·
"ὢ πόποι, ἦ μάλα δή με παλαίφατα θέσφαθ' ἱκάνει
πατρὸς ἐμοῦ, ὃς ἔφασκε Ποσειδάων' ἀγάσασθαι
ἡμῖν, οὕνεκα πομποὶ ἀπήμονές εἰμεν ἁπάντων.

147 ὡς σὺ κελεύεις **a**   152 μέγα: μὴ Aristophanes   πόλιν **a** (also 158, 177)
173 ἀγάσεσθαι Aristarchus   174 ἀμύμονες **a**

φῆ ποτε Φαιήκων ἀνδρῶν περικαλλέα νῆα   175
ἐκ πομπῆς ἀνιοῦσαν ἐν ἠεροειδέϊ πόντωι
ῥαισέμεναι, μέγα δ᾽ ἧμιν ὄρος πόλει ἀμφικαλύψειν.
ὡς ἀγόρευ᾽ ὁ γέρων· τὰ δὲ δὴ νῦν πάντα τελεῖται.
ἀλλ᾽ ἄγεθ᾽, ὡς ἂν ἐγὼ εἴπω, πειθώμεθα πάντες·
πομπῆς μὲν παύσασθε βροτῶν, ὅτε κέν τις ἵκηται   180
ἡμέτερον προτὶ ἄστυ· Ποσειδάωνι δὲ ταύρους
δώδεκα κεκριμένους ἱερεύσομεν, αἴ κ᾽ ἐλεήσηι
μηδ᾽ ἡμῖν περίμηκες ὄρος πόλει ἀμφικαλύψηι."
ὣς ἔφαθ᾽, οἱ δ᾽ ἔδεισαν, ἐτοιμάσσαντο δὲ ταύρους.
ὣς οἱ μέν ῥ᾽ εὔχοντο Ποσειδάωνι ἄνακτι   185
δήμου Φαιήκων ἡγήτορες ἠδὲ μέδοντες,
ἑσταότες περὶ βωμόν.

Odysseus awakes to a disguised Ithaca

                    ὁ δ᾽ ἔγρετο δῖος Ὀδυσσεὺς
εὕδων ἐν γαίηι πατρωΐηι, οὐδέ μιν ἔγνω,
ἤδη δὴν ἀπεών· περὶ γὰρ θεὸς ἠέρα χεῦε
Παλλὰς Ἀθηναίη, κούρη Διός, ὄφρα μιν αὐτὸν   190
ἄγνωστον τεύξειεν ἕκαστά τε μυθήσαιτο,
μή μιν πρὶν ἄλοχος γνοίη ἀστοί τε φίλοι τε,
πρὶν πᾶσαν μνηστῆρας ὑπερβασίην ἀποτεῖσαι.
τοὔνεκ᾽ ἄρ᾽ ἀλλοειδέα φαινέσκετο πάντα ἄνακτι,
ἀτραπιτοί τε διηνεκέες λιμένες τε πάνορμοι   195
πέτραι τ᾽ ἠλίβατοι καὶ δένδρεα τηλεθάοντα.
    στῆ δ᾽ ἄρ᾽ ἀναΐξας καί ῥ᾽ εἴσιδε πατρίδα γαῖαν,
ὤιμωξέν τ᾽ ἄρ᾽ ἔπειτα καὶ ὣ πεπλήγετο μηρὼ
χερσὶ καταπρηνέσσ᾽, ὀλοφυρόμενος δ᾽ ἔπος ηὔδα·
"ὢ μοι ἐγώ, τέων αὖτε βροτῶν ἐς γαῖαν ἱκάνω;   200
ἦ ῥ᾽ οἵ γ᾽ ὑβρισταί τε καὶ ἄγριοι οὐδὲ δίκαιοι,
ἦε φιλόξεινοι καί σφιν νόος ἐστὶ θεουδής;
πῆι δὴ χρήματα πολλὰ φέρω τάδε; πῆι δὲ καὶ αὐτὸς
πλάζομαι; αἴθ᾽ ὄφελον μεῖναι παρὰ Φαιήκεσσιν
αὐτοῦ· ἐγὼ δέ κεν ἄλλον ὑπερμενέων βασιλήων   205
ἐξικόμην, ὅς κέν μ᾽ ἐφίλει καὶ ἔπεμπε νέεσθαι.
νῦν δ᾽ οὔτ᾽ ἄρ πηι θέσθαι ἐπίσταμαι, οὐδὲ μὲν αὐτοῦ

175 περικαλλέα: εὐεργέα **a**   180 παύεσθε **a**   183 πολύμηκες **a**   194 φαίνετο **a**
197λλ = 226 **a**   203 κτήματα **a**

καλλείψω, μή πώς μοι ἕλωρ ἄλλοισι γένηται.
ὢ πόποι, οὐκ ἄρα πάντα νοήμονες οὐδὲ δίκαιοι
ἦσαν Φαιήκων ἡγήτορες ἠδὲ μέδοντες,   210
οἵ μ᾽ εἰς ἄλλην γαῖαν ἀπήγαγον· ἦ τέ μ᾽ ἔφαντο
ἄξειν εἰς Ἰθάκην εὐδείελον, οὐδ᾽ ἐτέλεσσαν.
Ζεύς σφεας τείσαιτο ἱκετήσιος, ὅς τε καὶ ἄλλους
ἀνθρώπους ἐφορᾷ καὶ τίνυται, ὅς τις ἁμάρτηι.
ἀλλ᾽ ἄγε δὴ τὰ χρήματ᾽ ἀριθμήσω καὶ ἴδωμαι   215
μή τί μοι οἴχονται κοίλης ἐπὶ νηὸς ἄγοντες."

Appearance of Athena in disguise; Odysseus' false tale

ὣς εἰπὼν τρίποδας περικαλλέας ἠδὲ λέβητας
ἠρίθμει καὶ χρυσὸν ὑφαντά τε εἵματα καλά.
τῶν μὲν ἄρ᾽ οὔ τι πόθει· ὁ δ᾽ ὀδύρετο πατρίδα γαῖαν
ἑρπύζων παρὰ θῖνα πολυφλοίσβοιο θαλάσσης,   220
πόλλ᾽ ὀλοφυρόμενος. σχεδόθεν δέ οἱ ἦλθεν Ἀθήνη,
ἀνδρὶ δέμας ἐϊκυῖα νέωι, ἐπιβώτορι μήλων,
παναπάλωι, οἷοί τε ἀνάκτων παῖδες ἔασι,
δίπτυχον ἀμφ᾽ ὤμοισιν ἔχουσ᾽ εὐεργέα λώπην·
ποσσὶ δ᾽ ὑπὸ λιπαροῖσι πέδιλ᾽ ἔχε, χερσὶ δ᾽ ἄκοντα.   225
   τὴν δ᾽ Ὀδυσεὺς γήθησεν ἰδών, καὶ ἐναντίος ἦλθε,
καί μιν φωνήσας ἔπεα πτερόεντα προσηύδα·
"ὦ φίλ᾽, ἐπεί σε πρῶτα κιχάνω τῶιδ᾽ ἐνὶ χώρωι,
χαῖρέ τε καὶ μή μοί τι κακῶι νόωι ἀντιβολήσαις,
ἀλλὰ σάω μὲν ταῦτα, σάω δ᾽ ἐμέ· σοὶ γὰρ ἐγώ γε   230
εὔχομαι ὥς τε θεῶι καί σευ φίλα γούναθ᾽ ἱκάνω.
καί μοι τοῦτ᾽ ἀγόρευσον ἐτήτυμον, ὄφρ᾽ εὖ εἰδῶ·
τίς γῆ, τίς δῆμος, τίνες ἀνέρες ἐγγεγάασιν;
ἦ πού τις νήσων εὐδείελος, ἦέ τις ἀκτὴ
κεῖθ᾽ ἁλὶ κεκλιμένη ἐριβώλακος ἠπείροιο;"   235
   τὸν δ᾽ αὖτε προσέειπε θεὰ γλαυκῶπις Ἀθήνη·
"νήπιός εἰς, ὦ ξεῖν᾽, ἦ τηλόθεν εἰλήλουθας,
εἰ δὴ τήνδε τε γαῖαν ἀνείρεαι. οὐδέ τι λίην
οὕτω νώνυμός ἐστιν· ἴσασι δέ μιν μάλα πολλοί,
ἠμὲν ὅσοι ναίουσι πρὸς ἠῶ τ᾽ ἠέλιόν τε,   240
ἠδ᾽ ὅσσοι μετόπισθε ποτὶ ζόφον ἠερόεντα.
ἦ τοι μὲν τρηχεῖα καὶ οὐχ ἱππήλατός ἐστιν

216 οἴχωνται **a**   ἔχοντες **a**   228 del. Knight

οὐδὲ λίην λυπρή, ἀτὰρ οὐδ' εὐρεῖα τέτυκται.
ἐν μὲν γάρ οἱ σῖτος ἀθέσφατος, ἐν δέ τε οἶνος
γίγνεται· αἰεὶ δ' ὄμβρος ἔχει τεθαλυῖά τ' ἐέρση.   245
αἰγίβοτος δ' ἀγαθὴ καὶ βούβοτος· ἔστι μὲν ὕλη
παντοίη, ἐν δ' ἀρδμοὶ ἐπηετανοὶ πάρεασι.
τώ τοι, ξεῖν', Ἰθάκης γε καὶ ἐς Τροίην ὄνομ' ἵκει,
τήν περ τηλοῦ φασὶν Ἀχαιΐδος ἔμμεναι αἴης."
    ὣς φάτο, γήθησεν δὲ πολύτλας δῖος Ὀδυσσεύς,   250
χαίρων ᾗ γαίηι πατρωΐηι, ὥς οἱ ἔειπε
Παλλὰς Ἀθηναίη, κούρη Διὸς αἰγιόχοιο.
καί μιν φωνήσας ἔπεα πτερόεντα προσηύδα—
οὐδ' ὅ γ' ἀληθέα εἶπε, πάλιν δ' ὅ γε λάζετο μῦθον,
αἰεὶ ἐνὶ στήθεσσι νόον πολυκερδέα νωμῶν·   255
"πυνθανόμην Ἰθάκης γε καὶ ἐν Κρήτηι εὐρείηι,
τηλοῦ ὑπὲρ πόντου· νῦν δ' εἰλήλουθα καὶ αὐτὸς
χρήμασι σὺν τοίσδεσσι. λιπὼν δ' ἔτι παισὶ τοσαῦτα
φεύγω, ἐπεὶ φίλον υἷα κατέκτανον Ἰδομενῆος,
Ὀρσίλοχον πόδας ὠκύν, ὃς ἐν Κρήτηι εὐρείηι   260
ἀνέρας ἀλφηστὰς νίκα ταχέεσσι πόδεσσιν,
οὕνεκά με στερέσαι τῆς ληΐδος ἤθελε πάσης
Τρωϊάδος, τῆς εἵνεκ' ἐγὼ πάθον ἄλγεα θυμῶι,
ἀνδρῶν τε πτολέμους ἀλεγεινά τε κύματα πείρων,
οὕνεκ' ἄρ' οὐχ ὧι πατρὶ χαριζόμενος θεράπευον   265
δήμωι ἔνι Τρώων, ἀλλ' ἄλλων ἦρχον ἑταίρων.
τὸν μὲν ἐγὼ κατιόντα βάλον χαλκήρεϊ δουρὶ
ἀγρόθεν, ἐγγὺς ὁδοῖο λοχησάμενος σὺν ἑταίρωι·
νὺξ δὲ μάλα δνοφερὴ κάτεχ' οὐρανόν, οὐδέ τις ἡμέας
ἀνθρώπων ἐνόησε, λάθον δέ ἑ θυμὸν ἀπούρας.   270
    αὐτὰρ ἐπεὶ δὴ τόν γε κατέκτανον ὀξέϊ χαλκῶι,
αὐτίκ' ἐγὼν ἐπὶ νῆα κιὼν Φοίνικας ἀγαυοὺς
ἐλλισάμην, καί σφιν μενοεικέα ληΐδα δῶκα·
τούς μ' ἐκέλευσα Πύλονδε καταστῆσαι καὶ ἐφέσσαι
ἢ εἰς Ἤλιδα δῖαν, ὅθι κρατέουσιν Ἐπειοί.   275
ἀλλ' ἦ τοί σφεας κεῖθεν ἀπώσατο ἲς ἀνέμοιο
πόλλ' ἀεκαζομένους, οὐδ' ἤθελον ἐξαπατῆσαι.
κεῖθεν δὲ πλαγχθέντες ἱκάνομεν ἐνθάδε νυκτός·
σπουδῆι δ' ἐς λιμένα προερέσσαμεν, οὐδέ τις ἡμῖν

---

245 τ' ἐέρση: τ' ὀπώρη a   247 γεγάασι a   250 μείδησεν a Eustathius   254
μυθῶι a   269 ζοφερή a   270 ἀπηύρων a   272 κιὼν: θοὴν a: θοὴν κιὼν b

δόρπου μνῆστις ἔην μάλα περ χατέουσιν ἑλέσθαι,   280
ἀλλ᾽ αὔτως ἀποβάντες ἐκείμεθα νηὸς ἅπαντες.
ἔνθ᾽ ἐμὲ μὲν γλυκὺς ὕπνος ὑπήλυθε κεκμηῶτα,
οἱ δὲ χρήματ᾽ ἐμὰ γλαφυρῆς ἐκ νηὸς ἑλόντες
κάτθεσαν, ἔνθα περ αὐτὸς ἐπὶ ψαμάθοισιν ἐκείμην.
οἱ δ᾽ ἐς Σιδονίην εὖ ναιομένην ἀναβάντες   285
ὤιχοντ᾽· αὐτὰρ ἐγὼ λιπόμην ἀκαχήμενος ἦτορ."

True identities revealed

ὣς φάτο, μείδησεν δὲ θεὰ γλαυκῶπις Ἀθήνη,
χειρί τέ μιν κατέρεξε· δέμας δ᾽ ἤϊκτο γυναικὶ
καλῆι τε μεγάληι τε καὶ ἀγλαὰ ἔργα ἰδυίηι·
καί μιν φωνήσασ᾽ ἔπεα πτερόεντα προσηύδα·   290
"κερδαλέος κ᾽ εἴη καὶ ἐπίκλοπος, ὅς σε παρέλθοι
ἐν πάντεσσι δόλοισι, καὶ εἰ θεὸς ἀντιάσειε.
σχέτλιε, ποικιλομῆτα, δόλων ἆτ᾽, οὐκ ἄρ᾽ ἔμελλες,
οὐδ᾽ ἐν σῆι περ ἐὼν γαίηι, λήξειν ἀπατάων
μύθων τε κλοπίων, οἵ τοι πεδόθεν φίλοι εἰσίν.   295
ἀλλ᾽ ἄγε μηκέτι ταῦτα λεγώμεθα, εἰδότες ἄμφω
κέρδε᾽, ἐπεὶ σὺ μέν ἐσσι βροτῶν ὄχ᾽ ἄριστος ἁπάντων
βουλῆι καὶ μύθοισιν, ἐγὼ δ᾽ ἐν πᾶσι θεοῖσι
μήτι τε κλέομαι καὶ κέρδεσιν. οὐδὲ σύ γ᾽ ἔγνως
Παλλάδ᾽ Ἀθηναίην, κούρην Διός, ἥ τέ τοι αἰεὶ   300
ἐν πάντεσσι πόνοισι παρίσταμαι ἠδὲ φυλάσσω,
καὶ δέ σε Φαιήκεσσι φίλον πάντεσσιν ἔθηκα.
νῦν αὖ δεῦρ᾽ ἱκόμην, ἵνα τοι σὺν μῆτιν ὑφήνω
χρήματά τε κρύψω, ὅσα τοι Φαίηκες ἀγαυοὶ
ὤπασαν οἴκαδ᾽ ἰόντι ἐμῆι βουλῆι τε νόωι τε,   305
εἴπω θ᾽ ὅσσα τοι αἶσα δόμοισ᾽ ἔνι ποιητοῖσι
κήδε᾽ ἀνασχέσθαι. σὺ δὲ τετλάμεναι καὶ ἀνάγκηι,
μηδέ τωι ἐκφάσθαι μήτ᾽ ἀνδρῶν μήτε γυναικῶν,
πάντων, οὕνεκ᾽ ἄρ᾽ ἦλθες ἀλώμενος, ἀλλὰ σιωπῆι
πάσχειν ἄλγεα πολλά, βίας ὑποδέγμενος ἀνδρῶν."   310
    τὴν δ᾽ ἀπαμειβόμενος προσέφη πολύμητις Ὀδυσσεύς·
"ἀργαλέον σε, θεά, γνῶναι βροτῶι ἀντιάσαντι
καὶ μάλ᾽ ἐπισταμένωι· σὲ γὰρ αὐτὴν παντὶ ἐΐσκεις.

282 ὑπήλυθε: ἐπέλλαβε **a**   285 ἐϋκτιμένην **a**   293 δόλων ἄτερ **a**   295 παιδό-
θεν **a**: παῖδες **b**   307 ἀνασχέσθαι: ἀναπλῆσαι **a**

τοῦτο δ᾽ ἐγὼν εὖ οἶδ᾽, ὅτι μοι πάρος ἠπίη ἦσθα,
εἵως ἐνὶ Τροίηι πολεμίζομεν υἷες Ἀχαιῶν·   315
αὐτὰρ ἐπεὶ Πριάμοιο πόλιν διεπέρσαμεν αἰπήν,
βῆμεν δ᾽ ἐν νήεσσι, θεὸς δ᾽ ἐκέδασσεν Ἀχαιούς,
οὐ σέ γ᾽ ἔπειτα ἴδον, κούρη Διός, οὐδ᾽ ἐνόησα
νηὸς ἐμῆς ἐπιβᾶσαν, ὅπως τί μοι ἄλγος ἀλάλκοις,
[ἀλλ᾽ αἰεὶ φρεσὶν ᾗσιν ἔχων δεδαϊγμένον ἦτορ   320
ἠλώμην, εἵος με θεοὶ κακότητος ἔλυσαν·]
πρίν γ᾽ ὅτε Φαιήκων ἀνδρῶν ἐν πίονι δήμωι
θάρσυνάς τ᾽ ἐπέεσσι καὶ ἐς πόλιν ἤγαγες αὐτή.
νῦν δέ σε πρὸς πατρὸς γουνάζομαι· οὐ γὰρ ὀΐω
ἥκειν εἰς Ἰθάκην εὐδείελον, ἀλλά τιν᾽ ἄλλην   325
γαῖαν ἀναστρέφομαι· σὲ δὲ κερτομέουσαν ὀΐω
ταῦτ᾽ ἀγορευέμεναι, ἵν᾽ ἐμὰς φρένας ἠπεροπεύσηις.
εἰπέ μοι εἰ ἐτεόν γε φίλην ἐς πατρίδ᾽ ἱκάνω."
    τὸν δ᾽ ἠμείβετ᾽ ἔπειτα θεὰ γλαυκῶπις Ἀθήνη·
"αἰεί τοι τοιοῦτον ἐνὶ στήθεσσι νόημα·   330
τώ σε καὶ οὐ δύναμαι προλιπεῖν δύστηνον ἐόντα,
οὕνεκ᾽ ἐπητής ἐσσι καὶ ἀγχίνοος καὶ ἐχέφρων.
ἀσπασίως γάρ κ᾽ ἄλλος ἀνὴρ ἀλαλήμενος ἐλθὼν
ἵετ᾽ ἐνὶ μεγάροισ᾽ ἰδέειν παῖδάς τ᾽ ἄλοχόν τε·
σοὶ δ᾽ οὔ πω φίλον ἐστὶ δαήμεναι οὐδὲ πυθέσθαι,   335
πρίν γ᾽ ἔτι σῆς ἀλόχου πειρήσεαι, ἥ τέ τοι αὔτως
ἧσται ἐνὶ μεγάροισιν, ὀϊζυραὶ δέ οἱ αἰεὶ
φθίνουσιν νύκτες τε καὶ ἤματα δάκρυ χεούσηι.
αὐτὰρ ἐγὼ τὸ μὲν οὔ ποτ᾽ ἀπίστεον, ἀλλ᾽ ἐνὶ θυμῶι
ᾔδε᾽, ὃ νοστήσεις ὀλέσας ἄπο πάντας ἑταίρους·   340
ἀλλά τοι οὐκ ἐθέλησα Ποσειδάωνι μάχεσθαι
πατροκασιγνήτωι, ὅς τοι κότον ἔνθετο θυμῶι,
χωόμενος ὅτι οἱ υἱὸν φίλον ἐξαλάωσας.
ἀλλ᾽ ἄγε τοι δείξω Ἰθάκης ἕδος, ὄφρα πεποίθηις·
Φόρκυνος μὲν ὅδ᾽ ἐστὶ λιμήν, ἁλίοιο γέροντος,   345
ἥδε δ᾽ ἐπὶ κρατὸς λιμένος τανύφυλλος ἐλαίη·
[ἀγχόθι δ᾽ αὐτῆς ἄντρον ἐπήρατον ἠεροειδές,
ἱρὸν Νυμφάων, αἳ Νηϊάδες καλέονται·]
τοῦτο δέ τοι σπέος εὐρὺ κατηρεφές, ἔνθα σὺ πολλὰς

320–1 del. Munro: 320–3 Aristarchus   333–8 del. Aristarchus   342 χόλον pa
347–8 om. pa (= 103–4)   349 εὐρὺ: ἐστὶ pa

ἔρδεσκες Νύμφῃσι τεληέσσας ἑκατόμβας·   350
τοῦτο δὲ Νήριτόν ἐστιν ὄρος καταειμένον ὕλῃ."
ὣς εἰποῦσα θεὰ σκέδασ᾽ ἠέρα, εἴσατο δὲ χθών·
γήθησέν τ᾽ ἄρ᾽ ἔπειτα πολύτλας δῖος Ὀδυσσεὺς
χαίρων ᾗ γαίῃ, κύσε δὲ ζείδωρον ἄρουραν.
αὐτίκα δὲ Νύμφῃς ἠρήσατο χεῖρας ἀνασχών·   355
"Νύμφαι Νηϊάδες, κοῦραι Διός, οὔ ποτ᾽ ἐγώ γε
ὄψεσθ᾽ ὔμμ᾽ ἐφάμην· νῦν δ᾽ εὐχωλῇσ᾽ ἀγανῇσι
χαίρετ᾽· ἀτὰρ καὶ δῶρα διδώσομεν, ὡς τὸ πάρος περ,
αἴ κεν ἐᾷ πρόφρων με Διὸς θυγάτηρ ἀγελείη
αὐτόν τε ζώειν καί μοι φίλον υἱὸν ἀέξῃ."   360

Discussion of the situation on Ithaca and disguise of Odysseus

τὸν δ᾽ αὖτε προσέειπε θεὰ γλαυκῶπις Ἀθήνη·
"θάρσει, μή τοι ταῦτα μετὰ φρεσὶ σῇσι μελόντων.
ἀλλὰ χρήματα μὲν μυχῶι ἄντρου θεσπεσίοιο
θείομεν αὐτίκα νῦν, ἵνα περ τάδε τοι σόα μίμνῃ·
αὐτοὶ δὲ φραζώμεθ᾽ ὅπως ὄχ᾽ ἄριστα γένηται."   365
ὣς εἰποῦσα θεὰ δῦνε σπέος ἠεροειδές,
μαιομένη κευθμῶνας ἀνὰ σπέος· αὐτὰρ Ὀδυσσεὺς
ἆσσον πάντ᾽ ἐφόρει, χρυσὸν καὶ ἀτειρέα χαλκὸν
εἵματά τ᾽ εὐποίητα, τά οἱ Φαίηκες ἔδωκαν.
καὶ τὰ μὲν εὖ κατέθηκε, λίθον δ᾽ ἐπέθηκε θύρῃσι   370
Παλλὰς Ἀθηναίη, κούρη Διὸς αἰγιόχοιο.
τὼ δὲ καθεζομένω ἱερῆς παρὰ πυθμέν᾽ ἐλαίης
φραζέσθην μνηστῆρσιν ὑπερφιάλοισιν ὄλεθρον.
τοῖσι δὲ μύθων ἦρχε θεὰ γλαυκῶπις Ἀθήνη·
"διογενὲς Λαερτιάδη, πολυμήχαν᾽ Ὀδυσσεῦ,   375
φράζευ ὅπως μνηστῆρσιν ἀναιδέσι χεῖρας ἐφήσεις,
οἳ δή τοι τρίετες μέγαρον κάτα κοιρανέουσι,
μνώμενοι ἀντιθέην ἄλοχον καὶ ἕδνα διδόντες.
ἡ δὲ σὸν αἰεὶ νόστον ὀδυρομένη κατὰ θυμὸν
πάντας μέν ῥ᾽ ἔλπει καὶ ὑπίσχεται ἀνδρὶ ἑκάστωι,   380
ἀγγελίας προϊεῖσα, νόος δέ οἱ ἄλλα μενοινᾷ."
τὴν δ᾽ ἀπαμειβόμενος προσέφη πολύμητις Ὀδυσσεύς·

---

351 κατειλυμένον a   360 ἀέξειν a   365 ὅπως ἔσται τάδε ἔργα a   369 Φαίηκες
ἀγαυοί (= 120) a   369a = 121 a   376 φράζεο νῦν μνηστῆρσιν ὑπερφιάλοισιν
ὄλεθρον a

"ὢ πόποι, ἦ μάλα δὴ Ἀγαμέμνονος Ἀτρεΐδαο
φθίσεσθαι κακὸν οἶτον ἐνὶ μεγάροισιν ἔμελλον,
εἰ μή μοι σὺ ἕκαστα, θεά, κατὰ μοῖραν ἔειπες.   385
ἀλλ᾽ ἄγε μῆτιν ὕφηνον, ὅπως ἀποτείσομαι αὐτούς·
πὰρ δέ μοι αὐτὴ στῆθι, μένος πολυθαρσὲς ἐνεῖσα,
οἷον ὅτε Τροίης λύομεν λιπαρὰ κρήδεμνα.
αἴ κέ μοι ὣς μεμαυῖα παρασταίης, γλαυκῶπι,
καί κε τριηκοσίοισιν ἐγὼν ἄνδρεσσι μαχοίμην   390
σὺν σοί, πότνα θεά, ὅτε μοι πρόφρασσ᾽ ἐπαρήγοις."
    τὸν δ᾽ ἠμείβετ᾽ ἔπειτα θεὰ γλαυκῶπις Ἀθήνη·
"καὶ λίην τοι ἐγώ γε παρέσσομαι, οὐδέ με λήσεις,
ὁππότε κεν δὴ ταῦτα πενώμεθα. καί τιν᾽ ὀΐω
αἵματί τ᾽ ἐγκεφάλωι τε παλαξέμεν ἄσπετον οὖδας   395
ἀνδρῶν μνηστήρων, οἵ τοι βίοτον κατέδουσιν.
ἀλλ᾽ ἄγε σ᾽ ἄγνωστον τεύξω πάντεσσι βροτοῖσι·
κάρψω μὲν χρόα καλὸν ἐνὶ γναμπτοῖσι μέλεσσι,
ξανθὰς δ᾽ ἐκ κεφαλῆς ὀλέσω τρίχας, ἀμφὶ δὲ λαῖφος
ἕσσω, ὅ κεν στυγέηισιν ἰδὼν ἄνθρωπον ἔχοντα,   400
κνυζώσω δέ τοι ὄσσε πάρος περικαλλέ᾽ ἐόντε,
ὡς ἂν ἀεικέλιος πᾶσι μνηστῆρσι φανήηις
σῆι τ᾽ ἀλόχωι καὶ παιδί, τὸν ἐν μεγάροισιν ἔλειπες.
αὐτὸς δὲ πρώτιστα συβώτην εἰσαφικέσθαι,
ὅς τοι ὑῶν ἐπίουρος, ὁμῶς δέ τοι ἤπια οἶδε,   405
παῖδά τε σὸν φιλέει καὶ ἐχέφρονα Πηνελόπειαν.
δήεις τόν γε σύεσσι παρήμενον· αἱ δὲ νέμονται
πὰρ Κόρακος πέτρηι ἐπί τε κρήνηι Ἀρεθούσηι,
ἔσθουσαι βάλανον μενοεικέα καὶ μέλαν ὕδωρ
πίνουσαι, τά θ᾽ ὕεσσι τρέφει τεθαλυῖαν ἀλοιφήν.   410
ἔνθα μένειν καὶ πάντα παρήμενος ἐξερέεσθαι,
ὄφρ᾽ ἂν ἐγὼν ἔλθω Σπάρτην ἐς καλλιγύναικα
Τηλέμαχον καλέουσα, τεὸν φίλον υἱόν, Ὀδυσσεῦ·
ὅς τοι ἐς εὐρύχορον Λακεδαίμονα πὰρ Μενέλαον
ὤιχετο πευσόμενος μετὰ σὸν κλέος, εἴ που ἔτ᾽ εἴης."   415
    τὴν δ᾽ ἀπαμειβόμενος προσέφη πολύμητις Ὀδυσσεύς·
"τίπτε τ᾽ ἄρ᾽ οὔ οἱ ἔειπες, ἐνὶ φρεσὶ πάντα ἰδυῖα;
ἦ ἵνα που καὶ κεῖνος ἀλώμενος ἄλγεα πάσχηι
πόντον ἐπ᾽ ἀτρύγετον, βίοτον δέ οἱ ἄλλοι ἔδουσι;"

384 φήσεσθαι a: πείσεσθαι b   398–401 del. Aristarchus   400 στυγέει τις ἰδὼν
ἄνθρωπον v.l. in Eustathius

τὸν δ' ἠμείβετ' ἔπειτα θεὰ γλαυκῶπις Ἀθήνη· 420
"μὴ δή τοι κεῖνός γε λίην ἐνθύμιος ἔστω.
αὐτή μιν πόμπευον, ἵνα κλέος ἐσθλὸν ἄροιτο
κεῖσ' ἐλθών· ἀτὰρ οὔ τιν' ἔχει πόνον, ἀλλὰ ἔκηλος
ἧσται ἐν Ἀτρεΐδαο δόμοις, παρὰ δ' ἄσπετα κεῖται.
ἦ μέν μιν λοχόωσι νέοι σὺν νηῒ μελαίνηι, 425
ἱέμενοι κτεῖναι, πρὶν πατρίδα γαῖαν ἱκέσθαι.
ἀλλὰ τά γ' οὐκ ὀΐω· πρὶν καί τινα γαῖα καθέξει
ἀνδρῶν μνηστήρων, οἵ τοι βίοτον κατέδουσιν."
ὣς ἄρα μιν φαμένη ῥάβδωι ἐπεμάσσατ' Ἀθήνη.
κάρψε μέν οἱ χρόα καλὸν ἐνὶ γναμπτοῖσι μέλεσσι, 430
ξανθὰς δ' ἐκ κεφαλῆς ὄλεσε τρίχας, ἀμφὶ δὲ δέρμα
πάντεσσιν μελέεσσι παλαιοῦ θῆκε γέροντος,
κνύζωσεν δέ οἱ ὄσσε πάρος περικαλλέ' ἐόντε·
ἀμφὶ δέ μιν ῥάκος ἄλλο κακὸν βάλεν ἠδὲ χιτῶνα,
ῥωγαλέα ῥυπόωντα, κακῶι μεμορυγμένα καπνῶι· 435
ἀμφὶ δέ μιν μέγα δέρμα ταχείης ἔσσ' ἐλάφοιο,
ψιλόν· δῶκε δέ οἱ σκῆπτρον καὶ ἀεικέα πήρην,
πυκνὰ ῥωγαλέην· ἐν δὲ στρόφος ἦεν ἀορτήρ.
τώ γ' ὣς βουλεύσαντε διέτμαγεν. ἡ μὲν ἔπειτα
ἐς Λακεδαίμονα δῖαν ἔβη μετὰ παῖδ' Ὀδυσῆος. 440

435 ῥωγαλέα: σμερδαλέα a

ΟΜΗΡΟΥ ΟΔΥΣΣΕΙΑΣ Ξ

Odysseus' arrival at Eumaeus' pig-farm

Αὐτὰρ ὁ ἐκ λιμένος προσέβη τρηχεῖαν ἀταρπὸν
χῶρον ἀν' ὑλήεντα δι' ἄκριας, ἧι οἱ Ἀθήνη
πέφραδε δῖον ὑφορβόν, ὅ οἱ βιότοιο μάλιστα
κήδετο οἰκήων, οὓς κτήσατο δῖος Ὀδυσσεύς.

τὸν δ' ἄρ' ἐνὶ προδόμωι εὗρ' ἥμενον, ἔνθα οἱ αὐλὴ   5
ὑψηλὴ δέδμητο, περισκέπτωι ἐνὶ χώρωι,
καλή τε μεγάλη τε, περίδρομος· ἥν ῥα συβώτης
αὐτὸς δείμαθ' ὕεσσιν ἀποιχομένοιο ἄνακτος,
νόσφιν δεσποίνης καὶ Λαέρταο γέροντος,
ῥυτοῖσιν λάεσσι καὶ ἐθρίγκωσεν ἀχέρδωι.   10
σταυροὺς δ' ἐκτὸς ἔλασσε διαμπερὲς ἔνθα καὶ ἔνθα
πυκνοὺς καὶ θαμέας, τὸ μέλαν δρυὸς ἀμφικεάσσας.
ἔντοσθεν δ' αὐλῆς συφεοὺς δυοκαίδεκα ποίει
πλησίον ἀλλήλων, εὐνὰς συσίν· ἐν δὲ ἑκάστωι
πεντήκοντα σύες χαμαιευνάδες ἐρχατόωντο,   15
θήλειαι τοκάδες· τοὶ δ' ἄρσενες ἐκτὸς ἴαυον,
πολλὸν παυρότεροι· τοὺς γὰρ μινύθεσκον ἔδοντες
ἀντίθεοι μνηστῆρες, ἐπεὶ προΐαλλε συβώτης
αἰεὶ ζατρεφέων σιάλων τὸν ἄριστον ἁπάντων·
οἱ δὲ τριηκόσιοί τε καὶ ἑξήκοντα πέλοντο.   20
πὰρ δὲ κύνες θήρεσσιν ἐοικότες αἰὲν ἴαυον
τέσσαρες, οὓς ἔθρεψε συβώτης, ὄρχαμος ἀνδρῶν.

αὐτὸς δ' ἀμφὶ πόδεσσιν ἑοῖς ἀράρισκε πέδιλα,
τάμνων δέρμα βόειον ἐΰχροές· οἱ δὲ δὴ ἄλλοι
ὤιχοντ' ἄλλυδις ἄλλος ἅμ' ἀγρομένοισι σύεσσιν,   25
οἱ τρεῖς· τὸν δὲ τέταρτον ἀποπροέηκε πόλινδε
σῦν ἀγέμεν μνηστῆρσιν ὑπερφιάλοισιν ἀνάγκηι,
ὄφρ' ἱερεύσαντες κρειῶν κορεσαίατο θυμόν.

ἐξαπίνης δ' Ὀδυσῆα ἴδον κύνες ὑλακόμωροι.
οἱ μὲν κεκλήγοντες ἐπέδραμον· αὐτὰρ Ὀδυσσεὺς   30
ἕζετο κερδοσύνηι, σκῆπτρον δέ οἱ ἔκπεσε χειρός.
ἔνθα κεν ὧι πὰρ σταθμῶι ἀεικέλιον πάθεν ἄλγος,

6 περισκέπτωι ἐνὶ χωρώι: κατωρυχέεσσι λίθοισι (= 9.185) **a**   12 μέλαν δρυὸς:
μεγάλους **a**   17 παυρότερον **p**   24 ἐΰχροον **a**   30 κεκληγῶτες **p**: κεκληγότες **a**
31 ἔκπεσε: ἔκβαλε **a**

ἀλλὰ συβώτης ὦκα ποσὶ κραιπνοῖσι μετασπών
ἔσσυτ' ἀνὰ πρόθυρον, σκῦτος δέ οἱ ἔκπεσε χειρός.
τοὺς μὲν ὁμοκλήσας σεῦεν κύνας ἄλλυδις ἄλλον   35
πυκνῇσιν λιθάδεσσιν, ὁ δὲ προσέειπεν ἄνακτα·
"ὦ γέρον, ἦ ὀλίγου σε κύνες διεδηλήσαντο
ἐξαπίνης, καί κέν μοι ἐλεγχείην κατέχευας.
καὶ δέ μοι ἄλλα θεοὶ δόσαν ἄλγεά τε στοναχάς τε·
ἀντιθέου γὰρ ἄνακτος ὀδυρόμενος καὶ ἀχεύων   40
ἦμαι, ἄλλοισιν δὲ σύας σιάλους ἀτιτάλλω
ἔδμεναι. αὐτὰρ κεῖνος ἐελδόμενός που ἐδωδῆς
πλάζετ' ἐπ' ἀλλοθρόων ἀνδρῶν δῆμόν τε πόλιν τε,
εἴ που ἔτι ζώει καὶ ὁρᾷ φάος ἠελίοιο.
ἀλλ' ἔπεο, κλισίηνδ' ἴομεν, γέρον, ὄφρα καὶ αὐτὸς   45
σίτου καὶ οἴνοιο κορεσσάμενος κατὰ θυμὸν
εἴπῃς ὁππόθεν ἐσσὶ καὶ ὁππόσα κήδε' ἀνέτλης."

Odysseus is welcomed into the farmhouse

ὣς εἰπὼν κλισίηνδ' ἡγήσατο δῖος ὑφορβός,
εἷσεν δ' εἰσαγαγών, ῥῶπας δ' ὑπέχευε δασείας,
ἐστόρεσεν δ' ἐπὶ δέρμα ἰονθάδος ἀγρίου αἰγός,   50
αὐτοῦ ἐνεύναιον, μέγα καὶ δασύ. χαῖρε δ' Ὀδυσσεύς,
ὅττι μιν ὣς ὑπέδεκτο, ἔπος τ' ἔφατ' ἔκ τ' ὀνόμαζε·
"Ζεύς τοι δοίη, ξεῖνε, καὶ ἀθάνατοι θεοὶ ἄλλοι,
ὅττι μάλιστ' ἐθέλεις, ὅτι με πρόφρων ὑπέδεξο."
    τὸν δ' ἀπαμειβόμενος προσέφης, Εὔμαιε συβῶτα·   55
"ξεῖν', οὔ μοι θέμις ἔστ', οὐδ' εἰ κακίων σέθεν ἔλθοι,
ξεῖνον ἀτιμῆσαι· πρὸς γὰρ Διός εἰσιν ἅπαντες
ξεῖνοί τε πτωχοί τε. δόσις δ' ὀλίγη τε φίλη τε
γίγνεται ἡμετέρη· ἡ γὰρ δμώων δίκη ἐστίν,
αἰεὶ δειδιότων, ὅτ' ἐπικρατέωσιν ἄνακτες   60
οἱ νέοι. ἦ γὰρ τοῦ γε θεοὶ κατὰ νόστον ἔδησαν,
ὅς κεν ἔμ' ἐνδυκέως ἐφίλει καὶ κτῆσιν ὄπασσεν,
οἷά τε ᾧ οἰκῆϊ ἄναξ εὔθυμος ἔδωκεν,
οἶκόν τε κλῆρόν τε πολυμνήστην τε γυναῖκα,
ὅς οἱ πολλὰ κάμῃσι, θεὸς δ' ἐπὶ ἔργον ἀέξῃ,   65
ὡς καὶ ἐμοὶ τόδε ἔργον ἀέξεται, ᾧ ἐπιμίμνω.
τώ κέ με πόλλ' ὤνησεν ἄναξ, εἰ αὐτόθι γήρα·

37 ὀλίγον a   67 αὐτόθ' ἐγήρα a

ἀλλ' ὄλεθ'. ὡς ὤφελλ' Ἑλένης ἀπὸ φῦλον ὀλέσθαι
πρόχνυ, ἐπεὶ πολλῶν ἀνδρῶν ὑπὸ γούνατ' ἔλυσε·
καὶ γὰρ κεῖνος ἔβη Ἀγαμέμνονος εἵνεκα τιμῆς   70
"Ἴλιον εἰς εὔπωλον, ἵνα Τρώεσσι μάχοιτο."
    ὣς εἰπὼν ζωστῆρι θοῶς συνέεργε χιτῶνα,
βῆ δ' ἴμεν ἐς συφεούς, ὅθι ἔθνεα ἔρχατο χοίρων.
ἔνθεν ἑλὼν δύ' ἔνεικε καὶ ἀμφοτέρους ἱέρευσεν,
εὗσέ τε μίστυλλέν τε καὶ ἀμφ' ὀβελοῖσιν ἔπειρεν.   75
ὀπτήσας δ' ἄρα πάντα φέρων παρέθηκ' Ὀδυσῆϊ
θέρμ' αὐτοῖς ὀβελοῖσιν, ὁ δ' ἄλφιτα λευκὰ πάλυνεν.
ἐν δ' ἄρα κισσυβίωι κίρνη μελιηδέα οἶνον,
αὐτὸς δ' ἀντίον ἷζεν, ἐποτρύνων δὲ προσηύδα·
"ἔσθιε νῦν, ὦ ξεῖνε, τά τε δμώεσσι πάρεστι,   80
χοίρε'· ἀτὰρ σιάλους γε σύας μνηστῆρες ἔδουσιν,
οὐκ ὄπιδα φρονέοντες ἐνὶ φρεσὶν οὐδ' ἐλεητύν.
οὐ μὲν σχέτλια ἔργα θεοὶ μάκαρες φιλέουσιν,
ἀλλὰ δίκην τίουσι καὶ αἴσιμα ἔργ' ἀνθρώπων.
καὶ μὲν δυσμενέες καὶ ἀνάρσιοι, οἵ τ' ἐπὶ γαίης   85
ἀλλοτρίης βῶσιν καί σφιν Ζεὺς ληΐδα δώηι,
πλησάμενοι δέ τε νῆας ἔβαν οἴκόνδε νέεσθαι,
καὶ μὲν τοῖς ὄπιδος κρατερὸν δέος ἐν φρεσὶ πίπτει.
οἵδε δέ τοι ἴσασι, θεοῦ δέ τιν' ἔκλυον αὐδήν,
κείνου λυγρὸν ὄλεθρον, ὅ τ' οὐκ ἐθέλουσι δικαίως   90
μνᾶσθαι οὐδὲ νέεσθαι ἐπὶ σφέτερ', ἀλλὰ ἔκηλοι
κτήματα δαρδάπτουσιν ὑπέρβιον, οὐδ' ἔπι φειδώ.
ὅσσαι γὰρ νύκτες τε καὶ ἡμέραι ἐκ Διός εἰσιν,
οὔ ποθ' ἓν ἱρεύουσ' ἱερήϊον οὐδὲ δύ' οἴω·
οἶνον δὲ φθινύθουσιν ὑπέρβιον ἐξαφύοντες.   95
ἦ γὰρ οἱ ζωή γ' ἦν ἄσπετος· οὔ τινι τόσση
ἀνδρῶν ἡρώων, οὔτ' ἠπείροιο μελαίνης
οὔτ' αὐτῆς Ἰθάκης· οὐδὲ ξυνεείκοσι φωτῶν
ἔστ' ἄφενος τοσσοῦτον· ἐγὼ δέ κέ τοι καταλέξω.
δώδεκ' ἐν ἠπείρωι ἀγέλαι· τόσα πώεα οἰῶν,   100
τόσσα συῶν συβόσια, τός' αἰπόλια πλατέ' αἰγῶν
βόσκουσι ξεῖνοί τε καὶ αὐτοῦ βώτορες ἄνδρες·
ἐνθάδε τ' αἰπόλια πλατέ' αἰγῶν ἕνδεκα πάντα
ἐσχατιῆι βόσκοντ', ἐπὶ δ' ἀνέρες ἐσθλοὶ ὄρονται.

82 τρομέοντες a   83 ποθέουσιν a   92 οὐδέτι a   94 οἴω: οἴα a   104
ἐσχατίην Aristarchus a   ὀρῶνται a

τῶν αἰεί σφιν ἕκαστος ἐπ' ἤματι μῆλον ἀγινεῖ,   105
ζατρεφέων αἰγῶν ὅς τις φαίνηται ἄριστος.
αὐτὰρ ἐγὼ σῦς τάσδε φυλάσσω τε ῥύομαί τε,
καί σφι συῶν τὸν ἄριστον εὖ κρίνας ἀποπέμπω."
ὣς φάθ'· ὁ δ' ἐνδυκέως κρέα τ' ἦσθιε πῖνέ τε οἶνον,
ἁρπαλέως ἀκέων, κακὰ δὲ μνηστῆρσι φύτευεν.   110

Odysseus suggests he may know about Eumaeus' master

αὐτὰρ ἐπεὶ δείπνησε καὶ ἤραρε θυμὸν ἐδωδῆι,
καί οἱ πλησάμενος δῶκε σκύφος, ὧι περ ἔπινεν,
οἴνου ἐνίπλειον· ὁ δ' ἐδέξατο, χαῖρε δὲ θυμῶι.
καί μιν φωνήσας ἔπεα πτερόεντα προσηύδα·
"ὦ φίλε, τίς γάρ σε πρίατο κτεάτεσσιν ἑοῖσιν,   115
ὧδε μάλ' ἀφνειὸς καὶ καρτερός, ὡς ἀγορεύεις;
φῆς δ' αὐτὸν φθίσθαι Ἀγαμέμνονος εἵνεκα τιμῆς.
εἰπέ μοι, αἴ κέ ποθι γνώω τοιοῦτον ἐόντα.
Ζεὺς γάρ που τό γε οἶδε καὶ ἀθάνατοι θεοὶ ἄλλοι,
εἴ κέ μιν ἀγγείλαιμι ἰδών· ἐπὶ πολλὰ δ' ἀλήθην."   120
    τὸν δ' ἠμείβετ' ἔπειτα συβώτης, ὄρχαμος ἀνδρῶν·
"ὦ γέρον, οὔ τις κεῖνον ἀνὴρ ἀλαλήμενος ἐλθὼν
ἀγγέλλων πείσειε γυναῖκά τε καὶ φίλον υἱόν,
ἀλλ' ἄλλως, κομιδῆς κεχρημένοι, ἄνδρες ἀλῆται
ψεύδοντ' οὐδ' ἐθέλουσιν ἀληθέα μυθήσασθαι.   125
ὃς δέ κ' ἀλητεύων Ἰθάκης ἐς δῆμον ἵκηται,
ἐλθὼν ἐς δέσποιναν ἐμὴν ἀπατήλια βάζει·
ἡ δ' εὖ δεξαμένη φιλέει καὶ ἕκαστα μεταλλᾶι,
καί οἱ ὀδυρομένηι βλεφάρων ἄπο δάκρυα πίπτει,
ἣ θέμις ἐστὶ γυναικός, ἐπὴν πόσις ἄλλοθ' ὄληται.   130
αἶψά κε καὶ σύ, γεραιέ, ἔπος παρατεκτήναιο,
εἴ τίς τοι χλαῖνάν τε χιτῶνά τε εἵματα δοίη.
τοῦ δ' ἤδη μέλλουσι κύνες ταχέες τ' οἰωνοὶ
ῥινὸν ἀπ' ὀστεόφιν ἐρύσαι, ψυχὴ δὲ λέλοιπεν·
ἦ τόν γ' ἐν πόντωι φάγον ἰχθύες, ὀστέα δ' αὐτοῦ   135
κεῖται ἐπ' ἠπείρου ψαμάθωι εἰλυμένα πολλῆι.
ὣς ὁ μὲν ἔνθ' ἀπόλωλε, φίλοισι δὲ κήδε' ὀπίσσω
πᾶσιν, ἐμοὶ δὲ μάλιστα, τετεύχαται· οὐ γὰρ ἔτ' ἄλλον
ἤπιον ὧδε ἄνακτα κιχήσομαι, ὁππόσ' ἐπέλθω,

111 ἐδωδῆς p

οὐδ’ εἴ κεν πατρὸς καὶ μητέρος αὖτις ἵκωμαι   140
οἶκον, ὅθι πρῶτον γενόμην καί μ’ ἔτρεφον αὐτοί.
οὐδέ νυ τῶν ἔτι τόσσον ὀδύρομαι, ἱέμενός περ
ὀφθαλμοῖσιν ἰδέσθαι ἐὼν ἐν πατρίδι γαίηι·
ἀλλά μ’ Ὀδυσσῆος πόθος αἴνυται οἰχομένοιο.
τὸν μὲν ἐγών, ὦ ξεῖνε, καὶ οὐ παρεόντ’ ὀνομάζειν   145
αἰδέομαι· περὶ γάρ μ’ ἐφίλει καὶ κήδετο θυμῶι·
ἀλλά μιν ἠθεῖον καλέω καὶ νόσφιν ἐόντα.”

Odysseus swears Eumaeus’ master will return

τὸν δ’ αὖτε προσέειπε πολύτλας δῖος Ὀδυσσεύς·
“ὦ φίλ’, ἐπεὶ δὴ πάμπαν ἀναίνεαι οὐδ’ ἔτι φῆισθα
κεῖνον ἐλεύσεσθαι, θυμὸς δέ τοι αἰὲν ἄπιστος·   150
ἀλλ’ ἐγὼ οὐκ αὔτως μυθήσομαι, ἀλλὰ σὺν ὅρκωι,
ὡς νεῖται Ὀδυσεύς. εὐαγγέλιον δέ μοι ἔστω
αὐτίκ’, ἐπεί κεν κεῖνος ἰὼν τὰ ἃ δώμαθ’ ἵκηται·
ἔσσαι με χλαῖνάν τε χιτῶνά τε, εἵματα καλά·
πρὶν δέ κε, καὶ μάλα περ κεχρημένος, οὔ τι δεχοίμην.   155
ἐχθρὸς γάρ μοι κεῖνος ὁμῶς Ἀΐδαο πύληισι
γίγνεται, ὃς πενίηι εἴκων ἀπατήλια βάζει.
ἴστω νῦν Ζεὺς πρῶτα θεῶν ξενίη τε τράπεζα
ἱστίη τ’ Ὀδυσῆος ἀμύμονος, ἣν ἀφικάνω·
ἦ μέν τοι τάδε πάντα τελείεται ὡς ἀγορεύω.   160
τοῦδ’ αὐτοῦ λυκάβαντος ἐλεύσεται ἐνθάδ’ Ὀδυσσεύς,
τοῦ μὲν φθίνοντος μηνός, τοῦ δ’ ἱσταμένοιο,
οἴκαδε νοστήσας, καὶ τείσεται ὅς τις ἐκείνου
ἐνθάδ’ ἀτιμάζει ἄλοχον καὶ φαίδιμον υἱόν.”
τὸν δ’ ἀπαμειβόμενος προσέφης, Εὔμαιε συβῶτα·   165
“ὦ γέρον, οὔτ’ ἄρ’ ἐγὼν εὐαγγέλιον τόδε τείσω,
οὔτ’ Ὀδυσεὺς ἔτι οἶκον ἐλεύσεται. ἀλλὰ ἔκηλος
πῖνε, καὶ ἄλλα παρὲξ μεμνώμεθα, μηδέ με τούτων
μίμνησκ’· ἦ γὰρ θυμὸς ἐνὶ στήθεσσιν ἐμοῖσιν
ἄχνυται, ὁππότε τις μνήσηι κεδνοῖο ἄνακτος.   170
ἀλλ’ ἦ τοι ὅρκον μὲν ἐάσομεν, αὐτὰρ Ὀδυσσεὺς
ἔλθοι, ὅπως μιν ἐγώ γ’ ἐθέλω καὶ Πηνελόπεια
Λαέρτης θ’ ὁ γέρων καὶ Τηλέμαχος θεοειδής.

140 αὐτὸς **a**   142 ἱέμενος: ἀχνύμενος **a**   152 ἔσται **a**   154 om. **pa**   164
φαίδιμον: νήπιον **a**

νῦν αὖ παιδὸς ἄλαστον ὀδύρομαι, ὃν τέκ' Ὀδυσσεύς,
Τηλεμάχου. τὸν ἐπεὶ θρέψαν θεοὶ ἔρνεϊ ἶσον,   175
καί μιν ἔφην ἔσσεσθαι ἐν ἀνδράσιν οὔ τι χερείω
πατρὸς ἑοῖο φίλοιο, δέμας καὶ εἶδος ἀγητόν,
τὸν δέ τις ἀθανάτων βλάψε φρένας ἔνδον ἐΐσας
ἠέ τις ἀνθρώπων. ὁ δ' ἔβη μετὰ πατρὸς ἀκουὴν
ἐς Πύλον ἠγαθέην· τὸν δὲ μνηστῆρες ἀγαυοὶ   180
οἴκαδ' ἰόντα λοχῶσιν, ὅπως ἀπὸ φῦλον ὄληται
νώνυμον ἐξ Ἰθάκης Ἀρκεισίου ἀντιθέοιο.
ἀλλ' ἦ τοι κεῖνον μὲν ἐάσομεν, ἤ κεν ἁλώῃι,
ἦ κε φύγῃι καί κέν οἱ ὑπέρσχῃι χεῖρα Κρονίων.
ἀλλ' ἄγε μοι σύ, γεραιέ, τά σ' αὐτοῦ κήδε' ἐνίσπες,   185
καί μοι τοῦτ' ἀγόρευσον ἐτήτυμον, ὄφρ' εὖ εἰδῶ·
τίς πόθεν εἰς ἀνδρῶν; πόθι τοι πόλις ἠδὲ τοκῆες;
ὁπποίης τ' ἐπὶ νηὸς ἀφίκεο; πῶς δέ σε ναῦται
ἤγαγον εἰς Ἰθάκην; τίνες ἔμμεναι εὐχετόωντο;
οὐ μὲν γάρ τί σε πεζὸν ὀΐομαι ἐνθάδ' ἱκέσθαι."   190

Odysseus' false biography: (i) early life

τὸν δ' ἀπαμειβόμενος προσέφη πολύμητις Ὀδυσσεύς·
"τοιγὰρ ἐγώ τοι ταῦτα μάλ' ἀτρεκέως ἀγορεύσω.
εἴη μὲν νῦν νῶϊν ἐπὶ χρόνον ἠμὲν ἐδωδὴ
ἠδὲ μέθυ γλυκερὸν κλισίης ἔντοσθεν ἐοῦσι,
δαίνυσθαι ἀκέοντ', ἄλλοι δ' ἐπὶ ἔργον ἔποιεν.   195
ῥηϊδίως κεν ἔπειτα καὶ εἰς ἐνιαυτὸν ἅπαντα
οὔ τι διαπρήξαιμι λέγων ἐμὰ κήδεα θυμοῦ,
ὅσσα γε δὴ ξύμπαντα θεῶν ἰότητι μόγησα.
ἐκ μὲν Κρητάων γένος εὔχομαι εὐρειάων,
ἀνέρος ἀφνειοῖο πάϊς. πολλοὶ δὲ καὶ ἄλλοι   200
υἷες ἐνὶ μεγάρωι ἠμὲν τράφεν ἠδ' ἐγένοντο
γνήσιοι ἐξ ἀλόχου· ἐμὲ δ' ὠνητὴ τέκε μήτηρ
παλλακίς, ἀλλά με ἶσον ἰθαγενέεσσιν ἐτίμα
Κάστωρ Ὑλακίδης, τοῦ ἐγὼ γένος εὔχομαι εἶναι.
ὃς τότ' ἐνὶ Κρήτεσσι θεὸς ὣς τίετο δήμωι   205
ὄλβωι τε πλούτωι τε καὶ υἱάσι κυδαλίμοισιν.

---

175 θεοὶ οὐρανίωνες a   176 χέρεια Aristarchus   177 δέμας: φρένας a   εἶδος:
ἦθος a   195 ἔποιεν: τράποιντο a   202 ἀλόχων a

ἀλλ' ἦ τοι τὸν κῆρες ἔβαν θανάτοιο φέρουσαι
εἰς Ἀΐδαο δόμους· τοὶ δὲ ζωὴν ἐδάσαντο
παῖδες ὑπέρθυμοι καὶ ἐπὶ κλήρους ἐβάλοντο,
αὐτὰρ ἐμοὶ μάλα παῦρα δόσαν καὶ οἰκί' ἔνειμαν.   210
ἠγαγόμην δὲ γυναῖκα πολυκλήρων ἀνθρώπων
εἵνεκ' ἐμῆς ἀρετῆς, ἐπεὶ οὐκ ἀποφώλιος ἦα
οὐδὲ φυγοπτόλεμος. νῦν δ' ἤδη πάντα λέλοιπεν·
ἀλλ' ἔμπης καλάμην γέ σ' ὀΐομαι εἰσορόωντα
γιγνώσκειν· ἦ γάρ με δύη ἔχει ἤλιθα πολλή.   215
ἦ μὲν δὴ θάρσος μοι Ἄρης τ' ἔδοσαν καὶ Ἀθήνη
καὶ ῥηξηνορίην· ὁπότε κρίνοιμι λόχονδε
ἄνδρας ἀριστῆας, κακὰ δυσμενέεσσι φυτεύων,
οὔ ποτέ μοι θάνατον προτιόσσετο θυμὸς ἀγήνωρ,
ἀλλὰ πολὺ πρώτιστος ἐπάλμενος ἔγχει ἔλεσκον   220
ἀνδρῶν δυσμενέων ὅ τέ μοι εἴξειε πόδεσσι.
τοῖος ἔα ἐν πολέμωι· ἔργον δέ μοι οὐ φίλον ἔσκεν
οὐδ' οἰκωφελίη, ἥ τε τρέφει ἀγλαὰ τέκνα,
ἀλλά μοι αἰεὶ νῆες ἐπήρετμοι φίλαι ἦσαν
καὶ πόλεμοι καὶ ἄκοντες ἐΰξεστοι καὶ ὀϊστοί,   225
λυγρά, τά τ' ἄλλοισίν γε κατεριγηλὰ πέλονται.
αὐτὰρ ἐμοὶ τὰ φίλ' ἔσκε, τά που θεὸς ἐν φρεσὶ θῆκεν·
ἄλλος γάρ τ' ἄλλοισιν ἀνὴρ ἐπιτέρπεται ἔργοις.
πρὶν μὲν γὰρ Τροίης ἐπιβήμεναι υἷας Ἀχαιῶν,
εἰνάκις ἀνδράσιν ἦρξα καὶ ὠκυπόροισι νέεσσιν   230
ἄνδρας ἐς ἀλλοδαπούς, καί μοι μάλα τύγχανε πολλά.
τῶν ἐξαιρεύμην μενοεικέα, πολλὰ δ' ὀπίσσω
λάγχανον· αἶψα δὲ οἶκος ὀφέλλετο, καί ῥα ἔπειτα
δεινός τ' αἰδοῖός τε μετὰ Κρήτεσσι τετύγμην.

Odysseus' false biography: (ii) disaster and recovery in Egypt

ἀλλ' ὅτε δὴ τήν γε στυγερὴν ὁδὸν εὐρύοπα Ζεὺς   235
ἐφράσαθ', ἣ πολλῶν ἀνδρῶν ὑπὸ γούνατ' ἔλυσε,
δὴ τότ' ἔμ' ἤνωγον καὶ ἀγακλυτὸν Ἰδομενῆα
νήεσσ' ἡγήσασθαι ἐς Ἴλιον· οὐδέ τι μῆχος
ἦεν ἀνήνασθαι, χαλεπὴ δ' ἔχε δήμου φῆμις.
ἔνθα μὲν εἰνάετες πολεμίζομεν υἷες Ἀχαιῶν,   240
τῶι δεκάτωι δὲ πόλιν Πριάμου πέρσαντες ἔβημεν

220 ὄλεσκον **a**   222 ἔ ἐν et alia **a**: ἔα ἐν Herodian   228 om. **a**: del. Knight

οἴκαδε σὺν νήεσσι, θεὸς δ' ἐκέδασσεν Ἀχαιούς.
αὐτὰρ ἐμοὶ δειλῶι κακὰ μήδετο μητίετα Ζεύς·
μῆνα γὰρ οἶον ἔμεινα τεταρπόμενος τεκέεσσι
κουριδίηι τ' ἀλόχωι καὶ κτήμασιν. αὐτὰρ ἔπειτα   245
Αἴγυπτόνδε με θυμὸς ἀνώγει ναυτίλλεσθαι,
νῆας εὖ στείλαντα, σὺν ἀντιθέοις ἑτάροισιν.
ἐννέα νῆας στεῖλα, θοῶς δ' ἐσαγείρετο λαός.
ἑξῆμαρ μὲν ἔπειτα ἐμοὶ ἐρίηρες ἑταῖροι
δαίνυντ'· αὐτὰρ ἐγὼν ἱερήϊα πολλὰ παρεῖχον   250
θεοῖσίν τε ῥέζειν αὐτοῖσί τε δαῖτα πένεσθαι.
ἑβδομάτηι δ' ἀναβάντες ἀπὸ Κρήτης εὐρείης
ἐπλέομεν βορέηι ἀνέμωι ἀκραέϊ καλῶι
ῥηϊδίως, ὡς εἴ τε κατὰ ῥόον· οὐδέ τις οὖν μοι
νηῶν πημάνθη, ἀλλ' ἀσκηθέες καὶ ἄνουσοι   255
ἥμεθα, τὰς δ' ἄνεμός τε κυβερνῆταί τ' ἴθυνον.
πεμπταῖοι δ' Αἴγυπτον ἐϋρρείτην ἱκόμεσθα,
στῆσα δ' ἐν Αἰγύπτωι ποταμῶι νέας ἀμφιελίσσας.
    ἔνθ' ἦ τοι μὲν ἐγὼ κελόμην ἐρίηρας ἑταίρους
αὐτοῦ πὰρ νήεσσι μένειν καὶ νῆας ἔρυσθαι,   260
ὀπτῆρας δὲ κατὰ σκοπιὰς ὤτρυνα νέεσθαι.
οἱ δ' ὕβρει εἴξαντες, ἐπισπόμενοι μένεῖ σφῶι,
αἶψα μάλ' Αἰγυπτίων ἀνδρῶν περικαλλέας ἀγροὺς
πόρθεον, ἐκ δὲ γυναῖκας ἄγον καὶ νήπια τέκνα,
αὐτούς τ' ἔκτεινον· τάχα δ' ἐς πόλιν ἵκετ' ἀϋτή.   265
οἱ δὲ βοῆς ἀΐοντες ἅμ' ἠοῖ φαινομένηφιν
ἦλθον· πλῆτο δὲ πᾶν πεδίον πεζῶν τε καὶ ἵππων
χαλκοῦ τε στεροπῆς. ἐν δὲ Ζεὺς τερπικέραυνος
φύζαν ἐμοῖς ἑτάροισι κακὴν βάλεν, οὐδέ τις ἔτλη
μεῖναι ἐναντίβιον· περὶ γὰρ κακὰ πάντοθεν ἔστη.   270
ἔνθ' ἡμέων πολλοὺς μὲν ἀπέκτανον ὀξέϊ χαλκῶι,
τοὺς δ' ἄναγον ζωούς, σφίσιν ἐργάζεσθαι ἀνάγκηι.
    αὐτὰρ ἐμοὶ Ζεὺς αὐτὸς ἐνὶ φρεσὶν ὧδε νόημα
ποίησ' – ὡς ὄφελον θανέειν καὶ πότμον ἐπισπεῖν
αὐτοῦ ἐν Αἰγύπτωι· ἔτι γάρ νύ με πῆμ' ὑπέδεκτο –   275
αὐτίκ' ἀπὸ κρατὸς κυνέην εὔτυκτον ἔθηκα
καὶ σάκος ὤμοιϊν, δόρυ δ' ἔκβαλον ἔκτοσε χειρός·
αὐτὰρ ἐγὼ βασιλῆος ἐναντίον ἤλυθον ἵππων

---

243 μητίετα: εὐρύοπα a   248 λαός: θυμός a   255 ἀσκεθέες a   258 στήσας a:
στήσαμεν b

καὶ κύσα γούναθ᾽ ἑλών· ὁ δ᾽ ἐρύσατο καί μ᾽ ἐλέησεν,
ἐς δίφρον δέ μ᾽ ἕσας ἄγεν οἴκαδε δάκρυ χέοντα.　　　　　280
ἦ μέν μοι μάλα πολλοὶ ἐπήϊσσον μελίῃσιν,
ἱέμενοι κτεῖναι — δὴ γὰρ κεχολώατο λίην —
ἀλλ᾽ ἀπὸ κεῖνος ἔρυκε, Διὸς δ᾽ ὠπίζετο μῆνιν
ξεινίου, ὅς τε μάλιστα νεμεσσᾶται κακὰ ἔργα.
ἔνθα μὲν ἑπτάετες μένον αὐτόθι, πολλὰ δ᾽ ἄγειρα　　　　285
χρήματ᾽ ἀν᾽ Αἰγυπτίους ἄνδρας· δίδοσαν γὰρ ἅπαντες.

Odysseus' false biography: (iii) fooled by a Phoenician

　　ἀλλ᾽ ὅτε δὴ ὄγδοόν μοι ἐπιπλόμενον ἔτος ἦλθε,
δὴ τότε Φοῖνιξ ἦλθεν ἀνὴρ ἀπατήλια εἰδώς,
τρώκτης, ὃς δὴ πολλὰ κάκ᾽ ἀνθρώποισιν ἐώργει·
ὅς μ᾽ ἄγε παρπεπιθὼν ᾗσι φρεσίν, ὄφρ᾽ ἱκόμεσθα　　　　290
Φοινίκην, ὅθι τοῦ γε δόμοι καὶ κτήματ᾽ ἔκειτο.
ἔνθα παρ᾽ αὐτῶι μεῖνα τελεσφόρον εἰς ἐνιαυτόν.
ἀλλ᾽ ὅτε δὴ μῆνές τε καὶ ἡμέραι ἐξετελεῦντο
ἂψ περιτελλομένου ἔτεος καὶ ἐπήλυθον ὧραι,
ἐς Λιβύην μ᾽ ἐπὶ νηὸς ἐέσσατο ποντοπόροιο,　　　　　295
ψεύδεα βουλεύσας, ἵνα οἱ σὺν φόρτον ἄγοιμι,
κεῖθι δέ μ᾽ ὡς περάσειε καὶ ἄσπετον ὦνον ἕλοιτο.
τῶι ἑπόμην ἐπὶ νηός, ὀϊόμενός περ, ἀνάγκηι.
ἡ δ᾽ ἔθεεν βορέηι ἀνέμωι ἀκραέϊ καλῶι
μέσσον ὑπὲρ Κρήτης· Ζεὺς δέ σφισι μήδετ᾽ ὄλεθρον.　　300
　　ἀλλ᾽ ὅτε δὴ Κρήτην μὲν ἐλείπομεν, οὐδέ τις ἄλλη
φαίνετο γαιάων, ἀλλ᾽ οὐρανὸς ἠδὲ θάλασσα,
δὴ τότε κυανέην νεφέλην ἔστησε Κρονίων
νηὸς ὕπερ γλαφυρῆς, ἤχλυσε δὲ πόντος ὑπ᾽ αὐτῆς.
Ζεὺς δ᾽ ἄμυδις βρόντησε καὶ ἔμβαλε νηῒ κεραυνόν·　　305
ἡ δ᾽ ἐλελίχθη πᾶσα Διὸς πληγεῖσα κεραυνῶι,
ἐν δὲ θεείου πλῆτο· πέσον δ᾽ ἐκ νηὸς ἅπαντες.
οἱ δὲ κορώνηισιν ἴκελοι περὶ νῆα μέλαιναν
κύμασιν ἐμφορέοντο· θεὸς δ᾽ ἀποαίνυτο νόστον.
αὐτὰρ ἐμοὶ Ζεὺς αὐτός, ἔχοντί περ ἄλγεα θυμῶι,　　310
ἱστὸν ἀμαιμάκετον νηὸς κυανοπρώιροιο

279 μ᾽ ἐσάωσεν a　　286 ἅπαντα a　　289 ἀνθρώπους a　　291 κτήματ᾽ ἔασι a
299 εὐκραέϊ a　　300 μήδετ᾽· βούλετ᾽ a

ἐν χείρεσσιν ἔθηκεν, ὅπως ἔτι πῆμα φύγοιμι.
τῶι ῥα περιπλεχθεὶς φερόμην ὀλοοῖς ἀνέμοισιν·

Odysseus' false biography: (iv) saved by the Thesprotians

ἐννῆμαρ φερόμην, δεκάτηι δέ με νυκτὶ μελαίνηι
γαίηι Θεσπρωτῶν πέλασεν μέγα κῦμα κυλίνδον.   315
ἔνθα με Θεσπρωτῶν βασιλεὺς ἐκομίσσατο Φείδων
ἥρως ἀπριάτην· τοῦ γὰρ φίλος υἱὸς ἐπελθὼν
αἴθρωι καὶ καμάτωι δεδμημένον ἦγεν ἐς οἶκον,
χειρὸς ἀναστήσας, ὄφρ᾽ ἵκετο δώματα πατρός·
ἀμφὶ δέ με χλαῖνάν τε χιτῶνά τε εἵματα ἕσσεν.   320
ἔνθ᾽ Ὀδυσῆος ἐγὼ πυθόμην· κεῖνος γὰρ ἔφασκε
ξεινίσαι ἠδὲ φιλῆσαι ἰόντ᾽ ἐς πατρίδα γαῖαν,
καί μοι κτήματ᾽ ἔδειξεν, ὅσα ξυναγείρατ᾽ Ὀδυσσεύς,
χαλκόν τε χρυσόν τε πολύκμητόν τε σίδηρον.
καί νύ κεν ἐς δεκάτην γενεὴν ἕτερόν γ᾽ ἔτι βόσκοι·   325
τόσσα οἱ ἐν μεγάροις κειμήλια κεῖτο ἄνακτος.
τὸν δ᾽ ἐς Δωδώνην φάτο βήμεναι, ὄφρα θεοῖο
ἐκ δρυὸς ὑψικόμοιο Διὸς βουλὴν ἐπακοῦσαι,
ὅππως νοστήσει᾽ Ἰθάκης ἐς πίονα δῆμον,
ἤδη δὴν ἀπεών, ἢ ἀμφαδὸν ἦε κρυφηδόν.   330
ὤμοσε δὲ πρὸς ἔμ᾽ αὐτόν, ἀποσπένδων ἐνὶ οἴκωι,
νῆα κατειρύσθαι καὶ ἐπαρτέας ἔμμεν ἑταίρους,
οἳ δή μιν πέμψουσι φίλην ἐς πατρίδα γαῖαν.

*Odysseus' false biography: (v) escape from treacherous sailors and
arrival in Ithaca*

ἀλλ᾽ ἐμὲ πρὶν ἀπέπεμψε· τύχησε γὰρ ἐρχομένη νηῦς
ἀνδρῶν Θεσπρωτῶν ἐς Δουλίχιον πολύπυρον.   335
ἔνθ᾽ ὅ γέ μ᾽ ἠνώγει πέμψαι βασιλῆϊ Ἀκάστωι
ἐνδυκέως· τοῖσιν δὲ κακὴ φρεσὶν ἥνδανε βουλὴ
ἀμφ᾽ ἐμοί, ὄφρ᾽ ἔτι πάγχυ δύης ἐπὶ πῆμα γενοίμην.
ἀλλ᾽ ὅτε γαίης πολλὸν ἀπέπλω ποντοπόρος νηῦς,
αὐτίκα δούλιον ἦμαρ ἐμοὶ περιμηχανόωντο.   340
ἐκ μέν με χλαῖνάν τε χιτῶνά τε εἵματ᾽ ἔδυσαν,

324 πολύκμητόν τε σίδηρον: ἅλις ἐσθῆτά θ᾽ ὑφαντήν a Eustathius   335 πολύμηλον a
337 φρεσὶν ἥνδανε βουλή: βουλὴ ἥνδανε θυμῶι a   338 δύηι ἔπι πῆμα γένηται Aristophanes

ἀμφὶ δέ με ῥάκος ἄλλο κακὸν βάλον ἠδὲ χιτῶνα,
ῥωγαλέα, τὰ καὶ αὐτὸς ἐν ὀφθαλμοῖσιν ὅρηαι.
ἑσπέριοι δ᾽ Ἰθάκης εὐδειέλου ἔργ᾽ ἀφίκοντο.
ἔνθ᾽ ἐμὲ μὲν κατέδησαν ἐϋσσέλμωι ἐνὶ νηῒ   345
ὅπλωι ἐϋστρεφέϊ στερεῶς, αὐτοὶ δ᾽ ἀποβάντες
ἐσσυμένως παρὰ θῖνα θαλάσσης δόρπον ἕλοντο.
αὐτὰρ ἐμοὶ δεσμὸν μὲν ἀνέγναμψαν θεοὶ αὐτοὶ
ῥηϊδίως· κεφαλῆι δὲ κατὰ ῥάκος ἀμφικαλύψας,
ξεστὸν ἐφόλκαιον καταβὰς ἐπέλασσα θαλάσσηι   350
στῆθος, ἔπειτα δὲ χερσὶ διήρεσα ἀμφοτέρηισι
νηχόμενος, μάλα δ᾽ ὦκα θύρηθ᾽ ἔα ἀμφὶς ἐκείνων.
ἔνθ᾽ ἀναβάς, ὅθι τε δρίος ἦν πολυανθέος ὕλης,
κείμην πεπτηώς. οἱ δὲ μεγάλα στενάχοντες
φοίτων· ἀλλ᾽ οὐ γάρ σφιν ἐφαίνετο κέρδιον εἶναι   355
μαίεσθαι προτέρω, τοὶ μὲν πάλιν αὖτις ἔβαινον
νηὸς ἔπι γλαφυρῆς· ἐμὲ δ᾽ ἔκρυψαν θεοὶ αὐτοὶ
ῥηϊδίως, καί με σταθμῶι ἐπέλασσαν ἄγοντες
ἀνδρὸς ἐπισταμένου· ἔτι γάρ νύ μοι αἶσα βιῶναι."

Odysseus again insists Eumaeus' master will return

τὸν δ᾽ ἀπαμειβόμενος προσέφης, Εὔμαιε συβῶτα·   360
"ἆ δειλὲ ξείνων, ἦ μοι μάλα θυμὸν ὄρινας
ταῦτα ἕκαστα λέγων, ὅσα δὴ πάθες ἠδ᾽ ὅσ᾽ ἀλήθης.
ἀλλὰ τά γ᾽ οὐ κατὰ κόσμον, ὀΐομαι, οὐδέ με πείσεις,
εἰπὼν ἀμφ᾽ Ὀδυσῆϊ. τί σε χρὴ τοῖον ἐόντα
μαψιδίως ψεύδεσθαι; ἐγὼ δ᾽ εὖ οἶδα καὶ αὐτὸς   365
νόστον ἐμοῖο ἄνακτος, ὅ τ᾽ ἤχθετο πᾶσι θεοῖσι
πάγχυ μάλ᾽, ὅττι μιν οὔ τι μετὰ Τρώεσσι δάμασσαν
ἠὲ φίλων ἐν χερσίν, ἐπεὶ πόλεμον τολύπευσε.
τώ κέν οἱ τύμβον μὲν ἐποίησαν Παναχαιοί,
ἠδέ κε καὶ ὧι παιδὶ μέγα κλέος ἦρατ᾽ ὀπίσσω·   370
νῦν δέ μιν ἀκλειῶς Ἅρπυιαι ἀνηρείψαντο.
αὐτὰρ ἐγὼ παρ᾽ ὕεσσιν ἀπότροπος· οὐδὲ πόλινδε
ἔρχομαι, εἰ μή πού τι περίφρων Πηνελόπεια

---

349 κεφαλήν δὲ Aristophanes **a**   353 δρύος **a**   πολυβενθέος **a**   369–70 omitted in many MSS (= 1.239–40, 24.32–3)

ἐλθέμεν ὀτρύνῃσιν, ὅτ᾽ ἀγγελίη ποθὲν ἔλθηι.
ἀλλ᾽ οἱ μὲν τὰ ἕκαστα παρήμενοι ἐξερέουσιν,   375
ἠμὲν οἳ ἄχνυνται δὴν οἰχομένοιο ἄνακτος,
ἠδ᾽ οἳ χαίρουσιν βίοτον νήποινον ἔδοντες.
ἀλλ᾽ ἐμοὶ οὐ φίλον ἐστὶ μεταλλῆσαι καὶ ἐρέσθαι,
ἐξ οὗ δή μ᾽ Αἰτωλὸς ἀνὴρ ἐξήπαφε μύθωι,
ὅς ῥ᾽ ἄνδρα κτείνας πολλὴν ἐπὶ γαῖαν ἀληθείς,   380
ἦλθεν ἐμὰ πρὸς δώματα· ἐγὼ δέ μιν ἀμφαγάπαζον.
φῆ δέ μιν ἐν Κρήτεσσι παρ᾽ Ἰδομενῆϊ ἰδέσθαι
νῆας ἀκειόμενον, τάς οἱ ξυνέαξαν ἄελλαι·
καὶ φάτ᾽ ἐλεύσεσθαι ἢ ἐς θέρος ἢ ἐς ὀπώρην,
πολλὰ χρήματ᾽ ἄγοντα, σὺν ἀντιθέοις ἑτάροισι.   385
καὶ σύ, γέρον πολυπενθές, ἐπεί σέ μοι ἤγαγε δαίμων,
μήτε τί μοι ψεύδεσσι χαρίζεο, μήτε τι θέλγε·
οὐ γὰρ τοὔνεκ᾽ ἐγώ σ᾽ αἰδέσσομαι οὐδὲ φιλήσω,
ἀλλὰ Δία ξένιον δείσας αὐτόν τ᾽ ἐλεαίρων."
    τὸν δ᾽ ἀπαμειβόμενος προσέφη πολύμητις Ὀδυσσεύς·   390
"ἦ μάλα τίς τοι θυμὸς ἐνὶ στήθεσσιν ἄπιστος,
οἷόν σ᾽ οὐδ᾽ ὀμόσας περ ἐπήγαγον, οὐδέ σε πείθω.
ἀλλ᾽ ἄγε νῦν ῥήτρην ποιησόμεθ᾽· αὐτὰρ ὄπισθε
μάρτυροι ἀμφοτέροισι θεοί, τοὶ Ὄλυμπον ἔχουσιν.
εἰ μέν κεν νοστήσηι ἄναξ τεὸς ἐς τόδε δῶμα,   395
ἕσσας με χλαῖνάν τε χιτῶνά τε εἵματα πέμψαι
Δουλίχιόνδ᾽ ἰέναι, ὅθι μοι φίλον ἔπλετο θυμῶι·
εἰ δέ κε μὴ ἔλθησιν ἄναξ τεὸς ὡς ἀγορεύω,
δμῶας ἐπισσεύας βαλέειν μεγάλης κατὰ πέτρης,
ὄφρα καὶ ἄλλος πτωχὸς ἀλεύεται ἠπεροπεύειν."   400
    τὸν δ᾽ ἀπαμειβόμενος προσεφώνεε δῖος ὑφορβός·
"ξεῖν᾽, οὕτω γάρ κέν μοι ἐϋκλείη τ᾽ ἀρετή τε
εἴη ἐπ᾽ ἀνθρώπους ἅμα τ᾽ αὐτίκα καὶ μετέπειτα,
ὅς σ᾽ ἐπεὶ ἐς κλισίην ἄγαγον καὶ ξείνια δῶκα,
αὖτις δὲ κτείναιμι φίλον τ᾽ ἀπὸ θυμὸν ἑλοίμην·   405
πρόφρων κεν δὴ ἔπειτα Δία Κρονίωνα λιτοίμην.
νῦν δ᾽ ὥρη δόρποιο· τάχιστά μοι ἔνδον ἑταῖροι
εἶεν, ἵν᾽ ἐν κλισίηι λαρὸν τετυκοίμεθα δόρπον."

---

377 χαίροντες... ἔδουσι a   381 ἤλυθ᾽ ἐμὸν πρὸς σταθμόν pa   389 ἐλεήσας a
396 εἵματα: οἴκαδε a   403 μετόπισθεν a   406 Κρονίων᾽ ἀλιτοίμην a   408
τετυκαίμεθα p

Arrival of the swineherds and dinner

ὣς οἱ μὲν τοιαῦτα πρὸς ἀλλήλους ἀγόρευον,
ἀγχίμολον δὲ σύες τε καὶ ἀνέρες ἦλθον ὑφορβοί.   410
τὰς μὲν ἄρα ἔρξαν κατὰ ἤθεα κοιμηθῆναι,
κλαγγὴ δ᾽ ἄσπετος ὦρτο συῶν αὐλιζομενάων.
αὐτὰρ ὁ οἷς ἑτάροισιν ἐκέκλετο δῖος ὑφορβός·
"ἄξεθ᾽ ὑῶν τὸν ἄριστον, ἵνα ξείνωι ἱερεύσω
τηλεδαπῶι· πρὸς δ᾽ αὐτοὶ ὀνησόμεθ᾽, οἵ περ ὀϊζὺν   415
δὴν ἔχομεν πάσχοντες ὑῶν ἕνεκ᾽ ἀργιοδόντων·
ἄλλοι δ᾽ ἡμέτερον κάματον νήποινον ἔδουσιν."
    ὣς ἄρα φωνήσας κέασε ξύλα νηλέϊ χαλκῶι·
οἱ δ᾽ ὗν εἰσῆγον μάλα πίονα πενταέτηρον.
τὸν μὲν ἔπειτ᾽ ἔστησαν ἐπ᾽ ἐσχάρηι· οὐδὲ συβώτης   420
λήθετ᾽ ἄρ᾽ ἀθανάτων· φρεσὶ γὰρ κέχρητ᾽ ἀγαθῆισιν.
ἀλλ᾽ ὅ γ᾽ ἀπαρχόμενος κεφαλῆς τρίχας ἐν πυρὶ βάλλεν
ἀργιόδοντος ὑός, καὶ ἐπεύχετο πᾶσι θεοῖσι
νοστῆσαι Ὀδυσῆα πολύφρονα ὅνδε δόμονδε.
κόψε δ᾽ ἀνασχόμενος σχίζηι δρυός, ἣν λίπε κείων·   425
τὸν δ᾽ ἔλιπε ψυχή. τοὶ δ᾽ ἔσφαξάν τε καὶ εὖσαν,
αἶψα δέ μιν διέχευαν· ὁ δ᾽ ὠμοθετεῖτο συβώτης,
πάντων ἀρχόμενος μελέων, ἐς πίονα δημόν.
καὶ τὰ μὲν ἐν πυρὶ βάλλε, παλύνας ἀλφίτου ἀκτῆι,
μίστυλλόν τ᾽ ἄρα τἆλλα καὶ ἀμφ᾽ ὀβελοῖσιν ἔπειραν,   430
ὤπτησάν τε περιφραδέως ἐρύσαντό τε πάντα,
βάλλον δ᾽ εἰν ἐλεοῖσιν ἀολλέα. ἂν δὲ συβώτης
ἵστατο δαιτρεύσων· περὶ γὰρ φρεσὶν αἴσιμα ἤιδη.
καὶ τὰ μὲν ἕπταχα πάντα διεμοιρᾶτο δαΐζων·
τὴν μὲν ἴαν Νύμφηισι καὶ Ἑρμῆι, Μαιάδος υἷι,   435
θῆκεν ἐπευξάμενος, τὰς δ᾽ ἄλλας νεῖμεν ἑκάστωι·
νώτοισιν δ᾽ Ὀδυσῆα διηνεκέεσσι γέραιρεν
ἀργιόδοντος ὑός, κύδαινε δὲ θυμὸν ἄνακτος.
καί μιν φωνήσας προσέφη πολύμητις Ὀδυσσεύς·
"αἴθ᾽ οὕτως, Εὔμαιε, φίλος Διὶ πατρὶ γένοιο   440
ὡς ἐμοί, ὅττι με τοῖον ἐόντ᾽ ἀγαθοῖσι γεραίρεις."

---

412 ὦρτο: ἦλθε **a**   419 εἰσάγαγον **a**   425 ἀναχαζόμενος **a**   428 πάντων
Aristarchus: παντόθεν MSS   429 ἀκτήν **a**   434 ἔσχατα **a**: ἔντεχνα **b**   436
ἐπαρξάμενος **a**   438 ἥνδανε **a**   439 ἔπεα πτερόεντα προσηύδα **a**

τὸν δ᾽ ἀπαμειβόμενος προσέφης, Εὔμαιε συβῶτα·
"ἔσθιε, δαιμόνιε ξείνων, καὶ τέρπεο τοῖσδε,
οἷα πάρεστι· θεὸς δὲ τὸ μὲν δώσει, τὸ δ᾽ ἐάσει,
ὅττι κεν ὧι θυμῶι ἐθέληι· δύναται γὰρ ἅπαντα."   445
ἦ ῥα, καὶ ἄργματα θῦσε θεοῖς αἰειγενέτηισι,
σπείσας δ᾽ αἴθοπα οἶνον, Ὀδυσσῆϊ πτολιπόρθωι
ἐν χείρεσσιν ἔθηκεν· ὁ δ᾽ ἕζετο ἧι παρὰ μοίρηι.
σῖτον δέ σφιν ἔνειμε Μεσαύλιος, ὅν ῥα συβώτης
αὐτὸς κτήσατο οἷος ἀποιχομένοιο ἄνακτος,   450
νόσφιν δεσποίνης καὶ Λαέρταο γέροντος·
πὰρ δ᾽ ἄρα μιν Ταφίων πρίατο κτεάτεσσιν ἑοῖσιν.
οἱ δ᾽ ἐπ᾽ ὀνείαθ᾽ ἑτοῖμα προκείμενα χεῖρας ἴαλλον.
αὐτὰρ ἐπεὶ πόσιος καὶ ἐδητύος ἐξ ἔρον ἔντο,
σῖτον μέν σφιν ἀφεῖλε Μεσαύλιος, οἱ δ᾽ ἐπὶ κοῖτον   455
σίτου καὶ κρειῶν κεκορημένοι ἐσσεύοντο.

Odysseus' false tale wins him a cloak

νὺξ δ᾽ ἄρ᾽ ἐπῆλθε κακὴ σκοτομήνιος· ὗε δ᾽ ἄρα Ζεὺς
πάννυχος, αὐτὰρ ἄη Ζέφυρος μέγας αἰὲν ἔφυδρος.
τοῖς δ᾽ Ὀδυσσεὺς μετέειπε, συβώτεω πειρητίζων,
εἴ πώς οἱ ἐκδὺς χλαῖναν πόροι ἤ τιν᾽ ἑταίρων   460
ἄλλον ἐποτρύνειεν, ἐπεί ἑο κήδετο λίην·
"κέκλυθι νῦν, Εὔμαιε καὶ ἄλλοι πάντες ἑταῖροι,
εὐξάμενός τι ἔπος ἐρέω. οἶνος γὰρ ἀνώγει
ἠλεός, ὅς τ᾽ ἐφέηκε πολύφρονά περ μάλ᾽ ἀεῖσαι,
καί θ᾽ ἁπαλὸν γελάσαι, καί τ᾽ ὀρχήσασθαι ἀνῆκε,   465
καί τι ἔπος προέηκεν, ὅ πέρ τ᾽ ἄρρητον ἄμεινον.
ἀλλ᾽ ἐπεὶ οὖν τὸ πρῶτον ἀνέκραγον, οὐκ ἐπικεύσω.
εἴθ᾽ ὣς ἡβώοιμι βίη τέ μοι ἔμπεδος εἴη,
ὡς ὅθ᾽ ὑπὸ Τροίην λόχον ἤγομεν ἀρτύναντες.
ἡγείσθην δ᾽ Ὀδυσεύς τε καὶ Ἀτρεΐδης Μενέλαος,   470
τοῖσι δ᾽ ἅμα τρίτος ἦρχον ἐγών· αὐτοὶ γὰρ ἄνωγον.
ἀλλ᾽ ὅτε δή ῥ᾽ ἱκόμεσθα ποτὶ πτόλιν αἰπύ τε τεῖχος,
ἡμεῖς μὲν περὶ ἄστυ κατὰ ῥωπήϊα πυκνά,
ἂν δόνακας καὶ ἕλος, ὑπὸ τεύχεσι πεπτηῶτες

461 λίην: βουλήν **a**

κείμεθα· νὺξ δ' ἄρ' ἐπῆλθε κακὴ βορέαο πεσόντος,   475
πηγυλίς· αὐτὰρ ὕπερθε χιὼν γένετ' ἠΰτε πάχνη,
ψυχρή, καὶ σακέεσσι περιτρέφετο κρύσταλλος.
ἔνθ' ἄλλοι πάντες χλαίνας ἔχον ἠδὲ χιτῶνας,
εὗδον δ' εὔκηλοι, σάκεσιν εἰλυμένοι ὤμους·
αὐτὰρ ἐγὼ χλαῖναν μὲν ἰὼν ἑτάροισιν ἔλειπον   480
ἀφραδίης, ἐπεὶ οὐκ ἐφάμην ῥιγωσέμεν ἔμπης,
ἀλλ' ἑπόμην σάκος οἷον ἔχων καὶ ζῶμα φαεινόν.
   ἀλλ' ὅτε δὴ τρίχα νυκτὸς ἔην, μετὰ δ' ἄστρα βεβήκει,
καὶ τότ' ἐγὼν Ὀδυσῆα προσηύδων ἐγγὺς ἐόντα
ἀγκῶνι νύξας· ὁ δ' ἄρ' ἐμμαπέως ὑπάκουσε·   485
'διογενὲς Λαερτιάδη, πολυμήχαν' Ὀδυσσεῦ,
οὔ τοι ἔτι ζωοῖσι μετέσσομαι, ἀλλά με χεῖμα
δάμναται· οὐ γὰρ ἔχω χλαῖναν· παρά μ' ἤπαφε δαίμων
οἰοχίτων' ἔμεναι· νῦν δ' οὐκέτι φυκτὰ πέλονται.'
ὣς ἐφάμην, ὁ δ' ἔπειτα νόον σχέθε τόνδ' ἐνὶ θυμῶι,   490
οἷος κεῖνος ἔην βουλευέμεν ἠδὲ μάχεσθαι·
φθεγξάμενος δ' ὀλίγηι ὀπί με πρὸς μῦθον ἔειπε·
'σίγα νῦν, μή τίς σευ Ἀχαιῶν ἄλλος ἀκούσηι.'
ἦ, καὶ ἐπ' ἀγκῶνος κεφαλὴν σχέθεν εἶπέ τε μῦθον·
'κλῦτε, φίλοι· θεῖός μοι ἐνύπνιον ἦλθεν ὄνειρος.   495
λίην γὰρ νηῶν ἑκὰς ἤλθομεν. ἀλλά τις εἴη
εἰπεῖν Ἀτρεΐδηι Ἀγαμέμνονι, ποιμένι λαῶν,
εἰ πλέονας παρὰ ναῦφιν ἐποτρύνειε νέεσθαι.'
ὣς ἔφατ', ὦρτο δ' ἔπειτα Θόας, Ἀνδραίμονος υἱός,
καρπαλίμως, ἀπὸ δὲ χλαῖναν θέτο φοινικόεσσαν,   500
βῆ δὲ θέειν ἐπὶ νῆας· ἐγὼ δ' ἐνὶ εἵματι κείνου
κείμην ἀσπασίως, φάε δὲ χρυσόθρονος Ἠώς.
[ὣς νῦν ἡβώοιμι βίη τέ μοι ἔμπεδος εἴη·
δοίη κέν τις χλαῖναν ἐνὶ σταθμοῖσι συφορβῶν,
ἀμφότερον, φιλότητι καὶ αἰδοῖ φωτὸς ἑῆος·   505
νῦν δέ μ' ἀτιμάζουσι κακὰ χροΐ εἵματ' ἔχοντα.]'
   τὸν δ' ἀπαμειβόμενος προσέφης, Εὔμαιε συβῶτα·
"ὦ γέρον, αἶνος μέν τοι ἀμύμων, ὃν κατέλεξας,
οὐδέ τί πω παρὰ μοῖραν ἔπος νηκερδὲς ἔειπες·
τὼ οὔτ' ἐσθῆτος δευήσεαι οὔτε τευ ἄλλου,   510

481 ἀφραδέως **a**: ἀφραδίηι **b**: ἀμαθία **c**   485 ἀνόρουσε **a**   495 del. Aristarchus
ἐνύπνιος **a**   500 βάλε **a**   501 δὲ θέειν: δ' ἰέναι **a**   503–6 marked with obeli **a**:
504–6 bracketed **b**

ὧν ἐπέοιχ᾽ ἱκέτην ταλαπείριον ἀντιάσαντα,
νῦν· ἀτὰρ ἠῶθέν γε τὰ σὰ ῥάκεα δνοπαλίξεις.
οὐ γὰρ πολλαὶ χλαῖναι ἐπημοιβοί τε χιτῶνες
ἐνθάδε ἕννυσθαι, μία δ᾽ οἴη φωτὶ ἑκάστωι.
αὐτὰρ ἐπὴν ἔλθηισιν Ὀδυσσῆος φίλος υἱός,   515
κεῖνός σε χλαῖνάν τε χιτῶνά τε εἵματα δώσει,
πέμψει δ᾽ ὅππηι σε κραδίη θυμός τε κελεύει."
   ὣς εἰπὼν ἀνόρουσε, τίθει δ᾽ ἄρα οἱ πυρὸς ἐγγὺς
εὐνήν, ἐν δ᾽ ὀΐων τε καὶ αἰγῶν δέρματ᾽ ἔβαλλεν.
ἔνθ᾽ Ὀδυσεὺς κατέλεκτ᾽· ἐπὶ δὲ χλαῖναν βάλεν αὐτῶι   520
πυκνὴν καὶ μεγάλην, ἥ οἱ παρακέσκετ᾽ ἀμοιβάς,
ἕννυσθαι ὅτε τις χειμὼν ἔκπαγλος ὄροιτο.
   ὣς ὁ μὲν ἔνθ᾽ Ὀδυσεὺς κοιμήσατο, τοὶ δὲ παρ᾽ αὐτὸν
ἄνδρες κοιμήσαντο νεηνίαι. οὐδὲ συβώτηι
ἥνδανεν αὐτόθι κοῖτος, ὑῶν ἄπο κοιμηθῆναι,   525
ἀλλ᾽ ὅ γ᾽ ἄρ᾽ ἔξω ἰὼν ὁπλίζετο· χαῖρε δ᾽ Ὀδυσσεύς,
ὅττι ῥά οἱ βιότου περικήδετο νόσφιν ἐόντος.
πρῶτον μὲν ξίφος ὀξὺ περὶ στιβαροῖς βάλετ᾽ ὤμοις,
ἀμφὶ δὲ χλαῖναν ἑέσσατ᾽, ἀλεξάνεμον μάλα πυκνήν,
ἂν δὲ νάκην ἕλετ᾽ αἰγὸς ἐϋτρεφέος μεγάλοιο,   530
εἵλετο δ᾽ ὀξὺν ἄκοντα, κυνῶν ἀλκτῆρα καὶ ἀνδρῶν.
βῆ δ᾽ ἴμεναι κείων, ὅθι περ σύες ἀργιόδοντες
πέτρηι ὕπο γλαφυρῆι εὗδον, βορέω ὑπ᾽ ἰωγῆι.

515–17 om. a   516 κεῖνός σε: αὐτός τοι a   δώσει: ἔσσει a   519 αἰγῶν τε καὶ
οἰῶν pa   521 μεγάλην: μαλακήν a   παρεκέσκετο a   526 κατελέξατο a: κατερέξ-
ατο b

COMMENTARY

BOOK 13

Book 12 ended with the final words of Od.'s long tale of his wanderings (books 9–12), and book 13 is then the hinge between those wanderings in a semi-mythical world and his return to the world of men. It covers the reaction to his story, his departure with honour from Scherie, his magical journey to Ithaca and his meeting with Athena on the shore. Eustathius (2.35.39 Stallbaum) tells us that the 'old' scholars called this book Ὀδυσσέως ἀπόπλους παρὰ Φαιάκων καὶ ἄφιξις εἰς Ἰθάκην.

Book division. As soon as the *Odyssey* became a written text, the restraints on the physical size of papyrus rolls would have meant that it was divided up in some way. What we do not know is when or by whom the current division was made, but the fact that the resulting books are much smaller than a papyrus roll can handle suggests the exigencies of that medium were not a principal factor. It has been suggested that the divisions were made by someone involved in the book-trade, perhaps to produce blocks which would be attractive to readers (cf. S. R. West 1967: 20). Olson 1995: 233 suggests that 'the abrupt manner in which Book IX begins and Book XII ends...does seem logical if one posits that buyers of books...were eager to read...Odyssey's apology in its entirety, but considerably less interested in the speeches by Alkinoos which accompany and frame it'.

In general, the books of *Od.* are shorter than those of *Il.*, perhaps to achieve 24 books to match the earlier epic. It has been suggested that the α–ω arrangement was an alphabetic, not a numerical, one, indicating Homer's comprehensivity: cf. 'I am alpha and omega.' The letters relate to the Ionic alphabet, which would seem to rule out an origin in any sixth-century recension made under the tyrant Peisistratus for the recital competitions at the Panathenaea: that alphabet was introduced to Athens only at the end of the fifth century. On the other hand, the division could antedate the use of the letters. [Plut.] *Vita Hom.* 2.4 says that the divisions were made 'not by the poet, but by grammarians around Aristarchus', but it has been argued that Aristarchus thought the 'end' (πέρας, τέλος) of *Od.* was 23.296 and so would have made a book-division at that point (see however Pfeiffer 1968: 116, 175–7). The first reference to the division is in the second century (Apollodorus of Athens, 3.557 Erbse).

For a critical assessment of the editor's choice of where to put the divisions, cf. Olson 1995: 228–39; for bibliography and discussion, S. R. West 1967: 18–25; N. J. Richardson 1993: 20–1; Haslam 1997: 57–9; and on *Il.*, Taplin 1992: 285–93.

1–15 The reaction to Od.'s story

That the Phaeacian episode is coming to its conclusion is indicated by the way that this section repeats a number of motifs from Od.'s original entry into Alcinous' palace (7.139–206); there is however little repetition of language. The silence that greeted his sudden arrival recurs (1 ≈ 7.154, cf. 144); Alcinous gives instructions (7–15 ~ 7.186–98); they go to bed before dealing with Od.'s return (17 ~ 7.188, 226–9); Od. prays for prosperity for the Phaeacians (44–6, 59–62 ~ 7.148–50); and Pontonous is ordered to mix a crater of wine for a libation (50–6 ~ 7.179–83, with 50–1 ≈ 7.179–80, 53–4 ≈ 7.182–3).

The scene also uses the motif of the giving of gifts as a response to an apt utterance by Od. This appears earlier in 8.385–445, where Od.'s praise for the Phaeacian dancers and his generally skilled diplomacy during the games leads Alcinous to demand gifts for him, and again shortly afterwards when Od. rewards Demodocus for his skill in narrating events at Troy (469–98; cf. 72–82 for the song). Later, Arete suggests gifts in admiration for Od.'s narrative in the 'intermezzo' in the tale of his wanderings (11.333–41; 333–4 = 13.1–2). In 14.508–12, Od.'s 'blameless tale' (508) of a Trojan exploit wins him a cloak; and in *H.Herm.* 437, Apollo declares the young Hermes' song worth fifty cows (this is reminiscent of the way early Indian and Celtic poets were rewarded with herds (cf. M. L. West 2007: 31)). It is hard not to see an element of self-reflexivity here, as Homer indicates discreetly how the best societies treat skilled speakers and narrators.

Though Alcinous graciously requests gifts to reward Od. for his narrative, his speech contains some troubling aspects, which suggest a somewhat arrogant attitude which will soon be picked up at the very end of the Phaeacian episode. His words have an element of troubling over-confidence which looks forward to Poseidon's anger later in the book. The phrase that he uses to describe his palace, χαλκοβατὲς δῶ 'bronze-based house', is elsewhere always used of Zeus's palace (8.321 and 4 × *Il.*). This use suggests a touch of arrogance, splendid though his house is; one might contrast Menelaus' demurral at Telemachus' suggestion that his palace rivals that of Zeus (4.71–9). Again, Alcinous speaks with risky confidence in suggesting that Od. will get back safely simply because he has come to his house (5–6); he seems to forget that it is Poseidon, not the Phaeacians, who rules the waves. There are troubling elements here which counterpoint the grand proceedings surrounding Od.'s departure. On this risky confidence, cf. further 165–87n.

1–2 The book begins in a striking manner. Od. stops his narration, and all sit in a magical silence as the torch-light casts shadows around the hall. The silence mediates the change from the excitement of Od.'s narration

of exotic adventures to the practicalities of getting him home. It may also
be imagined as having been observed, not just amongst Od.'s listeners in
the story but also amongst Homer's own audience: Virgil borrows the same
idea for the start of Aeneas' account of his wanderings: *Aen.* 2.1 *conticuere
omnes, intentique ora tenebant.*

1 οἱ δ'...σιωπῆι: this formula is used four times of the Phaeacians' reactions to Od. In addition to 11.333–4 mentioned above, it describes their
reactions to his arrival and speech of supplication to Arete (7.154), and to
his winning discus-throw and speech in the athletic competition (8.234).
Amazement accompanies Od.'s actions and utterances throughout his
time therefore: five of the seven occurrences of this (or a very similar)
formula in *Od.* involve Od.; it is also found of him in *Il.* 9.693. By contrast, on Ithaca, Od. avoids causing amazement, at least after the initial
surprise caused by his begging (17.367 ἐθάμβεον). On this phrase and its
varied use in the two epics, cf. Foley 1995; Kelly 2007: 85.   **ἄρα** 'as
you can imagine'. ἄρα can mark a natural result of an action or event:
cf. 33, and 8.326 where, after the gods see Ares and Aphrodite captured
in a compromising position in Hephaestus' nets, ἄσβεστος δ' ἄρ' ἐνῶρτο
γέλως 'as you might imagine, unquenchable laughter arose among them'.
ἀκὴν...σιωπῆι 'calmly in silence'. There is no tautology here: ἀκήν is
adverbial accusative of *ἀκή which appears originally to have denoted
'calm', cf. Hesych. α 2378 ἀκὴν ἦγες· ἡσυχίαν ἦγες; it may be connected
with words such as ἦκα 'gently, slowly'.   **ἀκὴν ἐγένοντο** is an example of
the use in epic of adverbs as predicates of verbs meaning 'to be': cf. *Il.*
6.130–1 οὐδὲ...δὴν ἦν 'he did not live long'; 9.551 Κουρήτεσσι κακῶς ἦν
'the Couretes had a hard time of it'. In these cases, εἶναι has its function as
a verb indicating existence rather than describing a quality (cf. *GH* II.9).

2 κηληθμῶι: the idea of song as 'enchantment' is a common one in Greek
literature. The charm can be of any kind, a simple delight, a medical cure
or a more sinister magical effect. There are innumerable examples: cf.
17.518–21 ὡς δ' ὅτ' ἀοιδὸς ἀνήρ...ὡς ἐμὲ κεῖνος ἔθελγε; 10.329 Od.'s ἀκήλητος
νόος, impervious to Circe's magic; 12.39–54 the Sirens' song; 14.387. Cf.
Walsh 1984; Finkelberg 1985–8; H. Parry 1992; Nünlist 1998: 126–34. On
the relationships between bard and audience in Homer, see Segal 1994:
113–41.   **ἔσχοντο:** middle in form, but passive in sense. In Homer, as in
a number of IE languages, the middle is used as a passive when, as here,
a state is described, especially one brought about by another person (*GH*
II.179–80; Introduction 5.3 §8.1.1).   **μέγαρα σκιόεντα:** the phrase is formulaic, appearing six times in *Od.* No doubt *megara* were in fact dark, being
lit only by torches and braziers (cf. 18.307, 354, 19.63–4), and smoky,
having but a single hole in the roof to let the smoke out, but here the
shadows are important in creating the effect of the scene. Similarly, this

formula is used three times (1.365, 4.768, 18.399) in the phrase μνηστῆρες
δ' ὁμάδησαν ἀνὰ μέγαρα σκιόεντα, of the Suitors reacting noisily to an event
that is unfortunate for them: there the shadows have a sinister quality;
here, the charm and unusualness of Od.'s story-telling creates a different but equally telling effect. In his *megara*, Homer preserves what looks
like a memory of the Mycenean palaces with their great halls, which were
the social centre and dining space of their owners. In Homer however, the
megaron seems to be used also for more everyday activities. Palaces were
not a feature of 8th-century Greek settlements as far as we know. Strictly,
μέγαρα in the plural indicates the palace in all its parts, μέγαρον the actual
hall, but this distinction is frequently blurred, not least for metrical convenience (cf. *GH.* 11.31, and 29–34 generally). On the *megaron*, a type of
construction also common in Near Eastern cultures, cf. Wace 1962: esp.
494; Knox 1973.

3 αὖτ(ε) 'in his turn'.   **ἀπαμείβετο φώνησέν τε:** lit. 'began his response
and said'. These two verbs are not synonymous, as is shown by the fact that
one is imperfect, the other aorist. (ἀπ)αμείβω means literally 'I act in my
turn'. The elements of this speech, orders to those present to go to sleep
and bring gifts, the safety of Od., sacrifice and return, are repeated from
Alcinous' first speech in 7.186–206; the repetition announces the coming
closure of the episode.

4 χαλκοβατές: presumably 'built on bronze'. The second element of the
adjective contains the root of βαίνω, but it is hard to find any parallels
concerning buildings among such adjectives (a list in Buck and Petersen
1944: 546): the adjectives tend to describe where or how someone or
something proceeds. Comparable however is *Il.* 4.2 χρυσέωι ἐν δαπέδωι
of Olympus. Essentially the word suggests something exotic and grandly
decorated. Such decoration is apparently unparalleled in eighth-century
Greece: bronze is found on Mycenean *tholos*-tombs, and two much later
bronze chambers in the Sicyonian treasuries at Olympia (Paus. 6.19.2, cf.
also 10.5.11). In Homer, bronze is found in both divine and the grander
forms of human architecture: Menelaus' palace displays χαλκοῦ στεροπήν
(4.72); Alcinous' has bronze(-clad?) walls and threshold, and gold and silver fittings (7.81–97); Zeus's palace is χαλκοβατές (8.321); Aeolus' palace
has a τεῖχος χάλκεον (10.3–4; also *Il.* 8.15; Hes. *Th.* 726); and Od.'s is
χαλκήϊον (18.328). Bronze is a feature of Near Eastern palaces, being
used to encase doors, columns and perhaps ceiling-beams: of his palace at
Calah, Ashurnasirpal II said 'I surrounded it with knobbed nails of bronze'
(Grayson 1976: 15 §619); in Nebuchadrezzar's palace, there were 'threshold, lintel and architraves...cast in bronze' (Wiseman 1985: 55; on the
possible Near Eastern influence on the depiction of palaces in Homer, cf.

Cook 2004, with 61 on bronze).   δῶ 'house'. The etymology is uncertain: it may be a long o-grade adverbial form connected with the adverb -δέ
'to' (cf. 17n. and the list in Risch 1974: 360); note the parallel use of both
ἡμέτερόνδε and ἡμέτερον δῶ (without a preposition) to mean 'to our house'.
Alternatively, it may be from a root noun *dōm connected with δόμος. Cf.
Beekes 362.

5–6 τῷ σ᾽ οὔ τι...ἂψ ἀπονοστήσειν 'for that reason, I think that you will
return home, without wandering back (in the direction you have come)':
i.e. 'because we will look after you, you will now get straight home, without
repeating your adventures' (so the scholia). οὐ grammatically negates ὀΐω
rather than παλίν πλαγχθέντα, in the same way that Greek negates the verb
of saying in οὔ φημι rather than the verb of the indirect speech as in English
('I say that...not...').

5 τῷ: the instrumental or ablative case of ὅς used adverbially; it picks up
ἐπεί. For the spelling and accent of this word variously rendered τώ, τῶ and
τῶι in the MSS, cf. M. L. West 1998: xxii.   **πάλιν πλαγχθέντα:** some take
πάλιν πλαγχθέντα as referring to return to Scherie, which is possible, but
'since you have come to my house, you will not come back again' makes
less good logical sense. εἰ καὶ μάλα πολλὰ πέπονθας also supports the idea
that Alcinous means he will not repeat his wanderings: the perfect indicates that they are over now, and the phrase echoes the opening of the
epic (1.1–2, 4). The uncompounded form is preferable, since there are
no other cases of compound verbs with πάλιν in Homer, and not many
after him.

7 ὑμέων: according to Alcinous in 8.390–1, 'twelve distinguished *basileis*
rule amongst the people, and I am the thirteenth' (*basileus* here, as regularly, means a local chieftain rather than a king). Alcinous rules therefore
as a kind of *primus inter pares* with this council of advisers (cf. 12 βουληφόροι,
186 ἡγήτορες ἠδὲ μέδοντες, and 8.1–17). His power ultimately rests upon
the acquiescence of the others: he may give commands (7 ἐφιέμενος τάδε
εἴρω), but he has to justify those commands by reference to his generosity to them (cf. 8n.). For this constitutional arrangement, cf. the γέροντες
in the Ithacan assembly who sit around the seat of Od. (2.14) and who
have not met since he left (2.26–7); and perhaps the old ἡγήτορες found
with Priam on the walls at Troy (*Il.* 3.146–53). For a useful survey of such
Homeric elites, see Raaflaub 1997: 633–4, 641–5.   **εἴρω** 'I bid', < the
IE root *uerh₁- (cf. Lat. *verbum*; Eng. *word*), whose derivatives in Greek and
other IE languages can have a formal, religious or juridical overtone: cf.
ῥήτρα 'spoken agreement, law' (as 14.393), ἄρρητος 'not to be spoken,
secret', and so 'numinous, sacred' (Beekes 393). This would lend authority to Alcinous' words, which are a formal and serious request: cf. 2.162

μάλιστα πιφαυσκόμενος τάδε εἴρω (Halitherses solemnly warns the Suitors that an omen portends Od.'s return), and 11.137 τὰ δέ τοι νημερτέα εἴρω (Teiresias ends his great prophecy to Od.).

8 γερούσιον αἴθοπα οἶνον: γερούσιος is 'reserved for the elders or chiefs' (cf. the Spartan *Gerousia*, the Council of Elders). The same half line appears in *Il.* 4.259, where Agamemnon similarly uses the fact that Diomedes is always kept supplied with wine to encourage him to get ready for battle. Compare too 4.343–8, where he contrasts Menestheus' and Od.'s readiness to be first at his feasts with their apparent shirking in the battle. There is also a γερούσιος ὅρκος referred to by Hector in *Il.* 22.119. Oaths and drinking together unite the group of *gerontes*, and impose obligations on the recipients.   **αἴθοπα:** used of wine and bronze in Homer, and derived from αἴθω, 'burn, flash'. When it is applied to wine it presumably refers to the reflection of light from the wine, so 'sparkling' (though not in the sense of 'fizzy'), 'glinting'; see on this and similar words Beekes 1995–6: esp. 16.

9 αἰεί 'regularly, repeatedly'; cf. 14.105 αἰεί... ἐπ' ἤματι 'regularly every day', and 7.99 where the Phaeacians are said to enjoy ἐπηετανόν lit. 'annual', and so 'abundant', eating and drinking.   **ἀκουάζεσθε** 'take delight in hearing, listen attentively to', a more expressive form of ἀκούω; cf. *H. Herm.* 422–3 ἵμερος ᾕρει... θυμὸν ἀκουάζοντα, of Apollo captivated by the lyre. For this intensive force of the suffix -άζω, cf. e.g. οἰνοποτέω : οἰνοποτάζω, and perhaps 277 ἀεκαζομένους.   **ἀοιδοῦ:** along with wine and food, a good host would also provide suitable entertainment, as is shown by the important role given in *Od.* to the singers Demodocus in Scherie and Phemius in Ithaca.

10 μὲν δή here strengthens the contrast between this clause and 13 ἀλλ' ἄγ'... (*GP* 257–9): 'the clothes, it is true,... but come now...'; more generosity is needed because Od. has entertained them more since the clothes etc. were originally given at Arete's behest (1–15n).

12 δῶρ': it is not entirely clear which gifts are referred to here, but gifts are ordered for Od. at 8.387–420 and 11.336–41. Gifts on departure are a standard gesture acknowledging the importance of the receiver: 3.349–55, 4.50, 8.455, 10.451, 14.132, 152–5, 395–6, 515–17 = 15.337–9, 16.78–80, 17.549–50, 556–8, 21.338–41, 23.155; Block 1985. On the Phaeacian gifts, cf. Scheid-Tissinier 1994: 170–7.   **Φαιήκων:** it has been suggested that this name is connected with φαιός 'grey, blackish', via φαικός 'bright', possibly a variant of φαιός influenced by another colour term λευκός (cf. Beekes 1547). The difference in meaning between the two adjectives makes this problematic, and why the Phaeacians should be 'grey' or the like is not clear from *Od.*

13 τρίποδα μέγαν ἠδὲ λέβητα: *lebetes* were shallow bowls placed on a tripod over the fire, and used for cooking meat (*Il.* 21.361–5) or washing hands and feet (*Od.* 1.136–8, 19.386–8). They were regularly given as prizes or marks of honour: the list of gifts Agamemnon is prepared to give Achilles to return to the fighting is headed by tripods, gold, *lebetes* and champion horses (*Il.* 9.122–4). Achilles brings out similar prizes for the funeral games for Patroclus: a woman and a tripod are first prize in the first competition, the chariot race (*Il.* 23.259–65); in Hes. *Op.* 656–9 Hesiod wins a tripod in a poetic competition. As worked metal objects, bowls and tripods were both useful and valuable.

14 ἀνδρακάς 'individually, each man in turn', = κατ' ἄνδρα. The word is found only here and in Aes. *Ag.* 1595.

14–15 ἀγειρόμενοι ... τεισόμεθ' 'we in turn shall indemnify ourselves, making a collection from the people'; the middle of τίνω 'repay' usually means 'avenge oneself on', but 'repay oneself' would be a basic meaning. The remark may seem at first sight to suggest an oppressive attitude to the demos by the nobles, particularly given Alcinous' point in the next line: it could be another hint that Scherie is not as ideal a society as it may seem (cf. 1–15, 165–87nn.). However, matters may be more complicated and less unattractive. Elsewhere there are cases where the demos does provide for the leaders: the Greek commanders drink δήμια 'at public expense' (*Il.* 17.248–51), Hector acknowledges the burden on the people of contributing to the war-effort (*Il.* 17.225–6), and Od. tells how, to entertain Idomeneus and his men, 'I collected barley and sparkling wine from the people (δημόθεν)' (*Od.* 19.197). In 21.16–17, we learn of a 'debt' that was owed to Od. by the 'whole demos' of Messene, because of the theft of his family's cattle. In 22.55–7, Eurymachus promises the Suitors will compensate Od., if he does not kill them, 'making amends κατὰ δῆμον' (though the meaning here is disputed); later Od. says the Achaeans will recompense him for the loss of his flocks eaten by the Suitors (23.356–8, cf. also 2.74–8). For passages distinguishing demos and political elite, see *LfgrE* s.v. δῆμος в 1f. These 'taxes' are clearly levied for special reasons, and in our case and 19.197 they enable the demos to be associated with the entertainment of a notable guest. Od. seems to acknowledge their role in his prayer that no κακὸν μεταδήμιον will befall the Phaeacians (46; cf. 62–3). Furthermore, wealth given to the *basileis* may well return to the demos in the form of public sacrifices and the accompanying feasting, rewards, prizes etc.: for a more extreme case of this, cf. *Il.* 18.300–2. However, if such exactions became excessive, then those imposing them could qualify for the epithets δημοβόρος 'people-devouring' (*Il.* 1.231) or δωροφάγος 'gift-eating' (Hes. *Op.* 39). See Donlan 1982: esp. 163–7, and the differing views of Donlan 1997: 661–3 and Thalmann 1998: 297–8.

15 ἀργαλέον…χαρίσασθαι 'because it is problematic for an individual to do a favour at a cost to himself', i.e. to look for no reward except thanks. χαρίζομαι means to do and acquire favour, to enter a arrangement of reciprocal benefits with a friend. The idea is that the kindnesses done by each side will normally even themselves out, but in this case Od. will not be able to repay the nobles, so they must look elsewhere.   **προικός:** προίξ 'gift' is cognate with words meaning 'to stretch out a hand' and so 'to give or take a gift' (Beekes 1236); προικός here means literally 'as a gift', a genitive of price, i.e 'at his own cost' or 'without reimbursement'.

16–62 Sacrifice and prayers for mutual prosperity

This scene provides the climax of Od.'s time in Scherie. His narratives have moved him from a shipwrecked nobody to a man of the highest 'heroic' qualities, which has encouraged the Phaeacians to offer him their highly privileged and magical help in returning home. He expresses an appropriate gratitude and wishes them the same kind of future prosperity that he hopes for himself. Sacrifice and prayers and the provision of food etc. to a departing honoured guest recur in the case of Telemachus on Pylos (3.418–86) and at Sparta (15.92–159), where they similarly mark his movement from the status of a rather timid youth to that of a man fit to stand by his father in battle.

The symmetrical structure of this passage is (i) gifts taken to the ships; (ii) sacrifice; (iii) Od.'s gracious words to Alcinous; (iv) libation; (v) Od.'s gracious words to Arete; (vi) gifts taken to the ships. A sacrificial feast provides the setting for Od.'s departure. Sacrifice and libations were a regular accompaniment to the start of a journey, as a means of seeking the gods' favour on the way. Greene 1995 points out how in *Od.* departures without offerings to the gods end in disaster: contrast this successful departure and that in 14.248–54 with the disastrous one in 14.293–309. The Phaeacians sacrifice to Zeus alone, but given Poseidon's potential anger the absence of any attempt to placate him is noteworthy.

16 ἐπιήνδανε 'pleased'; 3rd p.s. imperfect active of ἐπι-ανδάνω. The root of the verb is *swād-* (cf. Lat. *suauis*; Eng. *sweet*), here with the two nasal infixes in the present stem (cf. μανθάνω ἔμαθον).   **μῦθος:** in Homer, this word almost always refers to an authoritative utterance; cf. Martin 1989: 10–26; Lincoln 1999: 12–18.

17 κακκείοντες 'in order to go to bed', for κατα- by apocope (Introduction 5.3 §7.5.3); κείω is a future or desiderative of κεῖμαι.   **οἴκόνδε** 'to their home(s)'; -δε is a local deictic postposition, cognate with Eng. *to* and seen again in 19 νῆάδε 'to the ship', ὅ-δε, Lat. *in-de* (Beekes 307). The MSS sometimes have it as a free-standing form, sometimes attached to its noun.

18 ἦμος δ'... Ἡώς: dawns introduced by this formula tend to be significant less for their simple temporal indications than for the way they articulate the narrative; this dawn marks the start of the next episode after Od.'s long narration which began at 8.1. This phrase is a standard one for dawn: Homer uses unique expressions for dawns of especial significance (cf. 93n.).   **ἦμος** 'always connects a recurring point in cyclical time to a specific moment in the linear narrative' (Radin 1988: 293).   **ἠριγένεια** 'which comes early'. ἦρι is probably the locative *ἦερι from the root of ἠώς; cf. also the name Ἠερί-βοια and ἠέριος 'early', 'in the morning', as in 9.52, describing the Cicones when they attack (Beekes 525).   **ῥοδοδάκτυλος:** 'the "rose" part is probably a Greek refinement, but the spread hand as an image of the sun's rays may be inherited from older poetic tradition' (M. L. West 2007: 220). West notes the epithets 'with good fingers' and 'golden-handed' of the Vedic Sun-god Savitṛ, and the gold rings on the fingers of the Sun in a Latvian song.

19 νῆάδ': for -δε, cf. 17n.   **εὐήνορα** 'that makes men strong', as in 4.622 οἶνον; lit. 'with good, strong men' (Leumann 1950: 110 n. 73).

20 τά: i.e. the gifts. It is striking that the king himself stows the gifts personally (so the scholiasts); by contrast, for instance, it is Nestor's housekeeper who packs Telemachus' chariot (3.479–80). However, as Eustathius suggests (2.37.11–13), this is perhaps an index of the status that Od. has now reached: he compares the way that Aeolus himself tied up the bag of winds (10.20); compare too how Nestor escorts Telemachus and Peisistratus to bed (3.397–401).   **ἱερὸν μένος** has a counterpart in the Sanskrit phrase *iṣiréṇa mánasā* 'with strong spirit' (Rig-Veda 8.48.7; cf. M. L. West 2007: 89 for bibliography). That Skt. *iṣirá-* is used of divine power would help to explain how ἱερός in Greek can be used to mean both 'strong' and 'sacred' (see in general Beekes 580–1). Thus 'ἱερὸν μένος Ἀλκινόοιο from a diachronic point of view effectively means "the strong mind of Strong (ἀλκι-) Mind (νόος)"' (Katz 2010: 360). The phrase is also appropriate to introduce a scene of sacrifice. Periphrases such as ἱερὸν μένος Ἀλκινόοιο are a feature of Homeric style: cf. 2.409 ἱερὴ ἲς Τηλεμάχοιο, *Il.* 2.851 Πυλαιμένεος λάσιον κῆρ, 3.105 Πριάμοιο βίην, 11.690 βίη Ἡρακληείη.

21 ἰών: masculine referring to Alcinous, despite the neuter ἱερὸν μένος, as in 11.90–1 ἦλθε δ' ἐπὶ ψυχὴ Θηβαίου Τειρεσίαο | χρύσεον σκῆπτρον ἔχων, though the use of αὐτός in our passage eases the use of the masculine.   **ὑπὸ ζυγά:** with κατέθηχ'. The ζυγά were cross-beams which joined the two sides of the vessel and served as seats (Mark 2005: 118–19).

22 βλάπτοι 'get in the way of'; the subject is τά (20).

23 εἰς Ἀλκινόοιο: cf. εἰς Ἀΐδαο, ἐν Ἀλκινόοιο etc. The genitive here is a partitive, with which ἐν and εἰς were associated in words like ἐμ-ποδών 'under foot, in the way'. The traditional explanation, that e.g. δῶμα is to be understood, founders on passages like 4.581–2 εἰς Αἰγύπτοιο διιπετέος ποταμοῖο | στῆσα νέας 'I brought my ships to the swift-flowing river Aegyptus' (cf. *GH* II.104–5).

25 κελαινεφέϊ 'of the black cloud', abbreviated from *κελαινο-νεφής, a suitable aspect of Zeus to appeal to before a sea-voyage. The only other appearance of this line in *Od.* is, ironically, 9.552, where Zeus refuses Od.'s sacrifice before his departure from the island of the Cattle of the Sun, because he has the destruction of his men and ships in mind.

26 μῆρα 'thigh-bones'. These were cut out of the meat, covered in fat and burnt for the gods (cf. the description in 3.456–60; 14.427–8n.). The aetiological myth explaining why the gods got the inedible parts of the animal while men enjoyed the meat (contrast e.g. the Jewish practice of holocaust) is given in Hes. *Th.* 535–69, where Prometheus tricks Zeus into accepting the bones as the gods' portion.   **δαίνυντ(ο)...δαῖτα:** a 'cognate' accusative, where the verb and its object share the same root; cf. 50 κρητῆρα κερασσάμενος, 1.291 κτέρεα κτερεῖξαι; Introduction 5.3 §7.2.4.2.

27 θεῖος ἀοιδός: the importance of the poet in *Od.* is marked by this laudatory epithet, which is used twelve times (cf. also 17.385 θέσπιν ἀοιδόν). In *Il.*, where the figure of the poet is less prominent, this formula appears only in 18.604. Eustathius (2.37.16–17) ascribes the brevity of the description of this sacrifice and the lack of indication as to what Demodocus sang to the fact that the narrative shares Od.'s enthusiasm that night would come.

28 λαοῖσι τετιμένος 'honoured by the people' is essentially a translation of Demodocus' name (< δῆμος + δέχομαι); λαοῖσι is a dative of the agent, as regularly with perfect passive participles. For such 'translations', cf. e.g. 111 and 14.161nn., 3.383 (βοῦν) ἀδμήτην, ἥν οὔ πω ὑπὸ ζυγὸν ἤγαγεν ἀνήρ 'an untamed ox, that no man had yet brought under the yoke'. The element *demo-* in this name, and the facts that in *Od.* poets sing under compulsion (1.154), are ordered around (1.325–59) and even find themselves abandoned on deserted islands (3.267–71), may suggest that, in contradistinction to the picture of Demodocus as an honoured court poet, eighth-century poets led a more peripatetic existence, with ordinary people as much as aristocrats as their audiences (cf. P. W. Rose 1992: 112–19). In 17.383–5, poets are listed, alongside seers, doctors and craftsmen, amongst the δημιοεργοί 'public workers'.

28–35 Simile of the ploughman. This picture of Odysseus looking away and willing the sun to go down amid the celebrations of the others present

is a moving moment: he is in this paradisiacal place, with wondrous entertainment, but as always home is what matters to him. He is compared to
a ploughman toiling in the fields and longing for his supper, in a simile
which works as much by the 'dissonances' between 'vehicle' (the simile)
and 'tenor' (the thing that is being compared) as by the similarities. The
ploughman is obviously a poor man who has to work, Od. is surrounded
by treasure; the ploughman is hungry for his dinner, Od. is amid plenty;
the ploughman toils in a fallow field, Od. is at ease in luxury; the ploughman's journey home is short but painful, Od.'s will be quick and painless.
However, just as for the ploughman there will be another day of toil on the
morrow, so for Od. his homecoming will merely be the prelude to another
half-epic of toil. For other similes of this kind, cf. 14.308–9 and n., and the
comparison of stones clattering on shields to snow quietly blanketing the
world in *Il.* 12.278–89. On the 'spectrum' of similarity in Homeric comparisons, cf. Ready 2008.

Homer thus gives a twist to the motif of time being taken up in collecting gifts to honour a departing guest. This motif is also found in Near
Eastern culture where, as here, retaining a visitor in order that a suitable body of gifts could be collected was not a fault of hospitality but a
mark of special respect (Bryce 2003: 68). Similarly, a separate day is given
to the preparations for Telemachus' departures from Pylos (3.404–87)
and Sparta (15.1–188). Here however the extra day is the cause less of
delight at being honoured than frustration at the delay (cf. Introduction
p. 2 n. 8).

29 πολλά 'many times, often': Homer regularly uses the accusative neuter,
singular and plural, of adjectives as adverbs (cf. *GH* II.44–5).

30 ἐπειγόμενος: middle, because Od. wills the sun to set in his own interest,
cf. 2.97 (Penelope to the Suitors) μίμνετ' ἐπειγόμενοι τὸν ἐμὸν γάμον, 'stop
encouraging me to marry one of you'.   **δὴ γὰρ μενέαινε** 'because he was
very keen'. In expressions of this kind, δή emphasises the verb: cf. e.g.
10.160 (a stag comes to the river to drink) δὴ γάρ μιν ἔχεν μένος ἠελίοιο
'because the power of the sun was greatly oppressing him', 14.282 ἱέμενοι
κτεῖναι, δὴ γὰρ κεχολώατο λίην 'wanting to kill me, because they were very
angry'.

31 δόρποιο: this is usually the evening meal; cf. Aes. fr. 304 which lists the
day's meals as ἄριστα, δεῖπνα, δόρπα τε. Homer does not always maintain
such distinctions: cf. 20.390–2, where δεῖπνον and δόρπον are used of the
same meal. See however Russo, *CHO* on 21.428–30 for a general consistency of usage.   **λιλαίεται** can express a very strong desire for something,
as in Calypso's passion for Od. in 1.15 λιλαιομένη πόσιν εἶναι 'longing for
him to be her husband'. It thus corresponds to δή … μενέαινε of Od.

31–2 ὧι τε ... ἄροτρον 'for whom all day up and down the fallow field his two dark oxen drag his jointed plough'. ἕλκητον is the 3rd person dual of the present subjunctive: the subjunctive is very common in Homer in generalising relative clauses, particularly in comparisons and those involving ὅς τε as here (cf. *GH* II.245–6; Intro 5.3 §11.8.1).

31 πανῆμαρ 'all day long', only here in Greek until much later, though cf. Homeric αὖθ-, ἐνν-, ἐξῆμαρ; it is an adverbial accusative.

32 νειόν 'fallow land', i.e. 'land...which has been left out of cultivation in order that it may recuperate' (Gow on Theoc. 25.25). νειός is probably cognate with words like νέατος 'lowest', νειόθεν 'from below', and so would mean 'low-lying land' (Beekes 1002–3). Ploughing such land, compacted by rain and filled with weeds, would be especially burdensome. Once ploughed, νειός becomes fertile, hence passages like *Il.* 18.541 νειόν μαλάκην, πίειραν ἄρουραν, εὐρεῖαν τρίπολον 'the soft *neios*, fertile ploughland, broad and thrice ploughed', and 10.353 νειοῖο βαθείης.   βόε: the dual, which was gradually lost in all dialects, is sparingly used in Homer, even for things that make natural pairs, such as hands or eyes; the plural is almost always more common (cf. 372n.; *GH* II.24).   οἴνοπε: οἶνοψ is usually an epithet of the sea. Its meaning was uncertain in antiquity (cf. D schol. *Il.* 13.703 οἴνοπε· ἤτοι μέλανες ἢ ξανθοί), and continues so (bibliography in *LfgrE* s.v.). *wo-no-qo-so* (ϝοῖνοψ) and other epithets such as αἰόλος, κελαινός seem to be the names of cattle on a group of Mycenean tablets (KN Ch (see Killen and Olivier 1989: 50–2); cf. Ventris and Chadwick 1973: 105, and 213 for KN Ch 896). Risch 1992 suggested αἰόλος may have been a word once in ordinary speech which later became part of the poetic register. The dual (see last note), and the hiatus preserving the effect of the original digamma, together suggest that βόε οἴνοπε had a long pedigree. πηκτόν 'jointed'. This is a manufactured plough, more complex than the one-piece ἄροτρον αὐτόγυον with a natural plough-share growing out of the stock; Hes. *Op.* 432–4 recommends having both types. Cf. Gow 1914.

33 κατέδυ: this aorist (of καταδύνω), used amongst the present tenses in the simile, is a timeless or 'gnomic' aorist describing things that are generally true or happen regularly (cf. 173n.; Introduction 5.3 §9.2.1). The sun sets in the course of the simile, and when we return to the narrative, it finally sets for Od.: thus, as time passes in the simile, so it does in the narrative, and Homer can in an ellipse pass over naturally the long period during which Od. waited for the blazing sun to go down. On sunsets in *Od.*, cf. 14.457n.

34 δόρπον ἐποίχεσθαι 'so that he could go to dinner'. The infinitive expresses the basic idea of the verb, and in Homer is used with very great flexibility, frequently as here with the sense of purpose; cf. 65 ἡγεῖσθαι, and

307n. βλάβεται δέ τε γούνατ᾽ ἰόντι 'his knees are in pain as he goes'. The ploughman is finally free, but the pain in his knees remains, because the plough had to be kept constantly pressed into the earth: osteo-arthritis is a major problem in traditional agricultural societies. When Hesiod recommends that workers be allowed to rest after the harvest, it is their knees to which he makes specific reference (*Op.* 608). The knees are regularly associated with vigour: cf. 23.3 (of Eurycleia rejuvenated by the news that Od. has come) γούνατα δ᾽ ἐρρώσαντο, *Il.* 4.313–16, 19.166; Hes. *Op.* 587; and for a cross-cultural (if rather speculative) study of knees, vigour and procreation, Onians 1951: 174–86. βλάβεται is a possibly more recent form of the present than the usual βλάπτομαι, being found only here and *Il.* 19.82 and 166 in Homer (*GH* 1.311, but cf. Shipp 1972: 84).

36–45 Od. makes a double prayer: like that in 59–62, this speech balances wishes for happiness for himself and for prosperity for the Phaeacians. There is a chiastic ABBA pattern, weaving together wishes for divine help and prosperity and wishes concerning wives and friends/children. His prayers for the prosperity of the Phaeacians and his own return recall his first words in the palace at 7.146–52: the sentiments are similar, but the language different. There is of course irony in the wishes, given what is about to happen. For this kind of framing of the narration, cf. 49, 78, 88–92, 14.23nn. Such farewell speeches are naturally often in pairs: 5.203–24, 8.461–8, 15.151–9; de Jong 2001: 211.

36–7 This juxtaposition of two speech introductions is unique; 'the first addresses Odysseus' speech to the Phaeacians at large and the second directs it especially to Alcinoüs' (M. W. Edwards 1970: 31).

36 φιληρέτμοισι is a regular epithet of the Phaeacians but appropriate here, given the forthcoming sea-journey.

37 πιφαυσκόμενος 'making his position clear'. The root of this verb is *φαϝ- (as in φάος), and the basic meaning is 'bring to light'; it thus comes to mean 'reveal, expound', and in the middle 'make oneself clear'. The same root lies behind φημί.

38 This line is elsewhere used in *Od.* when Od. or another is acknowledging either Alcinous' authority in giving a command or the justness of his words (8.382, 401, 9.2, 11.355, 378). Its use here not in response to anything the king has said is perhaps another way in which Od.'s new status, cemented by the tale of his wanderings, is marked: he speaks as an equal, not as one acquiescing in the king's wishes.   κρεῖον: vocative, < *κρείοντ. The vocative of third-declension nouns was originally simply the stem, e.g. ὦ πόλι; where the stem had a final stop or stops, these were lost in Greek, as in γέρον < *γέροντ, γύναι < *γυναίκ, ἄνα < *(ϝ)άνακτ, etc.

ἀριδείκετε: lit. 'much pointed out', so 'famous', from *deik- 'show' (Beekes 309).   λαῶν: for the meaning of this word in Homer, cf. Haubold 2000: esp. 100–44.

39 πέμπετέ με 'escort me home', cf. 41 πομπή.   ἀπήμονα: proleptic in sense, 'so that I (get home) unharmed'. There is a similar wish expressed by Eum.'s wicked nurse at 15.436 ἀπήμονά μ' οἴκαδ' ἀπάξειν, but she does not get home.

40 φίλος in Homer is often no more than a possessive adjective ('his', 'mine' etc.), with no sense of affection involved; this may be the original meaning, though the etymology is unknown (cf. Beekes 1573–4; and the differing views of Hooker 1987 and Robinson 1990).

41 πομπὴ καὶ φίλα δῶρα: getting home is not enough for Od.; he is keen to arrive back with great wealth to enhance his status, as he should have done after Troy was sacked. For the expression and the importance of goods to Od., cf. 11.355–61, where he says that abundance of treasure will make him αἰδοιότερος καὶ φίλτερος ἀνδράσιν, and 19.413, where one reason Od. visits Autolycus is to get gifts; also 9.229, 18.281–2. They were equally important to Menelaus (4.90–1, 15.80–5), and Zeus himself ensures that Od. will have gifts to return with (5.36–40). Apart from trade, which was not an aristocratic activity, gifts or plunder were the only means of gaining wealth, as Od. points out in 23.357–8. Od. has lost the booty of his earlier exploits and is now in no position to recoup it by plunder. Poseidon's anger at Od.'s imminent return is not so much the result of that return but of the fact that he is coming home with more fine gifts than he could ever have got at Troy (134–8).

42 ὄλβια ποιήσειαν: the gods naturally look askance at mortals who are too prosperous and fortunate, which Od. acknowledges by his prayer that the gifts may be fortunate for him; there is a similar sentiment in Solon, fr. 13.7–13. It is however precisely these gifts which annoy Poseidon.

42–3 ἀμύμονα … φίλοισιν 'and may I find that my wife at home is blameless and my friends safe and sound'; the adjectives are predicative, cf. 15.15 πεμπέμεν, ὄφρ' ἔτι οἴκοι ἄμυμονα μητέρα τέτμῃς. Since antiquity, ἀμύμων has been taken to be a compound of ἀ + μῶμος 'without fault', a meaning which suits this and many other contexts, but which is singularly inappropriate when applied to Aegisthus (1.29) or the Suitor Antilochus (4.187). Heubeck 1987 sees a connection with ἀμεύσασθαι 'surpass' (and ἀμύνω) and translates 'who victoriously defeats his enemy'. For an extended treatment of the use of the word, cf. A. A. Parry 1973.

43 ἀρτεμέεσσι 'in good health', a rare word of unknown etymology, only here in Od. (also Il. 5.515, 7.308).

45 ἀρετήν: here 'prosperity, success'; cf. in a verbal form 8.329 οὐκ ἀρετᾶι κακὰ ἔργα 'bad deeds do not prosper', 19.114 ἀρετῶσι δὲ λαοί.

46 μεταδήμιον: on the role of the demos in the giving of gifts to Od., cf. 14–15n. The epithet is found only here and 8.293 in Homer, and is very rare elsewhere.

48 κατὰ μοῖραν ἔειπε: a common formula. Speeches are often judged thus by their appropriateness, cf. e.g. 14.509 οὐδέ τί πω κατὰ μοῖραν, and the similar 8.489, 14.363 (οὐ) κατὰ κόσμον said by Od. of Demodocus, and of Od. by Eum. Od. is generally a master at achieving the right tone when he speaks publicly to the Phaeacian nobility, which makes them happy to grant his requests or to honour him: cf. 7.226–7, 8.236–7, 381–7, 408–11; also 17.580, 20.350–2.

49 κήρυκα: perhaps best translated 'steward'. The κήρυκες performed a number of different functions, such as convening and controlling the assembly, attending at trials and sacrifices, bearing important diplomatic messages and so on. They were often of high status, though the fact that in 19.135 Penelope lists them with strangers and suppliants as δημιοεργοί suggests that there were different classes of κῆρυξ. See in general Adcock and Mosley 1975: 152–4. That Pontonous has an aristocratic name linked to the sea, like many of the Phaeacians (cf. the list in 8.111–20), shows that he is no mere menial servant. He frames Od.'s time in the palace: he was ordered to mix a *krater* when Od. was first welcomed in, and now mixes one as he leaves (7.178–83 ≈ 49–54; cf. 8.62–70 for his attendance on Demodocus).

50 κρητῆρα κερασσάμενος 'having mixed a mixing-bowl', a cognate accusative (cf. 26n.); κερασσάμενος is aorist middle participle of κεράννυμι. The Greeks always mixed wine with water in varying proportions, reducing its strength so that it could sensibly form the basis of extended drinking. Unmixed wine was the preserve of the gods, especially Dionysus, and barbarians. The custom of diluting wine seems to go back at least into Mycenean times: cf. *ka-ra-te-ra* MY Ue 611 (Ventris and Chadwick 1973: 233–4, no. 234). **μέθυ:** sometimes unmixed wine, but here the mixed form. In IE, the word originally meant 'honey, intoxicating drink', like 'mead' (from the same root). The word was transferred in Greek to wine; note μέθυ ἡδύ in Homer, and perhaps μελίφρονα οἶνον (53).

51 ἀνὰ μέγαρον, ὄφρ': for the scansion here, cf. Introduction p. 28.

52 πατρίδα γαῖαν: this is a very common formula, but the epithet indicates the importance of continuity in a family's (and especially a noble family's) tenure of its land; cf. 14.64n. It is not just a cliché therefore.

54 ἐπισταδόν possibly 'standing by each in turn'; for the idea of 'in turn', cf. 12.392 νείκεον ἄλλοθεν ἄλλον ἐπισταδόν, of Od.'s men quarrelling. Alternatively, it could mean 'expertly'. That the meaning of the word could fluctuate between the spheres of ἐφίσταμαι/ἐπίσταμαι 'stand before'/'understand' is suggested by 16.453 δόρπον ἐπισταδὸν ὁπλίζοντο, where the scholiasts translate ἐπισταδόν as ἐπιστημόνως 'expertly', as 12.307 δόρπον ἐπισταμένως τετύκοντο; cf. Beekes 445.

56 αὐτόθεν ἐξ ἑδρέων = ἐξ αὐτῶν τῶν ἑδρῶν; cf. 21.420 αὐτόθεν ἐκ δίφροιο. At 3.341, people stand to pour a libation, the difference probably being simply that there the sacrifice is still taking place and each man stands to go and pour a libation onto the tongues on the altar, whereas here they are sitting drinking after the sacrifice and feasting.   **ἀνὰ δ᾽ ἵστατο:** on this so-called 'tmesis', cf. Introduction 5.3 §7.5.1.

57 χερσί: the MSS fluctuate between singular and plural in such expressions, but the preponderance is the plural; cf. 3.51, 443, 15.120.   **δέπας** 'beaker, drinking cup', possibly a word borrowed from an Anatolian language (cf. Hieroglyphic Luwian *tipas*- 'heaven'; Beekes 317 (heaven is conceived as a vessel over the earth)). In Mycenean, *di-pa* is given the ideogram of a large bowl, but in Homer it is always a normal drinking-cup, except in the case of Nestor's cup in *Il.* 11.632–7.   **ἀμφικύπελλον** 'with a cup on either side', i.e. a vessel formed of two cups joined at the rim, of the kind found from Mycenean contexts (so also Aristotle, *HA* 624a, though he was working by popular etymology). In Troy II, which was originally but erroneously thought to be Homer's Troy, the discovery of slender cups with pairs of large handles rising from the base to two thirds of the way up the bowl led to a translation 'twin-handled' (so Aristarchus; cf. Ath. 482–3a; Hesych. α 4045). 'Depas amphikupellon' subsequently became a technical term in archaeology for this kind of cup, but etymologically this meaning is less likely; cf. Beekes 804. Cups of this kind are often used in Homer for formal gestures and special occasions, such as arrivals and departures, or as gifts or prizes: cf. 3.63, 8.89, 15.102, 120; *Il.* 23.219.

58 μιν (like ἔπεα) is governed by προσηύδα; φωνήσας is intransitive here. **ἔπεα πτερόεντα:** that words reach our ears by flight is an old IE idea (Nünlist 1998: 279–83; M. L. West 2007: 44–5). The use of the phrase here lacks some of the pregnant sense that it tends to have in *Il.*: cf. Kelly 2007: 143–8.

59–62 The pattern of this prayer is ABA, with prayers for Arete's and her people's happiness surrounding a reference to himself. The prayer is less grand than that to the king, as might be expected, and has a more personal and intimate tone.

60 τά τ' . . . πέλονται: lit. 'which go around amongst men', and so 'which are mankind's lot'. πέλομαι is cognate with words meaning 'turn, circulate' (cf. πόλος, ἀμφίπολος), whence it came to mean 'be involved in, find oneself amongst', and so 'become, be'. τά is an example of the neuter plural of relatives used with things which are viewed as a unit or group, cf. 14.73n.; *GH* II.21. For τά as a relative after nouns in other genders, cf. 409–10, 14.63, 226. τε is often used in a relative clause in epic to express what is always true: cf. 31–2n., 410; Ruijgh 1971: 358, 453–62.

61–2 This wish corresponds to that in 44–6 expressed to Alcinous; λαοῖσι again acknowledges the demos (cf. 14–15n., 46).

63–92 The journey to Ithaca

After a section where nearly half the lines were direct speech, straight narration now takes over for the voyage, on which Od., who has long been at the forefront of things with his tales and his final leading of the prayers, now becomes a silent figure borne magically home.

This section is in three parts, the last mirroring the first. A measured description of the preparations comes to a close with the quiet description of Od.'s sleep (79–80). This is then followed by a much more lively passage on the exceptionally fast speed of the ship, the pace changing suddenly in 81 where we are launched via an anacolouthon into the simile of the hurtling racing chariot (81–8). There is then another diminuendo which describes his sleep, summarising all that he has suffered in the epic so far (89–92).

There is something numinous about these preparations. It is night and Od. silently (σιγῇι, 76) prepares for sleep, which comes to him in its deepest form: it is so deep that he does not notice the speedy voyage and can be carried from the ship and placed on the shore without his waking (117–19). The sleep is 'closest to death' (80), and indeed his awakening after the night voyage will have something of a 'rebirth' about it, as he returns to a new life back in the world of human beings (cf. Segal 1967). That the journey takes place at night is also unusual: one might compare the voyage into the Underworld, which culminates at night (11.11–22). Greek ships, which had essentially no on-board accommodation, were usually beached for the night and the crews slept on the shore: as Eurylochus says (12.286–7), 'the winds that rise at night are problematic and destroy ships'. For the strategic use of night sailing, cf. 2.388–434 and 15.34 (Telemachus), 4.786 (Suitors), 5.270 (Od.'s skill at it).

Important journeys are often prefaced by a detailed description of the preparation of the tackle of the ship (cf. e.g. 2.414–29, 4.577–80, 780–5, 8.50–5, 11.1–5, 12.144–52, 15.282–95; de Jong 2001: 65–6). That this journey gets a unique treatment and not the standard motif is a further sign of its significance; the motif has anyway been used in the earlier preparations in 8.48–56. The unique sunrise in 93–4 also marks this episode as special.

This magical journey is the counterpart to the great two-day storm and nine days of 'destructive winds' which cast Od. and his men, so nearly home, into the world of monsters and the fantastic in the first place (9.67–84). The storm and the journey, both abnormal, serve to mark off the world of the fantastic from the world of men.

63–9 The procession to the ship becomes a formal πομπή, led by the king's herald (49n.) and involving the queen's attendants with her gifts. All of this marks Od.'s important status; for the 'accompaniment' motif as a marker of status, cf. Nagler 1974: 64–111.

63 ὑπὲρ οὐδὸν ἐβήσετο: this recalls his original arrival in the palace at 7.135 καρπαλίμως ὑπὲρ οὐδὸν ἐβήσετο. Crossing thresholds can have a symbolic significance, here marking Od.'s leaving of the fantasy world of the Phaeacians for good.   **ἐβήσετο:** one of a small number of aorists in epic that have the -s- of the sigmatic aorist but the thematic conjugation in -ε/ο- (contrast Att. ἐβήσατο); for a discussion of the forms, cf. *GH* 1.416–17.

66 δμωιάς: 'the most common way of referring to all kinds of dependent labourers in the poem, *dmōs* [and its feminine here] is a relatively neutral term ... used when slaves are viewed ... from the point of view of their function' (Thalmann 1998: 55, cf. 53–62 generally; also Mele 1968: 141–8; Gschnitzer 1976: 46–72).

67–9 τὴν μὲν ... τὴν δὲ ... ἡ δέ: despite the three particles, each pronoun here is in a different construction. The first is in apposition to δμωιάς; the second is (with χηλόν) the object of ὅπασσε, the subject of which is the queen; and the third is subject of its clause. There is a similar but more regular sequence in 10.352–9. Arete has already put such items into the chest at 8.441, which raises the essentially unanswerable (and not perhaps very involving) question whether these are different clothes, or whether Homer has forgotten the earlier passage. For a similar case, cf. 383–5n.

72 πόσιν καὶ βρῶσιν ἅπασαν stand in apposition to τά γ', though that in fact refers to all of Arete's gifts.

73 κὰδ δ' = κατὰ δέ, by apocope.

74 ἐπ' ἰκριόφιν 'on the deck'. The ἴκρια were the raised platforms or small decks in the bow and stern of a ship. Those in the stern seem to have been a place of honour (so Eustathius): it is there that Telemachus sits with Athena and with Theoclymenus (2.416–18, 15.285–6; Morrison and Williams 1968: 48). In mild weather, it would have been preferable to

being in the body of the ship, cramped by other sailors and dampened by
the bilge. -φι(ν) is a suffix, strictly a post-positional adverb, used in Homer
for all declensions, singular and plural, and with the force of a locative (as
here), ablatival genitive (as 14.134 ὀστέοφιν, 498 παρὰ ναῦφιν), dative (cf.
early Latin *ti-bei* = *tibi*), or instrumental (as 14.266 ἅμ' ἠοῖ φαινομένηφιν). It
is already present in Mycenean as a locative and instrumental ending. Its
very flexible use in epic is in part due to its usefulness in providing metrical variety or avoiding metrically impossible forms: ἰκρίοις for instance, as
a cretic (–◡–), would not fit the hexameter. Cf. *GH* 1.234–41; Shipp 1953:
1–17.   νήγρετον 'without waking', adverbial accusative, formed from a
combination of the negative prefix ν- (< n̥, whence also the negative suffix
ἀ-, Lat. *ne*) and ἐγρε- 'wake'.

75 πρυμνῆς 'in the stern'. This is most easily explained as a noun paratactically attached to νηός and functioning as an adverb; similar is 12.229–30
ἐπ' ἴκρια νηὸς ἔβαινον | πρώιρης 'they went onto the ship's decks in the prow'.
For the accent, cf. M. L. West 1998: xxi.   κατέλεκτο: 3rd p.s. athematic
aorist of καταλέχομαι 'lie down'.

77 κόσμωι along with σιγῆι (76) stresses the calm formality of this departure.

78 ἀνερρίπτουν ἅλα πηδῶι: this expression occurred when Alcinous first
promised to send Od. home (7.328), and returns at the moment the
promise is fulfilled. It appears only in these places in *Od.*

79 καί: 'apodotic', i.e. used apparently unnecessarily to join a subordinate
to a main clause (*GP* 308–9); cf. 144n. and Introduction 5.3 §12.3 on
the comparable apodotic δέ. καί used thus is mainly a feature of Homer
and lyric.   νήδυμος 'sweet' is a form of ἥδυμος, created by misdivision
of phrases like *Il.* 2.2 Δία δ' οὐκ ἔχεν ἥδυμος ὕπνος (*GH* 1.14; the same phenomenon gives us Eng. *an orange* from *a norange* (cf. Sp. *naranja*), and con-
versely *a newt* from *an ewt* (cf. Ger. *Eft*)). It is not therefore to be connected
with the negative ν- discussed in 74n. On the other hand, the synonymous
ἥδιστος in the subsequent line makes one wonder whether for Homer it
meant something else: Aristarchus derived it from νη- and δύω as = ἀνέκ-
δυτος 'inescapable'. For the repetition however, cf. e.g. *Il.* 15.237–8 ἴρηκι
ἐοικώς | ὠκέϊ φασσοφόνωι, ὅς τ' ὤκιστος πετεηνῶν.

80 θανάτωι ἄγχιστα ἐοικώς: such expressions emphasise the closeness
between vehicle and tenor, cf. 17.500 Ἀντίνοος δὲ μάλιστα μελαίνηι κηρὶ ἔοικε,
Il. 22.410 τῶιδε μάλιστ' ἄρ' ἔην ἐναλίγκιον. For the closeness of sleep and
death, cf. also *Il.* 16.672, where they are brothers; the comparison can
be reversed, as in *Il.* 11.241 κοιμήσατο χάλκεον ὕπνον 'he slept the bronze
sleep', of a warrior killed.

81–5 *Chariot simile.* The four-horse chariot was the fastest and most glamorous means of land transport the Greeks knew. It appears on monuments from the Late Geometric period onwards. A chariot-race is the first event in the Funeral Games for Patroclus, and it was also the grandest competition at the Olympic games. Its grandeur suits the nature of the escorted return given Od. by the Phaeacians. For the comparison of ships and horses, cf. 4.708–9 νηῶν...αἵ θ' ἁλὸς ἵπποι | ...γίγνονται; *Ep. Adesp.* 13W (*GEF* p. 292) ἡνίοχος νηὸς κυανοπρώιροιο 'charioteer of the dark-prowed ship'.

81 ἡ δ' (i.e. the ship) has no grammatical construction, as the horses to which it is compared take over as the subject of the sentence; it is picked up by 84 τῆς. Cf. 14.85–8n.   **τετράοροι** 'attached to a four-horse chariot', < τετρα- and ἀείρω 'attach'.

82 ὑπὸ πληγῇσιν: the basic meaning of ὑπό, 'under', gave rise to the meaning 'under the effect of' (*GH* II.140).

83 ὑψόσ' ἀειρόμενοι 'raising themselves up high', 'leaping upwards'. πρήσσουσι κέλευθον 'travel on their way'; cf. 9.491 ἅλα πρήσσοντες. This is a peculiarly epic use of πρήσσω (Attic πράσσω), and pre-dates the meaning 'strive to do, accomplish'. The root of the verb is πρᾱ-, related to the root of πείρω 'cross' (*per(h₂)-*), as in 91 κύματα πείρων, and πέρᾱ 'beyond' (Beekes 1229–30).

84 ὡς ἄρα τῆς...ἀείρετο: τῆς is 'its', i.e. the ship's. ἀείρετο is the third use of the root of ἀείρω in the passage.   **πρώιρη** 'prow' is Rochefort's change for the MSS' πρύμνη(ς) 'stern', which is impossible: any ship, however magical, which flies along with its stern in the air is heading nowhere but to the bottom. The rising of the prow corresponds to the rearing heads of the horses in a way that the rising of the stern would not. With the emendation, the first part of the line describes the rising prow, the second and 85 the waves churned up as the stern buries itself in the water. Perhaps πρυμνῆς in 75 played a part in the scribal error.

85 πορφύρεον 'foaming, seething' is probably to be connected with the verb πορφύρω 'seethe' (cf. Lat. *ferveo, fermentum*), not with πορφύρα 'purple dye'; cf. Pulleyn 2000 on *Il.* 1.482.

86 ἀσφαλέως θέεν ἔμπεδον: the two adverbs emphasise just how stable, despite the speed, this fabulous ship was. A modern reconstruction of the trireme, the main attacking Greek warship from the late-sixth century onwards, achieved a maximum of nine knots, well short of what we are to imagine here.

86–7 ἴρηξ | κίρκος: if Homer had a particular bird in mind, from the reference to its speed, it was most likely the peregrine falcon (cf. Arnott 2007: 66–8, 99 s.vv.). In phrases of this kind, the second word specifies the first: cf. βοῦς ταῦρος, σῦς σίαλος (cf. 14.41), σῦς κάπρος. Ships and birds are regularly associated: cf. M. L. West 1978 on Hes. *Op.* 628. The comparison of the ship's speed to a hawk 'assimilates it to the journeys made by the gods' (Saïd 2011: 182).

88–92 These touching lines set the seal on the first part of *Od.*, rounding off the narrative of *Od.*'s hardships on land and sea, and echoing the opening of the whole work: cf. 1.1–2 ἄνδρα … ὃς μάλα πολλὰ | πλάγχθη, 1.4 πολλὰ δ' ὅ γ' ἐν πόντωι πάθεν ἄλγεα ὃν κατὰ θυμόν. The irony is that we know that it may be the end of one set of troubles, but it is also the start of another.

89 θεοῖσ' ἐναλίγκια μήδε' ἔχοντα 'with an intelligence like (the intelligence of) the gods'; Greek regularly abbreviates such comparisons in this way. **μήδε':** possibly cognate with μῆτις, μέδομαι, words representing ideas of 'thought, control, cleverness' (Beekes 941), which are central to *Od.*'s and his family's success.

90 πρὶν μέν 'in the past, it is true'. πρίν is adverbial, and the phrase contrasts with δὴ τότε γ' in 92.

92 δὴ τότε γ' 'but at *that* moment'. 'Homer never opens a sentence or clause with δή, except when it precedes a temporal adverb or γάρ' (*GP* 228; cf. 30n.). The two particles emphasise the adverb. **λελασμένος:** perfect middle-passive participle of λανθάνω/λήθω. **ἐπεπόνθει:** in Homer, the pluperfect can emphasise the fact that the action of the verb is over, so these particular troubles of *Od.*'s really are in the past (*GH* II.200).

93–125 The arrival in Ithaca: Od. is left on the shore and
the Phaeacians depart

This section is in two contrasting parts: (i) the numinous description of the cave of Phorcys, and (ii) the matter-of-fact description of the Phaeacians' depositing of their cargo on the shore before departing. The pattern is similar to that found in the description of *Od.*'s departure (63–92n.). The scrupulousness and thoroughness of the Phaeacians is laudable, but will not impress Poseidon.

93 εὖτ' ἀστὴρ ὑπερέσχε 'when the (morning) star [i.e. Venus] rose'. This description of dawn is found only here in Homer. Its uniqueness emphasises that subsequent events mark an important new beginning, not just the next stage in the narrative: cf. 18 and n., and 63–92n. for the uniqueness of the description of the departure. The emphasis on brightness here contrasts with the darkness that accompanied the journey, and suggests a splendid homecoming, which expectation will be soon disappointed as the problems that Od. will face become clearer. In general, sunrises are described in more various and detailed ways than sunsets (14.457n.), presumably because they are used to launch new events whereas sunsets tend to bring events to a close. There are seven other unique sunrises (3.1–3, 5.1–2, 390, 6.48–9, 10.144, 15.495, 23.347–8), plus the pair 15.56 = 20.91.   φαάντατος 'brightest', from the root *phan- of φαίνω etc. The repeated α is an example of what ancient critics called diektasis (cf. GH 1.75–83). When Ionic contracted forms of words began to replace earlier uncontracted forms, in order to preserve the metrical shape of formulae a vowel was repeated, in the same way that a vowel was repeated in musical texts to indicate the quantity of the syllable. Thus, for example, an original ἡβάοντα (–––⏑) was contracted to ἡβῶντα (––⏑), which became ἡβώωντα to keep the metrical shape. φαάντατος is probably built on the aorist φαάνθην, itself created from φάνθην (GH 1.81). Other forms with diektasis in this book are 99 σκεπόωσι, 425 λοχόωσι; cf. 14.15 ἐρχατόωντο.   ὅς τε μάλιστα: μάλιστα regularly appears with relatives at line-end to mark the person or thing especially responsible for an action. The sense is 'the star which is the most obvious herald of the coming of dawn's light': there may be other signs, but this is the best. Cf. Il. 11.123–5 ὅς ῥα μάλιστα | ...οὐκ εἴασχ' Ἑλένην δόμεναι...Μενελάωι 'the man who most opposed the handing of Helen to Menelaus' (cf. Ebeling s.v. μάλα, μάλιστα (2)).

94 ἠριγενείης: lit. 'early-born'; for ἠρι-, cf. 18n. In IE tradition, 'the appearance of dawn is sometimes represented as a birth... All that remains [in Greek] of her being "born" is her epithet ἠριγένεια' (M. L. West 2007: 218–19).

96–112 The Harbour of Phorcys. This bay mediates the transition from the magic and fantastical world of the wanderings to the 'real' world: it is in the real world but yet has something other-worldly about it. More importantly perhaps, it is also a nucleus of themes and ideas that will inform the second half of the epic. For discussions of this description, see Hellwig 1964: 31–9; Elliger 1975: 107–56 (123–8 on this harbour); Andersson 1976: 37–52; S. Richardson 1990: 50–61; Byre 1994.

    1. *Interpretation.* Antiquity read this cave allegorically. Porphyrius of Tyre wrote a complex allegorical interpretation of this passage in his *On the Cave of the Nymphs in the Odyssey* (ed. Nauck 1886; Duffy et al. 1969); the scholia and Eustathius (2.41.17–36) also contain vestigial allegorical interpretations. Faced with the unusual features of the passage, Porphyrius wrote: 'Since this narration is full of such obscurities it can neither be a fiction

casually devised for the purpose of procuring delight, nor an exposition of a topical history [i.e. a real place]; but something allegorical must be indicated in it by the poet who likewise mystically places an olive near the cave' (1.4 tr. Taylor 1917). For an English translation, see Taylor 1917; Duffy *et al.* 1969. For discussion, see Pépin 1966; Lamberton 1986: 119–33; Alt 1998.

That the harbour is sheltered from the wind and ships can keep their positions without any restraint (97–100) marks it as a place where the sea, which has for so long dominated Od.'s existence, is temporarily at least stilled.

At the same time, several past episodes that threatened Od.'s return are also evoked. Off the Cyclopes' shore there was an island, where again ships did not need to be anchored, and a cave at the head of the harbour with a spring (9.136–41); as here, a god covers the island with mist (9.142–8). The cave with Nymphs and their weaving recalls Circe and her weaving (10.221–3), Calypso's cave, where she too weaves (5.63), and the cave on the island of the Sun, where the Nymphs have 'fine dancing-floors and seats' (12.317–18). There are also hints of the harbour of the Laestrygonians (10.87–94). These echoes suggest that the cave is not just the site of release from trouble, but also the start of different troubles.

On the mixing-bowls, amphoras and looms made out of stone (105–8) two points can be made. First, the drinking-vessels point to sympotic activity, the main locus of male social life, and the looms then stand for the female equivalent, weaving being one of the characteristic tasks of women in the *oikos*. A feast and weaving are two of the principal ways in which Od. and Penelope thwart the Suitors. The cave is a sort of microcosm of events past and future in Od.'s *oikos* therefore, and looks forward from this earliest moment of his time back on Ithaca to his eventual success.

Secondly, the cave is also a place where men and gods meet, but it marks both 'communion' and 'separation', figuring the mixed relationships that exist between the two worlds. First, 'communion'. The olive prepares for Athena's presence (cf. 102n.), for the subsequent scene of extraordinary intimacy between her and Od., and for her coming help in Od.'s revenge on the Suitors. Men and gods, via their own entrances, share in rites in the cave, symbolised by the sympotic vessels: Athena reminds Od. that he used to partake in such rites in 349–50. One thinks too of the rites called *theoxenia* 'entertainment of the god(s)', where men sacrificed and ate, believing the gods were actually present with them; couches and food and drink were put out for them.

As for 'separation', the distance between men and gods is marked by the fact that the two entrances are mutually exclusive; and the Nymphs clearly do not weave with men around. Furthermore, the fittings, made unusually out of stone, have a non-human, exceptional quality about them: you can't really have a stone loom. This separation figures examples of relationships between gods and men which are the counterpart to Athena's warm relationship with Od. The very next episode will show Zeus and Poseidon planning the destruction of the Phaeacians, even though (and partly because) they are Poseidon's kin.

2. *Archaeology*. This cave has been identified with a cave on Polis Bay on Ithaca, which contains a sanctuary in use from the Early Bronze Age down to Roman times. At 366–71, Od. stows the thirteen tripods given to him by the Phaeacians in this cave, and in the 1930s excavations there revealed ninth- and eighth-century bronze tripods (Deoudi 2008: 225–31), as well as a possibly second-century terracotta mask inscribed εὐχὴν Ὀδυσσέι. This raises the difficult question of whether knowledge of the cave and its cult of the Nymphs led our poet to construct this episode, or whether an earlier version of this story influenced the cultic practice in the cave. The former seems perhaps more likely: we do not know whether the episode existed in the ninth century when the cult starts, and this episode is perhaps not substantial enough on its own to have given rise to a major cult. If this is right, it shows that the poet was familiar with Ithaca (cf. also 106n.). Whether Od. was associated with the cave in the eighth century we do not know: in favour, Malkin 1998: 106–7; against, Antonaccio 1995: 154. See also Currie 2005: 52–3, and 48–57 generally on the question of the possible influence of Homeric epic on the institution of hero cults. On the archaeology of the cave, cf. also Benton 1934–5; Malkin 1998: 94–119; Deoudi 1999: 119. Against all these, Bittlestone 2005: 119–29 identifies the site as Atheras Bay on Paliki, the western peninsula of Cephalonia.

96 Φόρκυνος δέ τίς ἐστι λιμήν: new episodes in Greek (and Latin) literature are often marked by an *ecphrasis*, a formal description of a place or scene, regularly in the form 'There is a certain ...'; cf. e.g. 4.354 νῆσος ἔπειτά τις ἔστι, 15.402, 19.172; *Il.* 6.152, 11.711, 13.32; Thuc. 1.24.1; and a parody in Ar. *Kn.* 1059. Phorcys was the grandfather of Polyphemus; his daughter Thoosa bore the Cyclops to Poseidon (1.70–3). He is one of the manifestations of the Old Man of the Sea, like Proteus (4.349).

97 ἐν δήμωι: '*dêmos* (land, district, and people) designates the largest conceivable social unit' (Raaflaub 1997: 629).

98 λιμένος: a partitive genitive of place, indicating where the headlands came down to (*GH* II.52). **ποτιπεπτηυῖαι:** fem. nom. pl. perfect active participle, either of ποτι-πίπτω (i.e. προσ-, cf. 14.472n.) 'fall upon', so 'slope down to', or of ποτι-πτήσσω 'nestle'. We cannot know what the poet thought it meant, and the two meanings are not far apart.

99–100 αἵ τ᾽ ἀνέμων ... | ἔκτοθεν 'which keep out the great wave caused by the storm winds (so that it stays) outside'. ἀνέμων is a genitive of origin: cf.

Il. 2.396–7 κύματα ... παντοίων ἀνέμων, 723 ἕλκεϊ ... ὕδρου 'a wound caused by a hydra' (*GH* II.61).

100 δέ τ' describes a habitual action (*GP* 528).

101 ὅρμου μέτρον ἵκωνται 'they come to the anchorage, (which is) the end of their voyage'. The phrase seems a slightly awkward development of say 11.317 εἰ ἥβης μέτρον ἵκοντο (cf. 18.217, 19.532) 'if they had reached the point from which ἥβη begins to be measured' (Stanford on 18.217), i.e. 'the point which is maturity'; ὅρμου is then a kind of defining genitive. Cf. with σοφίης Solon, fr. 13.52, Thgn. 875, Pigres, fr. 1.2. Hes. *Op.* 648 δείξω ... μέτρα ... θαλάσσης and *Od.* 4.389 ὅς κέν τοι εἴπησιν ὁδὸν καὶ μέτρα κελεύθου are different.

102 ἐλαίη: the olive is a tree especially associated with Athena. It was, for instance, her gift to the city when she competed for the patronship of Athens with Poseidon. It recurs throughout *Od.* at significant moments: it forms the haft of the axe with which Od. skilfully makes the raft on which he sails from Calypso's island (5.236); he sleeps under a double olive on arrival on Scherie, its wild and cultivated branches representing the way that Scherie is the marginal place between the fantasy world of the wanderings and the 'real' world to which he will return (5.475–7); olive-wood forms the club which Od. uses to put out the Cyclops' eye (9.320); and an olive-tree forms the centre of Od. and Penelope's bed as described at the climax of their meeting (23.190–8). As on Scherie, this tree, presiding over the harbour and the symbol of Poseidon's counterpart and rival (cf. 102n. and Introduction pp. 4–6), marks the key moment of Od.'s escape from the influence of the sea.

103 ἄντρον: cave-sanctuaries are a feature of Minoan religion, and some of them continued to be used in Classical times; cf. Burkert 1985: 24–6. **ἠεροειδές** 'misty, murky', from ἀήρ, perhaps also with the ideas of 'foggy', 'damp', 'dark'. It is used of caves elsewhere in Homer only in 12.80, of Scylla's cave high on a misty mountain, and 13.347, 366. The epithet adds an air of mystery to the cave, and for Porphyry (§6) the juxtaposition of this negative epithet with the positive ἐπήρατον was a sign that the passage needed interpretation.

104 ἱρὸν Νυμφάων 'sacred to the Nymphs'; cf. e.g. 6.321–2 ἄλσος ... ἱρὸν Ἀθηναίης; for the genitive, see Introduction 5.3 §7.2.5.2.1. **Νηϊάδες:** the Nymphs of rivers and springs; the name is connected with νάω 'flow', and so possibly means 'daughters of the source' (cf. Beekes 1000). On Nymphs generally, cf. 14.435n.

105 κρητῆρές τε καὶ ἀμφιφορῆες: see 96–112n.   **ἔασι:** this use of the present tense (cf. also εἰσίν in 109) may indicate that the poet is suggesting the objects are still there in his time (Currie 2005: 53), a technique commonly found in Herodotus.

106 λάϊνοι: the Marmarospilia cave in southern Ithaca contains fine stalagmites and evidence for a cult of the Nymphs; the stalagmites may possibly have given the poet the idea of the stone vessels and looms in the cave of Phorcys. This would again point to the poet's familiarity with the island (cf. 96–112n.: 2. *Archaeology*).   **ἔπειτα** 'furthermore, in addition'; cf. 9.116 νῆσος ἔπειτα...τετάνυσται 'then there is an island that stretches out...' **τιθαιβώσσουσι:** a very rare word, of unknown meaning and etymology (cf. Beekes 1482), usually translated (following the scholia but without other justification) as 'store up honey'; it is used later, apparently in a different sense, in Nic. *Th.* 199; Lycophron 622; Antimachus, in *PMilan* 17.37. **μέλισσαι:** wild bees do nest in rocky clefts. For bees in a cave of a high significance, cf. those that attended the young Zeus in the Dictaean cave (Ant. Lib. 19 preserves the story from Boeus' *Ornithogonia*; cf. Call. *Hy.* 1.46–54); this cave was out of bounds to both men and gods. Bees are regularly associated with divinity: cf. Davies & Kathirithamby 1986: 69–70.

108 ἁλιπόρφυρα: garments dyed with the liquid produced by the boiling down of large numbers of the shellfish called the πορφύρα or *murex*, which were crushed and salted, and the resulting liquid strongly reduced; cf. Pliny, *NH* 9.125–41; *OCD* s.v. 'purple'. The colour was probably a reddish brown: it is used of a horse in *Il.* 23.454. It was the most expensive kind of dye, and so suitable for divine weavers (elsewhere, only Arete weaves such cloth, 6.53, 306). It is disputed whether words for 'purple' are connected with πορφυρέω 'boil' (against, Beekes 1223–4; cf. 85n.); if there is a connection, ἁλιπόρφυρα would be 'flashing like the sea' (Hainsworth, *CHO* on 6.53).   **θαῦμα ἰδέσθαι:** in *Od.* (though not *Il.*) 'typically used by mortal focalisers in connection with immortal persons or objects' (de Jong 2001: 167); cf. 6.306, 7.45, 8.366.

109 ἀενάοντα = αἰενάοντα 'ever-flowing'. ἀέ for ἀεί is hard to explain, but the lexicographical tradition attributes ἀέ to the epic poet Pisander (fr. 11 (*GEF* p. 186)) and it is plausibly restored in Pi. *Py.* 9.88; in Hes. *Op.* 595 some MSS read ἀεν(ν)άου (but others ἀιενάου, printed by West 1978) and Herodotus has ἀέναος.   **δύο δέ τέ οἱ θύραι εἰσίν:** Homer prefers to use the plural of θύρα, probably because an item made up of more than one part (i.e. folding or double doors) is involved (cf. 2n. on μέγαρα). For caves with two entrances, cf. Hades (19.562–7) and Soph. *Phil.* 16.

110 πρὸς βορέαο 'at the northern end', genitive of place (cf. 98n.). **καταιβαταί** 'where one can go down' (καταβαίνω); for καται-, which appears only in compounds (and is metrically useful), cf. παραί, χαμαί, πάλαι.

111 αἱ δ'...θεώτεραι 'those to the south belong, by contrast, to the gods'. The suffix -τερος expressed opposition before it began to be used to mark the comparative: cf. ἀρίστερος/δεξίτερος 'left'/'right', and κουρότε-ρος, which makes clearer the opposition between young and old, θηλύτερος 'female (not male)' etc. (*GH* 1.257). So here θεώτεραι contrasts the doors used by the gods with those used by men. It is found only here in Homer, and 111b–112 are effectively a translation of it (cf. 28n.).

113 πρὶν εἰδότες: i.e on one of their many sea-journeys, for which see 7.321–4.

114 ὅσον τ' ἐπὶ ἥμισυ πάσης 'as far (up the shore) as half of all (the ship)'. Cf. *Il.* 10.351–2 ὅσσον τ' ἐπὶ οὖρα πέλονται | ἡμιόνων 'as far as the furrows made by mules extend'; 21.251 ὅσον τ' ἐπὶ δουρὸς ἐρωή 'as far as the spear flies'. The exact explanation of our phrase is obscure, but one can perhaps understand τόσον with ἐπέκελσεν. τε is normal in such expressions giving measurements: *Od.* 10.112–13 γυναῖκα | ...ὅσην τ' ὄρεος κορυφήν 'a woman as big as a mountain peak'.

115 τοῖον...ἐρετάων 'because it was so driven forward by the hands of the oarsmen'. Some MSS have τοίων, but cf. 3.496 τοῖον γὰρ ὑπέκφερον ὠκέες ἵπποι, 24.62 τοῖον γὰρ ὑπώρορε Μοῦσα λίγεια.

118 αὐτῶι σύν τε λίνωι 'linen clothing and all', i.e. 'still wrapped in his linen clothing'. This is a 'sociative' dative, where αὐτός is added to empha-sise the notion of accompaniment expressed by the dative; cf. 14.77 αὐτοῖς ὀβελοῖσιν 'complete with their spits' and *Il.* 9.542 αὐτῆισιν ῥίζηισι 'roots and all'. In Homer, σύν accompanies the dative in these expressions much more than it does elsewhere. Od. is treated almost like a tiny child coming swaddled into the world for the first time; again, the idea of a new start is evoked.   **ῥήγεϊ σιγαλόεντι:** for the use of the epithet 'shining' of clothes, cf. Shelmerdine 1995.

119 κὰδ δ' ἄρ': cf. Introduction 5.3 §7.5.3.   **δεδμημένον:** perfect passive participle of δάμνημι 'overcome'.

121 διὰ μεγάθυμον Ἀθήνην: though in fact there was no mention of Athena at the time (17–23). This comment by the narrator shows that the gods could be behind events even when the story does not state explicitly that they were (cf. 125, 302, 305nn.).

122 πυθμέν' ἐλαίης: these are the last words of Od.'s great description of his making of the marriage-bed, which finally confirm his identity to Penelope

(23.204). These references to the olive frame the events of the second half of the work. For the olive in *Od.*, cf. 102n.

124 πρὶν Ὀδυσῆ' ἐγρέσθαι: πρίν is usually followed by the infinitive in Homer, never by the indicative as in Attic. It was originally an adverb, perhaps an old locative (Beekes 1234). The use with the infinitive comes from the infinitive's origin as a verbal noun: πρὶν ἐγρέσθαι thus means literally 'before the awakening' (*GH* II.314–15; Introduction 5.3 §10.5.1); ἐγρέσθαι is aorist middle infinitive.

125–64 The anger of Poseidon against the Phaeacians

Drama returns to the narrative with this sudden shift to Olympus in midline. *Od.* differs from *Il.* in that it has far fewer scenes in Olympus. There are four narrated by Homer, here, 1.26–95, 5.1–42 and 24.472–88 (i.e. at the very start, at the start of Od.'s involvement and at the very end); one by Demodocus (8.266–366, Ares and Aphrodite); and one by Od. based on information from Calypso (12.376–88, the Sun's reaction to the eating of his cattle); all bar that in book 24 occur in the non-Ithacan part of the poem. *Od.* keeps the scene of the narrative resolutely on earth.

This motif of divine anger and concern for honour has a number of striking counterparts in Greek and Mesopotamian epic, two featuring Poseidon.

1. *Il.* 5.330–431. Aphrodite complains to her mother Dione about her wounding by Diomedes, and Zeus consoles her. Cf. Burkert 1992: 96–8.
2. *Il.* 7.445–64. Poseidon complains to Zeus that the fame of the Greek wall will eclipse that of the wall he and Apollo built for Troy. Zeus gives advice to Poseidon, suggesting the destruction of the wall, and reassuring him his *kleos* is not in danger.
3. *Il.* 15.168–217. Iris tells Poseidon that Zeus forbids him to fight. He complains that Zeus is mistreating a ὁμότιμος (186), and that he should not operate beyond his proper sphere (τιμή) of the sky. After an angry speech he calms himself and backs down, but promises trouble should Zeus try to spare Troy.
4. *Od.* 12.472–88. Helios complains to Zeus and threatens to shine in the Underworld unless Zeus punishes (378 τεῖσαι, 382 τείσουσι) Od.'s men for eating his cattle. Zeus assures him that he will get his way (385–8). Cf. Segal 1992.
5. *Gilgamesh* VI–VII i. Aspects of 1 and 4 are found here. The goddess of love and war, Ishtar, complains to her parents Anu (chief of the older gods) and Antu about Gilgamesh's rejection of her advances: 'Father, Gilgamesh has shamed me again and again! Gilgamesh spelt out to me my dishonour, my dishonour and my disgrace' (VI iii; tr. Dalley 2000).

Unless she is given the Bull of Heaven as recompense and as a means of punishing Gilgamesh, 'I shall set my face towards the infernal regions, I shall raise up the dead, and they will eat the living!' (VI iii). Gilgamesh and his companion Enkidu kill it, and Anu insists Enkidu must die.

It is possible to feel uncomfortable that the genial Phaeacians are made to suffer by Poseidon, since they seem different from the more obvious villains, such as the Cyclops or the Suitors; one could think too that Poseidon's actions are petulantly vindictive, since he has long been annoyed by the Phaeacians' services to sailors, but has never done anything about it, and now seems to punish them simply because he cannot punish Od. This may be a natural reaction after hearing this section, but the subsequent section, with its reminder of how the Phaeacians have ignored warning oracles about Poseidon's likely reaction, presents another way of looking at the question (cf. 165–87n.).

125 οὐδ' ἐνοσίχθων: the shift in mid-line is unusual in Homer, if less striking than the next example at 187b (where see n. for such shifts). We suddenly realise that the gods have been watching the scene all the time (cf. 121n.). The concentration in this scene is totally on what is said: we are not told where the gods are nor what they are doing. ἐνοσίχθων, along with ἐννοσίγαιος (140) and possibly ἐννοσίδας (Pi.; cf. perhaps Myc. *e-ne-si-da-o-ne*), refers to Poseidon as the god of the earthquake. For the etymological problems, cf. Beekes 430.

127 πρῶτον ἐπηπείλησε: these threats are nowhere actually mentioned, but Poseidon gives ear to the Cyclops' prayer at 9.536, in answer to his request for vengeance.   ἐξείρετο 'began to enquire'; probably the imperfect (*GH* 1.394).

128 Ζεῦ πάτερ: there is a mildly comic side to Poseidon's use of this common honorific address to his brother. Different traditions made Zeus (*Il.* 13.355) or Poseidon (Hes. *Th.* 453–91) the elder brother.

129 τιμήεις: though Iliadic (especially Greek) warriors regularly worry about their τιμή, this is much less the case in *Od.* People wish to possess τιμή (e.g. Telemachus in 1.117, Penelope in 18.161) or to ensure the honour of others (e.g. Athena for Telemachus in 1.93–5, 13.422), but no-one is so stridently worried about their honour and status as is Poseidon here. ὅ τε 'because' regularly introduces causal clauses (*GH* II.285–6). It is an adverbial accusative meaning literally 'with regard to the fact that'. The causal ὅ τε seems better than the temporal ὅτε here.

130 τοί πέρ τοι: lit. 'the very ones who are, after all'; the first τοί is the relative, the second a particle. πέρ is an intensive particle, emphasising the word it follows (Munro 1891: 320–1): compare its use for 'although'.

The particle τοι 'is especially used where a speaker wishes to imply that he is saying as little as possible' (Munro 1891: 252), cf. *Il.* 4.405 ἡμεῖς τοι πατέρων μέγ᾽ ἀμείνονες εὐχόμεθ᾽ εἶναι 'it is we who claim to be much better than our fathers (to say no more about it)'. Poseidon means that he does not want to harp on the fact that the Phaeacians are his descendants, but even so it does make things worse that they of all people should fail to respect him. For their relationship, cf. 7.56–68.

131 νῦν… ἐφάμην 'I have always said'; νῦν can refer to a more or less protracted period, not just to the very recent past.

132 οὔ ποτ᾽ ἀπηύρων 'I never took away'. The form ἀπηύρων starts from ἀπηύρα, an old athematic aorist in -ᾱ (Introduction 5.3 §6.5.4), which was wrongly taken to be an imperfect of a contract verb in -άω, like e.g. ἐτίμα. From this was created a corresponding first-person imperfect form ἀπηύρων, on analogy with e.g. ἐτίμων < ἐτίμα-ον; cf. *GH* 1.356, 380.

133 πάγχυ 'completely', so here 'in any way'. Along with οὔ ποτ᾽ it emphasises Poseidon's claim to have observed strictly from the very start (πρῶτον) Zeus' decision on Od.'s survival; for this, cf. 1.65–7, 5.41–2. ὑπέσχεο καὶ κατένευσας: this passage is important for the concept of fate in *Od.* In *Il.* the possibility of fate being changed or circumvented is frequently held up, even if it never in fact is changed (see somewhat differently Allan 2006); but in *Od.*, the certainty of Od.'s fated return is for the most part much clearer. In 5.288–9 Poseidon himself acknowledges that Od. must survive: 'he is now close to the land of the Phaeacians, where it is fated (*aisa*) that he should escape the bounds of his misery'. So here Poseidon points out that he did not try to prevent Od.'s return, because Zeus had decreed it was to happen. All Poseidon could do was make life difficult for him, which is why he is now so angry, not because Od. has returned home, but because he has done so with more wealth, and so status, than he would have gained had he come home unmolested. Fate can be changed in *Od.*, but apparently only for the worse, usually through unintelligent actions, e.g. by Aegisthus, who ignores divine warnings (1.32–43), and Ajax, who boasts of the gods' inability to kill him (4.499–511).

135 εἰν Ἰθάκηι: before words beginning with two short syllables ἐν is lengthened to εἰν to avoid an impossible run of three short syllables, perhaps on analogy of εἰς Ἰθάκην and the alternative forms of the preposition ἐς/εἰς (W. F. Wyatt 1969: 90–2). ἄσπετα: lit. 'untellable', so 'countless', from α-privative + *sek^w-* 'speak, tell', which becomes *sep-* in Greek, seen in the zero grade in the aorist imperatives of ἐν(ν)έπω, ἐνί-σπ-ες, ἔσπετε; cf. also 14.33n.

136–8 Poseidon uses almost exactly Zeus's words to Hermes and Athena when he prophesied the wealth Od. will get from the Phaeacians (5.38–40), an irony the audience can appreciate but not Poseidon.

136 ἅλις: an adverb, 'in large quantities', cf. ἀολλής 'all together' (root *wel- 'turn, wind').

137 ἐξήρατ(ο): aorist middle of ἐξ-άρ-νυ-μαι 'carry off'.

138 λαχών: for the sharing of booty, cf. 14.232–3n.

139 νεφεληγερέτα: these forms in -ᾰ for -ης (cf. εὐρύοπα, ἱππότα, κυανοχαῖτα) are probably vocatives used as nominatives, and the fact that they are often to be found with names of gods suggests they may be old forms. The phrase in the vocative could easily have slipped with time into being used as a nominative, through familiarity and once the origin of the -a ending was forgotten. They are three times more common in *Il.* than *Od.* (*GH* 1.199–200).

140 ὢ πόποι: this exclamation conveys displeasure, complaint, disagreeable surprise. It shows that Zeus's remarks here are characterised by some exasperation at Poseidon's complaint. Poseidon has twice referred to his *time*, and Zeus's exasperation is further visible in his four-fold use of words from its root (ἀτιμάζουσι, ἀτίμησιν, τίει, τίσις). The exclamation is most common in epic, but it does appear in tragedy, mainly in lyrics. Cf. Kelly 2007: 220–3.   **οἷον ἔειπες:** exclamatory; 'what sort of thing you have said!', so 'what a thing to say!' This expression is used to mark 'the factual error, undesirability, or unlikelihood of the situation envisaged … by the previous speaker' (Kelly 2007: 185).

141 δέ here is the equivalent of 'because', as often in Homer's paratactic style (*GP* 169).

142 πρεσβύτατον: Poseidon is one of the older generation of gods born to Cronus by Rheia, along with Zeus, Demeter, Hera and Hades (Hes. *Th.* 453–8). Cf. 128n. for the uncertainty as to whether Zeus or Poseidon was the elder, which would determine whether one translates 'oldest' or 'most venerable'.   **ἀτιμίῃσιν ἰάλλειν** 'to bring into disrepute, dishonour'. ἰάλλω is 'to set in motion, throw', and the phrase here has no real parallel in Homer, the verb normally being used of physical objects like hands or arrows. The closest perhaps is 2.316 πειρήσω ὥς κ' ὔμμι κακὰς ἐπὶ κῆρας ἰήλω 'I shall try to set the dread fates upon you'. For the idea and the dative of the aim of a movement, cf. *Il.* 21.394 θεοὺς ἔριδι ξυνελαύνεις 'you are driving the gods to strife'. ἀτιμίῃσιν has a metrically lengthened iota to avoid a cretic.

143 εἴ περ 'if indeed', a common use, as in Euryalus' apology to Od. at 8.408–9 ἔπος δ᾽ εἴ πέρ τι βέβακται | δεινόν 'if anything insulting really has been said' (*GP* 487–8; Ebeling s.v. περ B.1 (p. 163)). Zeus points out that Poseidon is quite capable of dealing with mortals, but enters the caveat that they should be punished only if they really have acted inappropriately. This remark rather implies a feeling that Poseidon is somewhat over-ready to take against people, a feeling that is justified by past events (125–64n.). On Zeus in the poem, see Marks 2008.　**βίηι καὶ κάρτεϊ εἴκων:** i.e. letting his violence and power get the better of him; cf. 14.221n.

144 σοὶ δ᾽: 'apodotic' δέ, that is, δέ used apparently unnecessarily in a main clause after a subordinate clause; cf. Introduction 5.3 §12.3; and 79n. for καί so used.

145 ἔπλετο: the aorist of πέλομαι (cf. 60n.) is regularly used in the sense 'have become' and so 'be'.

147 αἶψά κ᾽ ἐγὼν ἔρξαιμι 'I have long wanted to get on and do'. The optative + κε can express something that was potentially the case in the past but not actually realised; the combination can thus express long-held desires. In Homer (unlike Attic) there is no distinction in the use of the present or past tenses in this construction, so that the potentiality here continues into the time of the utterance (*GH* II.220). Poseidon tactfully indicates that he does not need Zeus's prompting, just his permission.　**κελαινεφές** responds to Zeus's honorific epithets for Poseidon in 140: courtesies are maintained, whatever the tensions between the two gods.

148 ὀπίζομαι: ὄπις, cognate with ὄψομαι, ὄμμα (< *ὄπ-μα), is originally the (often vengeful) watch kept by the gods on men, cf. *Il.* 16.388 θεῶν ὄπιν οὐκ ἀλέγοντες 'taking no account of the watchfulness of the gods', *Od.* 14.82 οὐκ ὄπιδα φρονέοντες. As early as Hesiod it seems to have been used to mean the 'punishment' of the gods (*Op.* 187, 251, 706; *Th.* 222). The meaning 'respect (for the gods)' does not reappear until Hdt. 9.76.2 τούς οὔτε δαιμόνων οὔτε θεῶν ὄπιν ἔχοντας, but it is appropriate here, and the scholiasts translate αἰδοῦμαι. Once again (cf. 147n.) Poseidon speaks very respectfully before Zeus, the more powerful god.

149 αὖ has a contrastive force: '(I was afraid of your anger), but now…'; cf. Lat. *aut, autem.*

151 ἤδη: 'to really (ἦ) and truly (δή)', so 'immediately', as in *Il.* 3.98 φρονέω δὲ διακρινθήμεναι ἤδη Ἀργείους καὶ Τρῶας 'I am keen that the Greeks and Trojans should cease from combat immediately'.　**σχῶνται:** middle, 'hold themselves back, desist'.

152 μέγα δέ σφιν ὄρος πόλει ἀμφικαλύψαι: lit. 'to enfold onto their city a huge mountain', so 'to cover their city with a mountain'. With ἀμφικαλύπτω, the thing that is covered is in the dative, the covering in the accusative: cf. 14.349 κεφαλῆι δὲ κατὰ ῥάκος ἀμφικαλύψας. The infinitive depends on ἐθέλω (149). The phrase implies the obliteration of the city, not, as some have suggested, just the blocking of the harbour. For the punishment, cf. Apollo's covering Telphusa's stream with rocks (*H. Ap.* 382–3). The scholiast (Q) says that Homer covers them with a mountain 'so that we will not seek the location of the Phaeacians'. If it was Homer's intention to stop people seeking the 'true' locations of the places he describes, he was of course completely unsuccessful: as early as Thuc. 1.25.4, 3.70.4 the Phaeacians were being associated with Corcyra, and the attempts continue today. Eratosthenes said that 'a man could discover where Od. wandered, when he could discover the cobbler who sewed up the bag of winds', but many disputed this: for a flavour of the debate, cf. Strabo 1.2 (Eratosthenes is quoted in §15).

154 ὦ πέπον: almost the equivalent of the now essentially obsolete English expression 'old fruit', πέπον being the vocative of πέπων 'mature'. The precise tone with which this expression is used, which ranges from warm friendship to scorn, seems to be given by the context in which it appears (cf. *LfgrE* s.v.). Here it marks a moderation of Zeus' tone from the ὦ πόποι of 140: cf. the poignant κριὲ πέπον (9.447) addressed by the blinded Cyclops to his favourite ram.   **ὧς μέν: ὧς** 'thus' seems preferable to the ὡς of the better MSS; it looks forward to the advice in the next line, and μέν is emphatic (*GP* 361).

155 ἐλαυνομένην: *sc.* νῆα from 149.

156 πτόλιος: forms of πόλις with this variant spelling are found in Mycenaean, Arcadian, Cypriot, Cretan and Thessalian; its explanation is uncertain, but there may have been an IE form *tpelH- 'fortification' (Beekes 1219–20) which gave rise to the two spellings. Cf. also Ruijgh 1957: 75–8. **θεῖναι:** 'make', as often (e.g. 163); the IE root *$d^h eh_1$-had a variety of meanings beside 'put', such as 'lay down, create'. Zeus seems here to move from his initial mild exasperation at Poseidon's anger to the refining of his rather crude proposal simply to smash the ship to pieces (151); he suggests he turn the ship to stone as a permanent warning to others, not just as a one-off spectacular. For turning to stone as a punishment, cf. e.g. *Il.* 24.617; Forbes Irving 1990: 139–48. For gods setting up a stone to mark an event, cf. Zeus's erection at Delphi of the stone that Cronus had swallowed in his stead, so that it would be a σῆμα and a θαῦμα to men (Hes. *Th.* 497–500).

158 μέγα...ἀμφικαλύψαι: the text of the MSS has Zeus encourage Poseidon to cover the city with a mountain. However scholion H on 152 says that
'Aristophanes read μὴ δέ σφιν; Aristarchus opposed this in his commentaries'. This looks very much like an attempt to avoid the depiction of the
gods as vindictive: Hellenistic scholarship was often concerned with the
'decorum' of Homer's text. The reading was defended by Friedrich 1989,
partly because Zeus has no reason to be so hostile to the Phaeacians. He
has however every reason to keep his powerful brother happy, since he has
acquiesced in Od.'s return despite his great anger (125–64n.). Compare
Athena's determination to punish all the Suitors, even those who could
plead mitigating circumstances (17.360–4). Whether the Phaeacians were
spared or not was probably debated from the moment this passage was
first performed. The scholiast on 187 says '*So they prayed*: from what is
left unsaid (κατὰ τὸ σιωπώμενον) they were destroyed, since what the gods
authorise is of necessity fulfilled'.

160 βῆ ῥ' ἴμεν: simply 'he went', cf. βῆ δ' ἰέναι, ἔβαν οἶκόνδε νέεσθαι: the
infinitive can be explained as a kind of cognate accusative, 'he went his
way' (Palmer 1962: 153), or as completing the meaning of the main verb,
giving its consequence or its aim (cf. 34n.; *GH* II.301; Introduction 5.3
§§7.2.4.1, 10.5.2).   **γεγάασιν:** lit. 'have been born here', and so 'live
here'; the perfect describes a state reached in the past. This is 3rd p.pl.
perfect active of γίγνομαι, with -γα- (< -γγ-) showing the zero grade of the
root *gen-; contrast Attic γεγόνασι, with the *o*-grade.

161 ἤλυθε = ἦλθε; see 14.490n. for the suffix.

162 ῥίμφα διωκομένη 'swiftly pursuing its course', middle. This speed, irri-
tating to Poseidon, is matched by the speed with which he brings the
ship to an immediate halt, a contrast heightened by the repetition σχεδόν
ἤλυθε | σχεδὸν ἦλθ'.

164 χειρὶ καταπρηνεῖ 'with the flat of his hand'; before his death, Apollo
strikes Patroclus in the same way, causing his eyes to whirl and his armour
to fall to pieces (*Il.* 16.791–804).   **ὁ δὲ νόσφι βεβήκει** 'but he had already
gone on his way'; cf. *Il.* 1.221 ἡ δ' Οὔλυμπόνδε βεβήκει. The pluperfect
stresses the completion of an action (92n.), and the phrase strikingly conveys the ease with which Poseidon almost contemptuously destroys the ship
and passes on.

165–87 The end of the Phaeacians?

In this section, we are reminded that the Phaeacians have been ignoring oracles about Poseidon's likely reaction to their transgressing on his

sphere of operation; this may mitigate the worries raised by the previous scene (cf. 125–64n.). Alcinous himself recalled these oracles when telling Od. about the magical powers of his ships (8.564–71), going on to comment, with an insouciance whose folly is now clear, that 'the god may bring these prophecies to fruition, or they may be unfulfilled, as pleases his heart' (570–1). Furthermore, the tenses make it clear that these warnings were given repeatedly (172n.), which makes the failure of the Phaeacians to pay attention to them even more unwise. The first line of Alcinous' speech is the same as that used by the Cyclops when he has a similar realisation about oracles (9.507). Alcinous' realisation, like the Cyclops', comes too late, but at least the Cyclops had paid attention to the oracle and was wrong only in his expectation that it would be a mighty figure who would come to deprive him of his eye, not the weedy Od. (9.513–16). Circe too had an oracle about Od.'s arrival and is apparently similarly caught out, though without unfortunate consequences except his departure (10.330–2). Other characters who ignored divine warnings are Aegisthus (1.32–43), the Suitors (*passim*), and the Companions of Od., who eat the Cattle of the Sun despite a warning from Circe (12.127–41). The stories of all of these misguided people, apart from Aegisthus and the Suitors, formed part of Od.'s account given to the Phaeacians, which might have acted as a hint. Indeed, the whole of that account made it plain to them what happens to those who anger Poseidon. Seen in the light of these comparable cases, Poseidon's reaction becomes more comprehensible. The Phaeacian episode as a whole is part of *Od.*'s demonstration of the importance of correct hospitality, but it also makes clear how fulfilling one's duties to a guest can involve displeasing powerful forces.

The Phaeacian insouciance about these warnings chimes with a certain over-confidence generally about their relationships with the gods (cf. 1–15n.). Alcinous remarks on how 'in the past the gods have always appeared openly to us whenever we perform fine hecatombs, and have sat and dined with us. If a solitary traveller meets them, they do not hide themselves, because we are related to them, like the Cyclopes and the wild race of the Giants' (7.201–6; the reference to the Giants, punished for trying to usurp the Olympians' power, is inauspicious). His casual reference to his ships effortlessly transporting Rhadamanthus, a ruler of the Underworld, to see Tityos (7.318–26) almost smacks of 'name-dropping'. He speaks proudly too of the ἀρετή that Zeus has bestowed on us since the days of our forefathers' (8.244–5; cf. also 6.309, 7.5, 11, 71 etc.). The Phaeacians seem to see themselves as having a superhuman quality, which may not be entirely false, but which does not guarantee protection from divine displeasure.

There remains the question whether the sacrifice will dissuade Poseidon from his long-intended purpose (cf. Bassett 1933). The question

admits of no answer. Several considerations might bode ill for the Phaeacians: prophecies in Homer all come true. A similar sacrifice, offered by
Od.'s men to an equally angry Sun (12.340–365), is unsuccessful, as is the
Trojan women's offering to Athena of a robe to persuade her to stay the
spear of Diomedes (*Il.* 6.297–311). On the other hand, as Phoenix tells
Achilles, στρεπτοὶ δέ τε καὶ θεοὶ αὐτοί 'even the gods themselves are persuad-
able' by sacrifice, when men make mistakes (*Il.* 9.497). Homer leaves us
in eternal suspense. This narrative uncertainty has no comparable parallel
in Homer: the episode ends in mid-line, and in mystery.

165 ἔπεα πτερόεντ(α): this phrase is regularly used in requests for information (Kelly 2007: 154; cf. also 58n.; Calhoun 1935).

166 δολιχήρετμοι, ναυσικλυτοὶ ἄνδρες: the use of these grandiose formulaic
epithets, denoting the maritime skill that has brought them to this disaster,
has an ironic ring (cf. also 7.39, 8.191, 369, 16.227). On the accent of
ναυσικλυτοί, cf. Leumann 1950: 37; M. L. West 1998: xxviii.

167 ὧδε δέ τις εἴπεσκεν: lit. 'thus someone kept saying', i.e. 'people kept
saying'. This is the so-called 'public opinion' motif, where an individual
is said to say or ask something that is or will be generally thought; it is
common in both epics, in this form and others.   εἴπεσκεν: the formation
of aorists with the iterative suffix *-sk-* is a feature peculiar to Greek in Indo-
European: it is used to indicate repeated separate single acts (*GH* 1.323–5).
ἐς πλησίον ἄλλον 'to the neighbour beside him'; for a roughly comparable
use of ἄλλος, cf. 266n.

169 καὶ δὴ προὐφαίνετο πᾶσα 'after all, it was in full view just now'; καὶ δή
adds a further point in a vivid manner (*GP* 248).

170 τὰ δ' οὐ ἴσαν ὡς ἐτέτυκτο 'but they did not know how these things had
been brought about'. ἐ-τέ-τυκ-το is 3rd p. sg. pluperfect passive of τεύχω,
in the zero grade. The construction is the usual Greek 'I know you, who
you are'. οὐ ἴσαν is in hiatus as the verb εἶδον, οἶδα originally had a digamma
(cf. Lat. *uideo*). We as audience have had a graphic description of Poseidon lying in wait for the ship and slamming it with his hand (161–4), but
the Phaeacians see only the result. As often, the audience has better knowledge than the characters: we watch the Phaeacians' horrified bemusement
in the same way as the gods do.

171 ἀγορήσατο καὶ μετέειπεν 'addressed them and said': the two verbs are
not tautologous. The formula is used when Alcinous addresses the people
at large (7.185, 8.25), and nine times in *Il.* in similar contexts.

172 ὢ πόποι: ironically, Alcinous responds to Poseidon's actions with the
same expression as Zeus used when Poseidon first spoke of his annoyance

(cf. 140n.). Cf. also 175-7n.   ἦ μάλα δή...ἱκάνει 'Ah, yes indeed, there came to me oracles spoken long ago'. ἦ makes a sentence strongly assertive, and this is emphasised here by μάλα δή (cf. 383, 14.391; *GP* 285). The present ἱκάνει has a perfect sense as often, and παλαίφατα shows that the oracles have been known for a long time; the imperfects φάσκε (173) and φῆ (175) suggest that Nausithous gave the oracles on more than one occasion, all of which emphasises the fact that the Phaeacians were given fair warning.

173 πατρός: Nausithous. The story of how he brought the Phaeacians to Scherie from their original home near the dangerous Cyclopes, and established and organised their city and agriculture is told in 6.2-10 (cf. 7.56-63). **ἀγάσασθαι:** φάσκω is one of the verbs which in Homer are used with the aorist as well as the present and future infinitives to describe future events (*GH* 11.307). This is a clear case of the aorist used in its 'aspectual' sense, indicating a single act, and not as a tense indicating the time of the event (cf. 33n.). There is no need for Aristarchus' future here therefore, despite the futures which follow in 177-8.

174 ἁπάντων suggests that Poseidon's annoyance is not so much at the simple fact that they save travellers, as at their indiscriminate abuse of the privilege, which has so far not attracted any retribution (ἀπήμονες); the escorting of Od. laden with treasure is the last straw for the god.

175-7: as in 172, Alcinous' words are very close to those of Poseidon in 149-52, and his own words in 8.564-72.

178 τελεῖται: present, rather than future, since the process has already started, as is shown by the fate of the ship. In the comparable 8.570-1 (cf. last note), Alcinous was looking forward to possibilities in the future and used the optative: τὰ δέ κεν θεὸς ἢ τελέσειεν | ἤ κ' ἀτέλεστ' εἴη 'the god may bring these about, or they may not happen'. The second half of 178, with its echo of the earlier passage, ironically gives Alcinous his answer.

180 παύσασθε: the aorist conveys the sense of 'stop now, once and for all'.

181 προτί = πρός, which was probably created by the palatalisation of τ before ι; the sequence is roughly *ti* > *ty* > *s* (Beekes 1238).

181-2 ταύρους | ...κεκριμένους: twelve bulls is a grand offering of the most expensive sacrificial animal. No Homeric sacrifice has this number of victims, though what the number was of the 'many' sheep and cattle sacrificed by Achilles at Patroclus' pyre is not stated (*Il.* 23.166). For twelve as the number of sacrificial victims, cf. the twelve Trojan youths sacrificed by Achilles to Patroclus (23.175). Bulls are regularly offered to Poseidon, as at Pylos (*Od.* 3.5-8), and he appears as Ταύρεος in [Hes.] *Scut.* 104. All sacrificial animals were carefully selected, so the use of κεκριμένους here emphasises the especial care that is to be taken in this case.

182 ἱερεύσομεν: jussive short-vowel aorist subjunctive.   **αἴ κ᾽ ἐλεήσῃι:** lit. '(to see) if he might pity us', so 'in the hope that'. The if-clause does not in this construction depend on the main clause, but on the idea of purpose or desire explicitly or (as often in Homer) implicitly expressed in it (cf. Smyth §2354). A more explicit example is *Il.* 5.279 νῦν αὖτ᾽ ἐγχείηι πειρήσομαι, αἴ κε τύχωμι 'now I will make trial with my spear, (to see) whether I may hit you'. In Homer, ἔλεος does not just mean simply 'a feeling of pity for', for which οἶκτος is used, but tends to describe a more active desire to do something about a problem (Burkert 1955).

183 μηδ᾽...ἀμφικαλύψῃι continues the wish; for μηδέ after a positive clause, cf. 212 οὐδ᾽.

184 οἱ δ᾽ ἔδεισαν: the initial epsilon of the verb is scanned long because the root was *δϝει-, with two initial consonants. It is sometimes written ἔδδεισαν, but this is a purely graphic form, not an indication of pronunciation (*GH* 1.163). Cf. 202n. on θεουδής.

187a ἑσταότες περὶ βωμόν: the book opened with the pregnant pause after Od.'s narration, and now this episode ends tantalisingly in mid-line with the worried leaders around the altar, wondering, as we are, whether the sacrifice will be enough to placate Poseidon. This is the last we see of the Phaeacians. The episode began with an account of how Alcinous' father Nausithous saved his people from the troublesome Cyclopes (6.2–10; cf. 173n.). It now ends with his son possibly exposing them to final destruction, which suggests a lack of his father's foresight and wisdom. The wisdom of Alcinous and the Phaeacians is stressed (cf. 6.12, 7.73, 292; Austin 1975: 193–200), but should not be exaggerated: they do not have the wisdom of the survivor Od., who also escaped the Cyclopes but listened to the voice of the divine.

187–216 Odysseus awakes to a disguised Ithaca

Od.'s awakening here is as sudden as the change of location in the middle of the line (cf. S. Richardson 2005–6: 345–7, 356). He awakes to an island disguised by Athena. The disguise of the island may seem gratuitous, but disguise is emblematic of the second half of the poem, and Homer announces its importance by the way that everything in this book is disguised, island, goddess, Od. Cf. Introduction 1.2.

The disguising of the island also allows the poet to deploy a little ironic humour at Od.'s expense. He has slept and awoken before in unknown lands (NB 200 αὖτε) where he could not be sure of the nature of the inhabitants. The language reminds us of this: 200–2 repeat 6.119–21 from his arrival on Scherie. This humour is conjoined with sympathy for a man whose first experience on returning home after twenty years is to find that he has apparently not returned at all. His reaction is all the more comprehensible, because he has twice before awoken from sleep to unpleasant realisations, when his men opened the bag of winds (10.31–52), and when they ate the Cattle of the Sun (12.338–73). Od. has a tendency to a suspicious pessimism, as shown when Calypso says she will let him go (5.173–6) or when Ino offers help (5.356–9; cf. 5.219–24, 6.172–4, 7.208–25; Rutherford 1986: 153–5), but it is sometimes quite justified, given what he has been through.

187b ὁ δ᾽ ἔγρετο: just as the previous scene began in mid-line (125), so does this one, taking us from Scherie back to Ithaca. There are two other cases of such intralinear shifts, 15.495 (from Eum.'s farm to Telemachus down on the shore) and 17.182 (from the palace back to Eum.'s farm); cf. also *Il.* 1.430 (from Achilles brooding on the shore to Od. preparing a sacrifice for Apollo). In *Il.* 1.495, 5.29 and 18.35, the scene shifts in midline, but the action that takes place in the second part of the line is in some way a reaction to an event in the first, so the disjunction is not so great as here. On the treatment of space in *Od.*, see Saïd 2011: 100–10.

189–90 These lines are an example of a regular rhetorical feature of Homer, the *hysteron proteron*, in which the important feature is put first, regardless of the chronology of the events or of logic (cf. Bassett 1920). The disguise will in fact follow the explanation, but it is crucial to the rest of the story, whereas the explanations are a temporary expedient necessary to stop Od. rushing straight home and meeting disaster. For other examples of this feature, cf. 14.49, 201, 279, 322.

189 ἤδη δὴν ἀπεών 'after he had been away a long time'. The participle is better taken as a temporal not a causal one: he does not recognise the island because Athena has disguised it (NB 189 γάρ), not because he has been away for twenty years. That the phrase has a temporal sense in 14.330 supports such a sense here.   **δήν:** an accusative of a root noun *dwā-* indicating length, also found in δηρός '(too) long', and in the zero grade in Lat. *dū-dum* 'for a long time' (Beekes 326).   **περὶ ... ἠέρα χεῦε:** putting ἀήρ around something is epic's way of describing it as invisible. Translation is difficult, since 'it is misleading to translate ἀήρ "mist" in such contexts: mist is something visible, and ἀήρ is the very stuff of invisibility' (M. L. West 1966 on Hes. *Th.* 9); cf. 7.15, 140; Hes. *Op.* 223. For this motif of hiding in ἀήρ, compare the ἀήρ and ἀχλύς which Athena pours round Od. to make him invisible on the way to the Phaeacians' city (7.15, 41). The repetition of the motif helps recall her last piece of assistance.

191 ἄγνωστον 'unrecognisable'; αὐτόν is Od. There is no need to take this as meaning 'unable to recognise (the island)', on the grounds that Athena did not need to disguise the island in order to disguise Od. Moreover, there are few parallels for such an active meaning for this adjective, though cf. Pi. *Ol.* 6.67 ψευδέων ἄγνωστον 'unaware of lies' (some MSS read ἄγνωτον). Furthermore, 397 below ἀλλ' ἄγε σ' ἄγνωστον τεύξω πάντεσσι βροτοῖσι supports the passive sense. The line summarises what is to happen in the book as a preparation for the second part of the poem: Od. is to be in disguise and to learn what he needs to survive.

192–3 πρὶν…πρίν 'lest in advance his wife, people and friends should recognise him, before…' For the use of πρίν in Homer, cf. 124n. It is in origin an adverb, as here in the first clause; it then became a conjunction, as in the second clause. It has been thought a problem that, by disguising Od. from Penelope, Athena/Homer makes it impossible for Od. to recruit her to his cause, even though it is made clear that she is still loyal to him (337–8; cf. 11.181–3). This has the advantage however of leaving the recognition by Penelope as the climax of the poem. Cf. Emlyn-Jones 1984: 1–2; Murnaghan 1987: 118–46.

193 πᾶσαν…ἀποτεῖσαι 'repay the Suitors for all their transgression'; the subject is Od. ὑπερβασίη is found six times in Homer, but is not common after him, until much later.

194 τοὔνεκ' ἄρ' 'and so it was for that reason', summarising the previous lines.   **ἀλλοειδέα φαινέσκετο πάντα** 'everything kept appearing in a different form', i.e. wherever he looked, he did not see what he would have expected on Ithaca. The repeated looking is conveyed by the imperfect iterative (a form which is a feature of Homer and Ionic; Introduction 5.3 §6.4). ἀλλοειδέα is essentially the reading of all MSS, but it is problematic because of the two synizeses, -οει- and -εα, of which the first would be a rare case of synizesis between vowels after the loss of the digamma where the first vowel is not ε (cf. *GH* 1.37–8, 56). It has been variously emended, but is defended by Cassio 2004, who argues that it is only the written form that is unmetrical. The word was pronounced /alleydea/, but written ἀλλοειδέα 'because of the orthographic pressure exerted *in primis* by all the other Homeric compounds of this type where a disyllabic -οει- was metrically necessary (θεοειδής, ἠεροειδής, ἰοειδής etc.)' (2004: 91). That φαινέσκετο is the correct reading, rather than the MSS' alternative φαίνετο, is made almost certain by the unlikelihood that a correct φαίνετο would have been corrupted into the less familiar frequentative; it is much more likely that φαίνετο was an attempt to mend the metrical problems caused by ἀλλοειδέα.

197 πατρίδα γαῖαν: here focalised from the narrator's point of view, since Od. is unaware that it is his fatherland.

198–9 In *Il.*, these lines (only here in *Od.*) are used at two moments of great distress, of Ares, when he suddenly learns of a son's death (15.113–14), and of Patroclus, when he realises that the Trojan success is such that he must persuade Achilles to fight (15.397–8). For the gesture, cf. also *H.Dem.* 245 (Metaneira fearing Demeter is killing her only child); *Il.* 12.162. Cf. 220n. for another striking expression for Od.'s grief.

198 ὣ πεπλήγετο μηρώ 'he smote both his thighs'. ὣ is the accusative dual of ὅς 'his, hers', the possessive of ἕ (Introduction 5.3 §4.1). πεπλήγετο is a reduplicated aorist middle of πλήσσω (*GH* 1.397).

199 ὀλοφυρόμενος: this word marks very considerable mental turmoil, like that of Eurycleia when she asks Telemachus how, as an only son, he can risk going in search of his father (2.362), or that of Eurylochus when he is told by Od. to take him to Circe's cave, despite what he has seen there (10.265).

200–2 For this question, cf. 6.119–21, 9.175–6.

200 τέων = τίνων.   αὖτε: though this is a common word, it can sometimes indicate a certain weariness at the repetition of some action or event, as in 5.356–7 ὤ μοι ἐγώ, μή τίς μοι ὑφαίνῃσιν δόλον αὖτε | ἀθανάτων 'Oh no! I hope some god is not weaving a trick aganst me *again*!'

201–2 ἦ ῥ᾽…ἦε 'are they…or are they…?' This combination is a regular way to express alternative questions in Homer. Both forms relate to the affirmative particle ἦ 'truly' (172n.): ἦ is the proclitic form; ἦε is < ἦ + the disjunctive (ϝ)ε 'or' (cf. Lat. *-ue*).

202 θεουδής 'god-fearing' < θεο- + *δϝει-; the diphthong ου marks the lengthening of the omicron before the double consonant in the second part of the compound (cf. 184n.).

203 πῆι δὴ χρήματα: once again, Od.'s thoughts turn immediately to the safety of his treasure (even, it seems, before his own safety), indicating its importance in his scheme of values (cf. 41n.).

203–4 φέρω… | πλάζομαι: φέρω is unproblematically a deliberative present subjunctive ('where am I to take…?'). πλάζομαι however, from its form, should be a present indicative, because there are in Homer very few short-vowel present subjunctives of thematic verbs, and even these few are questionable (*GH* 1.458). On the other hand, the parallelism of πῆι δή…πῆι δέ suggests strongly that πλάζομαι is being used as a subjunctive like φέρω.

204 αἴθ' ὄφελον: the subject is the χρήματα, rather than Od. (for the plural verb with a neuter plural subject, cf. 14.73n.), as suggested by the contrasting ἐγὼ δέ and ἄλλον in 205; Od. means that even if he had not taken the Phaeacians' gifts, he could easily have got their equivalent from some other king elsewhere. The aorist (and imperfect) of ὀφέλλω began to function like the optative to express unrealisable wishes, and so came to mean 'I ought to have (but didn't)'. The addition of αἴθε is a later strengthening of this sense of regret (*GH* II.227–9).

205–6 ἐγὼ δέ κεν... | ἐξικόμην 'I could have come'. Aorist and imperfect indicatives with ἄν/κε express what could have been in the past; this explains also ἐφίλει 'would have treated me as his friend' (imperfect, because expressing a continued friendship) and ἔπεμπε in the next line. This development is connected with the use of this combination in conditionals (*GH* II.226–7).

206 ἔπεμπε νέεσθαι: cf. 34n. for the infinitive of purpose.

207 οὔτ' ἄρ πηι θέσθαι ἐπίσταμαι: lit. 'I neither know how to put them anywhere'; cf. 12.433–4 οὐδέ πηι εἶχον | οὔτε στηρίξαι ποσὶν ἔμπεδον οὔτ' ἐπιβῆναι 'I didn't have anywhere either to fix my footing or to stand on'; for this use of the infinitive to express ability, possibility etc., cf. *GH* I.303–4.

207–8 οὐδὲ μέν... | καλλείψω, μή πως... γένηται: lit. 'nor again will I leave them here: may they not become prey...', so 'but I will not leave them here, so that they do not...'. This example shows clearly how what were historically separate expressions paratactically joined in Homer could come very close to syntactic ones, producing in this case the purpose-clause construction (cf. Introduction 5.3 §11.1.2). For οὐδὲ μέν, cf. *GP* 362.

208 μοι: a 'dative of disadvantage'.   **ἕλωρ** 'prey' is a striking expression when used of treasure, as the word elsewhere in Homer is always used of corpses which are at the mercy of the enemy or of wild beasts.

209 ὦ πόποι: cf. 140n.

209–10 οὐκ ἄρα... | ἦσαν 'so they were not!' ἄρα often indicates a sudden realisation of something: the trickery (as he sees it) of the Phaeacians finally strikes home. The imperfect (usually of εἰμί and often with a negative) is frequently used in this sense, as the speaker thinks back to the time when matters appeared otherwise: '(when I thought they were), the Phaeacians weren't right-thinking' (for a similar use of the imperfect of things not the case in the past, cf. 204n.). Illustrative is Hes. *Op.* 11–12 οὐκ ἄρα μοῦνον ἔην Ἐρίδων γένος... | εἰσὶ δύω 'so there was not a single kind of Strife (as I thought in the past), there are two (as I now see)' (cf. *GP* 36–7; Bakker 1993: 16–23).

209 πάντα: 'completely', adverbial accusative.

211 ἄλλην: i.e. 'than the one I expected'; cf. 9.261–2 οἴκαδε ἱέμενοι, ἄλλην ὁδόν, ἄλλα κέλευθα | ἤλθομεν 'trying to get home, we followed a different path and different ways', said by Od. when explaining how they came to the Cyclopes' land.   **ἦ τέ μ' ἔφαντο** 'and yet they really told me'. ἦ (cf. 172n.) can have a concessive force, cf. *Il.* 11.362–3 ἐξ αὖ νῦν ἔφυγες θάνατον, κύον· ἦ τέ τοι ἄγχι | ἦλθε κακόν 'you escaped death this time, you dog, but yet disaster came near you'; τε adds a little confirmation (*GH* II.344).

212 εὐδείελον is of uncertain meaning. García-Ramón 1998–9 argues for a connection with δείελος 'late afternoon', giving it the meaning of 'well visible, distinct in the late afternoon, at sunset'. Alternatively, it has been connected with δῆλος and taken to mean 'conspicuous, standing out in the light'. In *Od.*, the adjective is used only of Ithaca (6 ×).   **οὐδ' ἐτέλεσσαν** 'but they did not fulfil their promise'. In Homer οὐδέ regularly follows a positive clause: cf. 16.379 φόνον αἰπὺν ἐράπτομεν οὐδ' ἐκίχημεν 'we plotted dread murder but did not succeed'; 14.524.

213 τείσαιτο: it is ironic that Od. curses his benefactors the Phaeacians to Zeus's punishment, at the very moment when Poseidon is contemplating punishing them for another reason, with Zeus's encouragement; and it is all the more ironic that Poseidon's reason is that the Phaeacians have been too happy and willing to help suppliants like Od. get home.   **ἱκετήσιος** '(god) of suppliants'. In this guise Zeus saw to it that, if someone success-fully supplicated another by physically grasping their chin or knees, that person did indeed do what the suppliant wanted. To be supplicated there-fore involved a religious obligation to fulfil the request, which was not to be taken lightly: Phaedra in Euripides' *Hippolytus*, despite being des-perate to keep the matter quiet, reveals her passion for Hippolytus when the Nurse seizes her hand in supplication (333–5). Od. had formally sup-plicated Arete when he first arrived in the palace, and asked for help in getting home (7.142–52), so he could reasonably call on Zeus to note the failure to fulfil his request. He will again employ supplication when Athena appears disguised as a youth (231). On supplication, cf. Gould 1973; Naiden 2006.

214 ὅς τις ἁμάρτηι 'whoever may do wrong', a generalising relative (cf. 31–2n.) with an almost conditional sense of 'if anyone ...' (Introduction 5.3 §11.8.3). For the singular after the plural ἀνθρώπους, cf. 3.355 ξείνους ξεινίζειν, ὅς τίς κ' ἐμὰ δώματ' ἵκηται: the shift in number is eased by the parat-actic style of composition.

215 ἀριθμήσω καὶ ἴδωμαι 'let me count and see', jussive aorist subjunctives; ἴδωμαι is a middle, as Od. does it on his own behalf. Again, Od. is deeply concerned with his treasure (cf. 203).

216 μή τί μοι οἴχονται: since the Phaeacians have in fact gone, the indicative οἴχονται is better than the subjunctive (though both would originally have been written OIXONTAI); the indicative is often found in such expressions after verbs of seeing, as in Pl. *Tht.* 145b ὅρα μὴ παίζων ἔλεγε 'make sure he wasn't speaking in jest' (the implication being that he was; cf. K–G ii.395). τι is object of ἄγοντες: such unemphatic words regularly stand in second position in their sentence.

217–49 Appearance of Athena in disguise

The rest of this book contains a remarkable scene where a goddess and a mortal chat together like good friends and equals. Gods seldom reveal themselves openly to mortals (cf. *Il.* 1.197–200, 5.121–3; N. J. Richardson 1974: 185), but even when they do, the meetings do not end in this kind of familiarity. On the relationship between the two, cf. Clay 1983: 186–212; Introduction pp. 6–8. For striking parallels between Athena's role here and in the *Od.* generally and the role of the goddess Durga in the *Mahābhārata*, cf. N. Allen 2001.

The motif of meetings with a helpful young person, often on the shore, is regularly repeated in *Od.* Od. has had this experience a number of times before, and the fact that the young people he meets are not always what they seem may contribute to his caution on this occasion: Hermes appeared as a young man on his way to Circe's cave and gave him the magical protective herb *moly* (10.275–309), and Athena, disguised as a young girl, gave him advice about dealing with the Phaeacians on his way to Alcinous' palace (7.18–77).

The scene closest to the present one is Od.'s meeting with the young Nausicaa on Scherie (6.141–315). Comparison of the two scenes illuminates them both. On Scherie, confronted by a young girl alone on an unknown shore, and mindful perhaps of Circe and Calypso with their magical powers, Od. was very cautious. Because he was naked, he decided not to embrace her knees but simply began with 'I supplicate you' (149). He kept open the question of whether she was a deity in a tentative yet highly laudatory passage (149–69); and expressed his admiration, calling her 'my lady' (ἄνασσα) and asking for her pity (175). He told her a brief tale, which was true, and made some humble requests.

In the current scene these elements are varied in an amusing way. Od. is unaware that this time he really *is* dealing with a goddess so, remembering perhaps that the last young person, Nausicaa, turned out to be no god and no threat, and emboldened by being this time properly dressed and prosperous, he addresses and supplicates the youth as a god in a rather more cursory manner than he did Nausicaa. However, any sense he has that the young man is without spirit is deflated by his rather patronising reply, which contrasts with Nausicaa's sympathetic promise of help. Od. then discovers that the youth is this time a god.

As well as looking back to these other examples, this scene is also a forerunner of Od.'s meeting with the young Telemachus. There is also pathos, since this apparent son of an *anax* (223) could so easily have been his own son (and perhaps in some versions of the story was), but Od. is not yet permitted any such pleasure. It is a good example too of how Homer can use such type-scenes not just to expand the narrative, but also to increase the emotional complexity of the work.

For other examples of the motif, cf. 4.363–425 (Menelaus protected from the seals' stench by Eidothea, daughter of Proteus); 10.105–11 (Od.'s men meet a daughter of the king of the Laestrygonians); and 14.317–20 (Od.'s fictional meeting with a helpful son of the king of Thesprotia).

219 τῶν μὲν . . . πόθει 'he was missing none of them, he saw'; for ἄρα, see 209–10n. The root *ποθ- often expresses a longing or desire for something that one has lost or that is absent.

220 ἑρπύζων 'creeping along' is used in Homer 'always of persons weighed down by age or deep distress' (LSJ); cf. also *Il.* 23.225 (Achilles by Patroclus' pyre) and *Od.* 1.193 (Laertes).   **πολυφλοίσβοιο θαλάσσης:** in *Il.* this formula is predominantly used, as here, where characters are unhappy, reluctant or apprehensive, as 1.34 (Chryses returns from his rude dismissal by Agamemnon), 2.209 (the Greeks return to the assembly having discovered they cannot go home after all), 6.347, 9.182 and 23.59. The only exceptions are 13.798 (the Trojans charge enthusiastically), and *Od.* 13.85.

221 σχεδόθεν . . . Ἀθήνη: expressions of this kind, followed by a description of her disguise, are formulaic for Athena when she is bringing help; cf. 2.267, 16.157–8, 20.30.

222 ἀνδρὶ . . . ἐϊκυῖα νέωι: for Athena's disguises, see 313n. Athena is the only character in *Od.* besides Od. to assume a disguise (Doherty 1991: 134). For gods appearing as young mortals, cf. *H.Hy.* 7.1–6 (Dionysus) and *H.Ap.* 448–50.   **δέμας:** 'in the context of divine disguise, *demas* alone occurs – never *eidos* or *phuê phuê*', perhaps because it marks the human form in an unchanging, static form (Clay 1974: 130).   **ἐπιβώτορι** 'herdsman', cognate with βό-σκω 'pasture'; only here in Greek. The scholiasts explain a prince acting as a shepherd as a feature of ancient life, but cf. Introduction pp. 6–7 for another suggestion.

223 οἷοί τε...ἔασι: lit. 'of what sort the sons of princes are'. One could understand τοίωι in the previous clause, but Homer regularly uses clauses introduced by οἷος in this slightly loose manner: cf. 14.392, 491. For τε, see 31–2n.

224 λώπην 'mantle', from λέπω 'peel'. This is a particularly fine cloak; cf. the much-admired cloak described by Od. at 19.233 οἷόν τε κρομύοιο λοπὸν κάτα ἰσχαλέοιο 'like the skin on a dried onion'.

225 ἄκοντα: the javelin is a small piece of 'reality', a reminder that shepherding was not an idyllic occupation and that wild animals and marauders had to be kept at bay (cf. 14.531).

226–35 Does Od. recognise Athena here or not? The scene is more effective if he does not. At 22.207–10, he rejoices at the sight of Athena disguised as Mentes, and replies 'thinking it was Athena', but the absence of any comparable clear indication in our passage militates against claims of recognition. Od.'s delight comes from meeting so unthreatening a person as the youth (so the scholiast; cf. also his fears in 200–2), and his great caution in 254–5 better suits one who is not sure whom he is talking to. For a similar failure of recognition, cf. 1.123, where Telemachus addresses the disguised Athena as a masculine ξεῖνος.

228 πρῶτα 'in the first place', adverbial accusative.

229 χαῖρε...ἀντιβολήσαις: for the shift between the imperative, the usual mood of suppliants, and the optative, cf. *Il.* 3.406–8 (an angry Helen to Aphrodite) ἧσο παρ᾽ αὐτὸν..., μηδ᾽...ὑποστρέψειας Ὄλυμπον 'go and sit by him, and don't go back to Olympus'; cf. Pearce 1996: 285, 287. The optative marks the more polite or tentative wish.

230 σάω 'save', a 2nd p.s. present active imperative, probably an athematic form from σάωμι, since thematic *σάο-ε would have given *σάου. Thematic Ionic/Attic imperatives like 3.58 δίδου may hide earlier athematic *δίδω etc. (cf. Munro 1891: 14–15; *GH* I.307, 466–7).

232 ἐτήτυμον 'truly': the neuter of this adjective is regularly used as an adverb, as in 4.157 κείνου μέν τοι ὅδ᾽ υἱὸς ἐτήτυμον 'you know, he really is that man's son'.

233 ἐγγεγάασιν: cf. 16on.

234 ἤ πού τις νήσων εὐδείελος, ἠὲ κτλ. 'I imagine it is some highly visible island, or...' The suggestions put forward with ἤ που show a certain confidence, and avoid the suggestion that he is lost and somewhat cluelessly vulnerable. ἦε is disjunctive: see also 201-2n. Od. is careful to apply two laudatory epithets to the land, to please the prince; on εὐδείελος, see 212n.

235 κεῖθ': i.e. κεῖται. ἁλὶ κεκλιμένη 'sloping down to the sea'.

236-49 *Athena's description of Ithaca.* The earlier part corresponds to other descriptions of Ithaca, which make it 'rough' (9.27, 10.417, 463), 'rocky' (1.247, 15.510, 16.124, 21.346), 'grazed by goats', 'attractive but not suitable for horses' and 'lacking good meadows' (4.605-7); but the idyllic coda does not correspond (apart from 'grazed by goats', 246); cf. e.g. Elliger 1975: 118-23 (see Luce 1998: 184-204 for a different view). There is no reason to suspect the text – these contradictions are exactly the point: Athena is trying to confuse Od., and so jumbles real and contradictory features together; she is not trying to be an accurate tour-guide.

She stokes Od.'s bemusement by obfuscating use of what rhetoricians called *epanorthosis* or *correctio*, the withdrawing or qualification of a statement as soon as it is made. Having broadcast the island's wide fame in 238-41, she moderates her picture in 242-4: 'not that it isn't rough, and you can't ride horses there – yet it isn't *too* poor –, but then again it doesn't have broad pastures; there is though an abundance of corn ... ' The corrections give a good impression of someone making things up as she goes along, whilst not worrying too much about being wholly convincing because she knows she has her auditor at her mercy: note too her *faux naïf* final remark suggesting uncertainty about exactly where Troy is (249). Athena then crowns her speech with an idyllic and eulogistic picture, which is quite at variance with the reality that Od. knows from experience.

If the lack of correspondence to Ithaca's actual geography in Athena's description can be accounted for, those in Od.'s apparently authoritative description in 9.19-26 are less easy to explain. The problems in these passages have led to a plethora of theories from antiquity onwards about the identities of the group of islands which includes Ithaca; there is a summary in Bittlestone 2005: 550-62. In some ways, in a work of fiction, the 'real' identity of Ithaca does not matter any more than the location of Camelot does for the appreciation of stories about King Alfred. The question continues to fascinate some however, and Bittlestone 2005 has recently revived Volterras' theory of 1903 that 'Ithaca' was in fact Paliki, now the western peninsula of Cephalonia, but once perhaps a separate island; cf. the critical assessment by Graziosi 2008.

236 γλαυκῶπις: a regular epithet of Athena, but of uncertain meaning. It may mean 'with eyes that are grey/blue/clear' or 'of bright appearance': cf. Perotti 1989; Pötscher 1997.

237 νήπιός εἰς... εἰλήλουθας is the Cyclops' contemptuous response to Od.'s suggestion that he respect the gods (9.273), and Proteus' daughter addresses Menelaus with νήπιός εἰς, ὦ ξεῖνε when she sees him doing little to resolve his problems in Egypt (4.371). These suggest a rather patronising tone for the shepherd's words. Generally, the precise tone of νήπιος depends on the circumstances: cf. Edmunds 1990.

238 εἰ δή... ἀνείρεαι 'if you really *are* asking about this island'; the youth moderates his suggestion of Od.'s extraordinary ignorance in the first clause.   **τήνδε τε γαῖαν:** τε is hard to explain. One might expect γε, implying 'this island of all islands'. Ruijgh 1971: 839 suggests that rhapsodes replaced here (and 15.484) an original γε with τε, to produce something more euphonious than γε γαῖαν.

238–9 οὐδέ τι λίην | οὕτω νώνυμός ἐστιν 'it is not so very little known' (lit. 'without name'; for the negative prefix *n-*, cf. 74n.). For οὐδέ, cf. 212n. Athena starts with an understatement, becomes more emphatic in μάλα πολλοί, and then widens the scope of those who know the island effectively to the whole world. This is calculated to increase Od.'s confusion even further: how can he not know *this* place of all places?

241 μετόπισθε: lit. 'behind', and so here 'to the west'.   **ἠερόεντα:** cf. 103n on the similar ἠεροειδές.

242–4 For a translation of these lines, see 236–49n.

242 ἦ τοι μέν: this combination of particles is used of strong expressions of opinion (*GP* 389).

243 λυπρή 'poor', from λύπη 'pain, poor condition', is a hapax in Homer, like βούβοτος (246), but the presence of two such words is not a strong argument for deletion of the lines: cf. 14.10n. for a similar collocation of hapaxes in one passage.   **τέτυκται:** the perfect of τεύχομαι regularly means no more than 'be' (*GH* ii.6; cf. 14.138, 234).

244 ἀθέσφατος 'unlimited'; lit. 'that which has not been stated or decided by a god', and so 'something that does not fit in a given order' (Fraenkel 1923: 281–2).

248 Ἰθάκης γε: Athena unkindly keeps until the very end of her speech the one thing Od. wants to hear, the name of the island; this is ironically emphasised by γε and by its position between the pauses after ξεῖν' and at the main caesura.   **ἐς Τροίην:** she also rather cruelly exploits her knowledge of the identity of the man before her, by suggesting that the fact that Ithaca was known even in *Troy* shows just how ignorant he is. The reference to Troy's distance from Ithaca, made to a man who is all too aware of how far it is, and the pretended uncertainty in φασίν in 249 add to the humour.

There is a similarly humorous use of this kind of geographical uncertainty by Alcinous in 7.321–4.

250–86 Od.'s cautious use of a false tale

This speech inaugurates the use by Od. of the 'false tales' which are a particular feature of the second half of *Od.*: the others are told to Eum. (14.191–359), Eum. and the swineherds (14.462–502), Antinous (17.419–44), Amphinomus (18.125–50), Melantho (19.71–88), Penelope (19.165–307) and Laertes (24.265–314). His successful lie to the Cyclops that his name was 'No-man' (9.366) is a seed of this feature. Od.'s false tales are regularly tailored to their audience (cf. e.g. 14.191–359n. para. 1). This particular tale gives a clear picture of how formidable a man Od. is, warning the youth against any ideas he may have of stealing the treasure, through the recital of what happened to the last man who tried that. The warning is reinforced by the fact that that man was the son of one of the most powerful of the Greeks.

250 πολύτλας δῖος Ὀδυσσεύς: though this is a very regular formula for Od. (5× *Il.*, 37× *Od.*), its last use was at 8.446, and there is pathos in its use here as he realises that, after all he has suffered, he is finally home (cf. 311n.).

251–2 χαίρων... Ἀθηναίη: lit. 'rejoicing in his ancestral land, that Pallas Athena said (*sc.* that it was his land)', i.e 'delighted that Pallas Athena said it was his ancestral land'. Cf. the way Greek says 'I know you, who you are' (cf. 170n.).

252 αἰγιόχοιο is traditionally translated 'aegis-bearing', but the meaning is in fact uncertain: for 'aegis-bearing' one would expect *αἰγιδοῦχος. Most take the second element as from ϝέχω 'ride' (cf. Lat. *ueho,* Eng. 'wagon'). There are a number of possibilities:
(1) 'who waves the aegis', with αἴξ being equivalent to αἰγίς; cf. γαιήοχος 'who moves the earth';
(2) 'who rides the storm winds', with a development from 'goat' to 'storm wind', perhaps through the fear caused when the aegis is shaken: cf. *Il.* 2.146–7 Ζέφυρος... λάβρος ἐπαιγίζων 'the west wind rushing wildly on', Aes. *Cho.* 591–2 ἀνεμοέντ' αἰγίδων... κότον 'the anger of stormy hurricanes';
(3) 'who rides the storm bird', with αἴξ not 'goat' but a bird which announces a storm (so M. L. West 1978: 366–8); the epithet would be connected with Zeus's role as a weather-god.

253–4 καί μιν φωνήσας... μῦθον: it is very unusual for such a speech introduction not to be followed immediately by direct speech. This sudden breaking off in the text from the expected speech mirrors and graphically conveys Od.'s own sudden change of mind not to speak the truth.

254 οὐδ' ὅ γ'... ὅ γε: Homer sometimes emphasises the contrast between two ideas by repeating the pronoun in disjunctive sentences of this kind; cf. *Il.* 1.189–91 μερμήριξεν | ...ἦ ὅ γε... | τοὺς μὲν ἀναστήσειεν, ὁ δ' Ἀτρεΐδην ἐναρίζοι 'considering whether he should break up the Greeks' assembly and slay Agamemnon' (*GH* 11.159). **πάλιν...μῦθον** 'but he took back what he was about to say'. The phrase is used at *Il.* 4.357 where Agamemnon, having accused Od. of cowardice, takes back the insults he had hurled at him. Here Od. has not said anything that he could take back, so the μῦθος must refer to what he had in mind to say. λάζομαι is cognate with λαμβάνω. Delighted though he may be to be home, Od. is not fool enough to reveal his identity to the first person he meets. The discrepancy between Od.'s own knowledge of what Ithaca looks like and the youth's claim that this still unfamiliar island is Ithaca has made him suspicious. This is perhaps the most striking example in *Od.* of the topos of 'unspoken thoughts': for other examples, cf. de Jong 2009.

255 ἐνὶ στήθεσσι νόον: for the chest as the seat of intellectual activity, cf. 13.330, 17.403 ἐνὶ στήθεσσι νόημα, 3.18 μῆτιν ἐνὶ στήθεσσι, 5.191 θυμὸς ἐνὶ στήθεσσι. **νωμῶν** 'deploying'. Only here, and in 18.216 and 20.257 (of κέρδεα), is this verb used of things other than physical objects, such as parts of the body and weapons.

256 πυνθανόμην Ἰθάκης γε 'yes, I used to hear of Ithaca.' γε can have the sense 'yes' in replies (*GP* 130). Od.'s reply is subtly ambiguous. Saying that Ithaca was famous not just in Troy but Crete too (καί), another famous land, could be words designed to win over the youth by flattery of his country. On the other hand, the claim to come from somewhere as grand as Crete (see next note) could also be something of a put-down: 'I think we'd heard of Ithaca.' This would be supported by the use of τηλοῦ ὑπὲρ πόντου, which rather unnecessary bit of geographical precision suggests that the youth himself might be νήπιος enough to need to be told where Crete is; it picks up and responds to the youth's mocking τηλοῦ in 249. This ambiguity is unlikely to be lost on Athena, and no doubt contributes to her exasperation expressed in 291–5. **ἐν Κρήτηι:** Od. claims to hail from Crete also in his tale to Eum. (14.199–206) and in his first story to Penelope (19.172–84). In the other tales (listed in 250–86n.), he does not refer to Crete. The choice of Crete may have been determined by a variety of factors: see Tsagalis 2012: 314 n.19 for a list. It may have featured prominently in other versions of the story (see Danek 1998: 269, 285–6), and Homer may be attempting to replace these with his own version: 'the

Odyssey must frame these as "lies" because they do not fit its own narrative arc, but taken on their own, these miniature epic episodes could have featured in independent Cyclic poems' (Martin n.d.: 13; cf. more speculatively Reece 1994). Crete seems to have weathered the 'Dark Ages' better than many places (cf. Morris 1997: 555–7), and so may have had a certain reputation for prosperity and prestige. At the same time, the fact that Od. feels the need to describe it in some detail to Penelope may suggest an element of mystery about it. Finally, stories about Minos inaugurated for it a reputation for adventurous sea-borne activity (cf. Thuc. 1.4). Demeter in *H.Dem.* 122–33 similarly uses Crete for a false story, which has echoes of Od.'s tales in this book and the next in its references to pirates and escape from ships (cf. N. J. Richardson 1974: 188 ad 120–1). For possible Cretan influence on the *Odyssey*, see Levaniouk 2012.

258 τοίσδεσσι: an unusual form of τοῖσδε, with the case-ending added also to the -δε suffix. This kind of formation is found six times in Homer, and sporadically also in a number of dialects: cf., beside Ionic (Homer and Democr. fr. 175), Lesbian τωνδέων (Alc. fr. 130.21), Argive τωνδεων (Wathelet 1970: 293–4). **τοσαῦτα:** Od. begins to build up a picture of his wealth and importance, by the suggestion that the great pile of treasure is only half of his fortune, so he has back-up should anything happen to it.

259 φεύγω 'I am in exile'. Exile as a result of a killing is a recurrent theme in both epics: cf. 14.380 (an Aetolian), 15.272–3 (Theoclymenus), 23.118–20 (general); *Il.* 13.695–7 (Medon), 15.431–2 (Lycophron), 23.85–8 (Patroclus). Od.'s tales, though false, presumably give an idea of how precarious life was for an exile. In no case is there talk of pursuit by the relatives of the dead man, so it may be that the loss of livelihood, wealth and status entailed by exile was felt to be sufficient revenge for the victims. **Ἰδομενῆος:** Od. claims to have killed the son of a very important and dangerous man. Idomeneus was the king of the Cretans, with eighty ships (*Il.* 2.645–52), and 'like a boar in strength' (4.253); the sight of him brings great joy to Agamemnon's face in a tricky moment in battle (4.255). He also plays a major role in the battle by the ships (*Il.* 13.210–515), and is one of the nine who offer to fight Hector in single combat (7.165). He chooses Od. as his companion for the night-raid in *Il.* 10.242–7. Od. associates himself with him again in *Od.* 14.237–8 and 19.181–91, in his tales to Eum. and Penelope. On Idomeneus in Od.'s tales, cf. Haft 1984.

260 Ὀρσίλοχον: he appears to have been made up by Od.; he is not to be confused with the three other men in Homer called Ortilochus (*Il.* 5.547, 549; *Od.* 3.489 etc.); on these names, see García-Ramón 2002.   **πόδας**

ὠκύν: only here in *Od.*; in *Il.* it is used solely of Achilles at line-end. Giving Orsilochus Achilles' epithet adds to his status, and 261 reinforces the point.

261 ἀλφηστάς: a word of uncertain meaning from antiquity onwards, but probably a combination of ἄλφι- 'barley' + *ed-* 'eat' (cf. ὠμ-ηστής). **νίκα:** unaugmented 3rd p.s. imperfect.

262–3 οὕνεκά με … | Τρωϊάδος: Od. now casually drops in the information that he is a veteran of the Trojan War, as an added disincentive to any thoughts of robbery the youth may have.

262 στερέσαι = Attic στερῆσαι, 'to deprive'. It is perhaps from an earlier, athematic, form of the verb, *στέρημι, which gave way to στερέω (not found in Homer); cf. *GH* I.347.

265 οὕνεκ' ἄρ 'since, you see'; this gives the reason for Orsilochus' desire to take Od.'s wealth, and looks back to 262. This whole sentence is a good example of the flexibility of Homeric syntax, where elements are added onto one another in a string.

266 ἄλλων ἦρχον ἑταίρων 'I commanded my men apart' (i.e. not under Idomeneus' control); cf. 5.489 (a farmer buries a brand) ἀγροῦ ἐπ' ἐσχατιῆς, ὧι μὴ πάρα γείτονες ἄλλοι 'at the edge of his field, where his neighbours are absent apart'; similar is 13.167 ἐς πλησίον ἄλλον. Od.'s independence and lack of fear of authority are made clear.

267 κατιόντα: with ἀγρόθεν. The line, with προσ- for κατ-, is the same as that used by Nestor in his proud account of his performance in battle in *Il.* 11.742.

268 λοχησάμενος: the choice of ambush as the means of Orsilochus' murder plays humorously on his name, 'Ambush-raiser'. Od. three times claims success in ambushes in his false tales (also 14.217–21, 469–71), and the exploit of the Wooden Horse is similarly described as an ambush (λόχον, 11.525); all of this looks forward to his 'ambush' of the Suitors. *Od.* represents skill in ambushing as a positive ability, and Idomeneus in *Il.* 13.275–91 tells how it sorts the brave from the coward. However, in *Il.* 4.391–8, 6.188–90 and 11.369–95 it is presented as a cowardly tactic. In hoplite warfare, which is beginning to develop at the end of the eighth century, the warrior was ideally expected to face his enemy openly and to eschew trickery. *Il.* and *Od.* seem to preserve an earlier ideology. See in general A. T. Edwards 1985: 15–41. **σὺν ἑταίρωι:** this could hint to the youth that Od. might not be alone this time either.

270 ἀπούρας: aorist active participle (cf. 132n.).

272 Φοίνικας: from the end of the second millennium the Phoenicians were a great trading nation, first in the eastern Mediterranean and then in the western; there is evidence for their activities from Morocco to Nineveh. In Homer they can be spoken of as deceivers. In *Il.* 23.743, they are πολυ-δαίδαλοι 'tricky'. Od. claims to have been tricked by 'a Phoenician of deceptive ways, a grasping man, who did much harm to people' (*Od.* 14.288–9). Eum. describes them as 'famed for their ships, grasping fellows, bringing countless baubles in their black ship' (15.415–16), and πολυπαίπαλοι 'very crafty' (15.419; cf. 15.415–84 generally for their role in his abduction). For the purposes of this story, Od. adopts in 277 a more positive view of them, perhaps to show that even the Phoenicians did not try to trick a man like him. Archaeology, with its evidence for complex trading patterns and civic organisation, suggests that Homer's picture of the Phoenicians is a caricatural one, a view produced perhaps at a time when Greeks at once emulated and yet defined themselves against the socially highly organised Phoenicians (see Winter 1995; that Homer's picture of the Phoenicians is not wholly negative is argued by Peacock 2011). On the Phoenicians and Greeks generally, see Lane Fox 2008: *passim*, and 47–78, 339–48 on the Phoenicians in Homer; also Dougherty 2001: 102–21 on their relationship with the Phaeacians in *Od.* (speculative at times); Woolmer 2011. Archaeological evidence points to Phoenician activity on Crete in the tenth century, in an inscribed bowl from Tekke near Cnossus and a shrine at Kommos: cf. Sznycer 1979; Shaw 2000, 2006: 139–40.

273 μενοεικέα 'plentiful'. The basic meaning is 'that which suits (ἔοικα) the spirit (μένος)', and so it means 'agreeable, satisfying', as in 409 βάλανον μενοεικέα 'tasty acorn', and then 'plentiful', as also in *Il.* 23.139 μενοεικέα . . . ὕλην.

274 ἐφέσσαι: sigmatic aorist active infinitive of ἐφ-έζω. It seems more natural to take this as 'settle, establish in'; in this sense it usually takes the dative, but the simple ἕζομαι regularly takes an accusative, e.g. 14.295 ἐς Λιβύην μ' . . . ἐέσσατο. Alternatively, as the scholia suggest, it could mean, in a *hysteron proteron* with καταστῆσαι, 'put on board ship', but 'ship' is actually expressed in the only place where that meaning is certain, 15.277 νηὸς ἔφεσσαι.

275 Ἐπειοί: for these people, cf. Nestor's tale in *Il.* 11.656–803, 2.619 and *Od.* 15.298.

276 ἦ τοι 'truly, I tell you'. In conjunction with another particle, τοι is used to bring a point home, the other particle keeps its usual force; ἦ here is emphatic (*GP* 548–9, 553–4). The emphasis on the fact that it was adverse weather conditions that prevented the Phoenicians from fulfilling their promise (and not deviousness) suggests that an audience would naturally have expected trickery from such men; the honesty of the Phoenicians is held up as an example to the youth, as they get a better press here than usual (cf. 272n.).

278 ἱκάνομεν: from here onwards, Od. shifts from a first-person-singular narrative to a first-person-plural one, moving himself from the marginal position of a suppliant needing Phoenician help to that of a full member of the team of sailors.   **νυκτός** 'at night'; genitive of the time when the event took place.

280 μάλα περ χατέουσιν ἐλέσθαι 'though we were very desirous of taking it'. For περ, see 130n.; χατέουσιν is the dative plural of the present participle and agrees with ἡμῖν (279). Again, Od.'s toughness in adversity is stressed.

281 αὔτως 'just as we were'; cf. 336, 14.151.   **ἐκείμεθα** 'we settled down to sleep'. The imperfects of κεῖμαι and ἧμαι can be used to describe not just the act of lying or sitting down, but also the result of doing so (*GH* II.191). **νηός:** take with ἀποβάντες.

285 Σιδονίην: Sidon was, with Tyre, one of the most important Phoenician cities, and in Homer and elsewhere 'Sidonian' is regularly a synonym for 'Phoenician'. Cf. *DCPP*, s.v. 'Sidon'.   **ἀναβάντες:** *sc.* νῆα.

286 ἀκαχήμενος: perfect middle participle of ἄχνυμαι, ἀκαχίζω, cognate with ἄχος. After a story full of warning, Od. ends rhetorically with words designed to evoke pity: the Phoenicians return to their wealthy city; Od. is left alone in a strange place.

287–310 Athena's exasperation at Od.'s continual trickery

The tone of Athena's speech moves from grudging but affectionate admiration (287–92), to exasperation (at her failure to trick him?, 293–5), to complicity (296–9), to an almost childish pleasure at his not having recognised her (299–302), and finally to a pragmatic approach to his problems (303–10). The familiarity between goddess and man is remarkable. One can contrast the much more matter-of-fact way in which she treats Achilles in *Il.* 1.194–222. Kirk 1985: 74 (on 197) describes her tugging Achilles' hair there as 'perhaps the most remarkable of all corporeal interventions by a god or goddess in the *Iliad*', but it is not such a familiar gesture as touching Od. with her hand as here; equally matter-of-fact is her treatment of Od. himself, when she encourages him to stop the Greek flight to the ships in *Il.* 2.169–81.

287–8 μείδησεν … κατέρεξε: this affectionate gesture of smiling and reaching out to touch someone is used in *Od.* when that person has responded to a speech by treating it suspiciously or a bit too seriously. For a close parallel compare Calypso in 5.180–1, after Od. has replied suspiciously to her suggestion that he build a raft to get home, and asks her to swear an oath that she is not tricking him. Similarly, Menelaus uses it when Telemachus responds to his offer of horses and a prolonged stay with an elaborate justification for his refusal, including disparagement of Ithaca (4.609–10); Menelaus sees Telemachus' speech as a sign of great breeding, but obviously thinks it a little overdone. In the more tragic *Il.*, the gesture of touching is used four times, but never with the smile. It appears always in a context of parental concern and consolation: Thetis uses it twice with Achilles (1.361, 24.127), Dione with her daughter Aphrodite when she is wounded by Diomedes (5.372), and Hector with Andromache as, 'laughing through her tears', she cuddles the baby Astyanax (6.485). This is the only place in *Od.* where Athena permits herself a smile. Generally in Homer, 'smiles express superiority, conciliation and love' (Levine 1982: 104), all of which are in play here.

288 ἤϊκτο: probably 3rd p.s. pluperfect middle-passive of εἴκω 'to be like', though this is a disputed form (*GH* 1.479). The pluperfect would stress the fact that Athena had made the change before she smiled and touched Od. (see 92n.). Athena, although she here reveals by her words who she is, still does not appear to Od. in her divine form, but rather as a striking woman. This is the only place in Homer where a divinity exchanges one disguise for another in the middle of a scene. The continued disguise could perhaps point to a limit to the familiarity she is prepared to show, but cf. Introduction pp. 6–7 for the suggestion that the two disguises look forward to the meetings with Telemachus, Eurycleia and Penelope. In less pregnant scenes, Athena will adopt this second disguise when she comes to Eum.'s farm (16.157–8) and to Od. in the hall (20.30–1).

289 καλῆι τε…ἰδυίηι: beauty and skill in domestic affairs were valued attributes in a woman in aristocratic circles; Penelope is a skilled weaver, and skill in household tasks is Athena's gift to the daughters of Pandareus when the gods prepare them for their wedding (20.72; cf. 24.278). Just how highly such skills were valued in serving women is suggested by the prize given by Achilles of 'a highly skilled woman, worth four oxen' (*Il.* 23.704–5; cf. also *Od.* 15.418).

291 ὅς: relative pronouns with the optative can have a conditional sense (*GH* ΙΙ.248); cf. also 214n., 14.404n.; and 13.391n. on ὅτε so used.

292 καὶ εἰ θεὸς ἀντιάσειε 'even if it were a god (who) ran into you'. This sentence marks the end of her masquerade as a mere mortal; the subsequent words announce her as the superior (if rather exasperated) figure that she is.

293 σχέτλιε: the particular force of this epithet depends on its context, and different performers would have invested it with different qualities. It can be applied to characters 'whose actions exhibit an unsupportable obstinacy' (Kelly 2007: 309), but it can also combine sympathy with exasperation in varying degrees, as in *Il.* 22.86, where Hecuba uses it to characterise Hector's bold but foolish intention to fight Achilles face to face, or Soph. *Ant.* 47, where Ismene's reaction to Antigone's intention to bury Polynices is ὦ σχετλία, Κρέοντος ἀντειρηκότος; 'you poor fool – when Creon has forbidden it?' Cf. also Dickey 1996: 164. Despite Athena's exasperation here, Od. will be no less cautious later, when in a similar scene, again disguised as a woman, she comes to him in the hall to spur him to revenge (20.30–53). There too she calls him σχέτλιε (20.45), and is annoyed that, though he does this time recognise her as a goddess (20.37), he is still not prepared to trust her completely.   **ποικιλομῆτα:** Athena is made to apply to Od. an epithet found of him alone, six times in *Od.* and in *Il.* 11.482, in the line-ending δαΐφρονα ποικιλομήτην. It is as if she knows the formulaic system and can make a jest about it. Elsewhere, the epithet is used as a positive term, but here it is a jesting insult. Cf. Austin 1975: 40–63 on the differences between the use of formulaic addresses by the poet and the characters.   **ἆτ'** 'insatiable', a contraction of ἄ(ϝ)ατος < *ἀϝάω 'injure, damage' (ἄατος, the uncontracted form, is often given by the MSS). The adjective thus means being so affected by a thing or emotion that it clouds one's judgement: cf. *Il.* 5.388 ἄτος πολέμοιο. δόλων ἆτ' is also said of Od. by the Trojan Socus in *Il.* 11.430.   **οὐκ ἄρ' ἔμελλες** 'I see you had no intention'. With future expessions of this sort, ἄρα tends to mark 'surprise attendant on disillusionment' (*GP* 35–6): the speaker realises that there was no way things could have been different. Here there is also a dash of amusement.

294 οὐδ' ἐν σῆι περ ἐὼν γαίηι 'not even though you are in your own land'; in negative sentences οὐδέ functions with περ in the same way as καί does in positive ones to produce a concessive sense (*GH* II.339; 130n.).

295 πεδόθεν 'from the bottom (of your heart)'. This is an unusual metaphorical use of this word, which is normally used of physical things, such as Olympus shaken to its core (e.g. Hes. *Th.* 680); its unusualness gives particular force to the goddess's remark.

296–7 εἰδότες ἄμφω | κέρδε(α) 'since we are both skilled in cunning', a causal participle. For this use of οἶδα, cf. 405n.

297 ὄχ' ἄριστος: ὄχα is an adverb derived from ἔξοχα, an adverbial accusative plural of the adjective ἔξοχος, which means literally 'that which very much (ἐξ) has it', i.e. 'surpassing'; it is an *o*-grade form of the root of the verb ἔχω. Cf. Leumann 1950: 133–6.

299 οὐδὲ σύ γ᾽ ἔγνως 'and *you* didn't recognise': Athena seems to want to find a way of claiming that she won the recent contest of wits.

300 Παλλάδ᾽ Ἀθηναίην: allowing herself a touch of divine arrogance, Athena names herself (by now rather unnecessarily) in a grand manner in the very middle of her speech. This adds to the sense that she is 'protesting too much'.

300–1 ἥ τέ τοι αἰεὶ | … παρίσταμαι: a good example of τε used of habitual actions.

302 καὶ δέ 'and what's more': 'a natural enough combination, the former particle denoting that something is added, the latter that what is added is distinct from what precedes' (*GP* 199). Athena's actions on Scherie are a special case of her general care for him; cf. *Il.* 24.370–1 ἀλλ᾽ ἐγὼ οὐδέν σε ῥέξω κακά, καὶ δέ κεν ἄλλον | σεῦ ἀπαλεξήσαιμι 'I shall do you no harm; indeed, I would protect you from another.' Strictly speaking, Athena is never said to have influenced the Phaeacians to make Od. their friend, though she does ensure his safe arrival at the palace, by encouraging Nausicaa to go to the shore to wash clothes (*Od.* 6.1–55) and herself guiding him (7.18–81): either the goddess is here and in 305 being defensive about her failure to offer more than minimal support during Od.'s wanderings (of which Od. is shortly to complain in 314–23), or this is another example of how Homer does not reveal everything the gods actually do (cf. 121n.).

303 ἵνα τοι σὺν μῆτιν ὑφήνω 'so as to weave a plot with you'. ὑφήνω is 1st p.s. aorist active subjunctive of ὑφαίνω. Weaving is regularly associated with trickery amongst the Greeks. Athena, the goddess of μῆτις 'cunning intelligence', was credited with the invention of the civilising arts (weaving, cultivation etc.), which enabled man to survive in a hostile world. Cf. 102n.

304 Φαίηκες: Athena makes it clear she knows what has been happening.

305 ἐμῆι βουλῆι: again (cf. 302n.), nothing was specifically said about Athena prompting the Phaeacians to give Od. treasure, and indeed this was something he was particularly keen on himself (cf. 41n.).

306–7 εἴπω … ἀνασχέσθαι 'and so that I might tell you how many troubles it is your fate to bear in your well-built house'; the aorist infinitive is timeless. The joking is now over, and Athena begins to reveal to Od. what he must face: he may be home, but his troubles are far from over.

307 τετλάμεναι 'be resilient', a zero-grade perfect active infinitive connected with τλήσομαι, ἔτλην etc. The perfect here describes a state achieved (160n.), and the idea is 'put yourself into, and stay in, a state of endurance' (cf. the perfect imperative τέτλαθι). This, like ἐκφάσθαι and πάσχειν later, is an infinitive of command. The imperatival infinitive is often used to express 'what the person addressed is to do as *his* part in a set of acts' (Munro 1891: 206). See in general Pearce 1996 (esp. 292–7), for the 'tone of authority' that this construction conveys.   καὶ ἀνάγκηι: lit. 'even by necessity', so 'because you must'; καί is emphatic.

308 τωι = τινι. Athena's insistence here is marked by the way she first forbids him to tell anyone, then adds 'of men or women', and then 'all of them' emphatically placed in enjambment. Od. has been warned by Agamemnon too not to reveal all to his wife at once (cf. 11.441–3).

309 οὕνεκ' 'that'; cf. Introduction 5.3 §11.2.2.

310 ὑποδέγμενος 'enduring'. This is probably a participle of an athematic present *δέγ-μαι = δέκομαι (Attic δέχομαι). The existence of such athematic forms is confirmed by the 3rd p.pl. present δέχαται (< *δέκ-νται, *Il.* 12.147); contrast the thematic forms δέχονται, δεχόμενος. Cf. *GH* 1.296.

311–28 Odysseus justifies his cautious use of trickery and complains at the lack of help from Athena during his wanderings

Od.'s speech is made to correspond to Athena's in ideas and language. Like hers, it begins with the difficulty (312 ἀργαλέον ~ 291 κερδαλέος) of recognising (312 γνῶναι ~ 299 ἔγνως) trickery when one meets it (312 ἀντιάσαντι ~ 292 ἀντιάσειε). Od. thus subtly returns the compliment Athena paid him on the difficulty of penetrating his disguises, by suggesting she is just as good as he is at disguise. He then acknowledges her help at Troy (314–15), before going on to cast doubt on her claims of having helped him after that, at least until he finally reached Scherie (316–23). She criticised him for never giving up his trickery even in his own land (293–5); he suggests that she is still tricking him in saying he is in that land at all (324–8). The success of his rhetorical skill here is shown by the fact that it provokes Athena only to further admiration (330–2). The intimacy between goddess and mortal in the subsequent discussion deepens, and the equality between them is marked by the way that, taking the episode as a whole, they both speak roughly the same number of lines (cf. 14.148–64, 410nn. for the importance of the number of lines spoken by different characters).

311 πολύμητις Ὀδυσσεύς: the formulaic epithet is particularly appropriate to Od.'s diplomatic skills here. See also 253–4, 382nn. for other examples of a significant choice of formula to introduce a speech by Od.; the formulae that introduce Athena's speeches are not similarly significant (cf. M. W. Edwards 1970: 5).

312 γνῶναι: only certain privileged mortals are allowed to recognise the presence of gods in Homer; cf. Turkeltaub 2007.

313 παντὶ ἔϊσκεις: this claim is well borne out by both epics. For Athena's disguises, cf. 1.105 (Mentes), 2.383 (Telemachus), 2.401, 22.206, 24.503 (Mentor), 3.372 (sea-eagle), 6.22–3, 7.20 (girl), 8.8 (herald), 194 (man), 13.222 (prince-shepherd), 13.288, 16.157, 20.31 (woman), 22.240 (swallow); *Il.* 2.280 (herald), 4.87 (Laodochus), 7.59 (vulture), 17.555 (Phoenix), 22.227 (Deiphobus). Only during the battle in the hall does Od. immediately see through the goddess's disguise (22.207–10).

314 ἠπίη: in Homer, ἤπιος generally refers to parental affection, an idea which is relevant here; cf. e.g. 14.139–44.

315 εἵως: for this spelling, see M. L. West 1967: 135–9.   **πολεμίζομεν:** unaugmented imperfect.

316 αὐτὰρ ἐπεί: Od. is not quite correct here. Though he did not know it at the time, Athena did in fact help him in the great storm Poseidon brewed to detain him after his leaving of Calypso, and finally saved him from destruction (5.382–7, 426–37). This was however only after Ino Leucothea had first intervened to advise him and give him her *kredemnon*, which helped him survive (333–81, 459–63).

317 ἐκέδασσεν = ἐσκέδασσεν, aorist of (σ)κίδνημι 'scatter'; the alternation *sk-/*k-* may be old, but it is also metrically useful (*GH* I.110).

318 ἴδον ... ἐνόησα: there seems little difference between these two words, as elsewhere, e.g. 16.160 οὐδ' ἄρα Τηλέμαχος ἴδεν ἀντίον οὐδ' ἐνόησεν; Hes. *Op.* 267.   **κούρη Διός:** this is the only time in Homer where this formula is used by a character rather than the narrator, and the only time it is used in an address. κοῦραι Διός in the plural is found twice, but each time in a prayer, not normal conversation (356, 17.240). The unusual deployment of an honorific phrase acknowledging Athena's distinguished ancestry is designed to soften Od.'s refutation of the goddess's claims.

320–3 These lines were deleted by Aristarchus: 320 because of the use of the third-person possessive adjective ᾗσιν (from ὅς, 198n.) to mean 'my'; 321 because 'when Athena is before him he attributes his safety to the gods', which is impolite; and 322–3 because Od. did not at the time know that it was Athena who was helping him on Scherie (7.14–81).

In 320, ᾗσιν 'my' rather than 'his, hers, its' is indeed problematic. In Vedic, the comparable form *sva-* is used for all persons, singular and plural. In Homer, there are two other places where ὅς may be being used archaically as a first- or second-person pronoun (cf. *GH* I.273). Most

promising is 9.27–8 οὔ τοι ἐγώ γε | ἧς γαίης δύναμαι γλυκερώτερον ἄλλο ἰδέσ-
θαι 'I cannot see a land sweeter than my/one's own' where, with the first-
person δύναμαι, 'my' is more natural than 'his own' in the sense of 'one's
own'. More ambiguous is 4.191–2 (Nestor's son Peisistratus to Menelaus)
Νέστωρ φάσχ' ὁ γέρων, ὅτ' ἐπιμνησαίμεθα σεῖο | οἷσιν ἐν μεγάροισι 'old Nestor
said we would remember you in his/our halls': the first-person plural verb
supports 'our', but 'his' could refer to Nestor as speaker; 'our' is perhaps
more natural.

Aristarchus' objection to 321 is rather like his objection to the destruction of the Phaeacians (158n.): decorum must be maintained in Homer's
narrative. We have already seen that Od. is prepared to speak his mind to
Athena, and he has also shown that he is not aware of what actually happened, so a presumption on his part that it was the other gods who saved
him is perfectly reasonable.

As for the objection to 322–3, it is not unparalleled for Homer to make
Od. aware of something he could not know (cf. e.g. Bassett 1938: 128–37).
Alternatively, one could imagine that Od. worked out from 302 that the
person who escorted him was in fact Athena (A–H–C ad loc.).

Though these objections are not fatal to the lines, the run of them is
nonetheless awkward. Particularly awkward are the two juxtaposed until-
clauses in 321–2. Without 320–1, 322 πρίν γ' ὅτε 'until' would naturally
follow from 318 ἔπειτα 'from then on'. On balance, 320–1 are an odd
parenthesis, and are probably best deleted.

320 φρεσὶν ᾗσιν ἔχων δεδαϊγμένον ἦτορ: for the φρένες as the seat of the ἦτορ,
cf. *Il.* 8.413 τί σφῶϊν ἐνὶ φρεσὶ μαίνεται ἦτορ;, 17.111–12. On φρένες in Homer,
see Sullivan 1988, esp. 166 on this combination; Clarke 1999: 61–126,
esp. 102 on this passage; also 255n. for the chest as the seat of intellectual
activity.   **δεδαϊγμένον:** perfect passive participle of δαΐζω 'tear, lacerate'.
δαΐζω is mainly used of physical things, but cf. the same phrase at *Il.* 17.535,
and the similar ones in 9.8 and 14.20 of a *thymos* torn by uncertainty as to
what to do.

322–3 These lines refer to 7.14–81, where however there is no suggestion
that Od. did recognise the goddess under her disguise as a girl.

322 πρίν γ' ὅτε 'until the time when'. Literally this means 'in the past
when': πρίν was originally an adverb, whence the use of ὅτε with it (cf.
GH II.264; 90, 124nn. above).

324 πατρός 'in the name of your father'. πρός + the (ablatival) genitive of
people is used to give the origin either of things (e.g. 11.302 τιμὴν πρὸς
Ζηνὸς ἔχοντες), or of authority (*Il.* 6.456 πρὸς ἄλλης ἱστὸν ὑφαίνοις 'you may
weave at the command of another'), and so it is used of the person in
whose name and authority supplication takes place (*Il.* 1.338–9 μάρτυροι

ἔστων | πρός τε θεῶν 'let them be my witnesses before the gods'; *GH* ɪɪ.134). Od. uses this potent supplication by Zeus (cf. 213n.) to make Athena drop her trickery and tell him the truth about where he is. She will oblige, but not immediately: the game between them goes on.

326 ἀναστρέφομαι: the shift to the indicative rather than another infinitive depending on ὀῖω emphasises Od.'s conviction that he is being fooled; cf. 10.284–5 οὐδέ σέ φημι | αὐτὸν νοστήσειν, μενέεις δὲ σύ γ' ἔνθα περ ἄλλοι 'I say that you will not return, but you will remain where the others are.'

327 ἵν'…φρένας ἠπεροπεύσῃς: cf. Helen's remarkably angry words to Aphrodite at *Il.* 3.399 τί με ταῦτα λιλαίεαι ἠπεροπεύειν; 'why are you so keen to deceive me in this way?', and Zeus's to Prometheus in Hes. *Op.* 55. For gods damaging a mortal's φρένες, cf. e.g. *Il.* 15.724; Sullivan 1988: 150–4.

328 εἰ ἐτεόν γε: sceptical formulae like this recur in recognition-scenes; cf. 22.45, 23.36, 107–8; Wakker 1994: 352–3.

329–60 Athena justifies her behaviour and reveals the island

Despite the obvious passion in Od.'s supplicatory request for the truth, Athena pauses to comment affectionately on his extraordinary caution and the way this binds him to her. She then acknowledges the truth of Od.'s complaint about her absence during his wanderings, before finally assuring him he is home and then dispelling the mist that disguises the island.

331 τώ σε καὶ οὐ δύναμαι 'it is just for that reason that I simply cannot'; for this emphatic use of καί, cf. *Il.* 3.176 τό καὶ κλαίουσα τέτηκα 'which is the very reason why I am wasting away with weeping' (Munro 1891: 241; *GP* 307–8).

332 ἐπητής: a rare word of uncertain meaning, though here 'wise, sage' seems most likely; it may be connected with the root **sep-* 'care for' (cf. 14.33n.; Beekes 439). It is also found in 18.128, where Od. says of the Suitor Amphinomus ἐπητῆι δ' ἀνδρὶ ἔοικας, shortly after calling him πεπνυμένος. The noun in 21.306 οὐ γάρ τευ ἐπητύος ἀντιβολήσεις seems to mean 'courteous treatment'. It was presumably a word of commendation whose precise meaning had been lost by Homer's time: for such words, cf. Silk 1983.   **ἀγχίνοος:** only here in Homer.

333–8 These lines were deleted by Aristarchus, because Od. has not given any evidence that he intends to test Penelope. However, Athena does not know what intentions he has, and having found him on the shore presumes that, as usual, he is being cautious. She is also impressed that he did not immediately make enquiries about his wife and family as soon as he met her, thus revealing his identity. She is however being slightly kind in her remarks about Od.'s caution, since this was not much in evidence say at the door to the Cyclops' cave, and indeed he himself will tell her at 383–5 that he *would* in fact have rushed off if she had not warned him. Cf. Erbse 1972: 158–60. The sentiments here are very close to the way in which Od. will complain to Penelope about her (to him) overly cautious attitude to a returning husband in 23.100–3: husband and wife are both characterised by their caution. For such rebukes in Homer, see Minchin 2002.

333–4 κ'...ἵετ(ο) 'would have been on his way'; for the imperfect + ἄν/κε expressing potential duration in the past, cf. 205n.

333 ἀλαλήμενος: perfect middle participle of ἀλάομαι 'wander'; for the reduplicated form, cf. ὄλλυμι, ὄλωλα. The recessive accent on this perfect middle form was considered by ancient grammarians to be an aeolism (*GH* I.190).

334 ἰδέειν: aorist infinitives in -έειν (cf. also βαλέειν, θανέειν) have been explained as created in Ionic from Aeolic infinitives in -έμεν, on the analogy of forms of contract verbs like φιλέειν (*GH* 1.492–3). Nikolaev 2013 however now suggests that they were created on analogy with so-called 'liquid futures' in -έω, which had active infinitives in both -εῖν and -έειν. ἰδέειν, βαλέειν etc. were created by making the situation in the aorist mirror that in the future, thereby enabling poets to adapt to something like contemporary Ionic speech formulae which sound changes had rendered metrically problematic or which contained Aeolic forms in -έμεν which they wished to replace.

335 οὔ πω 'not at all', as often in epic.   **δαήμεναι** 'to learn', that is, from others rather than seeing for himself (so also πυθέσθαι). δαήμεναι is an infinitive of the aorist passive ἐδάην, formed on the root *δα- 'teach' (cf. δι-δά-σκω).

336 πρὶν...πειρήσεαι: the verb is 2nd p.s. aorist middle subjunctive (short-vowel) of πειράω, the middle emphasising the point that Od. will carry out the test for himself, not trusting another to do it for him. πρίν is normally used with the infinitive in Homer (124n.), but appears six times with the subjunctive and once with the optative (*GH* II.264–5).

337–8 ὀϊζυραὶ...χεούσῃ 'for her, miserable nights and days go by as she weeps'. The same words are used by Od.'s mother in the Underworld at 11.182–3; cf. 11.444–6 for a similar reassurance by Agamemnon, and 379–81 below. This confirmation that his mother's words are still true so many years later is bitter-sweet for Od.: he knows that Penelope is still faithful, but is reminded of the cost to her of his absence. That, despite all these reassurances, Od. is still wary of Penelope shows how cautious he has become as a result of his wanderings.

339 τό 'this' looks forward to ὅ 'that' in 340.   ἀπίστεον: 1st p.s. imperfect of ἀπιστέω; 'only here; probably a symptom of the influence of contemporary Ionic' (Hoekstra, *CHO* ad loc.).

340 ἤιδε(α): 1st p.s. pluperfect of οἶδα. Athena's confidence here coincides with the general certainty of Od.'s return which pervades the epic: there is never any real doubt but that he will return. We are told early on that it is fated that he should return in a particular year, and as soon as that year comes, the gods set about arranging it (1.16-27). Zeus assures Athena that he could never forget Od. and that Poseidon will come round (1.64-79), which he does. Cf. also 133n.

341 οὐκ ἐθέλησα Ποσειδάωνι μάχεσθαι: cf. 6.328-31, where Athena hears Od.'s prayer as he goes towards Alcinous' palace, but does not appear to him because of *aidōs* for her uncle. This cautiousness contrasts with the gusto with which she confronts other gods in the *Iliad*. Poseidon, brother of Zeus and her uncle, is, as was clear earlier in the book, a powerful force to be reckoned with (125-64n.). Athena does ultimately get what she wants, and Poseidon has to back down, but she does so by cunning and diplomacy, which are necessary because simple disguise would not work, the gods being easily able to recognise each other (5.79-80).

342-3 Od. is all too aware of this, since he himself says that Poseidon gave ear to the Cyclops' curse (9.536).

344 Ἰθάκης ἕδος is a 'periphrastic' (i.e. 'roundabout') expression for 'Ithaca'; cf. *Il.* 24.144 ἕδος Οὐλύμποιο, *Od.* 11.263 Θήβης ἕδος; 13.20n.

345-8 Here 345 ≈ 96, 346-8 ≈ 102-4, from Homer's earlier description. Byre 1994: 9-10 points out that this repetition describes only what Od. knew or could see: the divine aspects remain the province of goddess, poet and audience. Some MSS and two papyri omit 347-8, and there is indeed a slight oddity in saying 'near it is a cave sacred to the Nymphs … and this is the tall wide cave where you sacrificed to the Nymphs'. It seems as though 347-8 were wrongly copied here from 102-3 in one part of the tradition. Without these lines, all the items in the description would be introduced by a demonstrative, which gives a more dynamic picture of Athena pointing out the various places one by one.

350 ἔρδεσκες: ἔρδω, from the same IE root *uerg- as ἔργον, ῥέζω, means 'to do', in Homer regularly 'to do (something important)', i.e. 'to sacrifice'. For the iterative imperfect with *-sk-, cf. Introduction 5.3 §6.4. In 358, Od. promises he will sacrifice to these Nymphs in future (for Od.'s regular blending of past, present and future thus, cf. Jones 1992: 89); the *Telegony* began with Od. sacrificing to the Nymphs before a journey to Elis, after the burial of the Suitors (*GEF* p. 166).   τελήεσσας: lit. 'having *telos*', but its meaning is not certain. It is often taken to be synonymous with τέλειος 'perfect', and it is very likely that the similarity in form led the poets so to understand it in contexts like this. The more literal meaning suits better its use of birds of omen (*H.Herm.* 544), but what it means when applied to Oceanus (Hes. *Th.* 242 = 959) is uncertain.   ἑκατόμβας has since antiquity been explained as a sacrifice of one hundred cattle, which is what its etymology suggests; this is however an enormous number for one sacrifice. More recently it has been connected with Sanskrit *shata-gu-* 'possessing one hundred cattle' (cf. Beekes 396–7), and so taken to mean a sacrifice intended to obtain a hundred cattle. Whatever its original meaning, by Greek times it is used for sacrifices that are not of one hundred animals or indeed of oxen (cf. Chantraine 2009: s.v. ἑκατόν). It means a grand sacrifice of some kind.

351 Νήριτον: another geographical puzzle (cf. 236–49, 14.355nn.). This mountain is referred to again in 9.21–2 and *Il.* 2.632, but Ithaca has no such mountain. The word means literally 'uncountable', < the negative ν- (74n.) + ἀρι- as in ἀριθμός; Ruijgh 1957: 161 compared Hesych. ν 521 νήριται· μεγάλοι. νήριτος is used as an epithet in Hes. *Op.* 511 (of ὕλη), and Leumann 1950: 243–7 argued that the epithet's meaning was lost and the word reinterpreted as a proper name for the mountain.   **καταειμένον** 'clothed', perfect passive participle of (κατα-)ἕννυμι < *Ϝέσ-νυ-μι, as in Latin *ues-tis.*

352 εἴσατο 'appeared', 3rd p.s. aorist middle of εἴδομαι.

353–4a ≈ 250–1, but this time Od. can really rejoice at his homecoming, now that it is certain.

354 κύσε δὲ ζείδωρον ἄρουραν: Od. did the same when he finally made land on Scherie (5.463).   **ζείδωρον** etymologically means 'spelt-giving' (< ζειαί), but the Greeks connected the first element with words such as ζωή 'life'.

355 χεῖρας ἀνασχών: this was the standard manner of praying in ancient Greece. Praying to one's gods on returning home was a natural act: cf. e.g. Aes. *Ag.* 810–13.

357 ἐφάμην 'I thought, expected', as often, cf. e.g. 10.562–3 φάσθε νύ που οἴκόνδε φίλην ἐς πατρίδα γαῖαν | ἔρχεσθ' 'you thought, I imagine, that you were going home to your country'.

358 καί 'in addition' (to the prayers); for the moment prayers must suffice.   **διδώσομεν:** a future built on the present stem, which suggests continued generosity; for the form, cf. κιχήσομαι 'I shall find' (< κιχάνω; *GH* 1.442). It is regular in such 'cletic' (from καλέω 'call') prayers to remind the deity

of an already existing relationship between them and oneself, the result
of previous mutual benefactions.

359–60 There is something mildly amusing about Od. making a promise
to the Nymphs which depends for its fulfilment on the goddess standing
next to him; but it allows Od. to display a continued cautiousness towards
the goddess. Athena shows in 362 that she has taken the point.

359 ἐᾶι: 3rd p.s. present subjunctive of ἐάω (< ἐά-ηι).   ἀγελείη 'leader
of the host', cf. Ἀθηνᾶι Ἀγελάαι on a fourth-century Attic inscription (*SEG*
21.527) and the masculine name Ἀγέλαος; it refers to Athena as a warrior
goddess. Cf. West on Hes. *Th.* 318.

361–91 Discussion of the situation on Ithaca

In the final scene, Athena enjoys casually dropping into the conversation
uncomfortable facts that are immensely important to Od., but of which
he is quite unaware (cf. 375–81, 411–15 and 425–8). To the end therefore, she insists on teasingly maintaining control of the situation and the
information that Od. has.

362 μελόντων 'be of concern'; 3rd p.pl. present imperative.

364 θείομεν: aorist short-vowel subjunctive of τίθημι (a scribal rendering of
*θήομεν, Palmer 1962: 97). Od.'s goods were also stored in a cave on Circe's
island (10.404, 424).   ἵνα...μίμνηι 'where they might stay safe/in order
that they should stay safe'. Clauses such as this show how subordinate
clauses involving place could have given rise to the use of ἵνα 'where' to
introduce a final clause; cf. Introduction 5.3 §11.1.2; *GH* II.268).   σόα
looks back to Od.'s request at the very start of this scene σάω μὲν ταῦτα,
σάω δ' ἐμέ (230).

365 ὄχ' ἄριστα γένηται 'how things might turn out for the best'. For ὄχα,
cf. 297n.; for this use of adverbial accusative + 'be', cf. 1n. With φράζομαι
ὅπως Homer uses subjunctives and futures (as 376 ἐφήσεις; *GH* II.294–5).

368 ἆσσον: this is the accent supported by ancient scholars and found in
the MS Venetus A of *Il.* Chantraine (*GH* I.190) suggests this form may
preserve the original vowel length and accent, as against the Ionic ἀσσον.

370 καὶ τὰ μὲν εὖ κατέθηκε: these words look back to their use in Alcinous'
original stowing of the gifts in the ship at 20, this last mention of the gifts
thus forming a ring with the first. The gifts will eventually be brought to
the palace for display and storage (23.355), with some no doubt left for
the Nymphs (cf. de Jong 2001: 333).   λίθον: for stones closing caves, cf.

the Cyclops' cave in 9.240–3. This episode begins and ends with reminiscences of that cave (cf. 96–112n.), but has been much happier for Od., now that Athena is able to help him. He went blindly into the Cyclops' cave and suffered, and could have met a similar fate in the palace had she not warned him (383–5).

372 τώ: the dual finds restricted use in Homer and is often used interchangeably with the plural (as τώ here but τοῖσι in 374; cf. 14.193n.; Introduction 5.3 §7.1.2). However it can also emphasise the closeness of the link between two people; cf. 16.1–3 Ὀδυσεὺς καὶ δῖος ὑφορβὸς | ἐντύοντ᾽ ἄριστον... κηαμένω πῦρ, | ἔκπεμψάν τε νομῆας, where the intimate business of preparing breakfast together has the dual, but the practical business of sending out the shepherds the plural; *GH* II.25–6.   **ἱερῆς:** i.e. to Athena. For the importance of the olive in *Od.*, cf. 102n.

375 διογενὲς... Ὀδυσσεῦ: now that all misunderstandings are cleared up, Athena finally addresses Od. by name, in a grand formulaic line (used 15× in *Od.*), which suggests he is now the hero returned to his homeland, ready to re-establish himself in his palace as king.

376 ὅπως... ἐφήσεις: cf. 365n.

377 τρίετες 'for three years'; neut. sg. adverbial accusative.

380–1 These lines are an early indication of the kind of trickery that Penelope has been using to keep the Suitors at bay. Antinous uses the same words in 2.90–1.

380 ἔλπει: the active voice of this verb means 'give hopes to someone'; the middle is 'give hopes to oneself, expect'.

382 πολύμητις: the use of this epithet when Od. is about to admit to nearly falling carelessly into a trap is nicely ironic.

383–5 Od.'s reaction here is problematic, because he acts as if he did not know what Athena tells him, though Teiresias has already told him about the Suitors (11.115–17, with verbal echoes of this passage). One cannot remove this problem by the suggestion that book 11 is a later addition, because some episode like that in Hades is presupposed by the fact that nowhere else in the epic Od. could have heard of the fate of Agamemnon. Homer may be 'nodding', but possibly memory of the earlier passage is simply suppressed, to give a more striking effect. There is humour as the grand address in 375 sets Od. up as a heroic figure about to embark on a successful venture, before Athena's news immediately and rather unkindly deflates him, by forcing him to reveal that he was quite unprepared for this first hurdle. Such anomalies are a feature of oral poems generally: cf. 67–9n. Alternatively, it may be that this is 'part of the rhetorical make-up of his whole speech. He takes up a position of dependence *vis-à-vis* the goddess', leaving her to do the planning (de Jong 2001: 335).

383 ὦ πόποι: see 140n.

383-4 ἦ μάλα δή... ἔμελλον 'I really was about to'. On these counterfactual statements which are used in Homer to change the course of the action and sometimes to pass comment on a character's actions, see Louden 1993. For the particles, see 172n.; for ἔμελλον, cf. 293n.

383 Ἀγαμέμνονος Ἀτρεΐδαο: Od. learnt the fate of Agamemnon from the man himself in Hades (11.385-466), and ὦ πόποι, ἦ μάλα δή γόνον Ἀτρέος were the similar words used there by Od. (436). The story of Agamemnon's fate counterpoints that of Od. throughout the first part of the poem: cf. 1.32-43, 298-302, 3.193-204, 232-5, 254-312, 4.91-2, 512-47, 11.409-56, and also 24.95-7, 191-202.

384 φθίσεσθαι...οἶτον: lit. 'to perish the fate', i.e. 'to suffer the fate', an 'internal' accusative (Introduction 5.3 §7.2.4.1).

386 μῆτιν ὕφηνον: see 303n.   **ἀποτείσομαι:** since ὅπως can be used with the future or the subjunctive (365n.), it is impossible to tell if this is future indicative or aorist subjunctive.

387 μένος...ἐνεῖσα: ἐνεῖσα is fem. nom. aorist active participle of ἐν-ίημι.

388 Τροίης...κρήδεμνα: κρήδεμνα lit. 'head-dress, mantilla' is regularly used for a city's battlements; on 'loosing *krēdemna*' in Homer, see Nagler 1974: 44-63.   **λύομεν:** unaugmented imperfect; given the intimacy of the situation here, the subject is perhaps better taken as 'the two of us' rather than 'we Greeks'.

389 αἴ κέ...παρασταίης 'supposing that you were to stand...' Unlike Attic, Homeric Greek uses εἰ κε/ἄν + optative often, as here, to mark a close parallelism between the condition and the thing that would be achieved if it were fulfilled (*GH* II.277-8). This closeness is sometimes emphasised: here καί 'certainly' stresses the link; cf. 17.223-5 τόν κ' εἴ μοι δοίης σταθμῶν ῥυτῆρα γενέσθαι | ...καί κεν ὀρὸν πίνων μεγάλην ἐπιγουνίδα θεῖτο 'supposing you gave him to me to guard my farmstead... *then* perhaps he might drink whey and thicken his thighs'.   **ὡς μεμαυῖα** 'being enthusiastic like that', i.e. 'as you were at Troy'. μεμαυῖα is the feminine participle of μέμονα 'be keen'.   **γλαυκῶπι:** this is the only time in either Homeric epic that anyone addresses Athena in this way; it again marks the extraordinary closeness between the two. The three-fold use of vocatives in this short speech might also suggest a certain clever flattery on Od.'s part: see also next note.

391 πότνα: a syncopated form of πότνια, via πότνυα. Metrical considerations may have played a part in its formation (*GH* 1.170), but it is found elsewhere in Homer only in 5.215 (Od. to Calypso, rejecting immortality) and 20.61 (Penelope to Artemis, asking for death or similar): all three occurrences seem to be connected with moments of great seriousness. The word is cognate with IE ones for 'goddess' (cf. Beekes 1226–7). **ὅτε ... ἐπαρήγοις** 'if you help me'; in ὅτε clauses, the optative gives a conditional colour (cf. *GH* ii.260; 14.404n.).   **πρόφρασσ(α):** the older feminine of πρόφρων, also found in 5.161, 10.386; *Il.* 10.290, 21.500. It is modelled on participial forms where *-nt-ya* > *-assa*; cf. Hesych. α 1334b <ἀέ>κασσα· ἄκουσα, Messenian and Arcadian εασσα = ἐοῦσα, Mycenean *a-pe-a-sa* = ἀπεασσαι = ἀποῦσαι, and names like *H.Hy.* 31.4 Εὐρυφάεσσα 'shining widely' (cf. Risch 1974: 136; Chantraine 2009: 281).

392–440 Disguise of Odysseus

Athena assures Od. of her help in the coming struggle: she will disguise him and send him to Eum.'s farm to get information, while she goes to fetch Telemachus. In fact however that help should not be exaggerated: 'her actual role in the Ithacan endgame is surprisingly limited: it is confined to Odysseus' supernatural disguise, the suggestion he visit Eumaeus, deflecting the suitors' spears in XXII, and some minor if persuasive psychological prompting all round' (Lowe 2000: 140). She combines reassurance with two more bombshells: that his son has left home (414–15), and is to be ambushed by the Suitors (425).

393 καὶ λίην 'certainly', as regularly at the beginning of a line.

394 τιν(α): by litotes, this implies not just 'someone', but 'everyone'. This is the 'distributive' use of τις; cf. 427–8 πρὶν καί τινα γαῖα καθέξει | ἀνδρῶν μνηστήρων 'beforehand the earth will cover all the Suitors' (and 167n.).

395 αἵματί τ' ... παλαξέμεν: as if to prove Athena right, there is a similar expression used of Od. after he has killed the Suitors, 22.402 = 23.48 αἵματι καὶ λύθρωι πεπαλαγμένον ὥς τε λέοντα. This is a line of striking unpleasantness. Expressions concerning the spattering of the brain are not common in epic. In *Il.* there are only six places where the brain figures in wounding, three with the formula ἐγκέφαλος δὲ | ἔνδον ἅπας πεπάλακτο 'and the brain within was spattered everywhere' (11.97–8 etc.). Such expressions also appear twice in emotional circumstances, in 9.458–9, what the Cyclops would do if he could find Od., and in *Il.* 3.300, a curse on anyone breaking the truce, that his brain should 'flow on the ground like wine'.   **ἄσπετον οὖδας:** for ἄσπετον, cf. 135n. The use of the adjective of a threshold is striking: it is usually found of really large spaces like the ether or the earth. The phrase recurs in 22.269 οἱ μὲν ἔπειτ᾽ ἅμα πάντες ὀδὰξ ἕλον ἄσπετον οὖδας, which marks the fulfilment of Athena's prediction here.

396 τοι: dative of disadvantage.

398 κάρψω 'I will shrivel'; cf. Hes. *Op*. 575 ἠέλιος χρόα κάρφει.   **γναμπ-τοῖσι** 'supple', not simply 'bent'; like καλόν and ξανθάς, it is a positive quality which is to be spoiled for the disguise.

400 ἔσσω < ϝέσ-σω: 1st p.s. future active of ἕννυμι; cf. 351n.   **ὅ κεν στυγέῃσιν ἰδὼν ἄνθρωπον ἔχοντα:** lit. 'which if (someone) saw he would be disgusted at the man who possessed it'. A problematic passage. Munro read ἄνθρωπον for the MSS' ἄνθρωπος, following a variant mentioned by Eustathius (see app. crit.). ἄνθρωπον leaves the clause without an expressed subject, but this is not unparalleled: cf. *Il.* 13.287 οὐδέ κεν ἔνθα τεόν γε μένος καὶ χεῖρας ὄνοιτο '(no-one) would then scorn your strength and power' and, with a participle, Hes. *Op.* 12 (on types of strife) τὴν μέν κεν ἐπαινή-σειε νοήσας 'one type (a man) would praise when he saw it in action' (cf. K–G 1.35–6). Against the MSS' ἄνθρωπος is that ἄνθρωπος = τις 'anyone' is hard to parallel until the New Testament. Once ἄνθρωπος for τις became a common usage, it would have been easy for ἄνθρωπος, with the help of the nominative ἰδών, to enter the text to make the sense clearer.

404–5 will be said again to Telemachus by Athena (15.38–9), a link between father and son.

404 συβώτην: this reference to a nameless swineherd gives no indication as to how important he is to be in the coming events; it is what narratology calls a 'seed', the planting of an apparently incidental idea in a narrative which will turn out to be significant later. There was another, apparently entirely casual, anonymous reference to a swineherd in 4.640, where the Suitors are surprised to find that Telemachus has gone to Sparta, not just to visit his flocks or swineherd.   **εἰσαφικέσθαι:** a command; cf. 307n.

405 ἐπίουρος 'guardian' < ὁράω, cf. 15.89 οὖρος, and ἔφ-ορος 'ephor', πυλ-ωρός 'gate-keeper'.   **ὁμῶς δέ τοι ἤπια οἶδε** 'and at the same time has kindly thoughts for you', rather than 'has kindly thoughts in the same way as you do'. That τοι goes with the verbal phrase not with ὁμῶς is supported by the dative in 15.557 ἀνάκτεσιν ἤπια εἰδώς (also of Eum.). The scholiast takes ὁμῶς to mean 'as before', as in *Il.* 9.605 οὐκέθ᾽ ὁμῶς τιμῆς ἔσεαι 'you will not be valued in the same way (as before)', which would suit Eum.'s claim that Od. 'loved me greatly' (14.146). This is possible, but it is Eum.'s current loyalty to Od. that he needs to be reassured about: the past is not particularly relevant.   **ἤπια οἶδε:** Homer regularly uses neuter plural adjectives thus to express attitudes; cf. 14.288 ἀπατήλια εἰδώς, 433 αἴσιμα ἤιδη, and with a noun 13.296–7 εἰδότες ἄμφω | κέρδε(α). In *Od.*, ἤπια οἶδε is used only of Eumaeus' relationship with Od. and Telemachus (cf. again 15.39, 557). The sense is 'to have thoughts of a certain kind': cf. Sullivan 1988: 95–8; Williams 1993: 28.

407 δήεις 'you will find'; δήω appears only in the present in Greek (except Hesych. ε457 ἔδηε· εὗρε), always with a future meaning.

408 Κόρακος... Ἀρεθούσηι: the scholia tell a tale of a Corax who died falling off a cliff when hunting, and of his mother's subsequent suicide at a spring. These places are not referred to again and their significance is unclear. They may merely add local colour, true or manufactured. Bittlestone 2005: esp. 130–7, 449–56 locates them on Cephalonia. Arethusa is the name of several springs in Greece, the most famous of which is still visible in Syracuse.

409 βάλανον: acorns are the traditional food of pigs; cf. 10.242–3 ἄκυλον βάλανόν τ'...οἷα σύες χαμαιευνάδες αἰὲν ἔδουσιν (the first two words both mean 'acorn'). Spanish *bellota* ('acorn') hams are still especially prized. **μενοεικέα:** see 273n. **μέλαν ὕδωρ** tends to refer to water that is deep, like the sea, as in 12.104 Χάρυβδις ἀναρροιβδεῖ μέλαν ὕδωρ; the spring provides rich acorns and plenty of water. The leisurely and attractive description of Eum.'s pigs makes the news of Telemachus' journey come as all the more of a surprise to Od.

410 τά refers back to the acorns and water (60n.). **ἀλοιφήν:** fat is valued in pork because it enriches the meat as it cooks, making it more tender and nourishing.

412 καλλιγύναικα: only here in *Od.*; in *Il.* it is used of Hellas (2.683) and Achaea (3.75).

413 καλέουσα: future participle indicating her purpose, as 415 πευσόμενος.

415 πευσόμενος μετὰ σὸν κλέος: lit. 'to make enquiries about news of you'; cf. the synonymous 17.43 μετὰ πατρὸς ἀκουήν. μετά + acc. is used of something that is sought. The phrase is a development of expressions such as 440 ἔβη μετὰ παῖδ᾽ Ὀδυσῆος 'she went to get...', *Il.* 11.227 μετὰ κλέος ἵκετ᾽ Ἀχαιῶν 'he went towards the noise made by the Achaeans'; κλέ(ϝ)ος, cognate with κλύω, is basically something that is heard. **εἴ που ἔτ᾽ εἴης:** lit. 'if you might still be alive anywhere', a potential optative; for the construction, cf. Introduction 5.3 §11.3.

417–19 Od. returns to his critical stance towards Athena, and the strength of his feelings about the danger to Telemachus comes out in the curt way he addresses her: she didn't look after him on his wanderings (ἠλώμην, 321), and now is doing the same to Telemachus (ἀλώμενος, 418), when she could easily have spared him the journey by telling him the truth. The diplomacy he showed earlier is lacking this time (311–28n.). Athena now has a rather more compelling reply than she did to Od.'s earlier complaint (cf. 329–60n.).

417 τίπτε; (= τί ποτε;) 'why on earth?' is naturally used in questions expressing surprise, exasperation, amazement etc.; cf. 9.494 (his men to Od. when he provokes the Cyclops) σχέτλιε, τίπτ' ἐθέλεις ἐρεθιζέμεν ἄγριον ἄνδρα;

418 ἦ ἵνα που 'no doubt so that'. ἦ is regularly used in suggesting answers to questions, as in *Il.* 1.202–3 τίπτ' αὖτ'...εἰλήλουθας; | ἦ ἵνα ὕβριν ἴδηι Ἀγαμέμνονος; (*GP* 283).

419 ἀτρύγετον: an epithet that has defeated ancient and modern attempts to etymologise it. The Homeric scholia derive it from ἀ-privative + τρυγάω, so 'unharvested, sterile', and Herodian (2.284) from ἄτρυτος 'what cannot be worn out, tireless'. Vine 1998: 62–4 relates it to a root *trug- 'dry', comparing the gloss Hesych. ε 6648 ἐτρύγη· ἐξηράνθη, and takes it to mean 'undryable'.   **οἱ:** dative referring to Telemachus.   **ἔδουσι:** 3rd p.pl. short-vowel present subjunctive (< *ἔδ-ο-νσι).

421 μὴ δή τοι...ἔστω 'come, there's really no need to be concerned about *him*'. For τοι, cf. 276n.; δή is used with imperatives when the command arises from what has just been said or done (*GP* 216–17). For a third time here (cf. 362, 393–4), Athena offers Od. reassurance; she may play with him to some extent, but she is in deadly earnest that he will succeed.

422 ἵνα κλέος ἐσθλὸν ἄροιτο: this is indeed what she said in 1.93–5. In *Il.*, κλέος is often to do with one's reputation in the future, but in *Od.* it is more to do with one's social status: Telemachus will not be more famous because of his trip to Sparta, but his position will be enhanced by his noble treatment by a man like Menelaus; cf. A. T. Edwards 1985: 71–93.

424 παρὰ δ' ἄσπετα κεῖται: for the importance of treasure as an enhancer of status, see 41n. Having seen earlier how much importance Od. attaches to his own gifts, Athena perhaps adds this detail to keep him happy. These gifts will play their part in getting Telemachus his κλέος.

425 ἦ 'yes, it is true'. For the third time, Athena calmly drops into the conversation news of a potential disaster, but this time Od. does not react, perhaps slightly tiring of this game, or just happy with Athena's reassurance in 427–8.   **λοχόωσι:** present indicative, with *diektasis*, cf. 93n. on φαάντατος.

427 τά γ' οὐκ ὄίω: lit. 'which I do not have in mind (as likely to happen)'; for ὄίω thus with the accusative, cf. 22.165–6 κεῖνος δὴ αὖτ' ἀΐδηλος ἀνήρ, ὃν ὀϊόμεθ᾽ αὐτοί, | ἔρχεται ἐς θάλαμον 'that villain, whom we had in mind ourselves (as likely to do it), is going into the chamber'.   τινα: see 394n.

429 ῥάβδωι ἐπεμάσσατ(ο): the verb is aorist middle of ἐπιμαίομαι. In the present it means 'seek', but in the more frequent aorist 'seek to touch'. This use of disguise as a beggar recalls Helen's story of how Od., again disguised as a beggar, entered Troy and killed many Trojans (*Od.* 4.240–64), a foreshadowing of what will happen in the palace. This phrase recurs when Athena changes Od. back for his meeting with Telemachus in 16.172 (cf. also 16.456). Apart from that moment, this disguise will remain in place until Athena makes Od. strikingly attractive for the climax of the recognition by Penelope (23.153–63). The motif of a character changed by the aid of a ῥάβδος before going to where pigs live is reminiscent of Circe, who fed his men magic herbs, struck them with a ῥάβδος and put them in pens, before trying to do the same to Od. (cf. 10.235–8, 317–19, 388–90). For such 'magic wands', cf. Hermes' herald's wand (5.47–8, 24.2–4; *Il.* 24.343–4) and Poseidon invigorating the two Ajaxes with his sceptre (*Il.* 13.59–61).

430–1, 433 ≈ 398–9, 401.

434–5 One could be forgiven for thinking that Athena is going a bit far in piling quite so much disagreeable and yet unprotective clothing onto Od. The weather is inclement, and an old animal-skin, a ragged scrap of clothing, a torn and dirty chiton soiled by smoke, and a threadbare deer-skin combine filth and permeability in an uncomfortable manner: the inadequacy of the clothes to the conditions becomes clear in 14.457–61. The clothes make a good disguise, but are they also the goddess's last throw in the game of cat-and-mouse that has informed the second half of this book?

434 ἄλλο: i.e. to replace the garment he had on. The expression is rather condensed, since Od. is not wearing a ῥάκος, but fine clothes.

435 ῥωγαλέα 'torn', an *o*-grade form from the root of ῥήγ-νυμι. For the neuter plural, cf. 60n.   **μεμορυγμένα** 'stained' < μορύσσω, only here in Homer and very rare elsewhere; cf. the name of the glutton Μόρυχος mentioned in comedy (Ar. *Ach.* 887).

436 ἕσσ(ε): 3rd p.s. aorist active of ἕννυμι; cf. 351n.

437 σκῆπτρον: it would be possible to see a symbolic hint at Od.'s real status in the choice of this word, instead of say ῥόπαλον, since σκῆπτρον is a regular word for a staff of often kingly authority. However, it is also a σκῆπτρον that Od. thrusts into the battered beggar Irus' hands, after he has defeated him in the fight (18.103).

438 πυκνὰ ῥωγαλέην: πυκνά is adverbial accusative, lit. 'thickly', so here 'in many places'. **ἐν δέ** 'and on it', adverbial. **στρόφος...ἀορτήρ** 'a cord as its strap', a slightly tautological expression. ἀορτήρ 'belt', a very rare word (also 17.198, 18.109), is an *o*-grade form cognate with ἀείρω 'attach'.

439 διέτμαγεν 'they parted', 3rd p.pl. aorist passive of δια-τμήγω, connected with τέμνω. The -ν suffix is an Aeolic form from original -ντ, which is preserved in Latin *ama-nt* etc. (cf. *GH* 1.471–2). **ἡ μέν:** this departure of Athena will be repeated in 15.1–2, when her story is picked up after the episode in Eum.'s hut. Olson points out that the fact that the book ends with a μέν-clause, which is picked up in 14.1 αὐτάρ ὁ, shows that 'the division here has nothing to do with Homer's own purposes' (1995: 234).

440 μετὰ παῖδ(α): see 415n.

BOOK 14

1–28 Odysseus' arrival at Eumaeus' pig-farm

This brief journey is not simply a narrative link between the end of the last book and Od.'s arrival at Eum.'s farmstead, but sets in motion Od.'s transition from the wilds of the seashore to the centre of the palace: cf. Introduction pp. 4–6. The rugged track, wooded landscape and hilltops sketch in the rough nature of the island (cf. 13.236–49n.), and prepare for the rural setting of the following episode.

On this episode with Eum., cf. G. P. Rose 1980; Roisman 1990; Reece 1993: 145–63; Olson 1995: 120–39; Louden 1997; Schmidt 2006. For its later reception, cf. Hall 2008: 131–43.

1 προσέβη τρηχεῖαν ἀταρπόν 'he went off (on) a rough path', an internal accusative, cf. 4.483 ἰέναι δολιχὴν ὁδόν 'go on a long journey'; Introduction 5.3 §7.2.4.1.

2 ἄν' 'up over'; ἀνά here combines the ideas of 'up onto' (cf. *Il.* 18.278 στησόμεθ' ἄμ πύργους) and 'across' (cf. *Il.* 5.87 θῦνε...ἄμ πεδίον).

2–3 ἧι...ὑφορβόν 'where Athena indicated to him (that) the swineherd (would be)'; πέφραδε is a reduplicated aorist of φράζω (cf. 13.198n.).

3 δῖον: δῖος is used in *Od.* seventeen times of Eum. and once of Philoetius, as well as of Mentor, Nestor, Orestes and a man of uncertain but perhaps servant status, Echephron (3.439). For the significance of this use of laudatory epithets for humble figures and of paradoxically laudatory epithets for the Suitors, cf. Introduction pp. 18–19; also 22 and 55nn. for other distinctive namings of Eum. In the past, the use of such grand expressions for servants caused problems: for some they were formulaic, for others justified by Eum.'s noble birth, for others they were intended to mock the poor. ὑφορβόν: on the significance of the fact that Eum. is a swineherd, cf. Introduction p. 4. ὑ- is the normal Greek reflex of IE *su- 'pig' (cf. Lat. *sus*); forms with σ- (7 συβώτης, 15 σύες) are possibly borrowed from a neighbouring IE language (cf. Chantraine 2009: s.v. σῦς; Beekes 1425).

3–4 ὅ οἱ βιότοιο...οἰκήων 'who, of those in his household, most cared for his livelihood'. βιότοιο is a partitive genitive depending on κήδετο, indicating the sphere in which the action of the verb takes place; cf. with ὀδύρομαι in 142, 174, and 1.69 Κύκλωπος κεχόλωται 'angry about the Cyclops' (*GH* II.56; Introduction 5.3 §7.2.5.2). οἰκήων is a another partitive genitive depending on the relative ὅ; οἰκεύς means a member of the household generally, and may include both slaves and free men (cf. Mele 1968: 135–9; Thalmann 1998: 64–6). A similar expression is used of Eurycleia, Eum.'s equivalent as the most loyal servant in the palace, in 1.434–5 καί ἑ [Τηλέμαχον] μάλιστα | δμωιάων φιλέεσκε.

5–28 *Eum.'s pig-farm.* In discussing the scenes here, reference is usually made to 'Eumaeus' hut', but this is misleading. It is true that he has a κλισίη 'hut, cabin' (194, 408), but so do Iliadic kings (2.19 etc.) and this κλισίη has a colonnaded entrance and the whole building is large enough to house several hundreds of pigs, so it should not be thought to be simply rudimentary. For the Homeric κλισίη, see Knox 1971. For *Od.*'s interest in the dwellings of all types of characters and the relationship between this dwelling and others, cf. Introduction pp. 19–20.

Eum. himself frames the description (5, 22–4), which falls into two roughly equal parts, the construction of the building (5–12) and the arrangement of the animals (13–22). The farmstead may lack the grandeur of a palace, but its solidity and order contrast with the chaos in *Od.*'s palace: yet here, as there, the depredations of the Suitors have a detrimental effect (17–19). The building is a symbol of Eum.'s solid character (cf. Austin 1975: 165–8): he is represented as an ideal servant, so it comes as a surprise to learn from his autobiography (15.390–484) that he is of noble birth (on which, see Minchin 1992). On the character of Eum., see variously e.g. Dimock 1989: 189–98; Olson 1995: 120–39; Ahl and Roisman 1996: 152–81.

With the stones, thorny pear-branches, thickly packed stakes and vicious dogs, Eum. is very careful about protecting his master's property, since he lives on the margins of the land (24.150 ἀγροῦ ἐπ᾿ ἐσχατιήν), exposed to marauders and pirates (for this problem, cf. 11.401–2 = 24.111–12; 83–8n.). His technical skill shows him as conscious of the need to look after himself: contrast Hesiod's man 'full of bright ideas', who unsuccessfully begs for a cart and ox on the grounds that 'his own cart is almost finished: fool! he does not realise that a cart needs a hundred timbers, which you should be careful to store up at home' (*Op.* 453–7). The idea of the importance of being prepared for everything runs through Hesiod's poem.

On the way that Homer tends to describe things in a narrative manner as here, cf. Minchin 2001: 114–19; cf. also A. T. Edwards 1993: 60–70.

5 ἄρ’ 'and so'; cf. 13.1–2n.   **εὗρ(ε):** Homer regularly introduces new characters by having someone come upon them 'in unguarded moments in their customary location and engaged in a telling activity' (Race 1993: 101), thus immediately suggesting their character. The narrative of Athena's visit to Sparta begins in a similar fashion, with verbal and phonetic echoes: 15.4–6 εὗρε δὲ Τηλέμαχον... | εὕδοντ’ ἐν προδόμωι... | ἤτοι Νεστορίδην... δεδμημένον ὕπνωι.   **προδόμωι...αὐλή:** the πρόδομος is the colonnaded entrance to a house, the αὐλή the courtyard in front of it, in this case where the pigs are kept. For the arrangement in Od.'s house, cf. 18.100–2.

5–6 ἔνθα... δέδμητο: ἔνθα refers not specifically to the πρόδομος, but to the site in general. The phrase recalls 9.184–5 περὶ δ’ αὐλὴ | ὑψηλὴ δέδμητο of the Cyclops' cave, where he too kept his animals. δέδμητο is the unaugmented pluperfect passive of δέμω 'build'.

6 περισκέπτωι: it is preferable to take this as meaning 'visible from all sides', from σκέπτομαι, rather than 'shut in, sheltered on all sides', from σκέπας 'shelter'. Later writers use the epithet in ways that suggest looking, as in 'worth-seeing' (of a παίγνιον, Call. *Epigr.* 5.8) or 'admired' (of a youth, *AP* 12.91.3), and the scholia take it in this way. One may compare too εὔσκεπτος 'easy to examine' (Pl. *Phlb.* 65d), ἀπερίσκεπτος/-ως 'thoughtless(ly)' (Thuc. 4.10.1, 108.4). ὑψηλη in 6 and καλή, μεγάλη and περίδρομος in 7, all of which point to something imposing and highly visible, would also support this interpretation. Putting the farmstead where it both commanded a good view and could be seen would offer advantages in terms of defending it and of making a bold statement about its importance. Furthermore, the fact that at 532–3 Eum. has to seek out a spot sheltered from the storm does not suggest the steading was very snug. This line also describes Telemachus' chamber (1.426), where again height and visibility are appropriate to a prince's rooms rather than sheltered insignificance. Finally, σκέπτομαι gave rise to many derivatives, whereas the few that arose from σκέπας are, apart from σκεπάζω, rare and late. Matters are less clearcut with περισκέπτωι ἐνὶ χώρωι used of Circe's cave (10.211, 253), which is not immediately visible but discovered ἐν βήσσηισι (210, 252). None of this of course tells us securely what the poet thought it meant.

7 περίδρομος 'detached, standing on its own', i.e. with a space running all round, cf. the hill in *Il.* 2.812 ἐν πεδίωι ἀπάνευθε, περίδρομος ἔνθα καὶ ἔνθα. This seems preferable to an active sense of 'running round', i.e 'circular', though the difference is not great.

8 αὐτὸς δεῖμα(το): a first indication that Eum. is very self-sufficient and willing to turn his hand to things that will benefit others.

9 νόσφιν δεσποίνης: νόσφι is lit. 'apart from', and so the phrase means probably 'without the assistance of his mistress', i.e. on his own initiative (cf. 451), as in *Il.* 9.348 πολλὰ πονήσατο νόσφιν ἐμεῖο (Achilles, speaking somewhat ironically, about how Agamemnon has managed without him). Less likely is 'without the knowledge of', for which cf. *H.Ap.* 105 where Iris is asked to bring Eileithuia secretly to Leda νόσφι... Ἥρης. Adverbs like νόσφι which are used as prepositions tend to take the genitive (*GH* II.147–9); the etymology of the νοσ- element is unknown (Beekes 1024–5).

10 ῥυτοῖσιν: in Greek only here and 6.266–7 ἀγορή...ῥυτοῖσι λάεσσι κατωρυχέεσσ' ἀραρυῖα (see *CHO* ad loc.). The meaning is uncertain: 'dragged (into place)' < ἐρύω is possible ('formally possible, but not semantically evident', Beekes 1296), and the scholia explain it by ἑλκυστοῖς and the like. Another possibility is 'quarried', but that would make it a synonym of κατωρυχέεσσι in the passage quoted above. The current passage contains a number of Homeric hapax legomena: 10 ἐθρίγκωσεν, ἄχερδος, 12 μέλαν, ἀμφικεάσσας (though uncompounded forms appear elsewhere), 15 ἐρχατόωντο, 16 τοκάδες, 24 εὔχροές, plus 15 χαμαιευνάδες (twice elsewhere): the unusual subject matter brings with it unusual words, and book 14 generally has a higher percentage of hapax legomena (1 per 9.9 lines) than all other *Od.* books (average 11.8), except 5 (6.4) and 6 (9.5); cf. in general Kumpf 1984, esp. 205–6, and also 203n. below. Shipp 1972: 340–1 collects the 'abnormal' features in this book. On hapaxes in Homer generally, see N. J. Richardson 1987.   **ἐθρίγκωσεν ἀχέρδωι** 'he topped it off with wild pear', the twigs of which end in a long sharp thorn. This feature corresponds to the coloured enamel coping of Alcinous' palace (7.87 περὶ δὲ θρίγχος κυάνοιο) and the stone on Od.'s (17.267).

11 σταυροὺς...ἔνθα 'and on the outside he made a continuous line of stakes on this side and that'. ἐκτός is adverbial; for ἐλαύνω, cf. Ar. *Ach.* 995 ἀμπελίδος ὄρχον ἐλάσαι 'plant a line of vines'.

12 τὸ μέλαν 'the bark'; the dark bark is stripped or cut away, leaving the harder internal wood. τό provides a clear case of the way the demonstrative force of ὁ, ἡ, τό was reduced to produce a true article (cf. Palmer 1962: 138; *GH* II.165; Introduction 5.3 §7.3.1–3).   **ἀμφικεάσσας:** aorist participle active of ἀμφι-κεάζω 'split off all round'.

13 ἔντοσθεν δ' αὐλῆς: for the genitive, see 9n. The segregation of the sexes here recalls the segregation of the Cyclops' sheep and goats (9.220–2). ποίει 'he set about building'; the imperfect describes the way the building took some time, so there is a slight contrast with the aorist δεῖμαθ' in 8, which views the building as a single act (cf. *GH* II.192–5).

15 ἐρχατόωντο: imperfect of ἐρχατάομαι 'be penned up', with *diektasis* (cf. 13.93n.).

17 πολλὸν παυρότεροι: though of course in reality one boar can service a good number of sows, natural history here gives way to symbolism, as this disparity in numbers between the sexes marks the deleterious effect of the Suitors on Od.'s property; as in the palace, the absence of the male leads to disorder which others have to mitigate. One can contrast the settled equality in numbers of Priam's sons and sons-in-law and their wives in their fifty chambers (*Il.* 6.243–50), or the six sons married to the six daughters in Aeolus' palace (*Od.* 10.5–7). τοὺς γὰρ μινύθεσκον 'for [the Suitors] were constantly depleting their numbers'; for the iterative suffix *-sk-*, cf. Introduction 5.3 §6.4.

18 ἀντίθεοι μνηστῆρες: cf. 3n.

19 ζατρεφέων 'well nourished, fat'. ζα- is an Aeolic treatment of δια-, an intensive suffix, via *δγα; they are not metrical equivalents but a genuine doublet. The number of words with this prefix is small and they appear old: cf. e.g. ζάης, ζάθεος, and also δάφοινος (*GH* I.169). For the -τρεφ- element, cf. 477n.

20 τριηκόσιοί τε καὶ ἑξήκοντα: one for each day of the year, and similar to the 350 cattle and sheep of the Sun (12.127–31), which the Companions like the Suitors tried to eat improperly. There does not seem to be any number-symbolism here.

21 κύνες: the presence of dogs at a farm is unsurprising; Hesiod specifically recommends a well-fed 'jagged-toothed' dog to keep thieves away at night (*Op.* 604–5), but the motif of 'dogs before the door' is important in *Od.* These dogs react to visitors in three different ways: they will nearly savage Od. (29–31); they fawn on Telemachus (16.4–10); but cower in fear at Athena (16.162–3). Dogs give an indication of the nature of the houses they guard: gold and silver ones guard the other-worldly palace of Alcinous (7.91–4); outside Circe's cave, there are wolves and lions, compared to dogs fawning on their master at dinner but actually men transformed (10.212–19); the fly-blown Argus neglected on the dung-heap mirrors the disarray in Od.'s own house (17.291–327). The motif appears also in modified forms. Before her meeting with Od., Penelope addresses Melantho as κύον ἀδεές 'fearless dog' because of her harsh attack on Od. (19.91; so

Od. in 18.338; cf. Louden 2011: 81). In 20.10–16, a simile of a mother-
dog's reaction to a stranger describes Od.'s heart's reaction to the folly of
the serving-girls. On dogs in *Od.*, see M. W. Edwards 1987; W. Beck 1991;
Goldhill 1991: 12–14. As well as real dogs, Near Eastern cities, palaces and
temples frequently had sculpted protective animals on the posts of door-
ways, such as the lions and sphynxes at Hattusha or the mythical beasts
found on Babylonian and Assyrian palaces: cf. Faraone 1987; Cook 2004:
67–8; Scodel 2005.

22 ὄρχαμος ἀνδρῶν appears in the *Iliad* of Achilles, Agamemnon and
Menelaus (7 × in all), but in the *Odyssey* of Eum. six times and Philoetius
twice, alongside Menelaus (6 ×) and Peisistratus (3 ×). Cf. 3n. on δῖον.

23 αὐτὸς δ'...πέδιλα 'he himself was making sandals to fit his feet'; Eum.
does not waste his free time, just as Hesiod's farmer is also imagined as
making his own clothes (*Op.* 536–46). After the buildings and then the animals inside, the narrative finally focuses on the man himself. There is no
physical description, but the narrative concentrates on his moral qualities,
which contrast with the wasteful idleness of the aristocratic youth. Sandals
frame the episode, since Eum. dons them to go to the city (16.154–5).

24 δέρμα βόειον: Hes. *Op.* 541–2 also recommends ox-hide πέδιλα for winter, stuffed with felt.   δὲ δή marks the contrast with αὐτὸς δέ, as it can
without a preceding μέν (*GP* 259).

25 ἄλλυδις ἄλλος 'each in a different direction'; for ἄλλος thus combined
with a cognate adverb, cf. LSJ s.v. II.2. ἄλλυδις is an Aeolic form (Wathelet
1970: 284–5).   ἀγρομένοισι 'herded together', aorist middle participle
of ἀγείρω with a passive sense; it has the zero grade of the root as is usual
in these archaic forms (*GH* 1.387).

26 οἱ τρεῖς· τὸν δὲ τέταρτον '(that is), three of them did this, but the
fourth...', an afterthought giving a slightly colloquial tone. For the use
of the article with numerals to mark different individuals or groups, cf.
3.298–300 ἀτὰρ νῆάς γε ποτὶ σπιλάδεσσιν ἔαξαν | κύματ'· ἀτὰρ τὰς πέντε νέας
κυανοπρωιρείους | Αἰγύπτωι ἐπέλασσε φέρων ἄνεμος 'the waves broke (most
of) the ships on the rocks, but five of them with their dark prows the wind
brought to Egypt' (*GH* II.162). We get a sense of the labour involved in
provisioning the idle Suitors.   ἀποπροέηκε: the simple verb is ἵημι (root
here *ἡ-); the subject is Eum.

27 ἀγέμεν: infinitive of purpose (cf. 13.34n.).   ὑπερφιάλοισιν is formulaic of the Suitors, but here can be read as giving Eum.'s own view of them.
ἀνάγκηι: 13.307n.

28 κορεσαίατο: 3rd p.pl. of the aorist middle optative of κορέννυμι 'to satisfy, sate, fill', governing the partitive genitive κρειῶν (*GH* II.51).

29–47 *The dogs attack Odysseus*

After the leisurely pace of the *ecphrasis* of the buildings, the narrative suddenly (NB ἐξαπίνης, 29) picks up speed as the dogs attack Od. Od.'s incaution in just walking up to the door recalls similar incaution before the Cyclops' cave (9.216); his Companions were similarly incautious at Circe's (10.231). It is a second lesson to him that, though he is home, caution is still needed: earlier he was about to blunder into the palace, but was saved by Athena's warning (13.383–5). Eum.'s saving of Od. from the dogs prefigures the way in which it is the servants who will stand by him in his triumph over the Suitors.

29 ὑλακόμωροι: the general sense of the word is clear from the root **ul-* 'bark' and the context, but the second element is more problematic. It is very probably not μῶρος 'mad' (cf. Ruijgh 1957: 93; the scholia derive it from μορέω 'toil'). The comparable 3.188 ἐγχεσιμώρους and *Il.* 4.242, 14.479 ἰόμωροι contain an IE element **meh₁-ro-* meaning 'great', found in names like Celtic *Nerto-marus*, Slavonic *Vladi-mir* etc. They would thus mean 'famous for…' (cf. Beekes 372–3). ὑλακόμωροι would be a mock-epic epithet (it is found only here and in 16.4 before Nonnus).

30 κεκλήγοντες: perfect participles with thematic -οντ- instead of -οτ- seem to be Aeolic (Wathelet 1970: 324–9). κεκλήγοντες appears five times in Homer, always with the variant κεκληγῶτες, the latter perhaps an attempt to get closer to the more familiar Ionic -ότες when a long penultimate vowel is needed. The only parallel for κεκλήγοντες is in fact the variant πεπλήγων preserved by the scholia on *Il.* 2.264 (*GH* I.430–1).

31 ἕζετο: for sitting down as a manoeuvre to avoid being savaged by dogs, cf. Arist. *Rhet.* 1380a24, Pliny, *NH* 8.146, Plut. *Mor.* 970E; Lilja 1976: 20. See Hainsworth 1961 for the ethology here.   **σκῆπτρον…ἔκπεσε:** for dropping objects as an expression of surprise etc. at cardinal moments, cf. 34, 16.13–14 (Eum. on the sudden arrival of Telemachus), 19.467–70 (Eurycleia on recognising Od.), 22.17 (Antinous on being shot).

32 ὧι πάρ σταθμῶι 'on his own farmstead'; for the possessive ὧι, cf. 13.198n. To be savaged by dogs on his home territory as soon as he was back would have been a cruel irony.

33 μετασπών 'chasing after them', aorist active participle of μεθ-ἕπω. This ἕπω 'busy oneself with', from the root **sep-* (here in the zero grade), is to be distinguished etymologically from ἕπομαι 'follow', from **sekʷ-* (cf. Latin *sequor*). Here however the sense is clearly more 'chased after' than simply 'took care of', which shows the influence from the more familiar ἕπομαι on its rarer counterpart, as in *Il.* 8.126 ἡνίοχον μέθεπε 'he went in search of a charioteer', and expressions like πότμον ἐπέσπον 'they met their fate'.

34 σκῦτος...χειρός: this second half-line is structurally, metrically and in meaning parallel to the end of 31. The use of similar expressions for Od. and Eum. constitutes the symbolic linking of master and servant.

36 πυκνῇσιν λιθάδεσσιν: this expression, with the very rare word λιθάς, appears in Homer only here and in 23.193, the description of Od.'s construction of his bed.   **ὁ δὲ προσέειπεν ἄνακτα:** ἄνακτα is how the author, not Eum. of course, sees it, but there is a frisson for the audience; cf. de Jong 1993: 291–7 on the rhetorical and emotional effects of the use of ἄναξ of Od. by the various characters. Compare the similar but more powerful use of ἄναξ in 19.358, where Penelope orders Eurycleia to wash Od., saying νίψον σοῖο ἄνακτος – where we expect a word for 'feet', but get instead ὁμήλικα 'contemporary'. ὁ δὲ προσέειπεν ἄνακτα is a unique expression for introducing a speech in Homer.

37–47 *Eum.'s first speech.* This brief utterance conveys the two salient aspects of Eum.'s character: his hospitable concern to show proper care for others (37–8, 45–7), and his devotion to his master (39–44). Hölscher 1939: 65 pointed out how people whom Od. meets have a habit of soon speaking of matters which concern him most: cf. 19.124–8, 369. From here onward, direct speech dominates more than in any other book of *Od.*: 76.7 per cent of book 14 is speech, the nearest to this is book 4 with 72.8 per cent (for figures, see D. Beck 2005: 282–3).

37 γέρον: though Eum. regularly calls the beggar 'old man', he does not do so after book 14, a sign of his changing attitude as the merits of the beggar become clearer.

37–8 ἦ ὀλίγου...ἐξαπίνης: 'the dogs really did nearly tear you apart on the spot!' The meaning is relatively clear, the grammatical explication less so. The problem is in ὀλίγου. The most natural sense would be 'nearly': there is no Homeric parallel, but cf. e.g. Thuc. 8.35.3 ὀλίγου εἷλον (τὴν πόλιν). ὀλίγου 'nearly' might be a shortened form of ὀλίγου δεῖ, found first in Hdt. 7.10γ.1 (Smyth §1399), but equally δεῖ may have been added later, to make this sense 'nearly' clearer. Alternatively, ὀλίγου could be 'quickly', a genitive of the time (so Stanford ad loc., *sc.* χρόνου; cf. e.g. δι᾽ ὀλίγου 'in a short time'); one would however expect ἄν/κε with the verb, as in the parallel 38 κέν...κατέχευας, and ἐξαπίνης would be tautological.

38 ἐλεγχείην: Eum.'s concern to avoid criticism of his treatment of others, and his immediate invitation to Od. to come inside and eat, align him early on with those figures who are characterised by their proper treatment of guests. That Eum. puts the shame that the dogs nearly brought him on a level (39 ἄλλα) with the loss of his godlike master further illustrates the breadth of his sense of decency. For the shame attendant on allowing a guest to be maltreated, cf. 18.220–5, and Hesiod's striking statement that harming a guest is the equivalent of seducing one's brother's wife (*Op.* 327–9). κατέχευας: for καταχέω in this metaphorical sense of pouring, cf. *Il.* 23.408 of ἐλεγχείην, *Od.* 11.433 αἶσχος, 22.463 ὀνείδεα.

39 καὶ δὲ...ἄλλα: καί emphasises ἄλλα; cf. 13.302n.

40 ἄνακτος ὀδυρόμενος: for the genitive, cf. 3–4n.   καὶ ἀχεύων 'and sorrowing for'. There is assonance and partial rhyme with 38 κατέχευας.

41 σύας σιάλους: σίαλος 'a fatted pig' is used with σῦς and on its own. For the form of such phrases, cf. 13.86–7n.   ἀτιτάλλω 'raise, nourish' is cognate with ἀταλός 'young, delicate', formed with expressive reduplication (cf. 92n.). It is usually employed in Homer not of parents but of others, such as nurses or foster parents, involved in the upbringing of young humans and animals, so its use here is a sign of Eum.'s affection for his beasts.

42 ἔδμεναι: infinitive of purpose; cf. 13.34n. Eum. contrasts the way he raises pigs for unnamed 'others' with the probable hunger of his master, the contrast marked by the way cognate words for eating frame the line. This is a small sign of his attitude to those 'others', though at this stage he is carefully unspecific about who they might be: he cannot know that Od. knows exactly what he means.   που 'no doubt, I imagine' here acknowledges that Eum. cannot be certain, but glumly presumes it to be true. Cf. 44n. for a slightly different sense.

43 ἐπ'...δῆμον: ἐπί marks the area through or over which something takes place; cf. *Il.* 7.88 πλέων ἐπὶ οἴνοπα πόντον. As often in Homer, δῆμος here refers to a people's land as opposed to the people themselves; cf. 24.12 δῆμον ὀνείρων; 13.97n. This is much rarer later; cf. Donlan 1999: 225–6. ἀλλοθρόων ἀνδρῶν: ἀλλοθρόων highlights one of the problems of wandering (in reality if not in epic, where everyone speaks Greek), the potential isolation caused by being amongst people speaking an unfamiliar language. Knowledge of other languages was rare in early Greece and the Near East, being largely restricted to professional interpreters and scribes: even someone like Herodotus manifestly knows very little about the languages of the peoples he describes, and indeed shows little interest in them (cf. Harrison 1998). Cf. Solon's sympathy for exiles 'no longer speaking the Attic tongue, because they have wandered so much' (fr. 36.11–12): language and identity go together, so travel and exile threaten both.

44 εἴ που: 'if, that is ...'; που is joined with εἰ, μή etc. to add a slight emphasis.   **ὁρᾶι φάος ἠελίοιο:** as opposed to being in the Underworld, where the sun never shines.

45 ἕπεο: 2nd p.s. present imperative of ἕπομαι (Att. ἕπου).   **κλισίηνδ':** for -δε, cf. 13.17n.   **καὶ αὐτός** 'you too', i.e. just as I have been telling you my problems.

47 εἴπηις: Eum. here follows the epic convention of not asking these questions before the guest has been fed and watered.

48-77 Odysseus is welcomed into the farmhouse

This description of homely hospitality, which makes what it can of what it has, had a profound influence especially upon Hellenistic and later writers: cf. esp. Callimachus, *Hecale*, and *Aitia* frr. 145-56 Massimilla = 54-60j Harder (*Molorchus*, where Heracles is entertained by old Molorchus before tackling the Nemean Lion); Ovid, *Met.* 8.618-724 (Baucis and Philemon). The pattern of meal followed by story-telling in the subsequent lines will be repeated when the swineherds arrive at 409.

49 εἷσεν 'he sat Od. down', sigmatic aorist of ἕζομαι, < *e-(s)ed-s-e. **ῥῶπας:** from ῥώψ 'brushwood'. The scene is a rustic variation on the honourable seating of guests, which is a common motif: a chair is brought by slaves for Helen and covered in a soft woollen rug at 4.123-4; cf. 1.130, 3.35, 4.51 etc. Eum. does the same for Telemachus: no distinction is made between beggar and prince, in seating and food (16.46-53).

50 ἐπί 'upon it'; a good example of the independent adverbial use of these preverbs/prepositions (Introduction 5.3 §7.5.1); cf. *Il.* 13.799 αὐτὰρ ἐπ' ἄλλα 'and others besides'.   **ἰονθάδος** 'shaggy', only here in Greek, from ἴονθος 'facial hair'.

51 αὐτοῦ ἐνεύναιον 'his own bed-clothes'. αὐτοῦ is literally 'of himself', acting as a reflexive third-person pronoun (*GH* II.158). ἐνεύναιος 'on which one makes one's εὐνή' appears only here and in 16.35 before the fourth century AD.

52 ἔπος τ' ἔφατ(ο) ἔκ τ' ὀνόμαζε: in *Od.* this expression is often (but not exclusively) used to introduce speeches between intimates, which is appropriate here, though Eum. does not know it. The expression has become largely formulaic, as is shown by the fact that, despite the presence of ὀνόμαζε, it is regularly used without a personal name following; cf. Calhoun 1935: 223-6; M. W. Edwards 1970: 10 n. 18.

53-4 Ζεύς...ἐθέλεις: there is gentle irony in Od. expressing the hope that the gods will give Eum. whatever he most wants, when he knows from 39-44 that what he most wants is Od.'s return. He thanks Telemachus in similar terms when he too immediately sees to his comfort on his arrival in the palace (17.354-5). These same words will be used with even greater irony when, after Od. has defeated the rival beggar Irus, one of the Suitors laughingly applies them to Od., not realising he is praying for his own destruction (18.112-13).

54 ὑπέδεξο: 2nd p.s. athematic aorist middle indicative of δέκομαι (Att. δέχομαι), from *δέκ-σο; cf. the 3rd p.s. in 275 ὑπέδεκτο.

55-71 *Eum.'s second speech.* Like the first, this begins with moral reflection (56-61) before turning to his absent master (62-71). There is a further remark about Eum.'s situation with regard to others in Ithaca (59-61), so that the speech thus continues the process of slowly 'drip-feeding' Od. with information. The vague 'others' (41) are now more precisely 'the new/young masters', and the implied criticism noted in 42n. is made a little more explicit: they inspire 'fear' (60). Eum. still cautiously keeps their actual identity close to his chest, not knowing whom he might be talking to. The last speech said simply that his master was lost; this speaks of his kindness to good servants and reveals that he is absent because he went to Troy. Eum. also indicates that he was himself a good servant, the success of whose work would normally have led to greater prosperity, but it is characteristic of him that this fact is kept to the very end.

The early part of the speech (56-61) contains a good deal of enjambment, which suggests a warm enthusiasm and a certain confidence. Once he gets to the subject of his master however the lines become end-stopped as a graver tone descends, enlivened only by the outburst about Helen in 68-9.

55 Εὔμαιε συβῶτα: on fifteen occasions Homer introduces a speech of Eum. by addressing him directly. All except 22.194 appear in books 14 and 16-17, and they account for all but five of Eum.'s speeches (the exceptions are 14.121, 401, 16.22, 36, 17.184). No other character is so addressed in *Od.*, and none so regularly in *Il.*, where such apostrophes are used for Patroclus (8 ×), Menelaus (7 ×), Phoebus (2 ×), Melanippus and Achilles (once each). Indeed, *Od.* generally uses authorial address in a more restricted way than *Il.*: there is only one invocation to a god (1.1; 6 × *Il.*), and only one address to the audience (22.12-14; 5 × *Il.*); cf. Block 1982: 11-12; Yamagata 1989. This is a first indication that Eum., unnamed so far, will be more important than epic convention might suggest for a swineherd. Eustathius suggested that this feature indicated affection on the part of the narrator (2.60.26-7 φιλῶν τῆς εὐνοίας τὸν δοῦλον). Cf. further A. M. Parry 1989: 324–5; Kahane 1994: 104–13, and 153–5.

The origin of the name Eumaeus is uncertain. Other names in -αιος can be abbreviations of longer names, as Πύλαιος < Πυλαιμένης. It might therefore derive from Εὐμενής (*e-u-me-ne* is a name found in Mycenean), which would be a suitable epithet for him. Another possibility is to connect it with μαίομαι 'seek' (cf. Οἰνόμαιος), so 'seeker after the good'. How exactly poet and audience took it, we do not know. On the way that this line, 121 and 401, all essentially meaning 'Eum. replied', appear to breach the 'principle of economy' of the Homeric formula, see M. W. Edwards 1970. On Homeric speech introductions generally, Riggsby 1992: 102–14.

56–7 οὔ μοι θέμις … ξεῖνον ἀτιμῆσαι: so Hes. *Op.* 717–8 'don't cast in a man's teeth destructive and depressing poverty, the gift of the immortal blessed ones'; cf. also Thgn. 155–7.

57 πρὸς γὰρ Διός: on πρός + genitive cf. 13.324n. The idea is that beggars come from unknown parts and, since no-one would willingly abandon his home, their wandering must have been caused by a great misfortune or crime: Zeus must somehow be involved, and so they should be treated with care. Gods themselves even travel in disguise to test mortals' attitude to strangers, as one of the Suitors points out to Antinous when he has thrown a foot-stool at Od. (17.483–7). Eum., like Nausicaa who uses the same words in 6.207–8, does not make the same mistake as the Suitors. His motivation however is not just fear of the gods (suggested by θέμις in 56), but also a sense of common decency: helping people need not cost much and it can give pleasure.

58 φίλη 'welcome'.

59–60 ἡ γὰρ δμώων δίκη … δειδιότων 'this is the condition servants find themselves in, because they are always afraid'. For ἡ one might expect a neuter pronoun, but ἡ takes the gender of δίκη. δίκη is a zero-grade form of the root of δείκνυμι, and means originally something like 'direction', and so 'way, manner, custom', and then in a more legalistic sense 'judgement'. For the meaning 'condition, circumstance' here, cf. 11.218 αὕτη δίκη ἐστὶ βροτῶν, ὅτε τίς κε θάνῃσιν, 4.691, 19.43 etc. The participle δειδιότων has a causal sense. Eum. is explaining ὀλίγη in 58: when young masters keep firm control, the servants have little room to manoeuvre. He thus skilfully shows himself at once (a) reluctantly less generous than he might be, (b) careful of his masters' resources, and (c) canny enough to know how to behave in tricky circumstances.

61 οἱ νέοι in enjambment is added almost as a corrective: 'when masters are in control – I mean the ones who are new/young'; Eum. does not wish this to be a general remark about all masters, as the contrast with τοῦ shows: for the article thus, cf. *GH* II.162–3. It is natural to take Eum. as thinking of the Suitors, but he will also express a worry about Telemachus' capacity for displeasure in 17.188–9, a worry borne out by Telemachus' words to him at 21.369–75, when he is slow to take the bow to Od.

61–7 Eum.'s trust that Od. would have rewarded him for his labours is shown to be justified by the rewards promised in 21.213–6; on which, cf. Introduction p. 23. Eum.'s counterpart Philoetius will speak with similar affection about Od.'s treatment of him when he meets Od. in 20.208–14.

61 ἦ γάρ 'you see, the fact is': γάρ explains why he has been talking about masters; ἦ emphasises what has happened to his master.   **κατὰ νόστον ἔδησαν** 'have held back his return', cf. 7.272 κατέδησε κέλευθον (so some MSS); this is a Homeric use of the verb. For the metaphor of binding, cf. 23.353 πεδάασκον ἐμῆς ἀπὸ πατρίδος αἴης 'they constrained me from my fatherland'.

62 ἐνδυκέως is used here to mean 'assiduously, graciously', but its origin was and is unknown (Beekes 422); it is used in a range of senses in poets and grammarians (cf. also 109).

63 οἵά τε: a generalising neuter plural relative referring back to the abstract κτῆσιν; cf. 13.410n.   **ἔδωκεν** gnomic aorist expressing what is generally the case. Eum. presents an idealised picture of the relationship between master and slave; his clear sense of his own worth and its just desserts reveals an independence of mind that reflects the former royal prince behind the slave.

64–5 64 is a parenthesis listing the gifts; ὅς in 65 then refers back to οἰκῆϊ in 63.

64 κλῆρον: 'a permanent share or allotment of the community's arable land, sufficient to maintain a family' (Donlan 1997: 656; cf. 656–8 for a useful summary on what is known of the *klēros* in the eighth century; see too M. L. West 1978 on Hes. *Op.* 340–1; Mele 1968: 179–96). Such shares were essential to independent existence and the stable continuity of an *oikos* over time. If one had no such inheritance, and was not in a position to get one by force or by joining a colony, then a gift of this kind was the only means of securing a πατρὶς γαῖα. Cf. the ungenerous gift supposedly made to Od. by his brothers in 14.208–10.   **πολυμνήστην** 'sought after by many suitors' is, given Penelope's problems, amusingly ironic for the audience, if not Od. An excellent servant could reasonably expect his master would reward him with an excellent wife: for the importance of a good soul-mate for a farmer, cf. Hes. *Op.* 695–705; *Th.* 607–12; also Semon. 7.83–93. Time in fact presses for Eum. to marry. We do not know his precise age, but he was brought up with the youngest (ὁπλοτάτην) of Od.'s younger sisters and sent to the fields when he reached maturity (15.361–70; cf. Severyns 1929). This implies he was younger than Od., who must be imagined as forty or so. If Eum. was in his thirties, then he was getting towards the end of the period which was thought the ideal time for marriage, which ranges variously in the sources from twenty-five to thirty-five: cf. Hes. *Op.* 696–7 μήτε τριηκόντων ἐτέων μάλα πόλλ' ἀπολείπων | μήτ' ἐπιθεὶς μάλα πολλά 'don't marry much before thirty nor much after it'; Solon, fr. 27.9; Pl. *Rep.* 460E, *Legg.* 772D.

65 κάμηισι...ἀέξηι: κάμηισι is a subjunctive in a general relative clause (cf. 13.31–2n.); when the θεὸς δέ clause is added paratactically, ἀέξηι keeps that mood.   ἐπί can be treated either as adverbial, 'in addition', or as part of a nascent compound verb with ἀέξηι.

66 τόδε ἔργον: i.e. the farmstead.

67 γήρα 'he had grown old' is an athematic aorist of γηράσκω (*GH* 1.380). Homer seems regularly to treat it as an imperfect (cf. 13.132n. for a similar case), but here, as in *Il.* 7.148 ἐπεί...ἐγήρα 'when he becomes old', it is an aorist.

68 ἀλλ' ὄλε(το): a bald statement of Eum.'s view of Od.'s fate. This conviction will be subtly eroded as the scene goes on: cf. 122–3, 172, 423–4nn.; G. P. Rose 1980: 287–92.   ὡς ὤφελλ(ε): lit. 'would that it were the case that'; cf. 13.204n. *sub fin.* (on the form ὤφελλον, cf. *GH* 1.314).   ἀπό φῦλον ὀλέσθαι: see Introduction 5.3 §7.5.1.

69 πρόχνυ 'completely, utterly': cf. *Il.* 21.459–60 ἀπόλωνται | πρόχνυ κακῶς. Despite the problem of the aspiration, πρόχνυ is almost certainly a compound of γόνυ in the zero grade, meaning literally 'forward on one's knees', cf. *Il.* 9.570 πρόχνυ καθεζομένη 'kneeling', and the adverb γνύξ in *Il.* (Beekes 1242). This would produce a pun with ὑπὸ γούνατ' ἔλυσεν at the end of the line: Helen's race would pay an appropriate penalty (for other possible puns in this book, cf. 204, 243–4, 316, 371; Ahl 2002). Later the adverb comes to mean simply 'very', as in A.R. 1.1118 πρόχνυ γεράνδρον 'very old'.   ὑπὸ γούνατ' ἔλυσε: the phrase describes the way that a man who is mortally wounded collapses at the knees. In *Il.* it is almost always used with the killer as the subject, but here and in 236 it is used of a person or thing indirectly responsible for the deaths (cf. also *Il.* 13.360).

70 καὶ γάρ apologises for the outburst and explains for the beggar's benefit why he suddenly cursed Helen and her race.   τιμῆς: questions of τιμή frame the speech (cf. ἀτιμῆσαι, 57).

72–9 *Eum. prepares the food.* Appropriately for a sacrifice with a single diner, this is described in slightly simpler terms than the many grander epic sacrifices; contrast the fuller version when the herdsmen come for their evening meal (413–56). Eum. however follows proper sacrificial practice, but he hastens to get the food to the beggar whom he clearly sees as in need of a square meal. There are verbal similarities with the food and drink offered to Telemachus on his return, but the beggar here gets a fresh sacrifice, while the prince has to make do with leftovers (16.49–53): Eum. does not believe in waste.

73 ἔρχατο: 3rd p.s. pluperfect passive of (ϝ)ἔργω 'shut in, confine, pen' (cf. 10.241 ἐέρχατο). It is an odd form, possibly simplified from (ϝ)ε(ϝ)έρχατο, but for unexplained reasons without an augment (cf. Leumann 1950: 179–80; *GH* I.421). A plural verb with a neuter plural subject is found when there is emphasis on the multiplicity of the subject; cf. 103–4 αἰπόλια ... βόσκοντ(αι) of the many flocks of Od., and *GH* II.17–18; Introduction 5.3 §7.1.1.   χοίρων 'young, suckling pigs'; these are too young to go out with their parents into the fields and are kept in a special stall.

74 δύ(ο): two pigs, even small suckling ones, are a generous lunch for one man; Eum. refuses to stint on his hospitality.

75 εὗσε 'singed', so that the bristles did not spoil the crackling. In the pig-sacrifices here and at 427–8, the singeing corresponds to the flaying of the ox in grander sacrifices (*Il.* 9.467).   μίστυλλεν 'divided up'; some parts were reserved for the gods and others for men.   ἀμφ' ὀβελοῖσιν ἔπειρεν: lit. 'he pierced them (so as to make them stick) round the spits' (Hoekstra, *CHO* ad loc.).

77 αὐτοῖς ὀβελοῖσιν: for the 'sociative' dative, see 13.118n. Normally, the roast meat is taken off the spits and served, sometimes in baskets as happens when Eum. later feeds the swineherds (430). Perhaps the meat is left on the spits because only Od. eats here; cf. also 78n. on the use of a simple cup for mixing the wine.   ἄλφιτα: barley was regularly scattered on meat at sacrifice.

78–110 Eum.'s third speech

The speech has at its start, end and middle the depredations of the Suit-ors, and the identity of the previously anonymous 'others' (41) and 'young masters' (60–1) is now revealed (81). Eum. drops his earlier caution and criticises them openly (82–3), before embarking on a moral discourse on such behaviour and its inevitable punishment at the hands of the gods (83–8). In this passage there is a clash between the end-stopping of the lines, which suggests an attempt at self-control, and the way in which his syntax breaks down, which indicates the strength of his passion. His depiction of Od. is also developed, as he proudly lists his master's wealth and power. Unwittingly, Eum. thus shows himself more and more a man admiring of and intensely loyal to Od.

78 κισσυβίωι: a specifically rustic cup (ἀγροικικῶι ἐκπώματι, scholia), of varied shape, used by the Cyclops (9.346) and Philoctetes in his cave (Soph. *Phil.* 35–6). Cf. Asclepiades Myrleanus, 'no-one in the city or amongst the moderate used a *skyphos* or *kissybion*, but only swineherds, shepherds and people in the countryside', and the other quotations in Ath. 476F–7E; cf. also Gow 1952 on Theoc. 1.27. As usual, wine is mixed with water for drinking (13.50n.), but here a simple cup is used rather than a mixing-bowl, presumably because only one person is drinking.   **κίρνη:** 3rd p.s. imperfect active indicative of κίρνημι 'mix'.

79 ἷζεν … ἐποτρύνων: Eum.'s solicitousness again comes out in the way he not only sits with the beggar while he eats, but dispels any reluctance he may have to take the generous gift of food.

80 τά τε: τά is a relative pronoun looking forward to χοίρε(α); for τε see 13.60n.

81 μνηστῆρες: Eum. lets slip the truth here, speaking as though the beggar knew as well as he what the situation was.   **χοίρε':** Eum. has been generous in cooking two piglets, but still hastens to apologise for the fact that he cannot give the beggar the mature pork the Suitors eat. Placed at the start of the line before a strong stop, χοῖρε' is emphasised in an almost scornful way. Later Eum. will be bolder in his use of the pigs (414–17).

82 οὐκ ὄπιδα … ἐνὶ φρεσίν: cf. 13.148n. for ὄπιδα. Philoetius makes a similar comment at 20.213–15. The verb φρονέω appears with its cognate φρήν only here in Homer.   **ἐλεητύν** 'compassion'. For the 'pitiless' waste of resources, cf. Antinous' complaint at 17.451–2 οὔ τις ἐπίσχεσις οὐδ' ἐλεητὺς | ἀλλοτρίων χαρίσασθαι 'there is no holding back or sparing of other people's goods in the making of gifts [to the beggar]'. The conspicuous waste of food offends against Greek notions of moderation and the gods' dislike of human excess.

83–8 There is here a critical view of piracy and raiding, which contrasts with its inclusion in a list of a hero's talents in *Il.* (cf. 6.414–28, 20.188–94), and in some places in *Od.* (1.398, 9.39–42, 14.258–72 = 17.427–41, 23.357). Here we get the view of those who are on the other end of piracy, a view also evinced by Nestor and the Cyclops in 3.71–4 = 9.252–5. In all three of Od.'s fictional stories of raiding there is disaster for the raiders. For Thucydides (1.4), piracy is one of the characteristics of the early age of Greece. On archaic Greek piracy and the difficulty of distinguishing between it and warfare, see de Sousa 1995: 180–1.

83 οὐ μέν 'but then'; the combination stresses the contrast between Eum.'s last remark about the Suitors and this truth about the gods (cf. *GP* 362).

85–8 These lines are rather loosely put together, and they have been variously punctuated. It seems easiest to print them as a single sentence, with two anacoloutha in 87 and 88. 85–6 appear to establish the villains as the subject of the sentence, but immediately a relative clause with generic subjunctives takes over the syntax and there is no main verb for that subject. (There is something similar in 13.81–3). 87 then introduces a contrast (δέ τε), but the verb is now in the indicative (ἔβαν), as if another indicative main verb had preceded. 88 then seems to start again with καὶ μέν (as in 85), but the men are now in the dative case. The fragmented syntax helps convey the fervour of Eum.'s attitudes to wrong-doing. The paratactic mode of composition can, to ears and eyes accustomed to more syntactic forms of language, appear strange, but it enables authors to make their points in a forceful and idiomatic manner: cf. Introduction 5.3 §11.1; *GH* II.351–64, esp. 353–5 on this type of passage; and 111–14, 149–51 below for other passages of this sort; Ruijgh 1971: 748–52.   **καὶ μέν ... καὶ μέν:** in each case, the meaning is most likely 'even', the second pair reinforcing the further point introduced by the first: 'the gods don't like wickedness; (this is true because) even violent criminals know it; (as is shown by the fact that) even they ultimately fear punishment'; cf. *GP* 390–1.

85 ἀνάρσιοι: lit. 'those who do not fit in', so 'those not conforming to society's norms', from the same root as ἀρ-αρ-ίσκω 'fit together'.

86 βῶσιν ... δώηι: for the subjunctive in generalising relative clauses, see 13.31–2n.   **σφιν:** Homer often replaces an expected second relative pronoun with a personal one.

87–8 πλησάμενοι δέ τε νῆας κτλ.: fear naturally strikes them when they have committed their crimes and are vulnerably exposed on the sea; the fate of Od.'s Companions illustrates their problem.

89 οἴδε δέ τοι ἴσασι 'you see, they [*sc.* the Suitors] know'; for τοι, see 13.130n.   **θεοῦ ... αὐδήν:** 'only here in the Homeric poems ... does *audê* mean something other than human speech and require the qualifying θεοῦ' (Clay 1974: 135).

90 ὄλεθρον: in apposition to τιν' ... αὐδήν in 89.   **ὅ τ(ι):** lit. 'with respect to the fact that', so 'because', an adverbial accusative neuter of the relative pronoun used as a conjunction; cf. *Il.* 6.125–6 πολὺ προβέβηκας ἁπάντων

| σῶι θάρσει, ὅ τ' ἐμὸν δολιχόσκιον ἔγχος ἔμεινας 'you have surpassed all the rest with your courage, because you awaited my long-shadowed spear'.

92 δαρδάπτουσιν 'devour', probably < *δαρ-δάρπτω (< δρέπω 'cull'), a present with expressive reduplication; cf. *GH* I.375–6; Risch 1974: 336, 340; Introduction 5.3 §6.1.3. This is strong language, since the verb is used elsewhere in Homer (except in the repetition of this line in 16.315) only of jackals savaging a deer (*Il.* 11.479).   **ὑπέρβιον** 'arrogantly', adverbial accusative; the adjective is used six times of the Suitors.   **ἔπι** = ἔπεστι; cf. *Il.* 14.216 ἔνθ' ἔνι μὲν φιλότης 'in it (is) sexual passion', where ἔνι similarly = ἔνεστι. In these examples, the verb 'to be' is omitted and the preposition is traditionally accented as barytone (cf. Munro 1891: 164, 167).

94 οὔ ποθ'…οἴω 'they don't sacrifice (only) one sacrificial victim, nor only two', i.e. they sacrifice far too many. For this expression, cf. 16.245–6 μνηστήρων δ' οὔτ' ἄρ δεκὰς ἀτρεκὲς οὔτε δύ' οἴαι, | ἀλλὰ πολὺ πλέονες 'truly there isn't just a group of ten Suitors or only two groups, but many more', and in a slightly stronger form 12.154–5 οὐ γὰρ χρὴ ἕνα ἴδμεναι οὐδὲ δύ' οἴους | θέσφαθ' 'it's not right that one or only two should know the decrees', where the meaning is 'all'. The plurals in those passages might offer some support for printing the plural οἴα here, but the dual is the *difficilior lectio*. Even the Suitors' sacrificing is rendered questionable by its excessive nature: cf. Athena/Mentes' criticism in 1.227–8 that, though it is an ordinary meal not a feast or a wedding, ὑβρίζοντες ὑπερφιάλως δοκέουσι | δαίνυσθαι 'they seem to feast excessively and arrogantly'. Indeed, the continuous feasting of the Suitors is not just excessive in itself but constitutes non-human activity: only Aeolus and his family feast continuously (10.8–11).

95 ἐξαφύοντες 'drawing it out', from the crater by means of long-handled ladles, cf. *Il.* 1.598 νέκταρ ἀπὸ κρητῆρος ἀφύσσων. ἐξ- implies they do it until the bowl is empty; this form is not found again until Oppian.

96 ἦ: emphatic, cf. 13.172n.   **οἱ:** Od.   **οὔ τινι τόσση:** *sc.* ἦν.

97–8 οὔτ' ἠπείροιο…Ἰθάκης 'neither on the dark mainland nor on Ithaca itself'; the genitives mark the area involved in the action or thought (cf. 3–4n.). In 20.187–8 animals are brought across the water for the Suitors.

98 ξυνεείκοσι 'twenty altogether', a hapax for Greek. Such forms may have arisen from expressions such as 9.429 σὺν τρεῖς αἰνύμενος 'taking them together in threes', where the adverbial σύν was eventually taken with the numeral (some editors print σύντρεις); cf. also Eur. *Tr.* 1076 συνδώδεκα, Pl. *Tim.* 54E σύντρεις; σύμπας (already in Mycenean) was perhaps an influence (cf. Leumann 1950: 75–6).

99 ἐγώ ... καταλέξω 'I would like to list it for you', a 'voluntative' subjunctive indicating a polite wish. When he is first introduced, Eum.'s counterpart, the cowherd Philoetius, will similarly describe his master's wealth in terms of cattle (20.209-21).

101 συβόσῐα: the lengthening is needed to accommodate to the hexameter a word with four short syllables.   αἰπόλια πλατέ(α) αἰγῶν 'wide(-ranging) flocks of goats'.

102 ξεῖνοι: i.e. Od.'s flocks are so large and numerous that his own men are not numerous enough to look after them all, and herdsmen have to be brought in from outside; cf. the use of ξένος later for mercenary soldiers (Xen. *Anab.* 1.1.10).

103 ἐνθάδε: i.e. on Ithaca, as opposed to the mainland (100).

104 ὄρονται: a present formed from the same root as ὁράω; cf. Myc. *o-ro-me-no* 'watching (over flocks)'; Beekes 1096.

105 τῶν is better taken as dependent on ἕκαστος rather than on μῆλον. αἰεί ... ἐπ' ἤματι 'on each and every day'. ἐπ' ἤματι means 'in a single day' (*Il.* 10.48, 13.234); the addition of αἰεί, with its sense of 'regularly, repeatedly' (13.9n.), changes the meaning slightly here. The temporal sense of ἐπί + dative is rare.   σφιν: the Suitors.

109-10 Od., taking his food and drink enthusiastically (ἐνδυκέως), grabbing at it (ἁρπαλέως) and saying nothing (ἀκέων), well imitates a hungry beggar.

109 ἐνδυκέως has a slightly different sense from that in 62, indicating a greater intensity.

110 φύτευεν: for this metaphorical use, cf. 5.340 (of Poseidon), 14.218, 15.178 etc. (of Od.); it is regulary used of evils in poetry (cf. LSJ s.v. A I 3). For Homer's treatment of unspoken thoughts of this kind, cf. de Jong 2009.

111–47 Odysseus suggests he may know about Eumaeus' master

Here Od. begins a series of references to Eum.'s master which test the swineherd's patience, a test he passes nobly by not being openly offended by Od.'s importunate insistence.

111-14 Who does what in these lines is problematic, but syntax and social conventions point to a solution. Whichever way they are construed, an unannounced change in the subject of the verbs is unavoidable.

Od. becomes the subject in 109. There is no indication of a change of subject at the start of 112, so Od. is the subject of δῶκε. He will then also be the subject of ἔπινεν, and indeed he has been drinking (109) whereas Eum. has not. ὁ δ' in 113 then indicates the change of subject, so it is Eum. who ἐδέξατο and χαῖρε. Od. then returns as subject in 114, despite the absence of an indication of a change of speaker, since the following speech is his. ὁ δ' ἐδέξατο, χαῖρε δὲ θυμῶι is then almost a parenthesis in the lines describing Od.'s actions. An unannounced change of speaker between 113 and 114 is less awkward than one between 111 and 112. There is a similar shift of subjects in 23.312–13 where Od. tells ὅσα Κύκλωψ ἔρεξε, καὶ ὡς ἀπετείσατο ποινὴν | ἰφθίμων ἑτάρων, οὓς ἤσθιεν οὐδ' ἐλέαιρεν 'what the Cyclops did, and how he [Od.] exacted a penalty for his brave companions, whom he [the Cyclops] ate and did not pity'. This is found also in prose: cf. Smyth §943. See also Currie 2013.

That Od. hands over the cup is supported by the convention whereby, after dinner, the guest offered a cup to his host. Od. gives a cup to Arete as he is about to leave Scherie (13.56–7), and he toasts his host Achilles after dinner (Il. 9.223–4); there is a kind of parody of it when Od. gives the Cyclops a cup of wine after he has made dinner of two of his men (Od. 9.345–6). Possibly relevant here is his handing Demodocus a piece of pork in 8.474–81 because of the excellence of his song. This gesture seems symbolically to acknowledge and 'repay' the hospitality the guest has received. Stanford suggests less plausibly that it is a characteristic of Od., who alone does it. This custom is to be distinguished from the giving of a cup first to a guest during or at the start of the meal. This is a mark of honour, as is explicit in the case of Athena on arrival at Nestor's palace (3.51–3; cf. 63 for Telemachus), and implicit in 447–8 below, where Eum. hands the cup to Od. In these cases, the sacrifice is still in progress and the meal and drinking have not begun.

111 αὐτὰρ...ἐδωδῆι 'when he had furnished his spirit with food'; ἤραρε is aorist of ἀραρίσκω. This line is found only here and at 5.95 (Calypso's entertaining of Hermes), of people finishing their meals, and in each case the eater is not accompanied in the meal by his host. The more usual αὐτὰρ ἐπεὶ πόσιος καὶ ἐδητύος ἐξ ἔρον ἔντο (7 × in Il., 14 × in Od.) is used of communal eating.

112 καί: apodotic, cf. 13.79n.   **σκύφος:** only here in Homer.

114 ἔπεα πτερόεντα: cf. 13.58n.

115–20 Od.'s second speech. Having spoken but two lines so far, Od. now permits himself six, and even takes the lead in asking a question about the identity of Eum.'s master. This introduces a repeated theme of this conversation, the possibility that the beggar has met Od. This is raised casually:

Od. is happy to let Eum. do the talking and the revealing. On the analogy
of other occasions where someone is entertained and then asked his identity (e.g. Athena/Mentes in 1.123–81, cf. 3.69–71, 10.325, 19.105), one
might have expected Eum. now to ask the beggar his name, but Homer
gets more out of the scene by unusually having the guest ask a question,
and having Eum. ask his question later (185–90). Homer thus makes the
audience wait to see how Od. will deal with the inevitable and problematic
request for his identity, and Eum. can reveal more about his attitude to
Od. and about the situation in the palace. Of course, in asking the identity of the man who bought Eum., Od. is in fact posing the conventional
question about the identity of the guest.

115 γάρ can introduce a question that asks for further information even,
as here, when there is a slight gap between it and the last utterance (cf.
GP 81–5). This is very rare in Homer and is possibly a colloquial feature:
compare the use of the conversational tic 'because' in English to introduce a remark, when what follows does not specifically explain anything
that precedes, but the speaker feels the need to link his remark into the
conversation.

117 φθίσθαι: perfect middle infinitive of φθίνω.

118 εἰπέ μοι...ἐόντα: 'tell me, in case by any chance I might know him,
since he is such a man (as one would remember)'.   **γνώω:** 1st p.s. aorist
active subjunctive of γιγνώσκω (*GH* 1.458).

119 Ζεὺς γάρ που τό γε οἶδε 'I suppose Zeus knows this at least'; the two
particles serve to make Od.'s utterance tentative, so that he does not give
the impression of pretending to know more than he does just to curry
favour.

120 εἴ κέ μιν ἀγγείλαιμι ἰδών 'whether I might be able to announce him [i.e.
say that he is on his way], because I have seen him'; the simple accusative
of the person with ἀγγέλλω is found only here. In this type of sentence,
the implication is usually that the possibility expressed is likely to be true
(cf. Leaf 1900–2 on *Il.* 5.183). This line inaugurates a series of occasions
on which Eum. will reject Od.'s suggestions, however strongly supported,
that his master will return: cf. 167, 363–71. The sequence will be repeated
in book 19 with Penelope.   **πολλὰ δ᾽ ἀλήθην:** for the audience, the echo
of the first line of the epic μάλα πολλὰ πλάγχθη gives a special overtone to
this phrase, which Eum. cannot access.

121–47 *Eum.'s fourth speech.* Since he very reasonably thinks the likelihood
of this frail beggar having met Od. is nil, Eum. replies obliquely, in an
attempt to forestall any ideas the beggar may have of making capital from
a lying tale about Od.: he has heard this too often before. He addresses

in reverse order the two parts of Od.'s speech, in which he (i) asked who
bought Eum. and (ii) suggested he may be able to bring news about his
master, in reverse order. Homer thus holds back the revelation of Od.'s
name until the climax of the speech (144). Lamentation for Od. frames
a central section with its repeated assertion that Od. is dead. Eum. thus
reinforces his own genuine grief at the loss of his master and reassures
Od. about Penelope's attitude to the situation.

Eum.'s words paint a grim picture of the hospitable Penelope worn
down by her insistence on always entertaining itinerant beggars, despite
her reward being repeated false claims about Od., which have left her
unable to believe anything or have any hope. The climax to this comes in
book 23 when, despite all the evidence, she does not immediately believe
Od. is who he says he is. The unpleasant picture of these beggars highlights the determined decency of Eum., willing to trust this one despite all
that has gone before. Hes. *Op.* 396–404 also paints an unattractive picture
of beggars who continually harass their neighbours for money, after bringing penury on themselves by idleness; cf. for the unwelcome presence of
beggars also Thgn. 278 στυγέουσ' ὥσπερ πτωχὸν ἐσερχόμενον.

122–3 οὔ τις... πείσει 'no-one who comes here on his wanderings with
news of that particular man is going to persuade'. For κεῖνον indicating the
absent Od., cf. 2.351 of Eurycleia κεῖνον ὀϊομένη. It is emphasised by its early
position and separation from its governing participle ἀγγέλλων: the family
may believe stories about other people, but not about Od. οὐ is used with
the potential optative (and subjunctive) in Homer to deny a possibility in a
stronger manner than would be the case with μή. This construction usually
has ἄν/κε, but for their absence cf. *Il.* 19.321 οὐ μὲν γάρ τι κακώτερον ἄλλο
πάθοιμι (cf. Munro 1891: 272).

122 ἀλαλήμενος: cf. 13.333n.

124 ἄλλως often means 'in vain', and so here, since the viewpoint of Penelope and Od.'s family is being given, 'pointlessly', i.e. 'just wasting our
time'.

125 ἀληθέα: the poet is playing on words for 'truth' and 'wandering'
in these lines: note also 120 ἀλήθην, 122 ἀλαλήμενος, 124 ἀλῆται, 126
ἀλητεύων. There is an even more complex and extended example of play
with ἀλάομαι and similar verbs in book 9, cf. Casevitz 1989. For another
such example, cf. 20.105–21, where a prayer by an ἀλετρίς ('grinding-
woman') convinces Od. that he will defeat the ἀλείτας ('sinners'). The
question of how far wanderers learn and speak the truth is one that runs
through the poem; cf. e.g. Goldhill 1991: 37–52 on this passage, and for
specific questions of narrative truth, Dougherty 2001: 62–78; on 'archaic
truth', Cole 1983.

127 ἀπατήλια βάζει 'speaks deceitfully'. βάζω is probably an old verb, since it is used only in poetry, does not appear with preverbs and is almost always used with neuter plurals like μεταμώνια, νήπια etc.

131 αἶψά κε...ἔπος παρατεκτήναιο 'even you would soon craft a story'. For the metaphorical use of the verb, cf. *Il.* 10.19 μῆτιν ἀμύμονα τεκτήναιτο. τέκτων is a standard IE metaphor for a poet: M. L. West 2007: 38–43. In performance, a rhapsode would have to decide what tone to give to these lines. Eum. could be made to show a world-weary knowledge of how beggars operate, which conveys his warning not to try the usual trick in a wry but knowingly friendly manner; or there could be an element of bluntness, designed to nip any such idea in the bud. Either way, Eum. then quickly changes the subject, to avoid any possibility of unpleasantness between the beggar and himself. There is also a nice self-referential joke in the use of ἔπος: it can mean simply 'story', which is what Eum. means, but it is also the word for a 'song' (cf. 8.91, 17.519), and Od.'s tales are precisely that in Homer's performance. Eum. will later be proved absolutely right about Od.'s willingness to craft a tale in order to get a cloak, when Od. spins his yarn about the ambush at Troy in 468–506.

132 χλαῖνάν τε χιτῶνά τε: the combination is appropriate to winter, as in Hes. *Op.* 536–7 καὶ τότε ἔσσασθαι... χλαῖνάν τε μαλακὴν καὶ τερμιόεντα χιτῶνα 'then [in winter] put on a soft tunic and a full-length cloak'. **εἵματα** 'as clothes', in apposition to χλαῖναν and χιτῶνα. The motif of the provision of clothes to visitors is very frequent, cf. 13.12n. **δοίη:** 'were likely to give', a true potential optative.

133–6 Eum. here gives a much more unpleasant picture of Od.'s fate than he did earlier. Greek culture often expresses a horror of being drowned and eaten by animals or fish, because this rendered proper burial and the subsequent tending of the tomb impossible; cf. e.g. Od.'s lament at 5.306–12, and 1.234–42, 14.365–71; *Il.* 21.318–23; Hes. *Op.* 687 δεινὸν δ' ἐστὶ θανεῖν μετὰ κύμασιν. Euripides' Cassandra makes the fact that the Trojans died at home, unlike the Greeks, one of her arguments for the counter-intuitive viewpoint that the Trojans are better off than the Greeks after the war (*Tr.* 374–83).

133–4 μέλλουσι...ἐρύσαι 'must have torn off'. μέλλω is used with the present and aorist infinitive of things that must be or are probably the case, now, in the future or in the past. The difference between present and aorist is aspectual, not temporal: here it is the context which tells us the past is involved (*GH* II.307–8).

134 ὀστεόφιν: for the suffix, cf. 13.74n. The scansion is -φῖν (ϝ)ερύσαι. **ψυχὴ δὲ λέλοιπεν:** probably intransitive 'has gone', since no object is expressed, as in 213 πάντα λέλοιπεν; contrast 426 τὸν δ' ἔλιπε ψυχή.

136 εἰλυμένα 'covered in', perfect passive participle of (ϝ)ειλύω; the root is *wel- 'turn', found e.g. in Lat. *uoluo.*

137 ἔνθ': i.e. wherever his body may lie.

138 τετεύχαται 'caused', 3rd p.pl. perfect passive of τεύχω; for the plural with κήδεα as subject here, cf. 73n. This perfect and 137 ἀπόλωλε 'stress Eumaeus' conviction that the situation is beyond remedy' (Hoekstra, *CHO* ad loc.).

139 ἤπιον: cf. 13.314n.   **ὁππόσ(α) ἐπέλθω:** lit. 'to whatever extent I might travel', so 'however far I might go': ὁπόσσα is an adverbial accusative, ἐπέλθω a prospective subjunctive.

140–1 The wistful reference to his home raises the possibility that Eum. is going to preface the story of who purchased him as a slave with facts about his early life. In fact however we will have to wait for another book before we learn about Eum.'s past (15.351–484). It would be against convention for the host's tale to come before the guest's, but keeping to the traditional order also allows Homer to make us wait for information about this remarkable swineherd.

142 νυ 'and so'. νυ(ν) is an enclitic form of νῦν, found mainly in Ionic prose and poetry (and seen in Lat. *nu-per, nu-dius*). Though mainly a particle of emphasis, it can have a mildly consecutive rather than temporal force (K–G ii.118; Ruijgh 1957: 57–67).   **τῶν** 'for them'; for the genitive depending on ὀδύρομαι, cf. 3–4n.

143 ἐὼν ἐν πατρίδι γαίηι: for Od., now at last home, there will be especial pathos in Eum.'s wish similarly to be in his native land.

144 ἀλλά μ' Ὀδυσσῆος: ἀλλά stands for the ὅσσον that might have been expected after 142 τόσσον. The shift to a main clause makes all the more striking the final speaking of Od.'s name, and also marks Eum.'s emotion. Up to now Od. has been referred to as 'he' or 'master'. Cf. 172–3n. for more names revealed by Eum.   **πόθος:** cf. 13.219n.

145 οὐ παρεόντ(α): the irony is particularly strong here and in 147 νόσφιν ἐόντα. Stanford (ad loc.) suggests the present tenses mean that Eum. still harbours hopes of Od.'s return, despite his gloomy remarks in 133–8.

146 αἰδέομαι: since antiquity the reason for Eum.'s reluctance has been a puzzle. The best solution is probably the second given by Eustathius (2.66.16): Eum. is saying 'I would not wish to call him Odysseus, because that is what a stranger would do; nor δεσπότης, for he was not that to me. So I call him ἠθεῖος, because of his brotherly kindness' (cf. also Bassett 1919). This makes good sense of the way that αἰδέομαι ὀνομάζειν is contrasted, through μέν... ἀλλά, with ἠθεῖον καλέω: ὀνομάζω and καλέω can mean the same thing, but here are slightly different. The reason for this contrast is Od.'s love for him, hence γάρ. Other possibilities are that the reluctance is a mixture of deference and a desire to avoid being taken in by strangers who would latch onto a name (as indeed Od. does) to claim knowledge they did not have (cf. Olson 1992, 1995: 127–8); or that there may be some influence from the idea that names have a magical power and are not to be bandied about without thought (cf. Austin 1972: 11–12); cf. also Fenik 1974: 28–30; and Clay 1983: 25–9 on the suppression of Od.'s name in the first part of the poem. περὶ...ἐφίλει 'he loved me very much'. περί, from a root *per- 'crossing' and cognate with παρά, πέρα 'beyond', comes to mean 'to the end', 'completely' (cf. GH II.124–5; Beekes 1176; Lat. per-ficio 'bring to completion', etc.).

147 ἠθεῖον: the meaning of this word (cognate with ἦθος, Lat. suetus) is hard to capture in English. Its use in Homer suggests it is appropriate for a close relative or friend talking to one of greater authority. It is found only here in Od., but in Il. it is used by Paris to Hector (6.518), Menelaus to Agamemnon (10.37), Athena to Hector when she is disguised as Hector's younger brother Deiphobus (Il. 22.229, 239), and in the form ἠθείη κεφαλή by Achilles to (the elder) Patroclus' ghost (23.94). Given that Eum. is younger than Od. (64n.), there is an approprateness in his use of it here, but the fact that, uniquely in Homer, the two people involved are of different classes makes that use of it all the more striking in its intimacy. Cf. Bettini 1988.

148–64 Odysseus' third speech

Up to this point, Od. has spoken eight lines and Eum. ten times that number. Od.'s silence well suits a polite beggar, and chimes with Hesiod's remark that greater charis attends one who does not speak too much (Op. 719–20). It also however enables him to test out Eum. and gain information about the situation in the palace. That Eum. speaks so much more need not be put down to simple garrulity, but rather to a desire to entertain an unfortunate, lonely beggar at dinner. Lamentations about a master who, for all he knows, means nothing to the beggar may not seem the most entertaining form of dinner conversation, but show the beggar that his host too has troubles and strengthen the bond between them.

In the course of this speech, Od. begins to move away from being a pathetically grateful beggar to one who takes greater control of things.

From now on he speaks far more than Eum., cannot be prevented from promising Od.'s return, is honoured at dinner and eventually gets himself a cloak for the night.

The speech fits the powerful speaker Od. has shown himself in *Il.* and earlier in *Od.* It begins with a rising tricolon describing Eum.'s scepticism (149–50), followed by the authoritative statement that Od. will come (151–2). A lower-key refusal of premature reward is then followed by even grander rhetoric. He begins with a quotation of Achilles' famous words about people who say one thing and think another: that these words come at the start of Achilles' great speech explaining his refusal to bow to Agamemnon (156n.) gives considerable weight to Od.'s words. He then swears an oath on three potent entities, Zeus, divinely sanctioned hospitality and Od.'s hearth, with punning assonance in ἴστω ... ἱστίη; 160 (where see n.) echoes lines elsewhere that have a prophetic quality. The speech reaches its climax with the grandiose 161–4, which themselves have a prophetic quality, in their use of the mysterious word *lykabas* and its accompanying rhetorically balanced explanation, before a final coda promises revenge.

149–51 There is no main clause for the three ἐπεί-clauses in 149–50, so ἀλλά in 151 has an 'apodotic' sense, 'even so', which is not infrequent in conditional sentences: cf. *Il.* 1.280–1 εἰ δὲ σὺ καρτερός ἐσσι ... | ἀλλ᾽ ὅ γε φέρτερός ἐστιν (cf. *GP* 11–13). ἀλλά is not used thus with ἐπεί in Homer, but cf. Hdt. 9.42.2 ἐπεὶ τοίνυν ὑμεῖς ... οὐ τολμᾶτε λέγειν, ἀλλ᾽ ἐγὼ ἐρέω. 149–50 will be partially repeated by Eurycleia when she tries to persuade Penelope that Od. really is back (23.71–2).

149 ἀναίνεαι 'you won't hear of it', rather than 'deny' which would be tautologous with οὐ ... φῇσθα (Hoekstra, *CHO* ad loc.).

150 κεῖνον: Od. here carefully avoids using the name that Eum. has just given him, as if the precise name were unimportant, but then brings it out in his emphatic 152 ὡς νεῖται Ὀδυσεύς. **δέ:** apodotic δέ (13.144n.) is often used in Homer to emphasise the connection between a subordinate and a main clause, so the sense here is 'it is just *because* you deny it completely ... that your heart is always mistrustful'.

151 ἀλλ᾽ ... ἀλλά: 'the elasticity of meaning of ἀλλά is one reason why classical poetry so readily allows it to be repeated at short intervals' (Jebb 1932 on Soph. *Phil.* 524–5; cf. *GP* lxii–iv). The two here have slightly different forces. The first picks up ἐπεί: 'even though you deny it ... yet I will say it directly'. The second creates a contrast between οὐκ αὔτως and σὺν ὅρκωι: 'not just directly, but with an oath'.   **αὔτως:** cf. 13.281n.   **σὺν ὅρκωι:** Od. can of course swear this oath without difficulty, but it is intended in context to be an earnest of the truth of what he is saying; Eum. is not impressed however (166–73).

152 ὡς νεῖται Ὀδυσεύς: the framing of these words between the beginning of the line and a full stop at the main caesura gives them great emphasis and portentousness. Od. plays with the precise meaning of νεῖται: the present often has a future sense, but need not, so for Eum. this means 'that Od. will come', for Od. it means 'that Od. is on his way'; cf. also 160n. on τελεῖεται.   **εὐαγγέλιον** 'reward for good news': it was traditional to reward messengers who brought good tidings, cf. e.g. Soph. *El.* 797–8.

153 αὐτίκ᾽…ἵκηται 'immediately, when he comes…', again with some irony, and contrasted with 155 πρὶν δέ.   **τὰ ἅ** 'his own'. ὁ ἡ τό are often used with possessives to mark a distinction, here between Od.'s own home and the many he has sojourned in (*GH* II.162). For ἅ, cf. 13.198n. on ᾧ.

154 ἔσσαι: aorist active infinitive of ἕννυμι, used as an imperative; cf. 13.307n. By insisting on the possibility of a cloak and tunic, Od. keeps up the role of the importunate beggar. The line has been deleted by some, because it is absent from many manuscripts and one of the papyri, and spoils the contrast between 153 αὐτίκ᾽ and 155 πρὶν δέ. Another version of it occurs in a very similar context at 396, where it is indeed better integrated into the context. Deletion is not necessary however as the line specifies what Od. has in mind as his εὐαγγέλιον.

155 πρὶν δέ: adverbial; cf. 13.90n.

156 This line repeats Achilles' remark to Od. himself at *Il.* 9.312, which continues ὅς χ᾽ ἕτερον μὲν κεύθηι ἐνὶ φρεσίν, ἄλλο δὲ εἴπηι 'who hides one thing in his heart but says another', and is followed as here by a forthright statement of what will happen in the future. For an audience who knew the line (cf. Taplin 1990; Mazur 2010–11), its repetition would be a powerful preface to his oath and testimony to Od.'s sincerity. At the same time such a quotation is a humorously grand way for a beggar to express himself, especially when he is indeed himself not being entirely truthful in his dealings with Eum.   **ὁμῶς Ἀΐδαο πύληισι** 'just as (I hate) the gates of Hades'; πύληισι is an instrumental dative which with ὁμῶς expresses accompaniment and the like (cf. *GH* II.149).

158 πρῶτα 'first of all', adverbial. It was traditional to start a prayer etc. with an appeal to Zeus as the highest god.

158–62 These lines recur in Od.'s oath to Penelope (19.303–7); the first two in his oath to Philoetius (20.230–1), and in Theoclymenus' to Penelope (17.155–6).

159 ἱστίη: Ionic for ἑστία 'hearth'. It appears only in *Od.* in Homer and only in connection with oaths (cf. the passages cited in last note); the normal word is ἐσχάρη (as in 420). The goddess Hestia first appears in Hes. *Th.* 454; the connection with Lat. *Vesta* is not certain (Beekes 472).

160 ἦ μέν τοι 'you may be sure'; cf. 13.242n.   **τελείεται:** strictly speaking, this is a 'prophetic' present, regularly used in confident statements about the future by oracles, seers etc.; but of course a normal present meaning 'are being brought about' is also exactly right here, since the process of Od.'s return is indeed under way. See also 152n. For the use of expressions like this in situations concerning prophecy, cf. 2.176 (Halitherses the seer) and 13.178 (Alcinous on his father's oracles).

161 λυκάβαντος: the etymology of the word, found only here (and in the identical 19.306-7) in Homer, is uncertain, with theories variously connecting it with *λυκ-* 'light' or λύκος 'wolf' and βαίνω. Later writers (e.g. A.R. 1.198, Bion 6.15) use it to mean 'year' (so too the scholia; this is defended by Ruijgh 1957: 147 and *LfgE* s.v.), but Stengel 1883 argued this was a misunderstanding caused by the idea that Od. would return at the end of his twentieth year of absence. He proposed that λυκάβας meant *Mondlauf*, 'cycle of the moon', and that the beggar means Od. would arrive in the next fortnight. Leumann 1950: 212 proposed 'the day of the new moon'. Stanford ad loc. and Austin 1975: 244-53 take it to mean the period of about a week around the time of the new moon when the moon does not shine ('the dark of the moon'): the night spent in Eum.'s farm is σκοτομήνιος (14.457), and the festival of Apollo which is being prepared in 21.257-68 is said by a scholiast on 20.155 to be that of Apollo Noumenius, 'of the New Moon'. Since the year is near its end, there is no real distinction here between 'year' and 'moon'. It is fairly clear that a period of time, rather than a particular day, is meant: this imprecision gives Od. some room for manoeuvre.

162 τοῦ μὲν...ἱσταμένου 'when the old moon is waning, and the new about to start'. In phrases like this, the original meaning of μείς, 'moon', can still be felt; cf. also ἡ ἕνη καὶ νέα (*sc.* ἡμέρα) 'the old and new day', i.e. the last day of the month (Ar. *Clouds* 1178). This line looks like an explanation of λυκάβας, which was possibly as unfamiliar to Homer's audience as it is to us (for such translations, cf. 13.28n.).

163 τείσεται ὅς τις: *sc.* αὐτόν as antecedent to ὅς τις.

165-90 Eumaeus' fifth speech

Od.'s authoritative words seem to take Eum. by surprise and his emotion is shown, not this time by grammatical confusion (83-8n.), but by some incoherence in his response. He first denies that he will pay any reward of a cloak to the beggar, because Od. is not coming home; then he tries to move to another topic because of the pain this topic causes him; then he suggests they forget the oath; but then expresses the wish that Od. *will* come home, thus contradicting his first remark. Having earlier told Od. about Penelope, he now sketches in the situation concerning the dangers to Telemachus, before finally succeeding in shifting the conversation away from what he thinks is only of interest to himself (NB ἐάσομεν in 183 as in 171), by asking Od. to tell his own personal story.

166–7 οὖτ'... | οὖτ': this combination is sometimes used where 'the thought implies a more elaborate relationship than that of mere addition' (*GP* 514); here the second οὖτε means 'because'.

167 ἔκηλος is regularly used of sympotic enjoyment in Homer (e.g. 21.289–90 ἔκηλος...δαίνυσαι, 309–10), though not in the sympotic poets.

168 πῖνε: this line and the next two show enjambments, the three words at the start of the lines being Eum.'s three most important points: 'just drink; don't remind me; it causes me pain'.   **παρέξ** 'besides'; there is no precise parallel for this meaning of παρέξ as an adverb, but compare the prepositional use in Archil. fr. 196.15 πάρεκ τὸ θεῖον χρῆμα 'besides the divine act'. παρα- is always the dominant element in this compound.

169 ἦ γὰρ θυμός 'you see, my heart really'; for ἦ, cf. 13.172n.

171 ἀλλ'...ἐάσομεν 'but come now, let us leave aside your oath'; for ἦ τοι cf. 13.242n. Eum. presumes the oath is false, so that it is an embarrassment; he tactfully suggests they pretend that it has not happened. This passage might imply that even after an oath had been sworn, the person to whom it was sworn could absolve the swearer from it.

172 ἔλθοι: the hope implied by this optative contrasts with his firm declaration in 167 that 'Odysseus will not come home'; Eum., despite his pessimism, has not entirely given up hope (cf. 68n.).

172–3 Πηνελόπεια κτλ.: here, for the first time, Eum. gives the beggar the names of Od.'s wife, father and son. Earlier, Penelope was just δέσποινα (127). The same discretion over names was shown in the case of Od. himself, referred to as 'master' until 144. The voluntary revelation of these names is a sign of Eum.'s growing intimacy with and confidence in the beggar. It also allows him once again to change an embarrassing subject (cf. 131n.).

173 Τηλέμαχος θεοειδής: this is the only verse-end name + epithet formula used for Telemachus, and it appears but five times (cf. also 16.20). This perhaps indicates that Telemachus has not yet reached the status of the other heroes who have a developed formulaic system (so Kahane 1994: 135–8).

174 αὖ: contrastive; cf. 13.149n.   **ἄλαστον** 'in a way I can never forget' (the root is *λαθ-, of λανθάνω, λήθη etc.); adverbial accusative.

175 ἔρνεϊ ἶσον: the comparison of young people to shoots is a commonplace in Greek and other literatures; cf. e.g. *Il.* 17.53–8, 18.56–7 = 437–8; *Od.* 6.160–9; Sappho, fr. 115; Eng. 'scion'.

176 χερείω 'worse', masculine accusative of χερείων, cf. *Il.* 3.11 ἀμείνω; the form is problematic (cf. *GH* 1.55; Risch 1974: 19). For the wish that a son will surpass his father, cf. *Il.* 6.476–81, and Ajax' more grudging version in Soph. *Aj.* 550–1.

177 δέμας καὶ εἶδος are better taken as accusatives of respect depending on ἀγητόν, a masculine accusative describing Telemachus, with the whole phrase in apposition to 175 τόν: cf. *Il.* 24.376 δέμας καὶ εἶδος ἀγητός. Alternatively, ἀγητόν could agree with the two nouns.

178 ἐΐσας 'well balanced, sensible'.

179 μετὰ πατρὸς ἀκουήν 'after news of his father'; cf. 13.415n.

182 Ἀρκεισίου: the father of Laertes, mentioned only here and 16.118, and in the patronymic at 4.755, 24.270, 517.

183 ἀλλ' ἦ τοι 'but really, I tell you' (*GP* 553).

183–4 κεῖνον μὲν ἐάσομεν ... φύγηι: 'let us not talk of him: he may either be captured, or he may escape'; ἁλώηι and φύγηι are potential subjunctives. This may seem a slightly heartless remark, but Eum. does not know to whom he is talking, and it enables Homer to hold over further news of Telemachus until later.

185 τὰ σ(ὰ) αὐτοῦ 'your own troubles'; the addition of αὐτοῦ etc. to possessive pronouns gives emphasis. Eum. shows himself aware that his troubles have taken up a good deal of their conversation, and that it is time for Od. to have a turn. It is at this point that Od. takes over from Eum. as the speaker of the majority of lines.   **ἐνίσπες:** cf. 13.135n. on ἄσπετα. The -ς suffix is of uncertain origin, but is found also in the imperatives δός, θές, πρόες.

187–90 The piling up of five quick-fire questions is a clear sign to the beggar that he should feel free to tell his tale at length. Eum. no doubt hopes that in his enthusiasm for telling his own tale the beggar will stop talking about Od. Only here and in 1.170–3 (Telemachus' words to Athena when she first comes to Ithaca) is the request for origins put in so elaborate a form.

187 τίς...τοκῆες;: a common formula, cf. 1.170, 10.325, 15.264, 19.105, 24.298.   **εἰς:** an alternative form to ἐσσί for the 2nd p.s. present indicative of εἰμί. It is either the Ionic form εἶ with the second-person singular marker -ς added to make it look more like a second-person form (*GH* 1.286), or a scribal representation of an archaic form ΕΣ (the root *ἐσ + ς; Palmer 1962: 118).   **πόλις:** the reference to someone's city in these expressions is an early sign of the importance of cities in the construction of people's identity, something which will remain true for much of Greek history. It also suggests that the polis was already an important concept in Homer' s time.

190 οὐ μέν...ἱκέσθαι: so in 1.173, 16.59, 224. The irony of the use of this expression here (and in 1.173 of Athena) is that Od. indeed did not arrive 'by any means the questioner can imagine' (Higbie 1995: 76). There is a similar, but grimmer, irony in Od.'s words to Elpenor, who fell drunk off Circe's roof and whom he is surprised to find in the Underworld (11.57–8): 'How did you come beneath the mirky darkness? You got here quicker on foot than I did with my black ship!'

191–359 Odysseus' fourth speech: his false biography

Od.'s stories are tailored to their hearers, the better to create a bond between them and them. His claim to be a rich man's son who has fallen on hard times chimes with Eum.'s own origins and fate. That his father 'honoured me equally with his legitimate sons', though he was born of a concubine (200–3), echoes the way that Eum., though a bought slave, was brought up by Anticleia alongside her own daughter Ctimene, and 'she honoured me only slightly less' (15.365). He achieved great things by his own talents, which mirrors Eum.'s own pride in his achievements (61–6, 15.371–3). Od. is taken in by a villainous Phoenician, just as the young Eum. was kidnapped by Phoenicians (15.415–84).

Od. is however careful not to paint too glorious a picture of himself. He is unable to do anything about his brothers' taking of the lion's share of their father's property (208–10). He goes to Troy, not from a desire for glory but through the pressure of public opinion (239). Seeking more adventures and wealth, he takes his men to Egypt, but they disobey his orders with disastrous results (259–65), and he has humiliatingly to beg for his life from the enemy king (276–80). His fortunes restored, he is deceived by a Phoenician's offer of a business opportunity, and saved from slavery only by a storm (288–315). Sent home by the Thesprotian king, he is tied up for sale by the crew, eventually managing to escape with difficulty

(334–59). This mixture of misfortune and achievement through effort, combined with an ironic self-awareness, is well designed to appeal to the sceptical Eum. At the same time, Od. suggests five times that the gods have kept an eye on him: 243, Zeus has malign plans for him; 273–4, he suggests how Od. can escape death at the hands of the Egyptians; 310–12, he puts a bit of mast into his hand in the storm; 348–9, the gods loosen his cords; and 357–8, the gods hide him from his pursuers. The suggestion is that Od. is someone special, who alone survives in apparently terminal situations because of divine help. Whether Eum. is convinced by these stories he keeps to himself, but they play their part in gradually establishing Od.'s credibility. On Eum. as an audience for Od.'s tales, cf. Dimock 1989: 189–98; Doherty 1995: 148–60; Louden 1997, 1999: 50–68; Minchin 2001: 209–16.

The speech falls into two main sections, his life on Crete (192–242) and his adventures abroad (243–359), the first essentially concerned with his character, the second with his experiences; as the second *Hypothesis* says, 'his words are about creating an image of himself (ἀναπλάττοντος ἑαυτόν) and setting out some of the things he has done'.

On Od.'s false tales, see e.g. Trahman 1952; Haft 1984; Reece 1994; Ahl and Roisman 1996: 152–66; Tsagalis 2012. For the mixture of truth, versions of the truth and falsehood in these tales, see e.g. Emlyn-Jones 1986; S. Richardson 1996; de Jong 2001: 353–4; for the recurrent elements in Od.'s tales, de Jong 2001: 596–7. On Crete and Egypt in the stories, see Lane Fox 2008: 338–45.

(i) 191–234 early life

192 τοιγάρ 'very well then': 'in Homer... τοιγάρ is only used by a person preparing to speak or act at another's request' (*GP* 565); cf. *Il.* 1.74–6 ὦ Ἀχιλεῦ, κέλεαί με... μυθήσασθαι | ... | τοιγάρ ἐγὼν ἐρέω. This line is normally used to introduce a true story, which indicates how keen Od. is that Eum. should believe him (Saïd 2011: 184).

193 εἴη... ἐδωδή 'would that we two had for a time both food...': ἐστί + dative is regularly used for possession.   **νῶϊν** 'us two' is the genitive-dative first-person dual. It is followed first by a plural (ἐοῦσι) and then by another dual (195 ἀέκοντ(ε)), in a manner not uncommon in Homer: cf. the striking *Il.* 21.115–16 χεῖρε πετάσσας | ἀμφοτέρας, 2.151 (of two eagles) πλησίω ἀλλήλοισι τιταινομένω (*GH* II.25–7). ἐπί + accusative indicates an extent of time (cf. 12.407 πολλὸν ἐπὶ χρόνον).

194 μέθυ: see 13.50n.

195 δαίνυσθαι ἀκέοντ(ε) 'so that we could dine quietly', an infinitive of purpose or consequence (cf. 13.34n.). For ἀκέοντ(ε), cf. 13.1n. on ἀκήν. **ἄλλοι…ἔποιεν** 'and that others were taking care of matters', i.e. that we could leave our duties to others for a time. For ἔποιεν, see 33n. on μετασπών.

196 καὶ εἰς ἐνιαυτὸν ἅπαντα 'even by the end of a whole year'; εἰς with expressions of time marks the limit of that time (*GH* II.104). Cf. the similar remark at 11.356, where Od. is encouraged to go on with more of his story: εἴ με καὶ εἰς ἐνιαυτὸν ἀνώγοιτ' αὐτόθι μίμνειν 'even if you were to tell me to remain here for a whole year'; also 4.595, 11.356. For this '(not) even + hyperbole' motif, cf. de Jong 2001: 112. Od. apparently eagerly takes up Eum.'s encouragement (186-90) to speak at length. The remark coming from a beggar may seem an exaggeration to Eum., but the audience knows there really is a great deal to tell.

197 κήδεα: the three main tales in *Od.* are all prefaced by remarks about recounting misfortunes at a feast. Od. begins his recital to the Phaeacians, 'I claim there is no greater fulfilment of delight than when … diners in the palace listen to a singer … But your heart has decided to ask me about my grievous troubles (κήδεα)' (9.5-7, 12-13); and Eum. says 'we too will drink and eat in the shelter taking pleasure in our grievous troubles (κήδεσι)' (15.398-9). These passages point to the way that dinner parties, along with festivals, became the most important locus for song in Greece (cf. E. L. Bowie 1986).

198 ὅσσα γε δή 'that is, all those very many'. γε δή is a rare combination in Homer and verse generally; the two particles are close in force, but γε emphasises the explanatory aspect of ὅσσα, while δή emphasises the magnitude of Od.'s troubles (cf. *GP* 245). Od.'s recital is going to be long, but he shows that he realises that Eum. is not a man of leisure with time to listen to the whole sorry tale.   **θεῶν ἰότητι** 'by the will of the gods', a formula that appears only in dialogue in Homer. The origin of ἰότης is unclear; cf. Beekes 595-6.

199 Κρητάων: the plural form Κρῆται appears only here and in 16.62; cf. the alternation Μυκήνη/Μυκῆναι, Θήβη/Θῆβαι, Ἀθήνη/Ἀθῆναι. By contrast, *Il.* 2.498 Θέσπειαν and 504 Πλάταιαν have a singular where later there was a plural. For a list of Homeric examples, cf. Ameis and Cauer 1895: 47. On Crete as a setting for Od.'s stories, cf. 13.256, 14.191-359nn.

201 τράφεν 'were brought up', 3rd p.pl. aorist passive of τρέφω. For the *hysteron proteron*, cf. 13.189-90n.

202 ὠνητή…μήτηρ: the situation seems similar to that in Near Eastern palaces: 'the Persians each have several legitimate wives (κουριδίας

γυναῖκας), but they also possess very many more concubines (παλλακάς)'
(Hdt. 1.135). The sons of the official wives were of higher status than those
of the *pallakai*.

203 ἰθαγενέεσσιν: the sons of his main wife. The initial element appears
to be from a root **id*ʰ*h₂e* 'here', cf. Lat. *ibi* 'there' and the similar αὐθι-
γενής 'born here, native'. There is no real English equivalent; 'legitimate'
is nearest, but not quite equivalent, since Od. would not necessarily have
been considered a νόθος 'bastard'. In this part of his speech, Od. shows a
fondness for compound words unique in Homer: cf. also 211 πολυκλήρων,
213 φυγοπτόλεμος, 217 ῥηξηνορίην, 223 οἰκωφελίη, 226 καταριγηλά, 228
ἐπιτέρπεται.

204 Κάστωρ Ὑλακίδης 'Beaver, son of the Barker'. Though one expects fic-
titious names to have some significance, it is hard to see any here, unless
Od. is deliberately producing an incongruous name for Eum.'s entertainment, perhaps with reference to his ὑλακόμωροι dogs. Another less likely
suggestion is a pun on dogs called καστόριαι (Xen. *Cyn.* 3.1). For puns
on names in *Od.*, cf. esp. 'Odysseus' in 1.60–2, 5.340, 423, 19.275, 407;
24.304–6 (a complex series of possible puns in Od.'s false tale to Laertes;
cf. Heubeck, *CHO* ad loc.); 14.316n.; and the evil servants Melanthius and
Melantho. For Homer's techniques in the revelation of names in scenes of
xenia, see Higbie 1995: 73–85. A guest is expected to name himself to his
host, so Od. is compelled to provide a false name, as with the Cyclops:
'crafty Odysseus turns the conventions of naming into a technique for survival' (Higbie 1995: 190).   **τοῦ ἐγὼ γένος εὔχομαι εἶναι** 'whose (son) I
claim to be by race'. γένος is an accusative of respect: cf. 15.267 ἐξ Ἰθάκης
γένος εἰμί; Ar. *Peace* 186 ποδαπὸς τὸ γένος δ' εἶ lit. 'where are you from as to
your race?'

205 θεὸς ὥς 'like a god'. Postpositive ὥς, found only in epic, makes a
preceding closed short syllable long because it probably originally had a
digamma (*GH* 1.125–6; Beekes 1683).   **δημῶι:** dative of the agent.

206 ὄλβωι … κυδαλίμοισιν: instrumental datives giving the reasons for the
honours shown to Castor (cf. Munro 1891: 137).

209 ὑπέρθυμοι: on how Od., as the secondary narrator of his travels in
9–12, does not avoid evaluative language in the way that Homer as primary narrator tends to, see de Jong 1992.   **ἐπὶ κλήρους ἔβαλοντο** 'made
straight for the property', i.e. immediately seized it for themselves; cf.
15.297 ἡ δὲ Φεὰς ἐπέβαλλεν. For κλῆρος, see 64n.

210 οἰκί(α) ἔνειμαν 'allotted me a place to live'; the force of μάλα παῦρα extends to οἰκία too, suggesting the property was not grand. This maltreatment by more powerful brothers is reminiscent of the behaviour Hesiod complains of in his natural brother Perses (*Op.* 37–9).

212 εἵνεκ' ἐμῆς ἀρετῆς: this idea, that a man's intrinsic qualities rather than the accident of his birth were what mattered, is a theme that runs through the poem. We see it in Eum. and Philoetius especially: cf. 8.169–77, 17.454–7, 18.3–4, 215–25, 19.244–8, and Introduction pp. 13 n. 39, 17–23. **ἀποφώλιος:** glossed by grammarians as ἀνεμώλιος, μάταιος 'vain, worthless'; it is not found in *Il.* and its etymology is uncertain (Beekes 119).

213 φυγοπτόλεμος: only here before Q.S. 1.740 and Hesych. φ 1011 φύξη-λιν. **νῦν δ' ἤδη πάντα λέλοιπεν** 'but now all that has gone'; for the intransitive use of λέλοιπε, cf. 134n. For use of the neuter, cf. 13.6on.

214–15 ἀλλ' ἔμπης... | γιγνώσκειν 'but I think that when you look at the stubble you can recognise it', i.e. its quality, as once having been associated with good grain. The scholia quote a proverb ἀπὸ τῆς καλάμης τὸν στάχυν '(you can tell the quality of) the corn from the stubble'; cf. the Latin *ex stipula cognoscere aristam* 'to recognise the ear from the stubble'. The phrase has a colloquial, country quality to it, which may be calculated to appeal to Eum. (so the scholiast). Od. compares his wizened body to what is left in the field after the harvest, suggesting that something of his old qualities may still be perceived despite the loss of the flower of his manhood.

215 δύη ἔχει ἤλιθα πολλή 'very much grief wildly besets me'. ἤλιθα is an adverb from ἠλεός 'mad'.

216 ἦ μὲν δή 'certainly'; this combination is used in forthright statements (*GP* 389). **Ἄρης τ' ἔδοσαν καὶ Ἀθήνη:** a plural verb between two singular subjects is called the *schema Alcmanicum*, because of that poet's regular use of it.

217 ῥηξηνορίην: only here in Greek, though cf. Achilles' epithet ῥηξήνωρ, 4 × in *Il.* **λόχονδε** 'for an ambush', an accusative indicating a purpose or end; for -δε, see 13.17n. On ambushes, see 13.268n.

218 κακὰ ... φυτεύων: see 11on.

219 προτιόσσετο = *προσ-όσσετο 'did not look for, did not consider'. For προτί, see 13.181n. ὄσσομαι shares the root *okʷ- with ὄσσε, Latin *oculus* 'eye(s)'; it usually means 'see' in a figurative as opposed to physical sense, as in 1.115 ὀσσόμενος πατέρ' ἐσθλὸν ἐνὶ φρεσί 'seeing his noble father in his mind's eye'.

220 ἐπάλμενος 'leaping out', athematic aorist middle participle of ἐφ-άλλομαι 'leap upon' (cf. *GH* 1.383, and 1.184 for the psilosis).

221 ἀνδρῶν … πόδεσσι 'whoever of my enemies was inferior to me at running', rather than 'whoever fled before me on foot'. ὅ τε = ὅς τε. πόδεσσι is probably an instrumental dative, cf. perhaps, with a comparable verb, 17.317 καὶ ἴχνεσι γὰρ περιήιδη 'he was also superior at following tracks' (*GH* II.68–9). Elsewhere εἴκω in the sense of 'be inferior to' has an accusative of the quality in question, as in *Il.* 22.459 τὸ ὃν μένος οὐδένι εἴκων 'yielding to none in his strength'. The phrase develops πρώτιστος: he was not only first but quickest too. In *Il.*, Od. wins (with a little help from Athena) the foot-race at the games for Patroclus (23.740–84); cf. also Achilles' formula πόδας ὠκύς as a military virtue.

222 τοῖος ἔα … ἔσκεν 'that's what I was like in war; but working on the land never appealed to me'. ἔα and ἔσκεν are both forms of the imperfect of εἰμί: ἔᾱ is by quantitative metathesis from ἦα (*GH* 1.287–8); ἔσκε has the iterative suffix *-sk-* (Introduction 5.3 §6.4), though oddly does not have an iterative sense (*GH* 1.290). When the two forms appear together, there is a tendency for ἔσκε to have a durative sense, as in 227 ἐμοὶ τὰ φίλ' ἔσκε 'these things were dear to me', and for ἔα (or ἦν) to be closer to an aorist, as here (cf. *GH* 1.320–1). ἔα ἐν has to be treated either as ἔ ἐν (found in some MSS) or as ἔα 'ν, both of which are awkward, but no ideal alternative has been produced.

223 οἰκωφελίη: only here before Theoc. 28.2; cf. 233 οἶκος ὀφέλλετο and 15.21. Though they may possibly have the same origin, this ὀφέλλω, a poetic verb meaning 'strengthen, increase', should be distinguished in use from ὀφείλω 'owe' (Beekes 1132–3; de Lamberterie 1992).

225 ἐΰξεστοι: well-polished javelins would fly better than rough-hewn ones.

226 λυγρά: for the neuter, see 63n.   **καταριγηλά** 'to be shuddered at' (cf. 481 ῥιγωσέμεν); only here. Od.'s delight in war is unusual for *Od.* where it is much less a feature than in *Il.* Line 227 also suggests there was something unusual about his tastes, which can only be explained by possible (που) divine influence.

227 τά … τά: the first is a demonstrative, the second a relative pronoun; cf. Introduction 5.3 §7.3.1, 4.

228 ἄλλος γάρ τ' ἄλλοισιν: for ἄλλος in such expressions, see 25n. τε is used as often in gnomic expressions. The line has been suspected as an interpolation because of the presence in -ταῖ ἔργοις both of a correction which neglects an original digamma and of an Attic dative, though one should probably not condemn all forms in -οις as Attic (*GH* 1.194–6). The line adds

little to the passage, and the presence of two γάρs in successive lines is not
a common occurrence (though cf. *Il.* 1.525–6, 2.30–1, 66–7, 22.50–1).
The addition of such gnomic statements to Greek texts by later scribes is
also not infrequent. However, all of this does not quite add up to enough
for deletion.

229 πρὶν μὲν γάρ: this is contrasted with 235 ἀλλ᾽ ὅτε δή. For πρίν, see
13.124n.   **Τροίης ἐπιβήμεναι:** as with verbs meaning 'touch, reach' etc.,
the genitive is often used with verbs of motion to indicate where an action
led to, as in 13.98 λιμένος ποτιπεπτηυῖαι.

230 εἰνάκις 'nine times'; εἰν- is the Ionic reflex of earlier ἐνϝ-, as ξεῖνος <
ξενϝος (cf. *GH* 1.161).   νέεσσιν illustrates the artificial and mixed nature
of the Homeric dialect, since it combines two Ionicisms, the shortening of
the stem-vowel νη- > νε- and the ephelcystic -ν, with the Aeolic suffix -εσσι
(cf. *GH* 1.206).

231 ἐς 'against'.   καί μοι μάλα τύγχανε πολλά 'and I had a lot of success';
cf. *Il.* 11.683 οὕνεκά μοι τύχε πολλά.

232–3 ἐξαιρεύμην ... | λάγχανον: the distribution of booty takes two forms;
the leader's importance is acknowledged by the fact that he is allowed to
choose what he most wants, but the rest is distributed by lot to ensure a
sense of fairness (for the latter, cf. 9.41–2, 548–9, 13.138). At other times,
the leader may be given a special prize (9.159–60, 550–1).

234 τετύγμην 'I became'; cf. 13.243n.

    (ii) 235–86 disaster and recovery in Egypt

235 ὅτε δή 'just at the moment when' (*GP* 219–20), picked up by δή τότε
(237). For a formal analysis of the phrases used to articulate these stories,
see Gaisser 1969: 27–31.   τήν γε στυγερὴν ὁδόν 'that well known hateful
expedition', i.e. against Troy. For the article in this sense, cf. 19.372 αἱ
κύνες αἵδε (Eurycleia on the absent Maids); *GH* 11.163–4. γε is emphatic.
εὐρύοπα: for this form of the nominative, see 13.139n.

236 ἐφράσα(το): perhaps a hint at those stories of the Trojan War in which
Zeus plans it specifically to reduce the population of the world; cf. *Cypria*,
fr. 1 (*GEF* pp. 80–2).

237 ἤνωγον 'insistently ordered' (*sc.* the Cretans); this is a pluperfect
form, but here seems to be meant as an imperfect (cf. 463, 471nn.).
The power of public opinion in 237–9 is striking: the fear of what people
might say recurs a number of times in *Od.*: Nausicaa fears men's reactions
if she is seen with a handsome stranger (6.273–84), and Penelope fears
the reaction of people if she leaves Laertes without a shroud (2.101–2 =

19.146–7 and 24.136–7; cf. also 16.75), a fear justified by the criticisms made by the Ithacans when they think she has married one of the Suitors rather than waiting for Od. (23.149–51). See also 21.321–9, 24.433–7. The suggested reluctance of Od. here to go to Troy chimes amusingly with those traditions that say he had indeed to be persuaded to take part in the expedition (*Cypria, Arg.* 5). None of the warriors in the Iliadic Catalogue of Ships has to be ordered to go by their communities.   Ἰδομενῆα: Od.'s casual claim to have been on a par with a great man recalls his tale recounted to the disguised Athena of his relations with Idomeneus (13.256–66), and will be repeated in the claimed close association with Od. and Menelaus in 470–1. It is not clear that either claim convinces Eum., who never refers to them.

238 νήεσσ' ἡγήσασθαι 'to lead the way in our ships'; cf. *Il.* 16.168–9 νῆες θοαί, ἧισιν Ἀχιλλεύς | ἐς Τροίην ἡγεῖτο.   **μῆχος** 'means, possibility', an old noun confined to poetry and the nominative-accusative singular; cognate with μηχανή.

239 ἀνήνασθαι: aorist middle infinitive of ἀναίνομαι 'deny, decline'. **χαλεπή . . . φῆμις** 'public opinion, which is hard to resist, compelled me'. **ἔχε:** cf. 10.160 (of a stag) ἔχεν μένος ἠελίοιο 'the sun bore down on him greatly'.

241–2 *Il.* and its sequel are despatched here in two lines; on the poem's attitude to the Trojan War, cf. Introduction pp. 23–6.

242 ἐκέδασσεν: for the form, see 13.317n. Nestor tells of the return of the Achaeans in 3.130–200.   **Ἀχαιούς:** i.e the other Achaeans; NB αὐτὰρ ἐμοί in the next line.   **θεός:** possibly no particular god is meant, but traditionally Athena was angered with the Greeks because of Ajax's treatment of her priestess Cassandra, and arranged a storm. The story was told in the *Iliupersis* (cf. *Arg.* 3; also Eur. *Tr.* 65–94).

243–5 There is a good deal of assonance in *m, t,* and *k* in these lines; cf. the repeated *p*'s in 267 and *s*'s in 350–1. These are however not characteristic of the speech as a whole, but perhaps add a little expressivity to their contexts.

243–4 μήδετο μητίετα Ζεύς̄ | μῆνα γὰρ οἶον ἔμεινα: there are two puns here, perhaps giving a sardonic tone to Od.'s remark, though Homer himself uses the first pun in *Il.* 7.478. μήδετο and μητίετα are possibly related, not just in sound but historically. On puns in this book, cf. 69n.

244 τεταρπόμενος: reduplicated aorist middle participle of τέρπομαι.

246 Αἴγυπτόνδε: in so far as the distinction is meaningful, here the name could refer to the country or the river; the river is more obviously meant in

257–8 and in 4.477, 581. The Greek name comes from the Egyptian name for the city of Memphis, 'Hikuptah'. Νεῖλος first appears in Hes. *Th.* 338. Before the middle of the seventh century, 'Greek awareness of Egypt seems to have been slight, but some Egyptian objects were reaching Greece, and these indicate the possibility that at times there was some more direct contact' (Boardman 1999: 112; cf. generally 141–53; Dickie 1995: 41–4; S. R. West, *CHO* 1.192).   θυμὸς ἀνώγει: this restless rushing off to Egypt after only a month at home, following a ten-year absence, well illustrates Od.'s description of himself in 222–6. ἀνώγει is the pluperfect of ἀνώγα; the ending is hard to explain (cf. *GH* 1.437; contrast 463n.).

249–50 ἐξῆμαρ... | δαίνυντ(ο): this same phrase is used of the Companions dining on the Cattle of the Sun (12.397–8), again shortly before a disaster caused by their folly. For the form of expression 'for six days...on the seventh' etc., cf. 10.80–1, 12.397–400. This long sacrifice is for a prosperous voyage, cf. 13.16–62n.

251 θεοῖσιν: θεοισ- is scanned as a single long syllable by synizesis of the two syllables. Od. uses a number of synizeses in this passage: cf. 255, 263, 287nn.   αὐτοῖσί τε δαῖτα πένεσθαι 'for the men to prepare as a meal for themselves'.

253 βορέηι ἀνέμωι ἀκραέϊ καλῶι 'before a fine north wind which blew from on high' (an instrumental dative). ἀκρ-αής is a compound of ἄκρος and ἄημι 'blow', cf. Hes. *Op.* 599 χώρωι ἐν εὐαεῖ 'in a well-ventilated spot'. The interpretation 'blowing from on high' (so the scholia), rather than 'blowing strongly', is supported by other ἄκρο-compounds such as ἀκρόπολις.

254 ὡς εἴ τε κατὰ ῥόον 'as if (we were sailing) downstream'. ὡς εἴ τε is regularly found in comparisons in Homer (cf. *GP* 522).   οὐδέ τις οὖν 'and so, as a consequence, not even one'; for οὖν thus, cf. *GP* 420.

255 ἀσκηθέες must be scanned as three long syllables, with synizesis of the epsilons; synizesis at the start of the fifth foot is very unusual; no MS offers ἀσκηθεῖς, which would avoid this.

256 ἥμεθα: for the sense 'sit doing nothing', while allowing other forces to steer the ship, cf. 9.78, 10.507 etc.

257 εὐρρείτην 'with abundant flowing water', a good description of the Delta.

258–72 Od. will repeat this story word for word (except 17.439 στῆναι for 270 μεῖναι) when he tries to persuade Antinous to give him food in 17.427–41. There are also echoes of the episodes in the land of the Cicones (9.38–61) and of the Laestrygonians (10.117–20, cf. 118). On the difference between the two versions, see Emlyn-Jones 1986: 4–7, esp.

6–7: 'in 14 Odysseus, while emphasizing his prosperous origins and ability, is at pains to project himself, not as a major Homeric hero engaged in a military operation, but as someone involved in an exploit which gets out of hand. This is surely calculated to appeal to Eumaios no less than Odysseus' action in supplicating the Egyptian King at 276ff., and the pointed reference to Zeus Xenios in 283 drives the point home' (cf. also 1986: 7–8 on the version in book 17).

258 ἀμφιελίσσας: regularly used of ships drawn up on a beach and fairly certainly a compound of ἑλίσσω 'turn'. Its precise meaning is uncertain however: possibly 'curved at both ends' or 'on both sides'; less probably perhaps 'turning both ways, manoeuvrable'.

259 ἦ τοι μὲν ἐγὼ κελόμην 'I *told* them'; contrast 262 οἱ δ'. For the emphatic use of these particles, cf. 13.242n. Od. insists that he gave these orders, which were disobeyed, so the blame does not lie with him. In the Cicones episode, the fault lay as much with Od. as with his men (9.40).

260 ἔρυσθαι 'look after, defend'; present infinitive of ἔρυμαι, the athematic predecessor of thematic ἐρύομαι.

262 ἐπισπόμενοι: aorist middle participle of ἐφ-έπω 'give rein to'; cf. 33n.

263 Αἰγυπτίων: three longs, the last two vowels joined in synizesis.

266 φαινομένηφιν: for -φιν, see 13.74n. The imagined timing here is a little obscure. The attack seems to take place over a period during the day, but the cry reaches the city early in the morning. The obscurity comes perhaps from the fact that the similar battle against the Cicones also started at dawn (9.56; even in that episode the chronology is not especially clear).

267 πλῆτο: 3rd p.s. aorist passive indicative of πίμ-πλη-μι 'fill'. For the alliteration of *p*, cf. 243–5n.   **ἵππων** 'charioteers', if like the Greeks the Cicones did not fight on horse-back: cf. *Il.* 18.153 λαός τε καὶ ἵπποι, 2.554 ἵππους τε καὶ ἀνέρας ἀσπιδιώτας.

268 ἐν δέ: 'during the course (of the battle)', the adverbial use of ἐν; cf. 13.438.   **τερπικέραυνος** may suggest how Zeus created the panic.

270 ἐναντίβιον: lit. 'showing force against (the enemy)', an adverb possibly formed from ἀντίβιος under the influence of ἐναντίον (Leumann 1950: 206).

272 τοὺς δ' 'others'.   **σφίσιν ἐργάζεσθαι ἀνάγκηι:** 'to work for them under compulsion', i.e. as slaves. ἐργάζεσθαι is an infinitive of purpose.

273–4 ὧδε νόημα | ποίησ(ε): 'created a thought thus', the thought being described in performance in 276–9.

274 ὡς ὄφελον 'how I wish', cf. 13.204n. This introduces an emotional parenthesis into the narrative.

275 αὐτοῦ ἐν Αἰγύπτωι: see 13.56n.   **ἔτι γάρ νυ:** νυ emphasises ἔτι; cf. 142n.   **ὑπέδεκτο** 'lay in store for'; cf. 22.470 (of birds caught in a net spread over their nesting-bush) αὖλιν ἐσιέμεναι, στυγερὸς δ' ὑπεδέξατο κοῖτος 'as they entered their roost, a hateful resting place was waiting for them'. For athematic forms like ὑπέδεκτο beside the more prevalent thematic ones, cf. 54n.

276 αὐτίκ'...ἔθηκα: this act of removing one's helmet as a means of supplication is not found elsewhere in battle in Homer; the putting on of helmets is regularly described in *Il.*, but not their removal thus. Hector removes his helmet because it was terrifying his son (*Il.* 6.466–73), and this passage and the current one suggest that the removal of the helmet marks one symbolically as no longer a combatant.

277 ὤμοιϊν: genitive(-dative) dual.   **δόρυ δ' ἔκβαλον:** casting away one's arms in battle was a serious matter, variously punished, for instance by loss of citizen rights in Athens. Plato is highly critical of the man who prefers a life of shame to defending himself when surrounded (*Legg.* 943d4–5b6), and Aristophanes constantly ridicules the ῥίψασπις Cleonymus (*Clouds* 353 etc.). Sympotic poets made fun of it: cf. Archil. fr. 6; Alc. fr. 428 (with Hdt. 5.95); Anac. fr. 381b. This is a striking example of the self-deprecating way in which Od. presents himself in these stories; cf. 191–359n. para 2. **ἔκτοσε:** an adverbial form (found only here in Greek) used as a preposition, as usual with the genitive (cf. 13n. on ἔντοσθεν).

279 κύσα γούνα(τα): though the act of supplication (cf. 13.213n. on ἱκετήσιος) often involves a form of self-abasement like grasping of knees or chin, supplicatory kissing is found only twice in Homer, and seems to suggest a form of self-abasement reserved for situations of great desperation. Athena says of Thetis that, when she beseeched Zeus to give glory to Achilles, 'she kissed his knees' (*Il.* 8.371). Athena was not there at the time, and Homer says simply that Thetis 'took hold of (λάβε) Zeus's knees and chin' (1.500–1), so it looks as though Athena chooses the most demeaning form of supplication to characterise Thetis' action, which threatens her intention to see Troy destroyed. In seeking Hector's body, Priam kisses 'the dreaded man-slaying hands of Achilles which had killed many of his sons' (*Il.* 24.478–9). Though Od. paints himself as a proud man, by admitting to adopting so demeaning a posture, he shows himself not so proud as to jeopardise his own survival.   **ἐρύσατο καί μ' ἐλέησεν:** a *hysteron proteron*; cf. 13.189–90n.

280 δίφρον: from δί(ς) + φέρω, and so literally something that could be carried by handles on either side. It was a structure that could be fitted to the chariot-frame on which driver and fighter were carried side by side, and so came to be used of the chariot itself and also of chairs.   **ἔσας** 'having put', sigmatic aorist active participle of ἕζομαι (cf. 49n.), here not 'sit' but 'place' ('they did not sit in chariots', scholia).

281 ἢ μέν: see 216n.

282 δὴ γὰρ κεχολώατο: for δὴ γάρ, see 13.30n. κεχολώατο is an Ionic 3rd p.pl. pluperfect of χολόω: for the ending, see Introduction 5.3 §6.3.2.5, 6; *GH* I.477.

283 ὠπίζετο: see 3.148n.

283–4 Διὸς ... | ξεινίου: relationships of *xenia* were under the protection of Zeus Xenios, so that breaches of them were thought liable to divine punishment.

285 ἑπτάετες: cf. the seven years spent with Calypso (7.259); 285a = 7.259a and 287 = 7.261. Seven is a typical number in stories; cf. also 249–50, 3.305–6.

286 ἀν᾽ Αἰγυπτίους ἄνδρας: ἀνά is often used of moving amongst groups; cf. *Il.* 1.10 ἀνὰ στρατόν etc. (*GH* II.91).   **δίδοσαν:** unaugmented 3rd p.pl. imperfect. This gift-giving is the result of Od.'s friendship with the king; cf. the gifts that Alcinous has his courtiers bring to Od. in 13.13–15.

(iii) 287–313 fooled by a Phoenician

287 ὄγδοον: < *ὄγδοϝος (cf. Lat. *octauus*). This must be scanned as a spondee; on this unusual kind of synizesis, see 13.194n.

288 Φοῖνιξ: see 13.272n.   **ἀπατήλια εἰδώς:** see 13.405n.

289 τρώκτης: lit. 'nibbler' (< τρώγω 'gnaw'), and so of grasping people generally. Eum. picks it up in his own tale of villainous Phoenicians (15.415–16); cf. also Ar. *Ach.* 257–8 φυλάττεσθαι σφόδρα | ...μή τις λαθών σου περιτράγηι τὰ χρυσία 'make quite sure no-one secretly pinches your gold jewellery'; *A.P.* 9.409.4 τρώκταις χερσί (of a usurer).   **ἀνθρώποισιν ἐώργει:** ἐώργει is the 3rd p.s. pluperfect of ἔρδω 'do'. Many MSS have ἀνθρώπους ἐώργει, which is unmetrical, but gives the expected second accusative and may hide an earlier ἀνθρώπους ἐ(ϝ)ε(ϝ)όργει (*GH* I.480). The dative may have been introduced to mend the metre once the digammas were lost.

290 παρπεπιθών 'having won over', the reduplicated aorist active participle of παραπείθω. In such compounds, παρά often has a negative sense, as in παράγω 'seduce', παραπαφίσκω 'deceive, lead astray' (cf. 488 παρά μ’ ἔπαγε). ὄφρ’ ἱκόμεσθα: the verb is probably an indicative, ὄφρα + aorist indicative being used to mean 'up to the point where, until' (*GH* 11.262).

292 τελεσφόρον εἰς ἐνιαυτόν 'for a complete year', rather than 'to the end of the year'. First, the reference to the start of an eighth year in 287 suits the former. Secondly, the elaborate precision of 293–4 might seem rather a grand way to mark the anniversary of Od.'s arrival at the Phoenician's house, rather than some more significant point, such as the start of a new year, but in 11.294–5 these same lines clearly mark the end of a year's enslavement of Melampus before he was able to drive off the cattle which won him his bride. The importance of complete periods of a year in folk tale again suggests a complete year: cf. 196 εἰς ἐνιαυτὸν ἅπαντα (and n.), 10.469–70 ἀλλ’ ὅτε δή ῥ’ ἐνιαυτὸς ἔην, περὶ δ’ ἔτραπον ὧραι, | μηνῶν φθινόντων, of the time with Circe, 19.151–3; M. L. West 1978: on Hes. *Op.* 561.

295 Λιβύην: 'Libya' is mentioned again at 4.85–90, where Menelaus describes it as a land of magically fertile sheep; he mentions it in the same breath as the major trading countries Cyprus, Phoenicia and Egypt, as well as Ethiopia and the mysterious 'Eremboi'. Lane Fox 2008: 145–7 suggests that the reference is to that part of Tunisia which was settled by Euboeans in the early eighth century: we find there place-names such as 'Euboea' and 'Pithecussae', the name of a Euboean settlement, now Ischia; cf. also Anderson and Dickie 1995: 44–5. ἑέσσατο: 3rd p.s. sigmatic aorist middle of ἕζομαι. This is either a recent creation influenced by the aorist of ἕνν-υμι, ἑέσσατο (as in 529), or an archaic form < *e-(s)ed-s-, cf. 49 εἶσεν (with n.) and 280 ἔσας. Cf. *GH* I.416, 481; for a similar case of such influence between verbs, cf. 306n.

296 οἱ σύν are not easy to distinguish in English translation: οἱ is 'to his advantage', and σύν an adverb meaning 'along with (him)' (i.e. it does not govern οἱ).

297 κεῖθι δέ 'but *in reality* when there'; δέ marks a strong contrast here, and κεῖθι is emphasised by its position at the start of the line. περάσειε: 3rd p.s. aorist active optative of πέρνημι 'sell'. ἄσπετον: see 13.135n.

298 ὀϊόμενός περ 'though I suspected (the truth)'; for the absolute use of ὀΐομαι thus, cf. 9.339 (the Cyclops pens up all his sheep) ἤ τι ὀϊσάμενος 'either being in some way suspicious...' ὀΐομαι implies a less strong belief than νομίζω or ἡγέομαι. For περ, see 13.130n.

300 μέσσον ὑπὲρ Κρήτης: the interpretation of the grammar and of the journey is difficult. μέσσον is probably best taken as an adverb 'in the open sea': cf. *Il.* 12.167–8 ὥς τε σφῆκες μέσον αἰόλοι ... | οἰκία ποιήσωνται, Eur. *Or.*

983 τὰν οὐρανοῦ μέσον χθονός τε... πέτραν, *Rh.* 530; cf. LSJ s.v. v 1. ὑπὲρ Κρήτης is most naturally 'beyond Crete', i.e. to the south (cf. 13.257 ὑπὲρ πόντου). Munro 1901 ad loc. however points out that there appears to be a contrast between this expression and the next line ἀλλ᾽ ὅτε δὴ Κρήτην μὲν ἐλείπομεν, 'so that the former clause must belong to the time *before* the ship was far on its way to Libya'; thus 'μέσσον implies keeping off the lee shore of Crete', i.e. to the north-west (cf. 3.170 καθύπερθε Χίοιο meaning 'on the windward side of Chios'). Others prefer a north or north-east passage. μέσσον is however a problem for such interpretations that involve the ship keeping close to the coast. As with the chronology of the Egyptian attack (cf. 266n.), the poet does not appear to have concerned himself too much with the precise details of the journey, which are not anyway the main interest of the story. For the Phoenicians and Crete, see 13.272n.   σφισι: the crew.

301–4 = 12.403–6, and **305–9** = 12.415–19 (with minor differences), from the storm that destroyed Od.'s Companions. Od. thus reworks his own material from his earlier version, so that there is an element of pathos in his going through that storm for a third time. This description, as regularly in the false tales, is briefer than that in the Phaeacian story-telling. For other major storms, cf. 5.291–387, 9.67–73, 12.312–17, 403–25; de Jong 2001: 594–5.

306 ἐλελίχθη 'was spun round'. This form acts as the aorist passive of ἐλίσσω (< *wel-). The earlier form *ἐ-ϝελ-ίχθη lost its digamma and was given a second lambda through the influence of ἐλελίχθη < ἐλελίζω, which has the similar meaning 'shake', but a different etymology (*GH* I.132).

307 ἐν δὲ θεείου πλῆτο: since lightning bolts can reach temperatures five times that of the sun, it is not surprising that the air can smell burned. The smell is regularly likened to that of sulphur: cf. e.g. 12.417; *Il.* 14.415; Lucr. 6.220–1; Virg. *Aen.* 2.698. For πλῆτο, see 267n.

308 κορώνηισιν: most likely 'cormorants' (cf. Arnott 2007: 115–16). The simile is notable not so much for the similarity between sailors and cormorants as for the difference that the cormorants are not drowning (cf. 13.28–35n. on simile of the ploughman). The grim irony here marks Od.'s lack of concern for men who were presumably in on the plot to sell him.

311 ἀμαιμάκετον: a word of unknown etymology and meaning. Ancient poets made varied use of it, applying it e.g. to fire, the sea and passion. They often associate it with μάχομαι. Here its use of a mast may suggest the meaning was something like 'solid, undamaged'. The scholia explain it as 'of incomparable size' (cf. *mak-* 'long'). It is probably very old: cf. Beekes 80. For the actions of the god(s) in this tale, see 191–359n. para. 3.

312 ἔτι 'even then'; cf. 338.

(iv) 313–33 saved by the Thesprotians

314 ἐννῆμαρ: this is a regular length of time for the duration of bad storms; cf. 7.253, 9.82, 10.28, 12.447.

315 Θεσπρωτῶν: in historical times, a people who lived in the area of the Acheron valley and Epirus, opposite Corfu, though the precise location can vary. For early references to them, cf. Hdt. 2.56, 8.47, Thuc. 1.46.4, 50.3. They appear a number of times in *Od.*, but have no epithet, which might suggest they were not a major part of the epic tradition, though Paus. 8.12.5–6 (quoted in *GEF* pp. 168–70) speaks of a cyclic epic, the *Thesprotis*, which dealt with Od.'s adventures there. See Malkin 1998: 120–55 for the Epirote appropriation of Od. into their history.   κυλίνδον: neuter singular present active participle agreeing with κῦμα.

316 Φείδων 'the Sparer'. Names that are significant in this way are known as 'speaking names' (from the German *redende Namen*); for other examples, cf. 449, 499; also 204n.

317 ἀπριάτην 'without payment', from ἐπριάμην 'I bought'. This is a feminine accusative adjective used as an adverb.   φίλος υἱός: for the motif of the young person met by a traveller, cf. 13.217–49n.

318 αἴθρωι ... δεδμημένον 'overcome by the clear cold air of the morning'. αἴθρος appears only here and in Alc. fr. 58.14, 134.11; for δεδμημένος, cf. 13.119n.

319 χειρὸς ἀναστήσας 'having raised me by (taking) my hand (conducted me)'. As in *Il.* 24.515 (the phrase's only other occurrence in Homer), the consequences of the raising have to be deduced from the context. The genitive is regular with verbs of touching or taking hold of.   ὄφρ(α) 'until', cf. 290n.

320 εἵματα ἕσσεν: cognate accusative (13.26n.); for ἕσσεν, see 13.436n.

321 Ὀδυσῆος: this claim to know about Od. is the ultimate point of the beggar's story, but he carefully leaves it until he has narrated a lengthy tale to impress Eum. with the fact that he is a man who has indeed travelled widely and not just a beggar. Eum. is not, as usual, impressed (363–5). In 19.269–99, Od. will make a similar claim to Penelope to know about Od., the Thesprotians and their king Phaedon; in 19.288–99, lines are repeated but in a different order from 329–35 here.

322 φιλῆσαι 'entertain'; cf. 1.123 πὰρ ἄμμι φιλήσεαι.

323 κτήματ(α): again material goods are seen as important markers of status; cf. 13.41n.

324 πολύκμητόν τε σίδηρον 'iron that is forged with much effort'. Iron was in use in Greece for jewellery from the Mycenaean period; by the turn of the millennium, it was used more widely (Sherratt 1992: 148–50). By Homer's time, it would have been common, but often stands beside gold and silver: cf. the same list in 21.10 and *Il.* 6.48; at 23.826–35, Achilles remarks on the value of the iron discus he puts up as a prize; cf. also 9.365–6. Its production was effortful because ancient furnaces could not produce cast iron, so objects had to be worked manually by chasing (engraving or gouging with a metal tool). The origin of the word σίδηρος is unknown: 'the Greeks got to know iron from Asia Minor, the Pontus and Caucasus, and it is likely that they took over the word for it from those areas as well' (Beekes 1329).

325 καί νύ κεν ... βόσκοι 'they really would support his heirs in turn until the tenth generation'. ἕτερόν γ' seems to mean 'his successor and each one after that', which is how the scholia explain it: ἕτερον ἐξ ἑτέρου διαδεχομένου παρὰ πατρὸς παῖδα. For νυ, see 142n.

326 κειμήλια: as the derivation from κεῖμαι shows, these are goods that are laid up in store.

327 Δωδώνην: situated in Epirus (cf. also 315n.), Dodona would be a natural oracle for an Ithacan about to return home to consult. It was reputedly the oldest oracle in Greece, founded on the orders of a talking dove (cf. Hdt. 2.52–7); evidence of settlement is found from the Early Helladic period onwards. Quite how divination was conducted is uncertain. Here the suggestion is that the oak-tree, for which Dodona was famous (Hes. fr. 240), spoke the oracles: compare the speaking oak-beam from Dodona which formed part of the Argo (Aes. fr. 20; A.R. 1.525, 4.580). Later sources say the priestesses prophesied in a trance (Pl. *Phdr.* 244a8-b2, 275b5–6; Aristeid. *Or.* 2.52), and there is evidence for the use of lots (Callisthenes, *FGrH* 124 F 22). Questions were scratched on tablets (some of which survive) and a positive or a negative answer was given; such an answer seems to be what is implied in 330. There is a further reference to the oracle in *Il.* 16.233–5, where Achilles prays to Zeus 'who rules wintry Dodona, where your prophets the Selloi (or Helloi) sleep on the ground with unwashed feet'. Cf., in general, Parke 1967: 1–163 (1–19 on Dodona in Homer). The oak as a source of divine knowledge at this ancient oracle can be compared to the way the oak was the most important tree in Celtic culture, and the Druids, who looked after sacrifice, justice and wisdom, took their name from that tree (< *dru-(w)id-*, 'oak-seer'; cf. (ϝ)ιδεῖν, Latin *uidere*).

330 ἢ ἀμφαδὸν ἦε κρυφηδόν: this is a hint to Eum. that his master might return in disguise, but it is not taken. Adverbs in -δον are old accusatives (*GH* I.248; Rau 2006).

331 ὤμοσε...ἀποσπένδων: this is a subtle move on Od.'s part. Twice before he has tried to use an oath to persuade Eum. to believe him, without success (cf. 151–64, 393–400). Rather than try a third time, he transfers the motif from himself to the fictional figure in the story. The libation lends authority to the oath.

332 νῆα...ἑταίρους: Alcinous spoke a similar line to Od. in 8.151 to reassure him that his homecoming would not be long delayed. κατειρύσθαι and ἔμμεν illustrate the difference between the perfect and present stems in Greek: the ship has been drawn down to the sea (and so is in a state of readiness); the men simply are ready.

333 πέμψουσι: the future here has a trace of purpose about it.

(v) 334–59 escape from treacherous sailors and arrival in Ithaca

334 πρίν: i.e. before Od. could return.   **τύχησε:** Homer has a number of later aorists in -ησα alongside earlier forms; for τύχησα beside τύχον, cf. also οὔτησε beside οὖτα (*GH* I.415–16).

335 Δουλίχιον: the identity of this island is an unresolved problem. By Virgil's time Dulichium and Ithaca seem to be interchangeable; cf. *Ecl.* 6.76 *Dulichias...rates*; Prop. 2.14.4 *cum tetigit carae litora Dulichiae*; a 'Maritime Itinerary' of the second or third century AD omitted Ithaca altogether: *Insulae Cephalenia Zacinthus et Dulichia: hic est mons Ithacus, ubi est patria Ulixis*. Bittlestone (2005: 40–1, 249–79, with Diggle on pp. 515–16), having identified Ithaca with the western part of Cephalonia, argues that the only place that Dulichium could be is the island we call Ithaca. Graziosi 2008: 179–80 however counters that it is more likely that 'the Roman poets, with Alexandrian learnedness and a nod to a well-known Homeric problem, treat Doulichion as a synonym for Ithaca'. Cf. also Burkert 1988.

336 ἠνώγει: the object is the Thesprotian sailors; με is object of πέμψαι. **βασιλῆϊ Ἀκάστωι:** in *Il.* the king of Dulichium is Meges (2.627, etc.); Acastus is not mentioned elsewhere and is presumably simply a fiction on Od./Homer's part. Epic uses a dative of the destination more frequently than prose.

337 κακὴ...βουλή: Od. reuses the motif of deceitful sailors intent on enslaving him from 295–7; cf. also 13.209–14.

338 ἀμφ' ἐμοί: ἀμφί lit. 'on both sides' comes to mean 'concerning' through its use with verbs of disputing and fighting over something (*GH* ii.87–8). **ὄφρ' ἔτι πάγχυ δύης ἐπὶ πῆμα γενοίμην** 'so that I might again come to the depths of despair'. The meaning is clear, but the transmitted text is problematic. γίγνομαι is used to mean 'arrive' infrequently in Homer (though commonly in Herodotus), but it is not found thus with ἐπί. For δύης πῆμα, cf. 3.152 πῆμα κακοῖο. Aristophanes emended rather drastically to δύηι ἔπι πῆμα γένηται 'that trouble might be added to woe'.

339 γαίης πολλὸν ἀπέπλω 'had sailed far from the land'; ἀπέπλω is 3rd p.s. of the athematic aorist of ἀποπλώω.

340 δούλιον ἦμαρ: in contrast to later Greek, words for 'slave' etc. formed from δουλ- are rare in Homer (*Il.* 3.409, 6.463; *Od.* 4.12, 17.323, 22.423, 24.252). 'Epic does not like to call slavery by its name' (Gschnitzer 1976: 14), because Homer wants to stress the function of these people and their human relationships rather than their status; cf. Introduction 1.2.

342–3a = 13.434–5a, where Athena does the same. This creates, for the audience, an amusing conjunction between the Od. in the story and the one before Eum.'s eyes; for Eum. the rags are meant to add credibility to Od.'s story.

343 ὄρηαι is 2nd p.s. of an athematic present middle *ὄρημαι = ὁράομαι. Athematic forms of what are elsewhere contract verbs are an Aeolic feature; cf. *GH* i.305–6.

344 εὐδειέλου: see 13.212n.   **ἔργ(α)** 'farmland'; cf. 222.

346 ὅπλωι 'ship's rope'. ὅπλον means basically 'a tool, implement', and so the tackle of a ship, weapons etc.

348 ἀνέγναμψαν: lit. 'bent back', so 'untied'; cf. Eng. 'bend' = both 'a knot (for tying two ropes together)' and 'to tie'.

349 κεφαλῆι ... ῥάκος: for the cases here, cf. 13.152n.

350 ἐφόλκαιον: it is very difficult to determine what part of the ship this is; the word appears only here in Greek. Once again (cf. 300n.), it looks as though the poet is not concerned with precise (and not very important) details. For discussion of the suggestions, cf. Mark 2005: 131–4; also Kurt 1979: 115–16. There are four possibilities.
(1) On grounds of etymology, most likely is a towing-bar, a crossbeam in the bow corresponding to the θρῆνυς in the stern. However, no model or picture shows such a feature in ships of or before Homer's time. If (unlike the θρῆνυς) the bar projected beyond the walls of the ship,

then καταβάς would mean that Od. used it as a stepping-stone for slip-
ping into the sea.

(2) Some sort of gang-plank. If the ship was, as usual with Homeric ships,
beached stern-first, then the gang-plank would have to have been
been in the bow for Od. to escape unnoticed into the sea: but the only
illustration of such a plank on a ship of Homer's time puts it in the
stern. Even if the ship was beached bow-first, as the Phoenicians were
in a hurry (347 ἐσσυμένως; cf. 13.113–15), gang-planks were pulled in
before sailing (e.g. Eur. *IT* 1352–3, 1382), and getting it over the side
would have been noisy. Finally, gang-planks were not dragged behind
ships, so using a word derived from ἕλκω would be odd.

(3) The grammarians and scholia explain the word as a small boat
(σανδάλιον = ἐφόλκιον, ἐφολκίς) trailed behind the ship. Mark 2005:
105 notes that this would have had to be towed to the front of the
ship when it was beached. Od. could have used it to get from the bul-
wark to the sea, but the beak of the ship would have been more stable
for such a manoeuvre.

(4) A quarter-rudder, but these were taken out of the boat to dry; getting it
down would have risked noise and it would not have supported Od.'s
weight.

The uncertainty here is characteristic: 'Homer is one of our best sources
of information on the various parts of ancient ships ... but ... a portion of
our information still consists of little more than names and hints that can
have more than one interpretation' (Mark 2005: 137).   **ἐπέλασσα:** 1st
p.s. aorist active of πελάζω 'bring towards'. Hoekstra (*CHO* ad loc.) notes
how the sigmas here seem to imitate the quiet lowering of his body into
the water (for such assonance, cf. 243–5n.).

352 θύρηθ(ι) ἔα ἀμφὶς ἐκείνων 'I was out (of the sea), far from them'. θύρηθι,
elsewhere only in *EM* 25.17, is literally 'outside the door'; for a meaning
'out of the sea', cf. 5.410 ἔκβασις ... ἁλὸς πολιοῖο θύραζε. Adverbs in -θι are
found only in Homer (and imitators) and Arcadian. ἀμφίς 'on both sides'
came to denote separation and distance, as in 19.221 ἀμφὶς ἐόντα (cf. *GH*
II.89); here it is used as a preposition with the ablatival genitive (cf. 9n. on
νόσφι).

353 δρίος 'thicket, copse', a hapax for Homer and very rare later; it has
been connected with δρῦς (cf. Beekes 354). This hiding in a thicket is reminiscent of his arrival on Scherie (5.474–87).

354 κείμην: see 13.281n.   **πεπτηώς:** perfect active participle of πτήσσω
'cower', 'crouch'.

355 ἀλλ' οὐ γάρ σφιν ἐφαίνετο 'but, you see, because it did not seem to them', the so-called 'anticipatory' γάρ, introducing an explanatory clause which precedes the clause it explains; cf. 1.301–2 καὶ σύ, φίλος, μάλα γάρ σ' ὁρόω καλόν τε μέγαν τε, | ἄλκιμος ἔσσ' (*GP* 68–73).

356 προτέρω 'further'; this is an old instrumental case used as an adverb, as ἄνω 'up', ἐπισχερώ 'successively'.   **πάλιν** 'back', with νηὸς ἔπι; it is not used of time in Homer.

359 ἐπισταμένου: Od. ends his tale with outright flattery of Eum.   **ἔτι γάρ νυ:** see 275n.

360–89 Eumaeus' sixth speech

Eum. begins sympathetically but, as if he cannot restrain his annoyance at the beggar's insistence on claiming association with Od., soon complains about it in somewhat fractured language (363–4). At the very end, he again mixes sympathy with a firm request that Od. stop trying to fool him. Ironically, in what he believes, he gets things quite the wrong way round: he seems to believe, or at least not to challenge, the false tales of adventure (cf. τοῖον 'a man of such qualities', 364), but he will have nothing to do with talk of Od.'s return. On 'scepticism' in *Od.*, cf. Zerba 2009.

The centre of the speech justifies his annoyance. He now avoids the palace unless summoned by the queen, because so many such beggars have come with claims to know about Od., culminating in an Aetolian whose false story bears similarities to Od.'s own. This Aetolian claims to have seen Od. in Crete (382 ~ 199), *chez* Idomeneus with whom he served (382 ~ 237); to have knowledge of Od. (382–5 ~ 321), including that he was repairing his ship for return (383 ~ 332) with great wealth (385 ~ 323–6). Only the Aetolian's reference to the Companions (385) has no counterpart. His claim to be in exile for killing a man also parallels a feature of Od.'s false tale to Athena (380–1 ~ 13.259–60).

Such a story is an obvious one to confect in such circumstances, but there is a possibility that Eum. is *himself* telling a false tale, carefully crafted to administer an inherent rebuke to Od. He makes up a man with a very similar story to Od.'s, criticism of which applies implicitly to the beggar; this avoids a direct rebuke, which is further testament to Eum.'s diplomacy and humanity. It is precisely such tales that have left him (almost) at the end of his patience with beggars, but he still takes them in.

Whether or not the Aetolian was fictional, that race may have been chosen for a pun on αἰτέω 'demand something': cf. Duris, *FGrH* 76 F 13 (*ap.* Ath. 253F), where Demetrius Poliorcetes is begged to save Greece from 'the Aetolian' (i.e. the Aetolian League), Αἰτωλικὸν γὰρ ἁρπάσαι τὰ τῶν πέλας, νῦν δὲ καὶ τὰ πόρρω 'because it is the Aetolian way to seize neighbours' property, and now they want things further afield'.

361-2 ἢ μοι μάλα κτλ.: Od. will use almost these same words in his response to Eum.'s tale of his life (15.486-7).

361 ἃ δειλὲ ξείνων: for the partitive genitive, cf. 443 δαίμονιε ξείνων; Ar. *Frogs* 835 ὦ δαιμόνιε ἀνδρῶν; δῖα γυναικῶν etc. This phrase will be used with a very different tone by Antinous in 21.288.

362 ὅσα δή: δή here emphasises the fact that it is the beggar's stories of suffering and wandering which have affected him, as opposed (363 ἀλλά) to his less well-chosen remarks on Od. (*GP* 218-19).   **ἀλήθης:** 2nd p.s. aorist indicative of ἀλάομαι 'wander'.

363 ἀλλὰ τά γ'...πείσεις 'but some of them, I think, were not (spoken) correctly – and you won't persuade me'. οὐ κατὰ κόσμον has no verb: it is as if Eum. began with the intention of saying explicitly οὐ κατὰ κόσμον εἶπες, but then checked himself and substituted the tentative 'I think', allowing the idea of 'saying' to be supplied from 362 λέγων. He thus ends up with this double parenthesis, which conveys at once his reluctance to criticise the beggar and his determination to put the topic of his master to one side. In 363-8, all the lines are enjambed with the next, the constant fragmenting of the regular rhythm of the metre reflecting the agitated state that Eum. is put in by the beggar's attempts to talk about his master's return. For Eum.'s expressive use of enjambement, cf. 55-71, 163nn.   **οὐ κατὰ κόσμον:** see 13.48n.

364 τί σε χρή: the asyndeton marks a reproachful question; cf. 16.187 οὔ τίς τοι θεός εἰμι· τί μ' ἀθανάτοισιν ἐΐσκεις; and, in a statement, *Il.* 2.23-4 εὕδεις Ἀτρέος υἱέ... | οὐ χρή...   **τοῖον ἐόντα** 'when you are a man such as you are'. Eum.'s use of this expression suggests that he is beginning to see there may be more to the beggar than meets the eye.

365 μαψιδίως 'recklessly': a strong word, which can convey considerable disapprobation; it is used of the Suitors' greed (2.58, 9.253) and of pirates (3.72, 17.451).

365-71 There are similar sentiments, similarly expressed, in Telemachus' words to Athena in 1.234-41 (368-71 = 1.238-41).

365-6 ἐγὼ δ'...ἤχθετο 'but I for myself know perfectly well (concerning) my master's return, that he was hated'; cf. 13.170n.

368 πόλεμον τολύπευσε: for the winding of carded wool as a metaphor for completing a war, cf. 1.238, 4.490, 24.95. τολυπεύω is always used metaphorically in Homer, though Penelope's 19.137 δόλους τολυπεύω, which introduces the story of her deceitful weaving, plays on the literal sense.

369–70 These lines recur at 1.239–40 and 24.32–3.

369 Παναχαιοί: i.e all the Greeks acting in unity. In *Il.* the word is always (bar 9.301) used with ἀριστῆρες.   τώ 'in that case'.   οἱ 'for him'.

370 ἤρατ(ο) must be the 3rd p.s. aorist middle of ἄρνυμαι 'take, gain'. The expected form is ἤρετο, but ἤρατο, the aorist of αἴρω 'lift, raise', may have had influence. The subject is Od.

371 Ἅρπυιαι ἀνηρείψαντο 'the Harpies have snatched him away'; the verb is ἀν-ερέπτομαι. The Harpies, 'Snatchers', are storm-demons who appear as women, with names evoking their fantastic speed: Podarge, Aello, Ocypete (*Il.* 16.150; Hes. *Th.* 267). They were used to explain sudden disappearances or death: cf. Penelope on the end of the daughters of Pandareus in 20.66–78. For their plaguing of Phineus, cf. Hes. frr. 151, 155; A.R. 2.178–434. There is probably a pun on their name (found also as Ἀρεπυῖαι) in the verb, but there is very likely no etymological connection (Beekes 139). On the varied spellings of this aorist in Greek, cf. M. L. West 1966 on Hes. *Th.* 990.

372 ἀπότροπος: the scholia define this as 'isolated, far from the city', which is very likely, though the interpretation may simply be taken from the next phrase. It is a hapax in Homer.

373 εἰ μή πού τι 'unless perhaps'. For the idea that normal relations between the people in Od.'s household have stopped in his absence, cf. 15.374–9 (Eum. regrets the ending of the easy commerce between mistress and servants), and 16.27–9 (Telemachus no longer visits his fields and flocks).

374 ὀτρύνῃσι: a subjunctive marking a repeated action; this is a rare example of the subjunctive in such clauses without ἄν/κε or τε (Palmer 1962: 166).

375 οἱ μέν: i.e. the people in the palace, who are then divided into two groups by ἠμέν... ἠδ(έ) (376–7).   τὰ ἕκαστα: the article appears with ἕκαστος elsewhere in Homer only in *Il.* 11.706, *Od.* 12.16, 165. Elsewhere in Greek, it seems to be confined to Attic prose and inscriptions (LSJ s.v. I 2).

377 νήποινον 'at no cost to themselves', i.e. without offering any recompense as one would expect in a recipient of hospitality: cf. ποινή used in quasi-legal contexts, such as *Il.* 18.498–9 ἐνείκεον εἵνεκα ποινῆς | ἀνδρὸς φθιμένου 'they were quarrelling about compensation for a dead man'. The complaint is made repeatedly about the Suitors' behaviour: cf. 1.160, 377, 2.142, 14.417, 18.280; and also 13.14–15n. This is the adverbial use of the neuter adjective (i.e. it is not an epithet of βίοτον); cf. 495 ἐνύπνιον (and in the feminine, 317 ἀπριάτην).

379 ἐξήπαφε: 3rd p.s. aorist indicative of ἐξαπαφίσκω 'trick completely (ἐξ)'.

380 ἀληθείς: for exile as the penalty for a killing, cf. 13.259n.

382 μιν: Odysseus.

383 ἀκειόμενον 'repairing'. This verb is used of the stitching of tailors, cobblers and spiders (Arist. *HA* 623a18 ἀκεσαμένη... τὸ διερωγός 'repairing the torn part (of its web))', and refers to the way that ships were sewn together with cords passed through holes drilled in the timbers (cf. Aes. *Supp.* 134–5 λινορραφής | τε δόμος and scholia; Morrison and Williams 1968: 50; Mark 2005: Index s.v. 'laced joinery'). In Homer and elsewhere generally, the verb usually retains something of its medical sense (cf. ἄκος): compare for 'wounded' ships, Hdt. 6.16.1 ἀδύνατοι ἦσαν αἱ νέες ὑπὸ τρωμάτων, 8.18 [νέες] τετρωμέναι.   **ξυνέαξαν:** 3rd p.pl. aorist indicative of ξυν-άγ-νυμι 'shatter'.

384 ἢ ἐς θέρος ἢ ἐς ὀπώρην 'by the end of the summer or the harvest'; for ἐς, cf. 196n. If this Aetolian came earlier in this year, the fact that the weather conditions described at the end of the book point to the onset of winter shows that his deadline has been missed and would make Eum.'s disillusionment fresh and still painful.

386 δαίμων: where Od. has grandly ascribed events to Zeus or the gods, Eum. uses a much more vague and general term, perhaps implying again a certain scepticism. Antinous does however name both θεοί and a δαίμων as responsible for Telemachus' survival in 16.364 and 370.

387 θέλγε: see 13.2n.

389 ἀλλὰ Δία...ἐλεαίρων: Eum. again stresses that his help is being given out of respect for the gods and for man's suffering; no other incentive is required.   **αὐτόν** 'you'. αὐτός on its own can be used as a personal pronoun referring to other than third persons: cf. *Il.* 24.503 αἰδεῖο θεούς, Ἀχιλεῦ, αὐτόν τ' ἐλέησον 'respect the gods, Achilles, and pity me'; *Od.* 10.27 αὐτῶν γὰρ ἀπωλόμεθ' ἀφραδίῃσιν 'we perished because of our own folly' (*GH* II.157).

390–400 Odysseus' fourth speech

In ordinary circumstances, Od.'s insistence on talking about Eum.'s master despite the man's pleas and hints would be thought insensitive, but it provides the audience with humour that is wry and not too unkind: after all, it is only a matter of time before Eum. learns the wonderful truth. Homer is thus enabled both to keep the audience in suspense about the moment of revelation and to expand his tale.

391 ἦ μάλα τίς...ἄπιστος 'you really have a mistrustful mind in your breast!' For ἦ μάλα τις thus, cf. 16.183 ἦ μάλα τις θεός ἐσσι 'you must be a god', 19.40; also 13.172n. For this motif of trying to persuade a doubter, cf. 149–51n.

392 οἷον 'given that'. This is best taken as an adverbial accusative in an independent clause meaning literally something like 'in regard to the manner in which', 'judging from the fact that', and so often best translated 'given': cf. 4.611 αἵματος εἰς ἀγαθοῖο...οἷ' ἀγορεύεις 'you are of good blood, (given) what sort of things you say'; and in the dative, 5.302–4 τὰ δὲ δὴ νῦν πάντα τελεῖται, | οἵοισιν νεφέεσσι περιστέφει οὐρανὸν εὐρύν | Ζεύς 'all of this will now come about, given the kind of clouds with which Zeus covers the broad heaven'; 15.281, 18.143 (cf. *GH* ii.238). The alternative is to take it as a masculine accusative with σ(ε), and so as the equivalent of ὅτι τοῖόν σε ὄντα... 'because being such as you are...', but this is awkward. **ὀμόσας:** in 158–64. The recalling of that oath leads into a repeat of the motif.

393 ῥήτρην 'compact'. In his attempt to swear an oath that will convince Eum., Od. uses a relatively infrequent word which has a strong technical legal overtone: cf. 13.7n. on the formal quality of words from the root *wrē-. It is used of the laws of Lycurgus at Sparta (Plut. *Lyc.* 6.1); in Tyrt. fr. 4.6, those involved in justice are encouraged to act εὐθείαις ῥήτραις ἀνταπαμειβομένους; and in a sixth-century inscription from Elis ϝρατρα is used of a formal treaty (*SIG* 9.1); cf. also Xen. *Anab.* 6.6.28.

393 ποιησόμεθ': short-vowel jussive subjunctive.

394 μάρτυροι: *sc.* 'will be'.

395 τεός: an Aeolic form = σός; cf. Introduction 5.3 §5.1.   **ἐς τόδε δῶμα:** by specifying Eum.'s farmstead rather than a more general 'home', Od. heightens the humour.

396 πέμψαι: infinitive of command.

397 ἰέναι: for this infinitive depending on πέμψαι and completing its meaning, see 13.160n.   **ὅθι...θυμῶι** 'where I am keen to be'; for ἔπλετο cf.

13.145n. Od. reassures Eum. that he will not hang around once he has been rewarded; cf. 15.308–9 'tomorrow I want to go to the city to beg, so that I don't trouble you and your companions'.

399 βαλέειν: infinitive of command (for the form, see 13.334n.). Eurycleia will make a similar offer in an attempt to persuade Penelope in 23.78–9.

400 καὶ ἄλλος 'any other'; καί is emphatic.   **ἀλεύεται:** a short-vowel aorist subjunctive of ἀλέ(ϝ)-ομαι 'avoid', where the -υ- represents the digamma; cf. *GH* 1.456.

401–8 Eumaeus' seventh speech

Od.'s speech provokes Eum. to a much more ironic and curt response. His exasperation is indicated by the return to the simple address ξεῖνε, which he used in the early stage of their relationship (56), before switching to the warmer and more sympathetic 361 ἆ δειλὲ ξείνων and 386 γέρον πολυπενθές. Later, the warmer tone will return in 443 δαιμόνιε ξείνων.

402 οὕτω γάρ κτλ. 'no, I won't, because in that way...'; For γάρ thus in responses, cf. *GP* 74–5 (though no examples from Homer are noted there for the negative reply). Compare Pheidippides' response to his father's request to sing some Aeschylus in Ar. *Clouds* 1366–7 ἐγὼ γὰρ Αἰσχύλον νομίζω | ... ψόφου πλέων 'no, I won't, because I think Aeschylus is just a lot of noise'. The examples in *GP* suggest there is a colloquial side to this usage. His exasperation is barely controlled in the heavily ironic '*that* would get me fame...' Characteristically he soon pulls himself up short with 'but now it's time for supper' (407).

403 ἐπ' ἀνθρώπους 'amongst men'; cf. 43n.

404 ὅς: a conditional relative = 'if I were to'; cf. 13.214n. ἄγαγον and δῶκα are indicative because they describe things Eum. has actually done, κτείναιμι and ἑλοίμην optative because they describe things that might happen.

406 πρόφρων ... δή 'with what assurance!' (Shewring): i.e., again with heavy irony, 'I could confidently pray to Zeus for help after committing *that* crime!' δή is ironically emphatic, as often (cf. *GP* 229–36). Some MSS divide not Κρονίωνα λιτοίμην but Κρονίων' ἀλιτοίμην giving 'I would deliberately sin against Zeus'; this is equally possible (the text was originally written without word-breaks), but produces a less striking statement and gives less weight to the particle.

407 νῦν δ': as he has several times before (131, 171, 183–4, 363), Eum. quickly gets them off a tricky subject, feeling perhaps that he has spoken ironically enough, or fearing he might go too far and spoil a developing friendship.

408 εἶεν 'should be', a potential optative, as 18.141 μή τίς ποτε πάμπαν ἀνὴρ ἀθέμιστος εἴη 'a man should not be wholly impious' (cf. *GH* II.216–18); there is also an element of wishing (Eum. has not eaten).   **λαρόν** 'tasty', probably < *λα(ϝ)-αρός or -ερός, and so connected with ἀπο-λαύ-ω 'enjoy'. **τετυκοίμεθα:** here τεύχομαι = 'make for ourselves'; contrast 234n.

409–56 Arrival of the swineherds and dinner

The other swineherds arrive to bring the conversation to an end. The narrative has been entirely in direct speech from the moment of Eum.'s first words at 37, except for 48–52, 72–9 and 109–14 (and lines meaning 'he said'). Though Od. began by humbly saying little (148–64n.), by this stage he has spoken 50 per cent more lines than Eum., which reflects the way he has taken gradual control of matters (cf. 13.311–28n.). Half of the rest of the book will be in direct speech. The pattern of meal and story-telling is repeated from the first half. Despite the arrival of the herdsmen, the narrative still concentrates on Od. and Eum.

The sacrifice, though it takes place in humble surroundings, is treated in the same kind of detail as those made by grand Iliadic heroes. Compare for instance *Il.* 1.458–61: 'when they had prayed and cast the barley-meal, they first bent back the head of the victim, cut its throat and flayed it; they cut out the thigh-bones and wrapped them in fat, folding it over double, and laid strips of meat on them'. Indeed, the division of the meat (432–8) is nowhere treated at quite such length: cf. e.g. *Il.* 1.458–68, 2.421–31, 7.314–22, 24.621–7; *Od.* 3.430–63; and contrast the much briefer 74–9. Whatever exasperation Od. has caused him, Eum. does not depart from the conventions of entertaining strangers properly (cf. 437n.). Again, *Od.* blurs the distinctions between aristocrat and pig-farmer (cf. Introduction pp. 16–23): only the reference to chopping sticks (418) provides a practical detail not found in the grander examples. The absence of any reference to the treatment of the thigh-bones, which is regular in epic sacrifice, is notable, though its significance is not clear.

This detailed emphasis on sacrifice is important, because in *Od.* correct performance of sacrifice is one of the great indicators of the moral status of those whose homes Od. comes to: the Cyclops unceremoniously eats his meat alive, Circe turns her guests into pigs, Calypso eats separate food (5.195–9), the Companions conduct a forbidden sacrifice (12.353–65), the Suitors ignore or maltreat Od. Eum. does everything correctly and his moral calibre is stressed (420–1, 433). Cf. Saïd 2011: 64–9 and, on the practical problems in this sacrifice, Petropoulou 1987.

410 ἀγχίμολον 'soon', an adverb from ἄγχι 'near' + μολεῖν 'go', used of time as well as place.

412 ὦρτο: 3rd p.s. athematic root aorist middle of ὄρ-νυμι 'rise'.

413 αὐτάρ picks up μέν in 411.   **ἐκέκλετο:** 3rd p.s. reduplicated aorist of κέλομαι 'order, encourage'.

414–17 Od.'s speeches have obviously had some effect on Eum. because, whereas before he was cautious about how he treated the pigs he is rearing for the Suitors (58–61), he now seems much more cavalier, calling for the best boar which would normally have gone to the palace (108, 189). This appropriation of the best boar because they have laboured to produce it is a very radical idea for the society depicted in *Od.*, and a striking declaration of independence. The fact that it is appropriated in order to honour a special guest mitigates this only slightly. That that guest is in fact the owner of the boar adds an element of irony (cf. A. T. Edwards 1993: 67–70).

414 ἄξε(τε) 'bring' functions as an aorist active imperative of ἄγω. It is a rare case of a 'mixed' aorist imperative created out of a future used as an imperative (almost all the verbs have *s*-futures): cf. *Il.* 8.505 ἄξεσθε, also οἴσετε, ὄψεσθε, λέξεο (*GH* 1.417–8; Risch 1974: 250). The expected aorist imperative from ἦξα, *ἄξατε does not appear to exist; the imperatives of the aorists ἤνεικα and εἶδον could not be used at the start of the line because they begin with a short syllable, which may account for the creation of the artificial forms.

415 πρὸς δ᾽ αὐτοὶ ὀνησόμεθ᾽ 'what's more, we'll enjoy it ourselves too'. πρὸς δέ is adverbial (cf. ἐν δέ, 13.438). Taking ὀνήσομεθα as a future indicative (of ὀνίνημαι) gives a more colourful sense than treating it as an aorist jussive subjunctive ('let us...').   **ὀϊζύν:** a strong word conveying the rigour of agricultural labours; Nestor uses it of the Greeks' travails at Troy (3.303).

418 κέασε: see 12n.   **νηλέϊ χαλκῶι:** the phrase is formulaic, but this is the only time it is used of cutting inanimate things (cf. 10.532, 11.45 for its use in killing sacrificial victims).

419 πενταέτηρον: for the humour in the use of this epithet, see Introduction p. 21.

420 ἐσχάρηι: a low altar. As usual in Homer, this is simply the house altar used for all the gods (423). In later literature it was often, though not exclusively, used for sacrifice to chthonic deities as opposed to the *bōmos*, a more upright structure used for the Olympians (cf. Scullion 1994 and 159n.).

421 ἄρ': this particle often comes later in its sentence than the second position, where particles tend to occur.

422 ἀπαρχόμενος: the technical term for starting a religious rite with the dedication of hairs from the animal's head. The point may be that the animal was thus rendered no longer inviolable, and so appropriate for sacrifice (Burkert 1985: 56; cf. Eitrem 1915: 344–72).

424 νοστῆσαι 'Οδυσῆα 'that Od. should return, for Od.'s return'. Infinitives in constructions of this sort tend to have not a temporal force but an aspectual one, so the aorist is often used in Homer where a future would be normal in English; cf. *GH* II.310; 14.133–4n. On the progress of Eum.'s thoughts about Od.'s return, see 68n.   **ὅνδε δόμονδε:** -δε (cf. 13.17n.) is sometimes added to possessive pronouns as well as the nouns (so also ἡμέτερόνδε, ὑμέτερόνδε).

425 ἣν λίπε κείων 'which he had left when he was splitting wood'. κείων, found only here, is perhaps a metrically lengthened form for κεῶν < *κεάων, related to κεάζω (cf. 418 κέασε). It is not the same as κείων in 532. In more formal sacrifices an axe would have been used for the slaughter (e.g. 3.449), and here we perhaps have, in the use of a piece of wood, a 'rustic' touch to this rite (cf. 77, 78nn.).

426 ἔσφαξαν 'they cut its throat', as was normal after the blow of the axe.

427–8 ὁ δ'...δημόν 'and the swineherd arranged the raw meat on the rich fat, making a first offering from all the limbs'. For ἀρχόμενος, cf. 422n. The meat is wrapped in fat either to be burned for the gods (429) or to be cooked for the men (430).

429 ἀλφίτου ἀκτῆι: ἀκτή is an archaic word of uncertain origin, possibly meaning 'corn' (cf. Hesych. α 2668 ἀκτή· τροφή) or 'ear of corn' (cf. Beekes 58). It is almost confined to epic where it is found in this formula (also ἀλφίτου ἱεροῦ ἀκτήν) and in Δημήτερος ἀκτήν. Sprinkling of meal is a regular feature of sacrifice.

432 ἐλεοῖσιν: Ath. 4.173a defines ἐλεός as 'cook's table', so 'dresser'; the word also appears in a sacrifice at *Il.* 9.215 εἰν ἐλεοῖσιν ἔχευε. It may be a word from everyday speech, cf. Ar. *Kn.* 152, 169.   **ἄν** = ἀνά (Introduction 5.3 §7.5.3).

433 δαιτρεύσων 'to distribute the meat'. The equal division of the meat at a Greek sacrifice was a frequent practice (cf. 20.281–2); equality was assured in grand city sacrifices by lot or even by weighing to ensure fairness (cf. A. M. Bowie 1995: 467). The equality of distribution signified the equality of status of those at the sacrifice. At the same time, it was also the custom to mark out certain people with special cuts of the animal (cf. 437).   **περί:**

probably here an adverb = 'very', as in 146.   αἴσιμα ἤιδη: see 13.405n.
on ἤπια οἶδε.

435 τὴν μὲν ἴαν: *sc.* μοῖραν from διεμοιρᾶτο in 434; cf. *Il.* 11.379 ἔς γε μίαν
βουλεύσομεν, where βουλήν is to be supplied from the verb (cf. *GH* 11.10).
ἴα = μία only here in Homer; it is an Aeolic feminine of ἰός 'that', possibly cognate with Latin *is*; *GH* 1.259. The weakening of the demonstrative
force led to the word meaning 'one'.   **Νύμφηισι καὶ Ἑρμῆι:** the Nymphs
who followed Artemis lived in the wilds, and Hermes was also a god of
boundaries and so of the marginal regions of the countryside; he was born
in the country and was famed for his sexual exploits with Nymphs (cf.
Burkert 1985: 158; Ar. *Thesm.* 977–8 'I call on Hermes of the fields, Pan
and the Nymphs dear to them'). These deities were therefore thought to
protect shepherds and their flocks and to ensure their fertility: the scholiasts remark 'Simonides [*sic*] says that they sacrifice to the Nymphs and
the son of Maia, because they are related to shepherds (ἀνδρῶν αἷμ' ἔχουσι
ποιμένων)' (= Semon. fr. 20, with the note in M. L. West 1992 ad loc.). Cf.
12.131–6 for the Nymphs who guard the Cattle of the Sun. For shrines of
the Nymphs on Ithaca, cf. 13.102–12 and 17.204–11; there is also a 'hill
of Hermes' at 16.471. Cf. Zusanek 1998: 1–105.

436 θῆκεν: perhaps 'put to one side', as if the gods were present; it would
be equivalent to παρέθηκεν.

437 νώτοισιν ... γέραιρεν: the chine was regularly given as a mark of favour,
because it was the choicest cut: cf. *H.Herm.* 122 νῶτα γεράσμια. Od. is given
it on Scherie (8.475–6), and Menelaus gives one to Telemachus (4.65–6),
which had been prepared for himself as γέρα 'a mark of honour'; cf. also
*Il.*7.321–2. Eum. follows the convention of giving a guest special treatment, even in the case of a beggar, to Od.'s pleasure (441–2).

440 Εὔμαιε: Homer appears to have Od.'s guard slip here when he uses
Eum.'s name, which Eum. has not told him before. According to Higbie 1995: 75, hosts do not identify themselves to guests in *Od.* (though
at 15.267 Telemachus does in fact reveal that he is the son of Od., if not
his actual name, to Theoclymenus, when the latter seeks his assistance on
his ship). The slip could thus be an indication of his admiration that Eum.
should give the best cut of meat to a beggar in his condition, even when
apparently not entirely convinced of his sincerity. Alternatively, one could
imagine that Eum.'s name was part of the racket accompanying the return
of the pigs (410–12). In his addresses to Eum., Od. moves from ξεῖνε (53)
to φίλε (115, 149) to his actual name here. For the first use of a name at a
crucial moment, cf. 16.204, when Od. finally persuades Telemachus that
he is his father.

443 δαιμόνιε ξείνων: δαιμόνιε is used in a great variety of ways in Greek (see Dickey 1996: 141–2), but its connection with δαίμων naturally allows it to be used to express surprise and to imply that there is something remarkable about the addressee.

444 οἷα πάρεστι 'such as they are'; Eum. modestly deprecates the value of what he has given Od. No high-status hero ever says this of the food he offers others.

446 ἦ ῥα 'so he spoke'. ἦ is a 3rd p.s. imperfect indicative, the only tense of this root in Homer. It is preserved in Attic (cf. ἦν δὲ ἐγώ, ἦ δὲ ὅς in Plato); a present ἠμί was created for it, on the analogy of φημί. **ἄργματα** 'first offerings', cognate with ἀρχή, ἄρχομαι (cf. 422n.). There is a problem as to how these relate to the actions described by ἀρχόμενος in 428. They are probably those parts already taken from the seven portions and set aside for the gods.

447 σπείσας: before wine is drunk, a little is given to the gods. This continued to be the practice in the more elaborate rituals at the start of the symposium. Again, the guest is marked out for special favour.

449 Μεσαύλιος 'he of the inner courtyard' (cf. 5n. on αὐλή), so 'Yardman' (Stanford), a suitable name for this servant. For such 'speaking names', cf. 13.28, 14.316nn.

450 κτήσατο illustrates how a servant of a royal master could have his own servants under him. Such a phenomenon is a feature of all slave-owning societies: 'nothing more confirmed the loyal slaves' acceptance of the condition of slavery and their own enslavement to the master than their willingness to own slaves themselves' (Patterson 1982: 184).   **οἷος** is explained by the next line.

452 Ταφίων: Homer never says exactly where these people come from, but they are presumably to be imagined as living not far away. Antinous' father joined them in attacking the Thesprotians (cf. 16.425–7 and 315n.). Athena disguises herself as Mentes, ruler of the Taphians, whom Telemachus does not recognise but correctly surmises is a *xenos* of his father (1.105, 174–84). They were known for their piratical raiding (15.426–9).   **πρίατο** 'bought'; this aorist has no present.

453–4 These lines regularly occur in the description of a feast in Homer and appear to have a long pedigree.

453 ὀνεία(τα) 'food, victuals', an archaic word cognate with ὀνίνημαι 'enjoy' (cf. 415n.).

454 ἔντο: 3rd p.pl. aorist middle indicative of ἵημι.

456 ἐσσεύοντο 'they began to hurry off' (inceptive imperfect); usually the sense is 'hurried away', but here they are stopped by Od.'s address in 462.

457–506 Odysseus' fifth speech: a second false story

Having seen the effect that claiming too often to have news about Od. has had on Eum., Od. here uses a different tactic, a reminiscence of having been chosen to accompany the great trickster on an ambush at Troy. There is thus a crescendo in the beggar's references to Od., from interest in who he might be (115–6), to a claim on oath that he will soon return (151–2), to claimed knowledge about him and a near meeting (321–33), to the offer to be killed if Od. does not return (391–400), to actual acquaintance with him here.

The tale is told to get Od. a cloak on a cold night. A formulaic feature of scenes of entertainment is the gift to a guest of clothes (13.12n.), which Homer here gives a novel treatment: in Eum.'s straitened circumstances such a gift has not been possible, and Od. needs a cloak, not as a traditional gift but because of the weather. Homer combines all of this with the motif of story-telling at a meal and the rewarding of the story-teller (13.1–15n.). For a subtle narratological analysis, see Lowe 2000: 145–7.

The story well characterises one who has been drinking. It has an amusing inconsequentiality, an ambush which grandly involves the beggar with Od. and Menelaus, and ends with them all sleeping until dawn. On this type of story in *Od.*, cf. Introduction pp. 21–2.

457 σκοτομήνιος 'dark because of the absence of the moon (μήνη)'; only found here and perhaps in Hes. fr. 66.5 νύκτ[ες ... σκοτο]μήνιοι (*suppl.* West). κακή suggests this epithet is an indication of the weather rather than the time of year; cf. also ἔφυδρος (458). Twenty-one sunsets are described in *Od.* This one is unique in its depiction of bad weather, and the most detailed. See 13.93n. and de Jong 2001: 42 for the variations.

458 ἄη: 3rd p.s. imperfect active of ἄημι 'blow'.   ἔφυδρος 'wet'; only here in Homer. The weather in Greece moves quite quickly from summer heat to winter storms, as Hesiod regularly notes: cf. especially *Op.* 619–26 (when the Pleiades set, 'then the blasts of all kinds of winds rage'), also 414–19, 492 and 670–7.

459 συβώτεω πειρητίζων: Eum. is heavily tested as to how he will receive the beggar, whether he will give him a cloak and whether (in book 15) he will keep him in his farm or send him off to the city; he always passes. Od. will similarly test others in the palace, such as the Suitors (17.360–4), the Maids (18.310–20), and Eum. and Philoetius (21.188–206). Indeed, Telemachus has to curb his father's desire to test people (16.305–20). In the end, it is Penelope who turns the tables and tests *Od.* (23.113–14, 173–206). Cf. 24.216–18, 236–319 for the testing of Laertes.

460 εἴ πως: see 13.415n.

461 ἐπεί ἕο κήδετο λίην 'since he showed so much concern for him'. ἕο is genitive of ἕ 'him'; for the genitive with κήδομαι, cf. 3–4n. The inadequacy of the garments that Athena piled onto him (13.431–8) becomes plain here and in 17.24–5.

462 κέκλυθι: aorist active imperative of κλύω, used alongside κλῦθι; the reduplication in this and the plural κέκλυτε is not satisfactorily explained. -θι is an imperative suffix used in athematic verbs more in Homer than Attic (*GH* 1.466).

463 εὐξάμενός τι 'somewhat boastfully': the beggar apologises for the claim to familiarity with Od. at Troy. The boastfulness is then excused by the wine he has drunk (NB γάρ). For εὔχομαι 'boast', cf. e.g. 11.261 ἥ δή καὶ Διὸς εὔχετ' ἐν ἀγκοίνῃσιν ἰαῦσαι 'she boasted that she lay in Zeus' arms'. Alternatively, εὐξάμενός τι ... ἐρέω could mean 'I will say what I have to say with something of a wish'. The difficulties with this are (i) that a wish (to be young again) follows shortly afterwards in 468–9, but that wish is not the point of the story; and more importantly (ii) that, if 488 οὐ γὰρ ἔχω χλαῖναν is the wish, then the point of the story appears half-way through the tale, which leaves the end as an anticlimax. With the first reading, it is the uncertainty about the point of the story which maintains Od.'s audience's interest in the denouement, and allows a much more gradual realisation. **ἀνώγει:** unlike ἀνώγει in 246, this is a present indicative, formed to the perfect ἄνωγα via the pluperfect ἀνώγει, which looks like an unaugmented imperfect; cf. *GH* 1.439 and 312; 471n. The excuse that wine is making him garrulous is cleverly chosen, since a certain amount of latitude in behaviour was permitted at dinners, when all are likely to be in a similar state and so sympathetic. There is a variant of this motif in 21.274–310, where Od., with a similar call to listen (275 κέκλυτέ μευ, μνηστῆρες) but without apology, asks to be allowed to try to string the bow, and Antinous accuses him of having drunk too much. For dislike of the man whose tongue gets out of control at the symposium, cf. Thgn. 295–8.

464 ἠλεός = 'crazy', as in 2.243 φρένας ἠλεέ. One can either see a transferred epithet (*hypallage*) here, the madness being transferred to the drinker, or with LSJ take it in the sense 'maddening'. This is unparalleled (the word is rare), but the scholia translate ἠλιθοποιός 'that makes one foolish'. **ἐφέηκε:** an uncontracted form = Attic ἐφῆκε 'sends off to, forces', a gnomic aorist. Stanford suggests that this, 465 ἀνῆκε and 466 προέηκεν constitute 'a drunken jingle'. **πολύφρονά περ μάλ'** '(a man) though he may be very sensible indeed'. For περ, cf. 13.130n.; μάλα often follows an adjective it emphasises.

465 ἁπαλὸν γελάσαι: what is meant by 'soft laughter' has been disputed since antiquity. ἁπαλός is rare in *Od.*: 21.151, 22.16 (the soft physique of the Suitors) and 13.223 (the young prince). In *H.Herm.* 281, the phrase is used of Apollo's indulgent laughter at the baby Hermes' trickery, and here too it could imply a gentle laughter that is still restrained. This would give a crescendo to the things Od. says wine provokes: singing (not unexpected at a symposium), gentle laughter, dancing (see next note) and finally remarks best left unsaid. Cf. Halliwell 2008: 86–7, 107–8.   **καί τ' ὀρχήσασθαι:** for the disapproval of inappropriate dancing at dinner, cf. Hippocleides, who danced away his marriage to the daughter of Cleisthenes, tyrant of Sicyon (Hdt. 6.129). καί τε is slightly redundant, as is the English equivalent 'and also' (*GP* 528).

466 ὅ πέρ τ' ἄρρητον ἄμεινον 'which really would be better left unsaid', *sc.* ἦν ἄν. περ and τε with a relative mark a strong identification between noun and relative: cf. *Il.* 5.477 (Sarpedon criticises the absence of Hector's close relatives in the battle) ἡμεῖς δὲ μαχόμεσθ', οἵ περ τ' ἐπίκουροι ἔνειμεν 'it is we, who really *are* your allies, who do the fighting' (cf. *GH* II.239–40).

467 ἀλλ' ἐπεὶ οὖν 'but since in fact'. οὖν in Homer almost always follows ἐπεί or ὡς and emphasises the fact of the event in the clause, usually looking back to something already mentioned, here the dangers of careless talk (cf. *GP* 417; this example should be added to the small number of 'causal' uses of ἐπεὶ οὖν listed there).   **τὸ πρῶτον** 'right at the start', 'already', i.e. 'since I've not even built up to careless talk, I might as well go on being incautious'.   **ἀνέκραγον:** an undignified action; the verb (κράζω, here in the aorist) is found only here in Homer.

468 εἴθ' ὡς ἡβώοιμι: this motif of wishing one were young again is something of a cliché amongst the old in both Homeric epics. It is found of Nestor (*Il.* 7.133–4, 11.670, 23.629–31), Menelaus (*Od.* 4.341–6) and Laertes (24.376–82); cf. also 17.313–15, where Eum. wishes it on behalf of the dog Argus. There is an element of humour in the use of a somewhat hackneyed epic topos by a tipsy old man.

468–9 ὡς... | ὡς 'in such a way ... as'.

469 ὑπὸ Τροίην 'up under the walls of Troy'.

470 ἡγείσθην: 3rd p. dual of the imperfect of ἡγέομαι.   **Ὀδυσεύς τε καί...Μενέλαος:** cf. 237 for a similar claim to a close association with Idomeneus.

471 τοῖσι δ' ἅμα 'together with them', cf. 25 ἅμ' ἀγρομένοισι σύεσσιν. **ἄνωγον** is the 3rd p.pl. pluperfect of the perfect ἄνωγα, formed with a thematic vowel; cf. γέγωνε beside γεγώνει, from γέγωνα 'shout'. Od. is careful to point out that he was specifically chosen by the great men.

472 ποτί 'towards, against'; though ποτί has a similar sense to προτί, πρός, it has a different origin.

473 περὶ ἄστυ: normally περί in this phrase means 'around', but here it must mean 'near', as it does in Herodotus (cf. J. E. Powell 1977: s.v. 3b, 4). **ῥωπήϊα** 'scrub, undergrowth', from ῥώψ as in 49.

474 πεπτηῶτες: see 354n.

475 βορέαο πεσόντος 'as the north wind fell upon us'. This is preferable to 'when the wind dropped', as in Od. 19.202 ἄνεμος πέσε, of the end of a storm. Cf. Hes. Op. 547 ψυχρὴ γάρ τ' ἠὼς πέλεται βορέαο πέσοντος, where 'dawn is cold when the north wind blows' is better than ' . . . when the north wind drops'; see also Hes. Op. 511 ἐμπίπτων, again of the north wind, Il. 23.216 ἐν δὲ πυρῆι πεσέτην of the winds Boreas and Zephyrus. Meteorologically too, the first is preferable. Though frost is kept away by wind, which might support 'dropped', much more than mere frost is involved here: **476 ἠΰτε πάχνη** suggests the kind of freezing precipitation that accompanies ice-storms. Furthermore, 'fell upon' suits better the piling up of the rigours of the climate in this passage.

476 πηγυλίς 'icy'; a hapax in Homer and generally rare.　　**πάχνη** 'frozen rain', again a hapax in Homer, is a kind of sleet or snow, which freezes on contact with cold objects (so e.g. Epicurus, Ep. Pythocl. 109.1). Naber's λάχνη 'down, wool' is neat but does not suit the viciousness of this storm.

477 περιτρέφετο 'congealed'. τρέφω is used of milk curdling to make cheese in 9.246, and of salt caking on shipwrecked sailors in 23.237; on this use, cf. Griffith 2010.

478–80 ἔνθ' ἄλλοι πάντες ... | αὐτὰρ ἐγώ: for this '(all) the others ... but X (alone)' motif, cf. 1.11–15, 2.82–4 etc.; de Jong 2001: 8.

479 σάκεσιν εἰλυμένοι ὤμους: the shields are possibly the large Mycenean ones which would shelter much of a body in a storm as in war. For εἰλυμένοι, cf. 136n.; ὤμους is an accusative of respect. In Il. 10.151–2 shields are used as pillows.

480 ἑτάροισιν 'with my companions', a locatival dative.

481 ἀφραδίηις 'in my folly'. It is hard to decide between this dative plural and the alternative ἀφραδέως, but the former is slightly the difficilior lectio, and other MSS readings (ἀφραδίηι, ἀμαθία) suggest a noun.　　**ῥιγωσέμεν**

ἔμπης 'that I would be in any way cold'. ῥιγωσέμεν is the future infinitive of ῥιγόω or ῥιγώω, a verb found only here in Homer (ῥιγέω is the usual form); the origin of ἔμπης is unknown (Beekes 417–18), but its meaning is clear. By painting this picture of himself as somewhat over-confident and improvident, Od. presumably aims to win over the herdsmen, who could feel amusedly superior to this self-styled Trojan warrior who did not know how to behave in the cold in which they spent much of their lives. Cf. Minchin 2007: 264–81.

482 ζῶμα 'belt'; cf. Lorimer 1950: 250.

483 τρίχα νυκτός 'the third part of the night'. τρίχα is an infrequent adverb meaning 'in three parts, ways', which is used only here and in the nearly identical 12.312 as the predicate of a verb. This is not easy to explain. For adverbs so used, cf. 13.1n., though this example is not quite parallel. τρίχα seems to be treated as an *a*-stem noun. The other comparable adverbs of number, δίχα, πένταχα and ἔπταχα (434), are not so used. For the three-fold division of the night in Homer, cf. *Il.* 10.251–3.   **μετά ... βεβήκει** 'had passed (the zenith)', and so were on their way to setting (so Eustathius μετεκινήθη, ὡς εἰκὸς πρὸς δύσιν).

485 νύξας: aorist active participle of νύσσω 'nudge'. That the beggar could treat Od. in so familiar a manner hints at his close relationship with the hero.   **ἐμμαπέως:** possibly 'quickly, immediately' (so the scholia), again suggesting that the Od. of the story respects him. The derivation and meaning are however uncertain. In Homer it appears only here and in *Il.* 5.836, where Sthenelus, pushed from his chariot by Athena, springs down ἐμμαπέως; cf. also *H.Aph.* 180 ὁ δ' ἐξ ὕπνοιο μάλ' ἐμμαπέως ὑπάκουσεν, [Hes.] *Scut.* 442. It is probably to be derived from μαπέειν 'grasp' (only in [Hes.] *Scut.* 231, 252, 304; cf. Beekes 903). Attempts to derive it from μάρπτω 'snatch' or μάψ 'rashly' are problematic etymologically or in terms of sense.

486 διογενές κτλ.: after the rather colloquial start to this story and its rather trivial subject matter, the grandiose formulaic address strikes an almost comic note, especially as it is used by Od. to himself. It appears fifteen times in *Od.*, nine times in books 10–11, and in the second half of *Od.* only here and in 16.167, 22.164 and 24.542. This distribution is explained by the fact that the people who have cause to address Od. in the second half of the epic do not know his name. The grandiose beginning is complemented by the unusual poeticisms ἥπαφε, οἰοχίτωνα and φυκτά (for this fondness for unusual words cf. also 203n.), which contrast with what look like much more colloquial, clipped expressions in 487–9: the clash of styles perhaps aims at a studied incompetence in story-telling, or may be put down to the drink.

487 οὔ τοι ἔτι 'I really won't…much longer': οὐ…ἔτι = οὔκετι; for τοι, cf. 13.276n.

487–8 ἀλλά…δάμναται '(because) the cold is killing me'. When two main clauses stand together, one is often logically though not grammatically subordinate to the other (for examples with δέ, see *GH* II.357–8).

488 δάμναται: the active and middle voices, though historically distinct in function, are used interchangeably (sometimes apparently for metrical reasons); compare *Il.* 5.278 οὐ βέλος ὠκὺ δαμάσσατο beside 106 οὐ βέλος ὠκὺ δάμασσεν (*GH* II.172–4). **παρά μ' ἤπαφε:** for ἤπαφε, see 379n.; for the force of παρά, 290n.

489 οἰοχίτων(α) 'wearing only a tunic', found only here in Homer and then in Nonnus. Adjectives in οἰο- are few in number, rare and poetic, the only other in Homer being οἰοπόλος 'lonely'. **ἔμεναι:** infinitive of result after ἤπαφε; cf. 13.160n. **οὐκέτι φυκτὰ πέλονται** 'there is no longer any way to escape (from my situation)'. For the infrequent use of the neuter plural thus as a predicate of verbs meaning 'to be', cf. 8.299 φυκτά, 11.456 οὐκέτι πιστὰ γυναιξὶν 'you can no longer trust women', 20.223 ἀνεκτά.

490 σχέθε 'had ready', unaugmented 3rd p.s. aorist active of ἔχω (root *sekʰ-). The suffix *-θε/-θο seems originally to have had a 'determinative' sense that looked towards the completion of the action: contrast βαρύθω 'be (actually) weighed down', and βαρύνω more generally 'weigh down'. It appears in a small number of aorists (e.g. ἦλθε). νόον σχέθε would therefore mean 'had a plan ready-made', whereas νόον ἔσχε would have meant simply 'made a plan'; σχέθε would thus emphasise the rapidity of Od.'s thought, which is then commented on in the next line. Cf. also 494 ἐπ' ἀγκῶνος κεφαλὴν σχέθεν 'he propped his head on his elbow (and kept it there)', *Il.* 4.113 and in general *GH* I.326–9.

491 οἷος κεῖνος ἔην βουλευέμεν '(because) such a man he was for planning'; for οἷος thus in explanations, cf. also 392n. βουλευέμεν is an infinitive of result, cf. the use of οἷός τε + infinitive. Od. indulges in a little self-flattery, which at the same time will please Eum. by its praise of his master's skills.

494 ἐπ' ἀγκῶνος κεφαλὴν σχέθεν: see 490n.

495 This line was athetised by Aristarchus, because it is odd both that we are not told the content of the dream and that officers should sleep on ambushes. However the line cannot easily be deleted, because of γάρ in the next line, which implies something before it to be explained. Furthermore, γάρ does in effect introduce the message of the dream: they have come too far. **θεῖος…ὄνειρος:** 'divine', because dreams were thought to be sent by gods. The same expression is used in *Il.* 2.56, where Dream himself comes to Agamemnon at Zeus' behest. There is humour in that grand passage being evoked in this rather trivial tale.   ἐνύπνιον 'in my sleep', a neuter adjective in the accusative used as an adverb; cf. 377n.

496 γάρ 'you see'. This use is not common in Homer, but is frequently found in later Greek after a statement that information has been received, as in Aes. *Ag.* 266–7 πεύσηι δὲ χάρμα μεῖζον ἐλπίδος κλύειν· | Πριάμου γὰρ ἡιρήκασιν Ἀργεῖοι πόλιν 'you are about to learn of a joy beyond what you expected to hear: you see, the Argives have taken Priam's city' (cf. *GP* 59).

496–7 ἀλλά τις εἴη | εἰπεῖν 'but still, perhaps there might be someone to tell'; the optative expresses a polite wish.

498 εἰ...ἐποτρύνειε 'to see whether he might encourage'; cf. 13.182n. παρὰ ναῦφι 'from the ships'; ναῦφι is an Aeolic form (contrast Ionic νηυ-); for -φι, see 13.74n.   νέεσθαι: here probably 'come', rather than 'return' (with the man who is sent)'.

499 ὦρτο: see 412n.   **Θόας** 'Mr Swift', an appropriate 'speaking name' for an eager messenger (cf. 416n.), as is acknowledged by 500 καρπαλίμως. Od. and Thoas are variously juxtaposed in mythical tradition: there is an Aetolian of this name and parentage listed after Od. in the Catalogue of Ships (*Il.* 2.638), who kills a man after Od. in the first battle (4. 527–35), and shares a line with him in 7.168, the list of those willing to fight Hector (other mentions of him in 13.215–38 and 15.281–300). He is linked with Od. also in *Ilias Parua*, fr. 7 (*GEF* p. 130) and Hes. *Catalogue* fr. 198; cf. also Apollod. *Epit.* 7.40. On the possible geographical origin of the name, see von Kamptz 1982: 326. The links between Od. and Thoas are discussed by Newton 1997–8 and Marks 2003.

500 φοινικόεσσαν: coloured with the dye made of shellfish; cf. 13.108n. This was the most expensive dye, so Od. is getting a fine cloak. The scansion φοινῑκ- (the noun is φοινῑκ-) became necessary after the insertion of the thematic vowel *o* into these forms: earlier *φοινικϝεσσα would have ended the line appropriately.

501 βῆ δὲ θέειν: see 13.160n. on βῆ ῥ' ἴμεν.

502 φάε δέ '(until) there appeared'; for δέ, cf. 487–8n. φάε is a thematic aorist from the root *φαϝ-, also found in φάος.

503–6 These lines were rightly condemned by Alexandrian scholars on the grounds that they spoil the cleverly indirect way in which Od. makes his request through this 'riddling' (αἰνιγματώδης) tale. The MSS mark the lines as suspicious. 503 (≈ 468) would round the speech off by ring-composition, but it comes in a little surprisingly after the natural end of

the story with the day breaking. The problems are greater in the other
lines. They scarcely deserve Eum.'s praise in 508–9 of their suitability.
Od.'s words here are unnecessarily unsubtle after the delicate humour of
what has gone before: he may have blamed drink for what he was about
to say, but there is no evidence of lack of subtlety in the hint conveyed by
the story. Especially unsubtle is 506 ἀτιμάζουσι, which the herdsmen have
done nothing to merit: he has not explicitly asked them for a cloak, and
the verb implies a strong disparagement, as in 13.141 and 14.164. Od.'s
over-explicit reference to himself as ἐῆος 'good' in 505, and so deserv-
ing, is unnecessarily petulant and does not sit well with his characterisa-
tion generally in the book, not least in his speeches. Furthermore, there
is little logic in saying in 503–4 'I wish I were young and strong again,
(because) then one of the herdsmen would give me a cloak'. It is not
clear whether this is a threat, or a complaint that they only respect the
young (so the scholia). Nor is it clear why they would want to help a fit
young man rather than a beggar in threadbare clothes on such a night.
The lines have the air of having been composed by someone who wanted
to round off the speech by echoing the start and summing up its argument, but thereby produced an unsatisfactory ending. As the Alexandrian
editors rightly sensed, 503–6 are crude, spoil the effect of Od.'s speech,
and should be athetised, but it is hard to say how they got into the text.

505 ἀμφότερον 'for two reasons', adverbial accusative; cf. *Il.* 4.60–1, where
Hera says that her work against Troy must not be wasted, ἀμφότερον γενεῆι
τε καὶ οὕνεκα σὴ παράκοιτις | κέκλημαι, 'both because of my ancestry and
because I am called your wife'.   **ἐῆος** 'good', genitive of ἐΰς (cf. the
adverb εὖ). The MSS give an aspirated form ἑῆος, but this is probably
the result of confusion with forms of the personal pronoun ἑός 'his'; cf.
Hainsworth, *CHO* on 8.325. This is one of three places where the word
could not be a possessive, along with 15.450 and *Il.* 19.342. In general, see
Nussbaum 1998: 85–159, esp. 92–104, 123–9 on this passage, and 146–59
on ἐῆος.

507–17 Eumaeus' eighth speech

As before, Eum. does not rise to the mention of Od. nor does he comment
on whether he gives the story any credence, but acknowledges the merits of
the story and does what he can in his restricted circumstances. He manages
neatly to combine hospitality with a clear indication to the beggar that he
will not get his hands permanently on a cloak. Eum.'s cautious and clear-
eyed view of beggars is again obvious: no amount of entertaining tales is
going to fool him. He does however give a very good reason why cloaks
are scarce, which reminds the beggar that he is dealing with men who are

themselves poor and also softens the remark, as does the promise of future reward from Telemachus. The cloak also turns out, as in the story, to be a very good one (521–2).

508 ὦ γέρον: a bald address, but the warmth here is in his complimentary remarks about the story.   **αἶνος:** a story with a message of some kind, moral or otherwise, as in Hesiod's fable of the hawk and the nightingale (*Op.* 202). In Homer, the word usually means 'praise' (21.110; *Il.* 23.652, 795): cf. Nagy 1999: 235–41.   **μέν τοι** 'in truth', 'really'. The combination, which is rare in Homer and has not yet come together to make the μέντοι of later Greek, has an affirmative sense; cf. 4.157, where Menelaus' recognition of Telemachus causes Peisistratus to say κείνου μέν τοι ὅδ᾽ υἱὸς ἐτήτυμον 'in truth, he really is that man's son'.

509 οὐδέ τί πω παρὰ μοῖραν 'nor in any way at all inappropriately'. πω is always found with a negative in epic: cf. *Il.* 1.108 ἐσθλὸν δ᾽ οὔτε τί πω εἶπας ἔπος. For μοῖρα here used of a story, cf. 8.496 κατὰ μοῖραν. For *Od.*'s tact as a speaker, cf. 13.48n.   **νηκερδές** < negative νη- (13.74n.) + κέρδος 'profit'; i.e. Od.'s tale is both fitting and will get its due reward. For the rewarding of a song with gifts, cf. 13.1–15n.

510–11 = 6.192–3, Nausicaa to Od.

511 ὦν ἐπέοιχ᾽... ἀντιάσαντα 'which a suppliant in distress ought not (to do without) when he comes one's way'; *sc.* μὴ δεύεσθαι depending on ἐπέοικε.

512 νῦν: the positioning of νῦν at the start of the line and before a strong stop is very rare in Homer, and indicates here a very curt and emphatic tone. There is only one other place in Homer where νῦν stands at the start of a line before a strong stop, 3.365–7, where there is no curtness but simple contrast ἔνθα κε λεξαίμην κοίληι παρὰ νηΐ μελαίνηι | νῦν· ἀτὰρ ἠῶθεν... εἶμι 'then I could collect the men by the hollow black ship for now, but at dawn I shall go'. νῦν before a stop is very rare generally: cf. *Il.* 15.254 θάρσει νῦν, 23.587 ἄνσχεο νῦν, *Od.* 15.440 σιγῆι νῦν. Monosyllables at the start of the line followed by a strong stop are naturally powerful: cf. e.g. Hephaestus' call to the gods to witness the adultery of Ares and his wife in 8.306–7 Ζεῦ πάτερ ἠδ᾽ ἄλλοι μάκαρες θεοὶ αἰὲν ἐόντες, | δεῦθ᾽, ἵνα..., 12.438–9 ἐελδομένωι δέ μοι ἦλθον | ὄψ· (of Od.'s keel and mast finally reappearing), *Il.* 2.214 μάψ, ἀτὰρ οὐ κατὰ κόσμον (of Thersites).   **δνοπαλίξεις:** perhaps 'will throw round yourself' or even 'knock about in' (Rieu). The verb is of uncertain meaning and derivation (a derivation from δονέω and πάλλω, both meaning 'shake', seems unlikely; cf. Beekes 343). Its only other occurrence before Oppian is *Il.* 4.472 ἀλλήλοις ἐπόρουσαν, ἀνὴρ δ᾽ ἄνδρ᾽ ἐδνοπάλιζεν 'they attacked each other, and man threw down man'. The scholia suggest ἀμφιέσεις, συρράψεις.

513 ἐπημοιβοί 'that we can exchange amongst ourselves'; elsewhere in Homer only in *Il.* 12.456, of bolts that work in opposing directions. In *Od.* 8.249 εἵματά τ' ἐξημοιβά are 'changes of clothes' as a luxury, something that the poor herdsmen cannot afford.

515–17 = 15.337–9. The better MSS do not have them here, but they make a gentler ending to Eum.'s remarks.

515 Ὀδυσσῆος φίλος υἱός: Eum. will be right about Telemachus' generosity, since an offer of clothes and a journey to wherever he wishes is one of the first promises he makes to Od. (16.78–81). The reference to Telemachus prepares for the move to Sparta in the following episode.

518–33 Eumaeus prepares for a night outside with the pigs

518–19 The spreading of sheep- and goat-skins on the bed provides a country counterpart to the spreading of mattresses, fine robes, rugs and fleeces in the aristocratic world (cf. 7.335–8, 19.317–19). That Od. is given a bed with coverings and a thick cloak, whereas the young swineherds seem to sleep on the ground, is another sign that Eum. now thinks of him as important enough to have special treatment.

520 κατέλεκτ': for the form, see 13.75n. This putting of Od. to bed under clothes closes by ring-composition both the long episode which began with his being put to sleep on the Phaeacian ship (13.73–6), and the events of this day, which began with Eum. spreading clothes for him to sit on, which also caused Od. pleasure (49–51).

521 ἥ οἱ παρακέσκετ' ἀμοιβάς 'which was set aside as his change of clothes' (cf. 513n.). παρακέσκετο is a frequentative form of παρακεῖμαι with *-sk- (see Introduction 5.3 §6.4). This reading of the majority of the MSS would represent one of only two examples of an augmented frequentative in Homer, apart from forms of φάσκω; contrast unaugmented 21.41 κέσκετ'. 20.7 ἐμισγέσκοντο is the other, but it is most probably a mistake (*GH* 1.482). ἀμοιβάς is a feminine nominative singular connected with ἀμοιβαῖος 'exchangeable'.

522 ὄροιτο: 3rd p.s. aorist middle optative of ὄρνυμι 'arise'.

523–33 *Coda.* The book ends as it began with Eum. preparing diligently to do his tasks, preferring to protect his pigs in the cold than sleep with his men within. The description recalls the arming scenes of heroes: see further Introduction p. 20.

524 οὐδέ: see 13.212n.

525 κοιμηθῆναι: an infinitive explaining the nature of the κοῖτος that displeased Eum.

526 ἰών expresses purpose, as 532 κείων.   **ὁπλίζετο** 'began to dress, equip himself'.

527 βιότου περικήδετο: looks back to a similar description of Eum. in 3–4; cf. 531n.   **νόσφιν ἐόντος:** 'though he was absent', in apposition to οἱ, with the genitive instead of the expected dative as often in Homer; cf. e.g. 9.256–7 ἡμῖν δ' αὖτε κατεκλάσθη φίλον ἦτορ | δεισάντων φθόγγον 'our heart was cast down when we were frightened by the noise'.

529 ἕσσατ': 3rd p.s. aorist middle indicative of ἕννυμι 'clothe'. The augment in short e- rather than long before a word originally beginning with ϝ, where metathesis of quantity is not involved, is problematic; cf. also ἐάγη, ἐάλη (*GH* 1.480). Contrast this form with 295 ἑέσσατο < ἕζομαι, where see note.   **ἀλεξάνεμον** 'that kept off the wind'; only here in Homer.

530 νάκην 'goat-skin'; only here in Homer. The goat- or sheep-skin was the characteristic garment of the country-dweller rather than the townsman: cf. Thgn. 53–6 new politicians in goat-skins have taken over the city; Men. *Epitr.* 12; Hesych. κ 1887, Suda κ 1114–15 κατωνάκη.

531 ἀλκτῆρα: lit. 'something to protect him against', with the same root as ἀλεξάνεμος (529), here in the form ἀλκ-. Protection against dogs looks back to the start of the episode (cf. 527n.).

532 κείων: on κείω, see 13.17.

533 ὑπ' ἰωγῆι 'in a place of shelter from', from ἄγνυμι 'break'; only here in Homer, but cf. 5.404 ἐπιωγαί 'sheltered spots'.

The narrative now moves to Sparta, and will return to this story in 15.301.

GLOSSARY OF LINGUISTIC TERMS

* indicates a form which does not appear in the evidence, but which is
reconstructed on historical principles.
< means 'is derived from'.
> means 'gives rise to'.

anacolouthon: a break in the expected run of the syntax, also called *non
sequitur*, cf. e.g. 13.81–5.
apocope: the 'cutting' off of the end of a word, as in the loss of the final
vowel in the prepositions such as ἄν for ἀνά, κάτ for κατά. Cf.
Introduction 5.3 §7.5.3.
apodotic: apparently superfluous use of καί and δέ to introduce a main
clause after a subordinate one. Cf. Introduction 5.3 §12.3; 13.144n.
aspect: a form of the verb indicating the kind of action involved, as
opposed to 'tense', which conveys the timing of the action. See
further Introduction 5.3 §9.1.
athematic verbs, nouns: forms of verbs and nouns where there is no *thematic*
or *stem* vowel between the root and the *suffix*. So, from τίθημι (root
θη-/θε-), τί-θε-μεν ἔ-θε-μεν, in contrast to λύ-ο-μεν; contrast *thematic verbs*.
Athematic nouns similarly add the ending to the stem, as in φύλακ-ς
(-ξ), φύλακ-α, φύλακ-ος etc., in contrast to λόγ-ο-ς, λόγ-ο-ν etc.
cognate: indicates that a word is historically related to another, as
'ἐπι-βώ-τορι "herdsman" is cognate with βό-σκ-ω "pasture"'
(13.222n.).
deictic: from δείκνυμι 'show', essentially synonymous with 'demonstrative'.
deliberative: used of subjunctives in questions such as ἴωμεν: 'Are we to go?'
desiderative: a form of the verb that indicates a wish that its action should
take place, as 13.17 κακκείοντες 'in order to, desiring to, go to bed';
often indicated by -s- before the endings, it is the origin of many
futures. Cf. Introduction 5.3 §6.6.1.
diektasis: see 13.93n.
elision: the loss of a vowel at the end of a word before another vowel, as
13.1 ἔφαθ' οἱ. Cf. Introduction 5.3 §4.2.
enclitic: a class of words, such as indefinite forms of τίς, some particles
such as γε, τε, most present indicative forms of εἰμί, closely
connected to the preceding word and where possible throwing their
accent back onto it, as 13.5 οὔ τι, 69 σῖτόν τε. Cf. *proclitic*.
enjambment: the running over of a sentence from one line to the next.
ephelcystic: used of the -ν which is sometimes 'brought in' at the end of a
word to lengthen a syllable or avoid hiatus, as 13.3 φώνησέν τε and
13.9 ἐμοῖσιν ἀκουάζεσθε. Also called '*n* moveable'.

frequentative: see *iterative*.

gnomic aorist: historically, the aorist does not express time, but *aspect*, and so can be used of things which are generally true or happen regularly. Cf. e.g. 13.33n. on κάτεδυ.

grade: used of variations (*a*-grade, *o*-grade, zero grade) in the root of a word. See Introduction 5.2a.

hiatus (cf. Lat. *hiare* 'gape'): two vowels and/or diphthongs standing together without any change to the first, as in 13.4 Ὀδυσεῦ ἔπει. See also *elision*, *synizesis*.

Hieroglyphic Luwian: a language of the Anatolian branch of Indo-European written in hieroglyphic rather than cuneiform characters.

IE: Indo-European, the language group to which Greek and Latin belong. It is the ancestor of a large range of languages, which together constitute the most widely spoken language family. They are divided into these groups: the extant Hellenic, Indo-Iranian, Italic, Celtic, Germanic, Armenian, Balto-Slavic and Albanian; and the extinct Anatolian (e.g. Hittite, Luwian and Lydian) and Tocharian (western China).

inceptive (cf. Lat. *incipio* 'begin', Eng. 'incipient'): used of imperfects indicating the start of an action, as 14.456 ἐσσεύοντο 'they began to hurry off'.

instrumental: old case indicating the object or person by which an event came about; subsumed into the dative.

iterative: a form of a verb, often with -*sk*-, indicating that an action took place many times (also called 'frequentative'), as 13.167 εἴπεσκεν 'kept saying'.

jussive: conveying an order (Lat. *iubeo*, *iussus* 'order, ordered'); used of subjunctives such as ἴωμεν 'let us go'.

laryngeal: see Introduction 5.3 §2c.

litotes: understatement; cf. 13.384n.

locative: old case indicating where something happened; subsumed into the dative.

paratactic: a style of writing or speaking in which clauses are juxtaposed to each other, rather than being linked by conjunctions in a syntactic manner. Cf. Introduction 5.3 §11.1; contrast *syntactic*.

partitive: type of genitive which shows the relationship of a part to a whole, e.g. 'first of all'.

postpositive: often used of prepositions, describes a word which is placed after rather than before the word it governs, as 14.205 θεὸς ὣς 'like a god'.

prefix: an element added to the beginning of a word, as the preposition in a compound verb, the augment etc. Cf. *suffix*.

preverb: a name for 'prepositions' when they still had an adverbial force
and were not directly connected to nouns and verbs. Cf.
Introduction 5.3 §7.5.

privative: an element that negates the meaning of a word, such as the ἀ- in
ἄ-λογος 'without *logos*, irrational', 13.135 ἄ-σπετος 'unsayable'.

proclitic: an accentless word closely connected with the following word,
such as prepositions or forms of the article beginning with a vowel.
Cf. *enclitic*.

proleptic: from λαμβάνω 'take', used of adjectives with a prospective sense,
i.e. whose meanings will come about in the future. Cf. 13.39n. on
ἀπήμονα.

psilosis: substitution of a smooth for a rough breathing, cf. e.g. 14.220
ἐπάλμενος from ἐπί + ἄλλομαι. This is a feature especially of the
Aeolic Lesbian dialect.

quantitative metathesis: the exchange of quantities between two vowels. Cf.
14.222n.; Introduction 5.3 §1.1.4.

reflex: a later form that develops out of an earlier form, as in 14.3n. 'ὑ- is
the normal Greek reflex of IE *su- "pig"', i.e. in Greek *h- is the
'reflex' of the original IE initial *s-.

root: the basic element of a word, as λυ- for λύω etc.

root aorist: an aorist formed by adding *suffixes* straight onto the *root*, as
14.412 ὦρ-το from ὄρ-νυμι.

short-vowel subjunctives: earlier forms of the subjunctive with the
alternation ε/ο in the *stem* vowel (e.g. 14.45 ἴομεν), rather than the
later η/ω.

sigmatic: used of aorists which have -s- before the endings, as in ἐ-λυ-σ-α.

stem: element added to the *root*, as the omicron in λύ-ο-μεν or the epsilon
in ἐλυ-ε-ς. See also *thematic verbs*.

stop: a consonant whose pronunciation involves the stopping of the flow
of air followed by its release, such as *k, g, t, d, p*.

suffix: an element, added to the end of a *root* or *stem*, which may be an
indication of person, as -μεν in λύ-ο-μεν showing the first person
plural, or an indication of case, as -α in ἄνδρ-α indicating the
accusative. Cf. *prefix*.

synizesis: < σύν + ἵζω 'together' + 'sit', the collapsing together of two
vowels or vowels and diphthongs (contrast *elision, hiatus*), as 14.251
θεοῖσι, where θεοισ- is scanned as a single long syllable. Cf.
Introduction 4.2.

syntactic (also *hypotactic*): a style of writing or speaking in which the
clauses are linked together by conjunctions; contrast *paratactic*.

thematic verb, nouns: verbs or nouns where there is a 'thematic' or *stem*
vowel between the *root* and the ending, as in λύ-ο-μεν, λύ-ε-τε,

λύ-ε-σθαι, in contrast to e.g. athematic τί-θε-μεν; cf. *athematic verbs*. For thematic nouns, cf. λόγ-ο-ς, λόγ-ο-ν, in contrast to φύλακ-α.

vocalic consonants: consonants with a vocalic element. Cf. Introduction 4.2.

zero grade: see *grade* and Introduction 5.2a.

WORKS CITED

Adcock, F. and Mosley, D. J. 1975: *Diplomacy in ancient Greece*, London.
Ahl, F. 2002: 'Wordplay and apparent fiction in the *Odyssey*', *Arethusa* 35: 117–32.
Ahl, F. and Roisman, H. M. 1996: *The Odyssey re-formed*, Ithaca and London.
Allan, W. A. 2006: 'Divine justice and cosmic order in early Greek epic', *JHS* 126: 1–35.
Allen, N. 2001: 'Athena and Durga: warrior goddesses in Greek and Sanskrit epic', in S. Deacy and A. Villing, eds. *Athena in the Classical World*, (Leiden) 367–82.
　2009: 'L'Odyssée comme amalgame: Ulysse en Ithaque et comparaisons sanscrites', *Gaia* 12: 79–102.
Allen, T. W. 1924: *Homer: the origins and the transmission*, Oxford.
Alt, K. 1998: 'Homers Nymphengrotte in der Deutung des Porphyrios', *Hermes* 126: 466–87.
Ameis, K. F. and Cauer, C. 1985: *Anhang zu Homers Odyssey Schulausgabe*, vol. III, 3rd edn, Leipzig.
Amory, A. 1963: 'The reunion of Odysseus and Penelope', in C. H. Taylor Jr., ed. *Essays on the Odyssey* (Bloomington) 100–21.
Anderson, Ø. and Dickie, M. W. (eds.) 1995: *Homer's world: fiction, tradition, reality*, Athens and Bergen.
Andersson, T. M. 1976: *Early epic scenery: Homer, Virgil, and the medieval legacy*, Ithaca.
Antonaccio, C. M. 1995: *An archaeology of ancestors: tomb cult and hero cult in early Greece*, Lanham.
Arend, W. 1933: *Die typischen Scenen bei Homer*, Berlin.
Arnott, W. G. 2007: *Birds in the ancient world from A to Z*, London and New York.
Austin, N. 1972: 'Name magic in the *Odyssey*', *ClAnt* 5: 1–19.
　1975: *Archery at the Dark of the Moon: poetic problems in Homer's Odyssey*, Berkeley, Los Angeles and London.
Bakker, E. J., 1993: 'Discourse and performance: involvement, visualization and "presence" in Homeric poetry', *ClAnt* 12: 1–29.
　(ed.) 2010: *A companion to the ancient Greek language*, Oxford.
Barnes, T. G. 2011: 'Homeric ἀνδροτῆτα καὶ ἥβην', *JHS* 131: 1–14.
Bassett, S. E. 1919: 'Note on Odyssey XIV.138–47', *CJ* 14: 385–6.
　1920: '"Ὕστερον πρότερον Ὁμηρικῶς (Cic. *Att.* 1.16.1)', *HSPh* 31: 39–62.
　1933: 'The fate of the Phaeacians (ν 125–87; cf. θ 565–7)', *CPh* 28: 305–7.
　1938: *The poetry of Homer*, Berkeley.
Beck, D. 2005: *Homeric conversation*, Cambridge, MA.

Beck, W. 1991: 'Dogs, dwellings, and masters: ensemble and symbol in the *Odyssey*', *Hermes* 119: 158–67.

Beekes, R. S. P. 1969: *The development of the Proto-Indo-European laryngeals in Greek*, Paris.

1995–6: 'Aithiopes', *Glotta* 73: 12–34.

Benton, S. 1934–5: 'Excavations at Ithaca. III: The Cave at Polis I', *ABSA* 35: 45–73.

Bettini, M. 1988: '"Hθεῖος', *RFIC* 116: 154–66.

Bittlestone, R. (with J. Diggle and J. Underhill) 2005: *Odysseus Unbound: the search for Homer's Ithaca*, Cambridge.

Block, E. 1982: 'The narrator speaks: apostrophe in Homer and Vergil', *TAPhA* 112: 7–22.

1985: 'Clothing makes the man: a pattern in the *Odyssey*', *TAPhA* 115: 1–11.

Boardman, J. 1999: *The Greeks overseas: their early colonies and trade*, 4th edn, London.

Bouvier, D. 2008: 'Formes de "retours à la liberté" et statut de l'"affranchi" dans la poésie homérique', in A. Gonzales, ed. *La fin du statut servile? (Affranchissement, libération, abolition)* (Besançon) 9–16.

Bowie, A. M. 1995: 'Greek sacrifice: forms and functions', in A. Powell, ed. *The Greek world* (London) 463–82.

2003: 'Fate may harm me, I have dined today: near-eastern royal banquets and Greek symposia in Herodotus', in C. Orfanos & J.-C. Carrière, eds. *Symposium: banquet et représentations en Grèce et à Rome* (Toulouse) 99–109.

Bowie, E. L. 1986: 'Early Greek elegy, symposium, and public festival', *JHS* 106: 13–35.

Bowra, C. M. 1966: *Heroic poetry*, London.

Bremer, J. M., de Jong, I. J. F and Kalff, J. (eds.) 1987: *Homer: beyond oral poetry: recent trends in Homeric interpretation*, Amsterdam.

Bryce, T. 2003: *Letters of the Great Kings of the ancient Near East: the royal correspondence of the Late Bronze Age*, London.

Buck, C. D. and Petersen, W. 1944: *A reverse index of Greek nouns and adjectives arranged by terminations with brief historical introductions*, Chicago.

Burkert, W. 1955: *Zum altgriechischen Mitleidsbegriff*, Erlangen.

1985: *Greek religion: archaic and classical* (tr. J. Raffan), Oxford.

1988: 'Imaginary words and epic tradition in the *Odyssey*', available at: www.classicalassociation.org/Audio/151–175.html, no. 175.

1992: *The orientalising revolution: Near Eastern influence on Greek culture in the early Archaic Age* (tr. M. E. Pinder and W. Burkert), Cambridge, MA.

1997: 'The Song of Ares and Aphrodite: on the relationship between the *Iliad* and the *Odyssey*', in Wright and Jones 1997: 249–62.

Byre, C. S. 1994: 'On the description of the Harbor of Phorkys and the Cave of the Nymphs, *Odyssey* 13.96–112', *AJPh* 115: 1–13.

Calhoun, G. M. 1935: 'The art of formula in Homer – ΕΠΕΑ ΠΤΕΡΟΕΝΤΑ', *CPh* 30: 215–27.

Carter, J. P. and Morris, S. P. (eds.) 1995: *The ages of Homer: a tribute to Emily Townsend Vermeule*, Austin.

Casevitz, M. 1989: 'L'humour d'Homère: Ulysse et Polyphème au chant 9 de l'*Odyssée*', in id., ed. *Etudes homériques* (Paris) 55–8.

Cassio, A. C. 2004, 'Spoken language and written text: the case of ἀλλοειδέα (Hom. *Od.* 12.194)', in Penney 2004: 83–94.

Cave, T. 1988: *Recognitions: a study in poetics*, Oxford.

Chantraine, P. 1945: *Morphologie historique du grec*, Paris.

 2009: *Dictionnaire étymologique de la langue grecque: histoire des mots, achevé par J. Taillardat, O. Masson et J.-L. Perpillou*, nouvelle éd., Paris.

Clarke, M. 1999: *Flesh and spirit in the songs of Homer: a study of words and myths*, Oxford.

Clay, J. S. 1974: 'Demas and aude: the nature of divine transformation in Homer', *Hermes* 102: 129–36.

 1983: *The wrath of Athena: gods and men in the Odyssey*, Lanham, New York and London.

Cole, T. 1983: 'Archaic truth', *QUCC* 13: 7–28.

Cook, E. F. 2004: 'Near Eastern sources for the palace of Alkinoos', *AJA* 108: 43–77.

Craik, E. M. (ed.) 1990: *'Owls to Athens': essays on classical subjects presented to Sir Kenneth Dover*, Oxford.

Currie, B. G. F. 2005: *Pindar and the cult of heroes*, Oxford and New York.

 2013: 'The supposed genitive Ὀδυσεῦς (Od. 24.398) and Homer's "awkward" parentheses', *JHS* 133: 21–41.

Dalley, S. (ed. and tr.) 2000: *Myths from Mesopotamia: Creation, the Flood, Gilgamesh and others*, rev. edn, Oxford.

Danek, G. 1998: *Epos und Zitat: Studien zu den Quellen der Odyssee*, Vienna.

Davidson, J. A. 1962: 'The transmission of the text', in Wace and Stubbings 1962: 234–65.

Davies, M. and Kathirithamby, J. 1986: *Greek insects*, London.

de Jong, I. J. F. 1985: 'Eurykleia and Odysseus' scar: *Odyssey* 19.393–466', *CQ* 35: 517–18.

 1992: 'The subjective style in Odysseus' wanderings', *CQ* 42: 1–11.

 1993: 'Studies in Homeric denomination', *Mnemosyne* 46: 289–306.

 2001: *A narratological commentary on the Odyssey*, Cambridge.

 2009: 'Between word and deed: hidden thoughts in the *Odyssey*', in Doherty 2009: 62–90 (= de Jong and Sullivan 1994: 27–50).

de Jong, I. J. F. and Sullivan, J. P. (eds.) 1994: *Modern critical theory and Classical literature*, Leiden, New York and Cologne.

de Lamberterie, C. 1992: 'Le problème de l'homonymie: les trois verbes ὀφέλλω en grec ancien', in Létoublon 1992: 201–17.

de Sousa, P. 1995: 'Greek piracy', in Powell 1995: 178–98.

Deoudi, M. 1999: *Heroenkulte in homerischer Zeit*, Oxford.

2008: *IΘAKI: die Polis-Höhle, Odysseus und die Nymphen*, Thessaloniki.

Detienne, M. and Vernant, J.-P. 1978: *Cunning intelligence in Greek culture and society*, Hassocks and New Jersey.

Dickey, E. 1996. *Greek forms of address: from Herodotus to Lucian*, Oxford.

Dickie, M. W. 1995: 'The geography of Homer's world', in M. Dickie and Ø. Andersen, eds. *Homer's world: fiction, tradition, reality* (Athens and Bergen) 29–56.

Dimock, G. E. 1989: *The unity of the Odyssey*, Amherst.

Doherty, L. E. 1991: 'Athena and Penelope as foils for Odysseus in the *Odyssey*', *QUCC* 39: 31–44.

1995: *Siren songs: gender, audiences, and narrators in the Odyssey*, Ann Arbor.

(ed.) 2009: *Oxford readings in Classical studies: Homer's Odyssey*, Oxford.

Donlan, W. 1973: 'The tradition of anti-aristocratic thought in early Greek poetry', *Historia* 22: 145–54.

1982: 'Reciprocities in Homer', *CW* 75: 137–75.

1997: 'The Homeric economy', in Morris and Powell 1997: 649–67.

1999: 'Changes and shifts in the meaning of *demos* in the literature of the archaic period', in id. *The aristocratic ideal and selected papers* (Wauconda) 225–36 (= *PP* 25 (1970) 381–95).

Dougherty, C. 2001: *The raft of Odysseus: the ethnographic imagination of Homer's Odyssey*, Oxford and New York.

Duffy, J. M., Sheridan, P. F., Westerink, L. G. and White, J. A. (eds.) 1969: *Porphyry: The Cave of the Nymphs in the Odyssey*, Buffalo.

Edmunds, S. T. 1990: *Homeric nēpios*, New York and London.

Edwards, A. T. 1985: *Achilles in the Odyssey: ideologies of heroism in the Homeric epic*, Königstein.

1993: 'Homer's ethical geography: country and city in the *Odyssey*', *TAPhA* 123: 27–78.

Edwards, M. W. 1969: 'On some "answering" expressions in Homer', *CPh* 64: 81–7.

1970: 'Homeric speech introductions', *HSCPh* 74: 1–36.

1975: 'Type-scenes and Homeric hospitality', *TAPhA* 105: 51–72.

1987: 'Topos and transformation in Homer', in Bremer, de Jong and Kalff 1987: 47–60.

1992: 'Homer and the oral tradition: the type-scene', *Oral Tradition* 7: 284–330.

Eitrem, S. 1915: *Opferritus und Voropfer der Griechen und Römer*, Kristiania.

Elliger, W. 1975: *Die Darstellung der Landschaft in der griechischen Dichtung*, Berlin.

Emlyn-Jones, C. 1984: 'The reunion of Penelope and Odysseus', *G&R* 31: 1–18.

1986: 'True and lying tales in the *Odyssey*', *G&R* 33: 1–10.

Emlyn-Jones, C., Hardwick, L. and Purkis, J. (eds.) 1992: *Homer: readings and images*, London.

Erbse, H. 1972: *Beiträge zum Verständnis der Odyssee*, Berlin.

Faraone, C. 1987: 'Hephaestus the magician and Near Eastern parallels for Alcinous' watchdogs', *GRBS* 28: 257–80.

Farron, S. G. 1979–80: 'The *Odyssey* as an anti-aristocratic statement', *StudAnt* 1: 50–101.

Fenik, B. 1974: *Studies in the Odyssey*, Wiesbaden.

Finkelberg, M. 1985–8: 'Enchantment and other effects of poetry in the Homeric *Odyssey*', *SCI* 8–9: 1–10.

Finley, M. I. 1978: *The world of Odysseus*, rev. ed. New York.

Foley, J. M. 1990: *Traditional oral epic: the Odyssey, Beowulf, and the Serbo-Croatian Return Song*, Berkeley, Los Angeles and London.

1991: *Immanent art: from structure to meaning in traditional oral epic*, Bloomington.

1995: 'Sixteen moments of silence in Homer', *QUCC* 50: 7–26.

(ed.) 2005: *A companion to ancient Epic*, Oxford.

Forbes Irving, P. M. C. 1990: *Metamorphosis in Greek myths*, Oxford.

Fraenkel, E. 1923: 'Homerische Wörter', in *ANTIDORON: Festschrift Jacob Wackernagel* (Göttingen) 274–82.

Friedrich, R. 1989: 'Zeus and the Phaeacians: *Odyssey* 13.158', *AJPh* 110: 395–9.

Gainsford, P. 2003: 'Formal analysis of recognition scenes in the *Odyssey*', *JHS* 123: 41–59.

Gaisser, J. H. 1969: 'A structural analysis of the digressions in the *Iliad* and the *Odyssey*', *HSCPh* 73: 1–43.

García-Ramón, J. L. 1998–9: 'Mycenaean "e-u-de-we-ro" /Eʰu-dewelo/ "having nice (late) afternoons", Homeric εὐδείελος and Cyrenaean Εὐεσπερίδες', *Minos* 33–4: 135–48.

2002: 'Mykenisch "o-ti-na-wo" /Ortinawos/ und vedisch "íyarti navam", homerisch ὀρτίλοχος/ὀρσίλοχος, *ὧρσε λόχον und λόχον εἶσε', in M. Fritz and S. Zeilfelder, eds. *Novalis indogermanica: Festschrift für Günter Neumann zum 80. Geburtstag* (Graz) 183–193.

Goldhill, S. 1991: *The poet's voice*, Cambridge.

Gould, J. P. 1973: 'Hiketeia', *JHS* 93: 74–103.

Gow, A. S. F. 1914: 'The ancient plough', *JHS* 34: 249–75.

(ed.) 1952: *Theocritus*, 2 vols., 2nd edn, Cambridge.

Grayson, A. K. 1976: *Assyrian royal inscriptions*, vol. II, Wiesbaden.

Graziosi, B. 2008: Review of Bittlestone 2005, *JHS* 128: 178–80.

Graziosi, B. and Haubold, J. (eds.) 2010: *Homer: Iliad book VI*, Cambridge.

Greene, E. S. 1995: 'The critical element in the embarkation scenes of the *Odyssey*', *GRBS* 36: 217–30.

Griffith, D. R. 2010: 'Τρέφειν γάλα (*Odyssey* 9.246)', *CPh* 105: 301–8.

Grottanelli, C. 1989: 'The roles of the guest in the epic banquet', in C. Zaccagnini, ed. *Production and consumption in the ancient Near East* (Budapest) 272–332.

Gschnitzer, F. 1976: *Studien zur griechischen Terminologie der Sklaverei*, part II: *Untersuchungen zur älteren, insbesondere homerischen Sklaventerminologie*, Wiesbaden.

Hackstein, O. 2010: 'The Greek of epic', in Bakker 2010: 403–23.

Haft, A. J. 1984: 'Odysseus, Idomeneus, and Meriones: the Cretan lies of *Odyssey* 13–19', *CJ* 79: 289–306.

Hainsworth, J. B. 1961: 'Odysseus and the dogs', *G&R* 8: 122–5.

1988: 'The epic dialect', in *CHO* I.24–32.

Hajnal, I. 1995: *Studien zum mykenischen Kasussystem*, Berlin and New York.

2004: 'Die Tmesis bei Homer und auf den mykenischen Linear-B Tafeln: ein chronologisches Paradox?', in Penney 2004: 146–78.

Hall, E. M. 2008: *The return of Ulysses: a cultural history of Homer's Odyssey*, London and New York.

Halliwell, F. S. 2008: *Greek laughter: a study in cultural psychology from Homer to early Christianity*, Oxford.

Harrison, T. 1998: 'Herodotus' conception of foreign languages', *Histos* 2, available at: www.dur.ac.uk/Classics/histos/1998/harrison.html.

Harsh, P. W. 1950: 'Penelope and Odysseus in *Odyssey* XIX', *AJPh.* 71: 1–21.

Haslam, M. 1997: 'Homeric papyri and transmission of the text', in Morris and Powell 1997: 55–100.

Haubold, J. 2000: *Homer's people: epic poetry and social formation*, Cambridge.

Haug, D. 2002: *Les phases de l'évolution de la langue épique: trois études de linguistique homérique*, Göttingen.

Hellwig, B. 1964: *Raum und Zeit im homerischen Epos*, Hildesheim.

Heubeck, A. 1987: 'ἀμύμων', *Glotta* 65: 37–44.

Higbie, C. 1995: *Heroes' names, Homeric identities*, New York and London.

Hölscher, U. 1939: *Untersuchungen zur Form der 'Odyssee': Szenenwechsel und gleichzeitige Handlungen*, Berlin.

Hooker, J. T. 1987: 'Homeric φίλος', *Glotta* 65: 44–65.

Horrocks, G. C. 1984: *Space and time in Homer: prepositional and adverbial particles in the Greek epic*, New York.

1997: *Homer's dialect*, in Morris and Powell 1997: 193–217.

Janko, R. 1982: *Homer, Hesiod and the Hymns: diachronic development in epic diction*, Cambridge.

(ed.) 1992: *The Iliad: a commentary*, vol. IV: *books 13–16*, Cambridge.

Jebb, R. C. (ed.) 1932: *Sophocles: the plays and fragments*, part IV: *Philoctetes*, Cambridge.

Jensen, M. S. 1980: *The Homeric question and the oral-formulaic theory*, Copenhagen.

Jones, P. V. 1992: 'The past in Homer's *Odyssey*', *JHS* 112: 74–90.

Kahane, A. 1994: *The interpretation of order: a study in the poetics of Homeric repetition*, Oxford.

2005: *Diachronic dialogues: authority and continuity in Homer and the Homeric tradition*, Lanham.

Katz, J. 2010: 'Inherited poetics', in Bakker 2010: 357–69.

Kazhdan, A. and Franklin, S. 1984: *Studies on Byzantine literature of the eleventh and twelfth centuries*, Cambridge.

Kearns, E. 1982: 'The Return of Odysseus: a Homeric theoxeny', *CQ* 32: 2–8.

Kelly, A. 2007: *A referential commentary and lexicon to Homer, Iliad VIII*, Oxford and New York.

Killen, J. T. and Olivier, J.-P. 1989: *The Knossos tablets*, 5th edn, Salamanca.

Kirk, G. S. 1962: *The Songs of Homer*, Cambridge.

(ed.) 1985: *The Iliad: a commentary*, vol. I: *books 1–4*, Cambridge.

Knox, M. O. 1971: 'Huts and farm buildings in Homer', *CQ* 21: 27–31.

1973: 'Megarons and ΜΕΓΑΡΑ', *CQ* 23: 1–21.

Köhnken, A. 1976: 'Die Narbe des Odysseus: ein Beitrag zur homerisch-epischen Erzähltechnik', *A&A* 22: 101–14.

Kumpf, M. M. 1984: *Four indices of Homeric hapax legomena together with statistical data*, Hildesheim.

Kurt, C. 1979: *Seemännische Fachausdrücke bei Homer: unter Berücksichtigung Hesiods und der Lyriker bis Bakchylides*, Göttingen.

Lamberton, R. 1986: *Homer the theologian: Neoplatonist allegorical reading and the growth of the epic tradition*, Berkeley, Los Angeles and London.

Lane Fox, R. 2008: *Travelling heroes: Greeks and their myths in the epic age of Homer*, London.

La Roche, J. 1898: 'Zahlenverhältnisse im homerischen Vers', *WS* 20: 1–69.

Lateiner, D. 1977: 'No laughing matter: a literary tactic in Herodotus', *TAPhA* 107: 173–82.

Lawrence, T. E. 1940: *The Odyssey of Homer*, Oxford.

Leaf, W. (ed.) 1900–2: *The Iliad*, 2 vols., 2nd edn, London.

Lehrs, K. 1882: *De Aristarchi studiis Homericis*, 3rd edn, Leipzig.

Létoublon, F. 1992: *La langue et les textes en grec ancien: actes du colloque Pierre Chantraine (Grenoble – 5–8 Septembre 1989)*, Amsterdam.

Leukart, A. 1994: *Die frühgriechischen Nomina auf -tās und -ās: Untersuchungen zu ihrer Herkunft und Ausbreitung (unter Vergleich mit den Nomina auf -eús)*, Vienna.

Leumann, M. 1950: *Homerische Wörter*, Basel.

Levaniouk, O. 2010: *Eve of the Festival: making myth in Odyssey 19*: Washington, DC.

2012: 'οὐ χρώμεθα τοῖς ξενικοῖς ποιήμασι: questions about evolution and fluidity of the *Odyssey*', in Montanari, Rengakos and Tsagalis 2012: 369–409.

Levine, D. B. 1982: 'Homeric laughter and the unsmiling suitors', *CJ* 78: 97–104.

Lilja, S. 1976: *Dogs in ancient Greek poetry*, Helsinki.

Lincoln, B. 1999: *Theorizing myth: narrative, ideology, and scholarship*, Chicago and London.

Lord, A. B. 2000: *The Singer of Tales*, 2nd edn by S. Mitchell and G. Nagy, Cambridge, MA and London.

Lorimer, H. L. 1950: *Homer and the monuments*, London.

Louden, B. 1993: 'Pivotal counterfactuals in Homeric epic', *ClAnt* 12: 181–98.

1997: 'Eumaios and Alkinoos: the audience and the "Odyssey"', *Phoenix* 51: 95–114.

1999: *The Odyssey: structure, narration, and meaning*, Baltimore and London.

2011: *Homer's Odyssey and the ancient Near East*, Cambridge.

Lowe, N. J. 2000: *The classical plot and the invention of western narrative*, Cambridge.

Luce, J. V. 1998: *Celebrating Homer's landscapes: Troy and Ithaca revisited*, Princeton.

Ludwich, A. 1884–5: *Aristarchs homerische Textkritik*, Leipzig.

Luther, A. (ed.) 2006: *Geschichte und Fiktion in der homerischen Odyssee*, Munich.

Malkin, I. 1998: *The returns of Odysseus: colonization and ethnicity*, Berkeley, Los Angeles and London.

Mark, S. E. 2005: *Homeric seafaring*, College Station.

Marks, J. R. 2003: 'Alternative Odysseys: the case of Thoas and Odysseus', *TAPhA* 133: 209–26.

2008: *Zeus in the Odyssey*, Cambridge, MA and London.

Martin, R. P. 1989: *The language of heroes: speech and performance in the* Iliad, Ithaca.

n.d.: 'Cretan Homers: tradition, politics, fieldwork', *classics@* 3 (online journal at chs.harvard.edu).

Mazur, P. S. 2010–11: 'Formulaic and thematic allusions in *Iliad* 9 and *Odyssey* 14', *CW* 104: 3–15.

Meillet, A. 1923: *Les origines indo-européennes des mètres grecques*, Paris.

Mele, A. 1968: *Società e lavoro nei poemi omerici*, Naples.

Minchin, E. 1992: 'Homer springs a surprise: Eumaios' tale at *Od.* o 403–84', *Hermes* 120: 259–66.

2001: *Homer and the resources of memory: some applications of cognitive theory to the Iliad and the Odyssey*, Oxford.

2002: 'Speech acts in the everyday world and in Homer: the rebuke as a case study', in Worthington and Foley 2002: 70–97.

2007: *Homeric voices: discourse, memory, gender*, Oxford.

Montanari, F., Rengakos A. and Tsagalis, C. (eds.) 2012: *Homeric contexts: neoanalysis and the interpretation of oral poetry*, Berlin and Boston.

Morris, I. 1997: 'Homer and the Iron Age', in Morris and Powell 1997: 535–59.

Morris, I. and Powell, B. (eds.) 1997: *A new Companion to Homer*, Leiden, New York and Cologne.

Morrison, J. S. and Williams, R. T. 1968: *Greek oared ships, 900–322 B C*, Cambridge.

Mumm, P. A. 2004: 'Zur funktion der homerischen Augments', in *Analecta homini universali dicata: Festschrift für Oskar Panagl zum 65. Geburtstag*, vol. 1, Stuttgart: 148–58.

Munro, D. B. 1891: *A grammar of the Homeric dialect*, 2nd edn, Oxford.

(ed.) 1901: *Homer's Odyssey: books XIII–XXIV*, Oxford.

Murnaghan, S. 1987: *Disguise and recognition in the Odyssey*, Princeton.

Nagler, M. N. 1974: *Spontaneity and tradition: a study in the oral art of Homer*, Berkeley.

Nagy, G. 1974: *Comparative studies in Greek and Indic meter*, Cambridge, MA.

1997: 'Homeric scholia', in Morris and Powell 1997: 101–22.

1999: *The best of the Achaeans: concepts of the hero in archaic Greek poetry*, rev. edn, Baltimore.

Naiden, F. S. 2006: *Ancient supplication*, Oxford and New York.

Nauck, A. (ed.) 1886: *Porphyrii philosophi Platonici opuscula selecta*, 2nd edn, Leipzig.

Newton, R. M. 1997–8: 'Cloak and shield in *Odyssey* 14', *CJ* 93: 143–56.

Nickau, K. 1977: *Untersuchungen zur textkritischen Methode des Zenodotos von Ephesus*, Berlin.

Nikolaev, A. 2013: 'The aorist infinitives in -έειν in early Greek hexameter poetry', *JHS* 133: 81–91.

Nünlist, R. 1998: *Poetologische Bildersprache in der frühgriechischen Dichtung*, Stuttgart and Leipzig.

Nussbaum, A. J. 1998: *Two studies in Greek and Homeric linguistics*, Göttingen.

Olson, S. D. 1989: 'The stories of Helen and Menelaus (*Odyssey* 4.240–89) and the return of Odysseus', *AJP* 110: 387–94.

1991–2: 'Servants' suggestions in Homer's *Odyssey*', *CJ* 87: 219–27.

1992: '"Name magic" and the threat of lying strangers in Homer's *Odyssey*', *ICS* 17: 1–7.

1995: *Blood and iron: stories and story-telling in Homer's Odyssey*, Leiden, New York and Cologne.

Onians, R. B. 1951: *The origins of European thought*, Oxford.

Palmer, L. R. 1962: 'The Language of Homer', in Wace and Stubbings 1962: 75–178.

Parke, H. W. 1967: *The oracles of Zeus: Dodona, Olympia, Ammon*, Oxford.

Parry, A. A. 1973: *Blameless Aegisthus: a study of ἀμύμων and other Homeric epithets*, Leiden.

Parry, A. M. (ed.) 1971: *The making of Homeric verse: the collected papers of Milman Parry*, Oxford.

1989: *The language of Achilles and other papers*, Oxford.

Parry, H. 1992: *Thelxis: magic and imagination in Greek myth and poetry*, Lanham.

Pasquali, G. 1952: *Storia della tradizione e critica del testo*, 2nd edn, Florence.

Patterson, O. 1982: *Slavery and social death: a comparative study*, Harvard.

Peacock, M. 2011: 'Rehabilitating Homer's Phoenicians: on some ancient and modern prejudices against trade', *AncSoc* 41: 1–29.

Pearce, T. E. V. 1996: 'The imperatival infinitive in Homer with special reference to A 20', *Mnemosyne* 49: 283–97.

Penney, J. H. W. (ed.) 2004: *Indo-European perspectives: studies in honour of Anna Morpurgo Davies*, Oxford.

Pépin, J. 1966: 'Porphyre, exégète d'Homère', in *Porphyre*, Entretiens Hardt XII, 229–72.

Perotti, P. A. 1989: 'Sur les adjectifs γλαυκός, γλαυκῶπις', *LEC* 57: 97–109.

Petropoulou, A. 1987: 'The sacrifice of Eumaeus reconsidered', *GRBS* 28: 135–49.

Pfeiffer, R. 1968: *History of classical scholarship: from the beginnings to the end of the Hellenistic age*, Oxford.

Pötscher, W. 1997: 'Die Bedeutung des Wortes γλαυκῶπις', *Philologus* 141: 3–20.

Powell, B. B. 1977: *Composition by theme in the Odyssey*, Meisenheim am Glan.

1997: 'Homer and writing', in Morris and Powell 1997: 3–32.

Powell, J. E. 1977: *A lexicon to Herodotus*, 2nd edn, Hildesheim.

Pucci, P. 1998: 'The song of the Sirens', in id., *The song of the Sirens: essays on Homer* (Lanham) 1–9.

Pulleyn, S. J. (ed.) 2000: *Homer: Iliad book one*, Oxford.

Raaflaub, K. A. 1997: 'Homeric society', in Morris and Powell 1997: 624–48.

Race, W. H., 1993: 'First appearances in the Odyssey', *TAPhA* 123: 79–107.

Radin, A. P. 1988: 'Sunrise, sunset: ἦμος in Homeric epic', *AJPh* 109: 293–307.

Rau, J. 2006: 'The Greek adverbs in -δην, -δον, -δα', *Glotta* 82: 211–20.

Ready, J. L. 2008: 'The comparative spectrum in Homer', *AJPh* 129: 453–96.

Redfield, J. M. 2009: 'The economic man', in Doherty 2009: 265–87 (= Rubino and Shelmerdine 1983: 218–47).

Reece, S. T. 1993: *The stranger's welcome: oral theory and the aesthetics of the Homeric hospitality scene*, Ann Arbor.
　1994: 'The Cretan Odyssey: a lie truer than truth', *AJP* 115: 157–73.
Richardson, N. J. (ed.) 1974: *The Homeric Hymn to Demeter*, Oxford.
　1983: 'Recognition scenes in the *Odyssey* and ancient literary criticism', *Papers of the Liverpool Latin Seminar* 4: 219–35.
　1987: 'The individuality of Homer's language', in Bremer, de Jong and Kalff 1987: 165–84.
　1993: *The Iliad: a commentary*, vol. VI: *books 21–4*, Cambridge.
Richardson, S. 1990: *The Homeric narrator*, Nashville.
　1996: 'Truth in the tales of the *Odyssey*', *Mnemosyne* 49: 393–402.
　2005–6: 'The devious narrator of the *Odyssey*', *CJ* 101: 337–59.
Riggsby, A. M. 1992: 'Homeric speech introductions and the theory of Homeric composition', *TAPhA* 122: 99–114.
Risch, E. 1974: *Wortbildung der homerischen Sprache*, Berlin and New York.
　1992: 'A propos de la formation du vocabulaire poétique grec entre le 12e et le 8e siècle', in Létoublon 1992: 91.
Robinson, D. 1990: 'Homeric φίλος: love of life and limbs, and friendship with one's θυμός', in Craik 1990: 97–108.
Roisman, H. M. 1990: 'Eumaeus and Odysseus – covert recognition and self-revelation', *ICS* 15: 215–38.
Rose, G. P. 1980 'The swineherd and the beggar', *Phoenix* 34: 285–97.
Rose, P. W. 1975: 'Class ambivalence in the *Odyssey*', *Historia* 24: 129–49 (= Emlyn-Jones, Hardwick and Purkis 1992: 193–209; Doherty 2009: 288–313).
　1992: *Sons of the gods, children of earth: ideology and literary form in ancient Greece*, Ithaca.
Rubino, C. A. and Shelmerdine, C. W. (eds.) 1983: *Approaches to Homer*, Austin.
Ruijgh, C. J. 1957: *L'élément achéen dans la langue épique*, Assen.
　1971: *Autour de τε épique: études sur la syntaxe grecque*, Amsterdam.
Rutherford, R. B. 1986: 'The philosophy of the *Odyssey*', *JHS* 106: 145–62.
　1991–3: 'From the *Iliad* to the *Odyssey*', *BICS* 38: 37–54.
　(ed.) 1992: *Homer: Odyssey books XIX and XX*, Cambridge.
Saïd, S. 2011: *Homer and the Odyssey* (tr. R. Webb; originally published in French in 1998), Oxford and New York.
Sasson, J. M. 2005: 'Comparative observations on the Near Eastern epic traditions', in Foley 2005: 215–32.
Schadewaldt, W. 1959: *Neue Kriterien zur Odyssee-Analyse: die Wiedererkennung des Odysseus und der Penelope*, Heidelberg.
Scheid-Tissinier, E. 1994: *Les usages du don chez Homère: vocabulaire et pratiques*, Nancy.
Schmidt, M. 2006: 'Der Welt des Eumaios', in Luther 2006: 117–38.

Scodel, R. 2005: 'Odysseus' dog and the productive household', *Hermes* 133: 401–8.

Scullion, S. 1994: 'Olympian and chthonian', *ClAnt* 13: 75–119.

Scully, S. 1990: *Homer and the sacred city*, Ithaca and London.

Segal, C. 1962: 'The Phaeacians and the symbolism of Odysseus' return', *Arion* 1: 17–64.

1967: 'Transition and ritual in Odysseus' return', *PP* 40: 321–42.

1992: 'Divine justice in the *Odyssey*: Poseidon, Cyclops, and Helios', *AJPh* 113: 489–518.

1994: *Singers, heroes, and gods in the Odyssey*, Ithaca and London.

Severyns, A. 1929: 'L'âge d'Eumée, porcher d'Ulysse,' *RBPh* 8: 853–5.

Shaw, J. W. 1989: 'Phoenicians in southern Crete', *AJA* 93: 165–83.

2000: 'The Phoenician Shrine, ca. 800 BC, at Kommos in Crete', in *Actas del IV Congreso International de Estudios Fenicios y Púnicos* (Cadiz) 1107–19.

2006: *Kommos: a Minoan harbor town and Greek sanctuary in southern Crete*, Princeton.

Shelmerdine, C. W. 1995: 'Shining and fragrant cloth in Homeric Epic', in Carter and Morris 1995: 99–107.

Sherratt, E. S. 1992: '"Reading the texts": archaeology and the Homeric question', in Emlyn-Jones, Hardwick and Purkis 1992: 145–65 (= *Antiquity* 64 (1990) 807–24).

Shipp, G. P. 1953: *Studies in the language of Homer*, 1st edn, Cambridge.

1972: *Studies in the language of Homer*, 2nd edn, Cambridge.

Sihler, A. L. 1995: *New comparative grammar of Greek and Latin*, New York.

Silk, M. S. 1983: 'LSJ and the problem of poetic archaism: from meaning to iconyms', *CQ* 23: 303–30.

Slings, S. R. 1998: 'ΔΕ or ΔΗ in a defixio from Olbia?', *Mnemosyne* 51: 84–5.

Spahn, P. 2006: '"Freundschaft" und "Gesellschaft" bei Homer', in Luther 2006: 163–216.

Stanford, W. B. and Luce, J. V. 1974: *The quest for Ulysses*, London.

Steiner, D. (ed.) 2010: *Homer: Odyssey books XVII and XVIII*, Cambridge.

Stengel, P. 1883: 'ΛΥΚΑΒΑΣ', *Hermes* 18.304–7.

Stewart, D. J. 1976: *The disguised guest: rank, role, and identity in the Odyssey*, Lewisburg.

Strasburger, H. 1997: 'The sociology of the Homeric epics', in Wright and Jones 1997: 47–70 (tr. of 'Der soziologische Aspekt der Homerischen Epen', *Gnomon* 60 (1953) 97–114).

Sullivan, S. D. 1988: *Psychological activity in Homer: a study of* phrēn, Ottawa.

Sutton, D. F. 1991: *Homer in the papyri*, Atlanta, available at: www.stoa.org/ homer/homer.pl.

Sznycer, M. 1979: 'L'inscription phénicienne de Tekke, près de Cnossos', *Kadmos* 18: 89–93.

Taplin, O. 1990: 'The earliest quotation of the *Iliad?*', in Craik 1990: 109–12.

1992: *Homeric soundings: the shaping of the Iliad*, Oxford.

Taylor, T. 1917 (tr.; orig. publ. 1789): *On the Cave of the Nymphs in the thirteenth book of the Odyssey: from the Greek of Porphyry*, London, available at: www.ccel.org/ccel/pearse/morefathers/files/porphyry_cave_of_nymphs_02_translation.htm.

Thalmann, W. G. 1998, *The swineherd and the bow: representations of class in the Odyssey*, Ithaca and London.

Thornton, A. 1970: *People and themes in Homer's Odyssey*, London.

Trahman, C. R. 1952: 'Odysseus' Lies (*Odyssey*, Books 13–19)', *Phoenix* 6: 31–43.

Tsagalis, C. 2012: 'Deauthorizing the Epic Cycle: Odysseus' false tale to Eumaeus (*Od.* 14.199–359)', in Montanari, Rengakos and Tsagalis 2012: 309–45.

Turkeltaub, D. 2007: 'Perceiving Iliadic gods', *HSCPh* 103: 51–81.

Turner, F. M. 1997: 'The Homeric question', in Morris and Powell 1997: 123–45.

van der Valk, M. (ed.) 1971–87: *Eustathii archiepiscopi Thessalonicensis commentarii ad Homeri Iliadem pertinentes*, vols. I–IV, Leiden.

Vanstiphout, H. L. J. 1992: 'The banquet scene in the Mesopotamian debate poems', in Gyselen R., ed. *Banquets d'Orient* (Bures-sur-Yvette) 9–22.

Ventris, M. and Chadwick, J. (eds.) 1973: *Documents in Mycenaean Greek*, 2nd edn by J. Chadwick, Cambridge.

Vidal-Naquet, P. 1981: 'Land and sacrifice in the Odyssey: a study of religious and mythical meanings', in R. L. Gordon, ed. *Myth, Religion and Society: structuralist essays by M. Detienne, L. Gernet, J.-P. Vernant & P. Vidal-Naquet* (Cambridge and Paris 1981) 80–94.

Vine, B. 1998: *Aeolic ὅρπετον and deverbative *-etó in Greek and Indo-European*, Innsbruck.

Volterras, G. 1903: *Kritiki meleti peri Omerikis Ithakis*, Athens.

von Kamptz, H. P. 1982: *Homerische Personennamen: sprachwissenschaftliche und historische Klassifikation*, Göttingen.

Wace, A. J. B. 1962: 'Houses and palaces', in Wace and Stubbings 1962: 489–97.

Wace, A. J. B. and Stubbings, F. H. (eds.) 1962: *A Companion to Homer*, Cambridge.

Wachter, R. 2000: 'Grammatik der homerischen Sprache', in J. Latacz *et al.*, eds. *Homer Ilias Gesamtkommentar: Prolegomena*, Leipzig: 61–108.

Wakker, G. 1994: *Conditions and conditionals: an investigation of Ancient Greek*, Amsterdam.

Walsh, G. B. 1984: *The varieties of enchantment: early Greek views of the nature and function of poetry*, Chapel Hill.

Wathelet, P. 1970: *Les traits éoliens dans la langue de l'épopée grecque*, Rome.

West, M. L. (ed.) 1966: *Hesiod: Theogony*, Oxford.

1967: 'Epica', *Glotta* 44: 135–48.

1973: 'Indo-European metre', *Glotta* 51: 161–87.

(ed.) 1978: *Hesiod: Works and Days*, Oxford.

1981: 'The singing of Homer and the modes of early Greek music', *JHS* 101: 113–29.

1982: *Greek metre*, Oxford.

1987: *Introduction to Greek meter*, Oxford.

1988: 'The rise of the Greek epic', *JHS* 108: 151–72.

1992: *Ancient Greek music*, Oxford.

1997: 'Homer's meter', in Morris and Powell 1997: 218–37.

(ed.) 1998: *Homeri Ilias*, vol. 1, Stuttgart and Leipzig.

2002: *Ancient Greek music*, Oxford.

2007: *Indo-European poetry and myth*, Oxford.

2013: *The Epic Cycle: a commentary on the lost Troy epics*, Oxford.

West, S. R. 1967: *The Ptolemaic papyri of Homer*, Cologne.

Willi, A. 2008: 'Genitive problems: Mycenaean *-Ca-o, -Co-jo, -Co* vs. later Greek -ᾱο, -οιο, -ου', *Glotta* 84: 239–72.

Williams, B. 1993: *Shame and necessity*, Berkeley, Los Angeles and London.

Willmott, J. 2007: *The moods of Homeric Greek*, Cambridge.

Winkler, J. 1990: *The constraints of desire*, New York and London.

Winter, I. J. 1995: 'Homer's Phoenicians: history, ethnography, or literary trope? [A perspective on early orientalism]', in Carter & Morris 1995: 247–71.

Wiseman, D. J. 1985: *Nebuchadrezzar and Babylon*, Oxford.

Woodhouse, W. J. 1930: *The composition of Homer's Odyssey*, Oxford.

Woolmer, M. 2011: *Ancient Phoenicia: an introduction*, London.

Worthington I. and Foley, J. M. (eds.) 2002: *Epea and grammata: oral and written communication in ancient Greece*, Leiden, Boston and Cologne.

Wright, G. M. and Jones, P. V. (eds.) 1997: *Homer: German scholarship in translation*, Oxford.

Wyatt, N. 2005: 'Epic in Ugaritic literature', in Foley 2005: 246–54.

Wyatt, W. F. 1969: *Metrical lengthening in Homer*, Rome.

Yamagata, N. 1989: 'The apostrophe in Homer as part of the oral technique', *BICS* 36: 91–103.

Zerba, M. 2009: 'What Penelope knew: doubt and scepticism in the *Odyssey*', *CQ* 59: 295–316.

Zusanek, H. 1998: *Die Nymphen: Untersuchungen zum dios-Begriff* vol. II, ed. S. Hoffmann, Frankfurt am Main.

INDEXES

II GREEK WORDS

For EU product safety concerns, contact us at Calle de José Abascal, 56–1°,
28003 Madrid, Spain or eugpsr@cambridge.org.

www.ingramcontent.com/pod-product-compliance
Ingram Content Group UK Ltd.
Pitfield, Milton Keynes, MK11 3LW, UK
UKHW020452240426
470322UK00016B/303